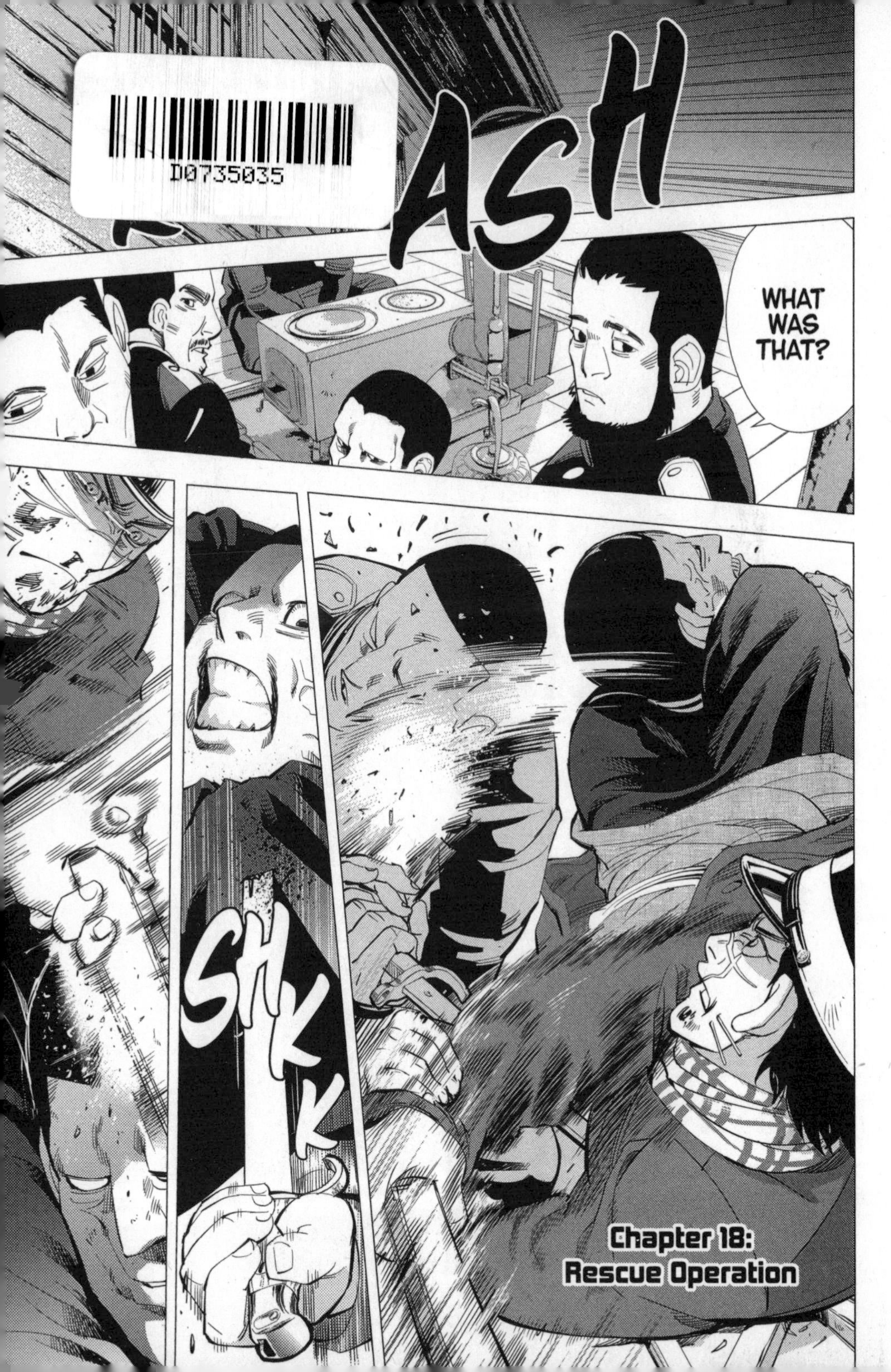
ASH
WHAT WAS THAT?
Chapter 18: Rescue Operation
SHKK

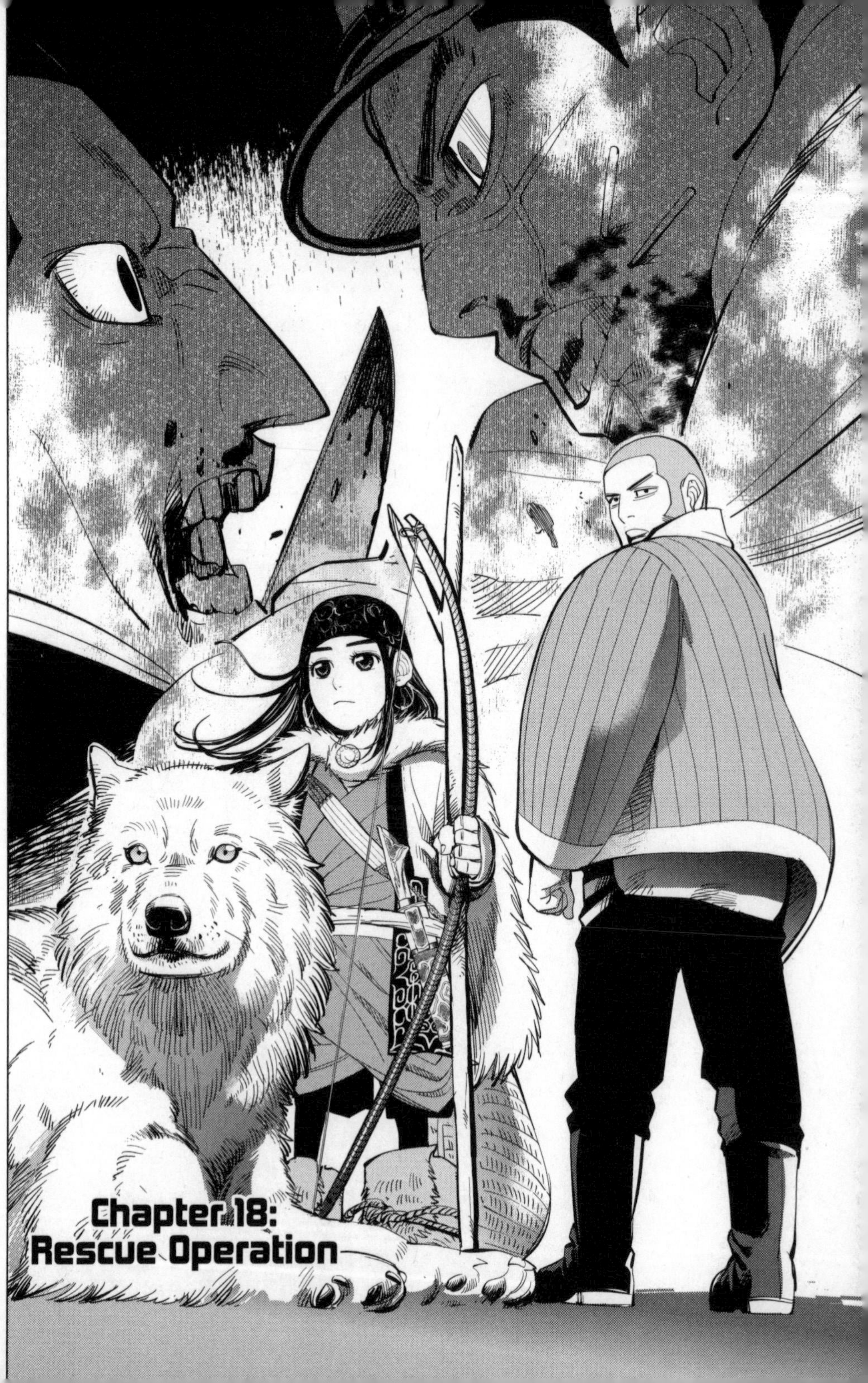
Chapter 18:
Rescue Operation

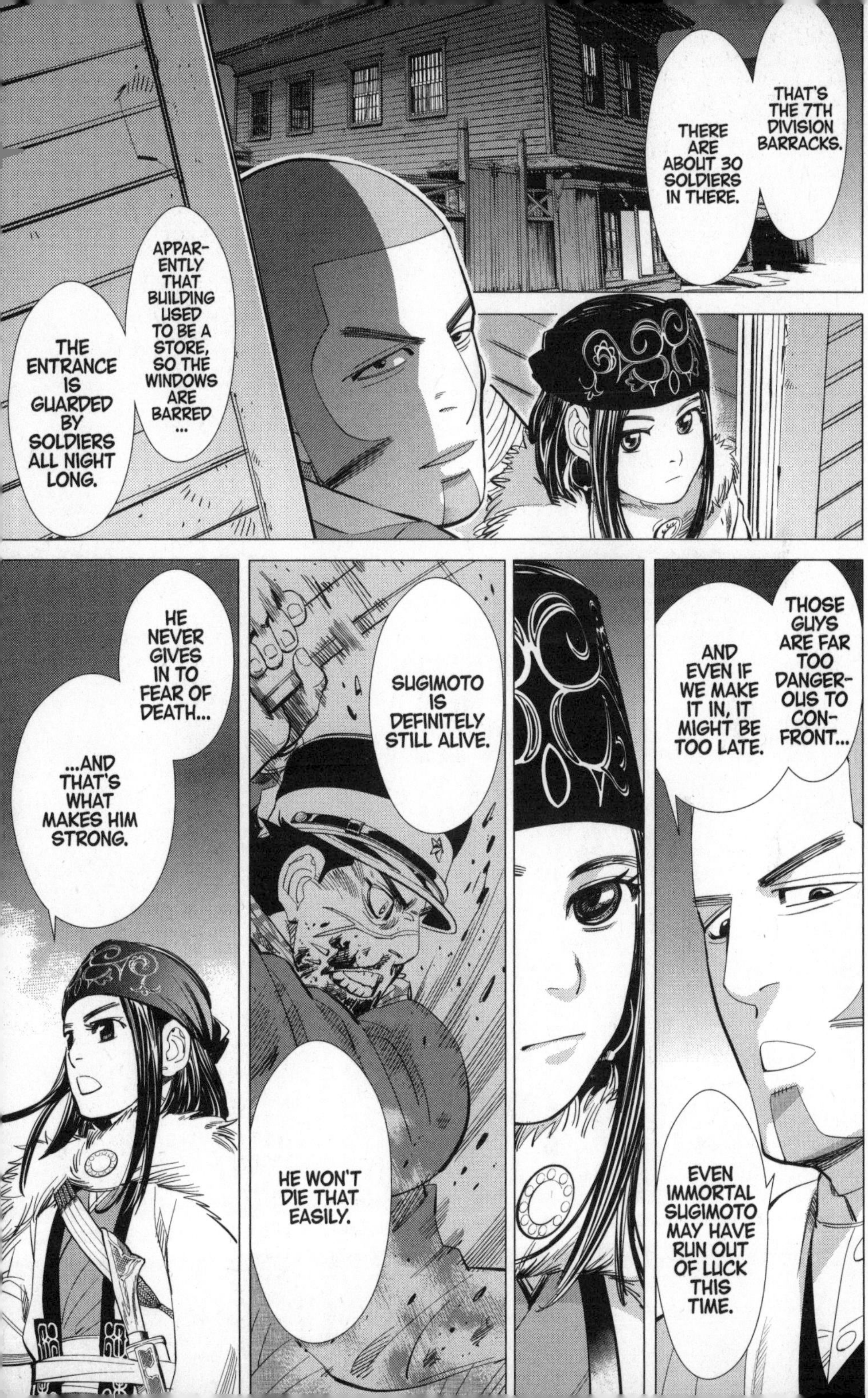
THAT'S THE 7TH DIVISION BARRACKS.
THERE ARE ABOUT 30 SOLDIERS IN THERE.
APPARENTLY THAT BUILDING USED TO BE A STORE, SO THE WINDOWS ARE BARRED...
THE ENTRANCE IS GUARDED BY SOLDIERS ALL NIGHT LONG.
THOSE GUYS ARE FAR TOO DANGEROUS TO CONFRONT...
AND EVEN IF WE MAKE IT IN, IT MIGHT BE TOO LATE.
EVEN IMMORTAL SUGIMOTO MAY HAVE RUN OUT OF LUCK THIS TIME.
SUGIMOTO IS DEFINITELY STILL ALIVE.
HE WON'T DIE THAT EASILY.
HE NEVER GIVES IN TO FEAR OF DEATH...
...AND THAT'S WHAT MAKES HIM STRONG.

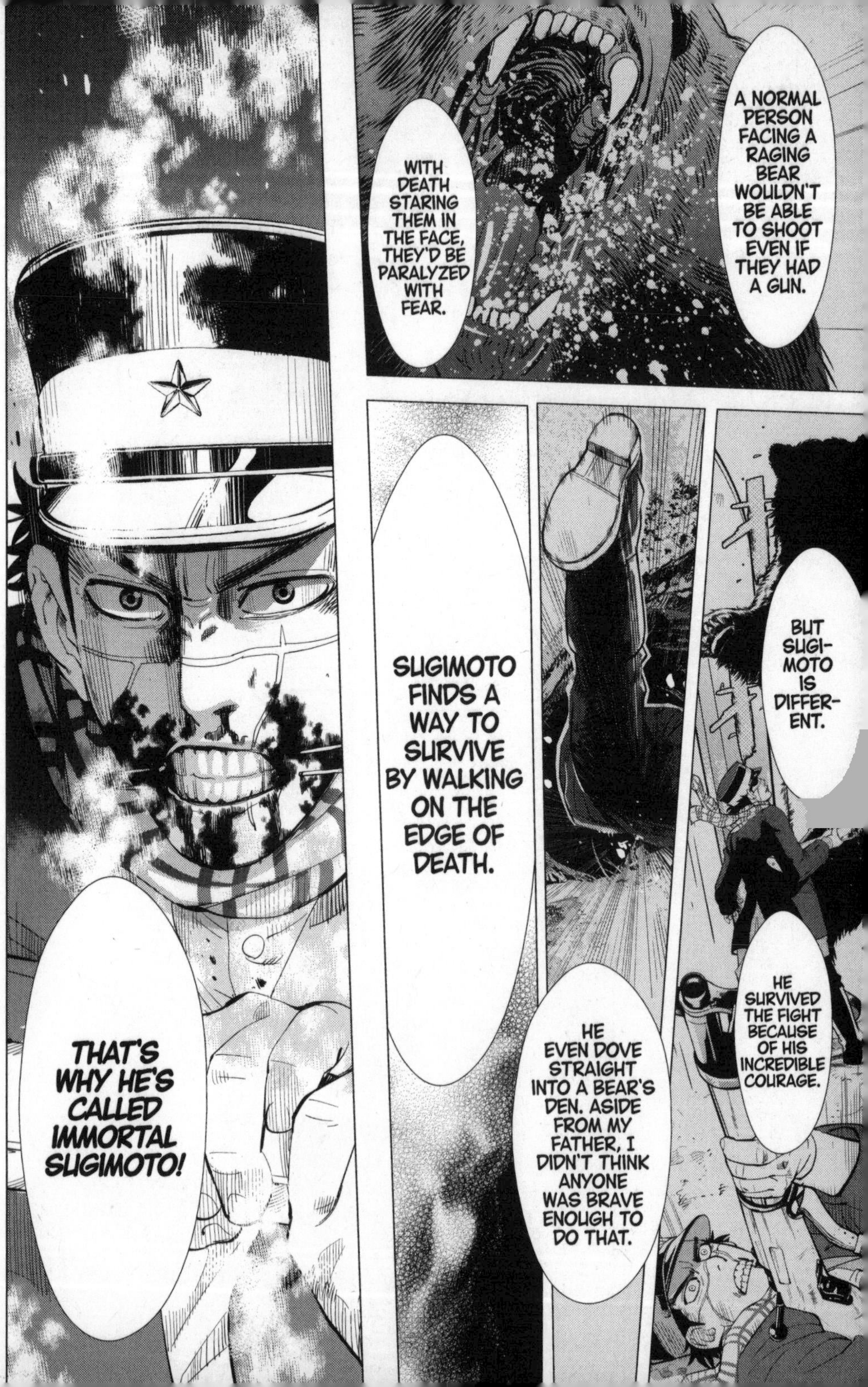
A NORMAL PERSON FACING A RAGING BEAR WOULDN'T BE ABLE TO SHOOT EVEN IF THEY HAD A GUN.
WITH DEATH STARING THEM IN THE FACE, THEY'D BE PARALYZED WITH FEAR.
BUT SUGI-MOTO IS DIFFER-ENT.
HE SURVIVED THE FIGHT BECAUSE OF HIS INCREDIBLE COURAGE.
HE EVEN DOVE STRAIGHT INTO A BEAR'S DEN. ASIDE FROM MY FATHER, I DIDN'T THINK ANYONE WAS BRAVE ENOUGH TO DO THAT.
SUGIMOTO FINDS A WAY TO SURVIVE BY WALKING ON THE EDGE OF DEATH.
THAT'S WHY HE'S CALLED IMMORTAL SUGIMOTO!

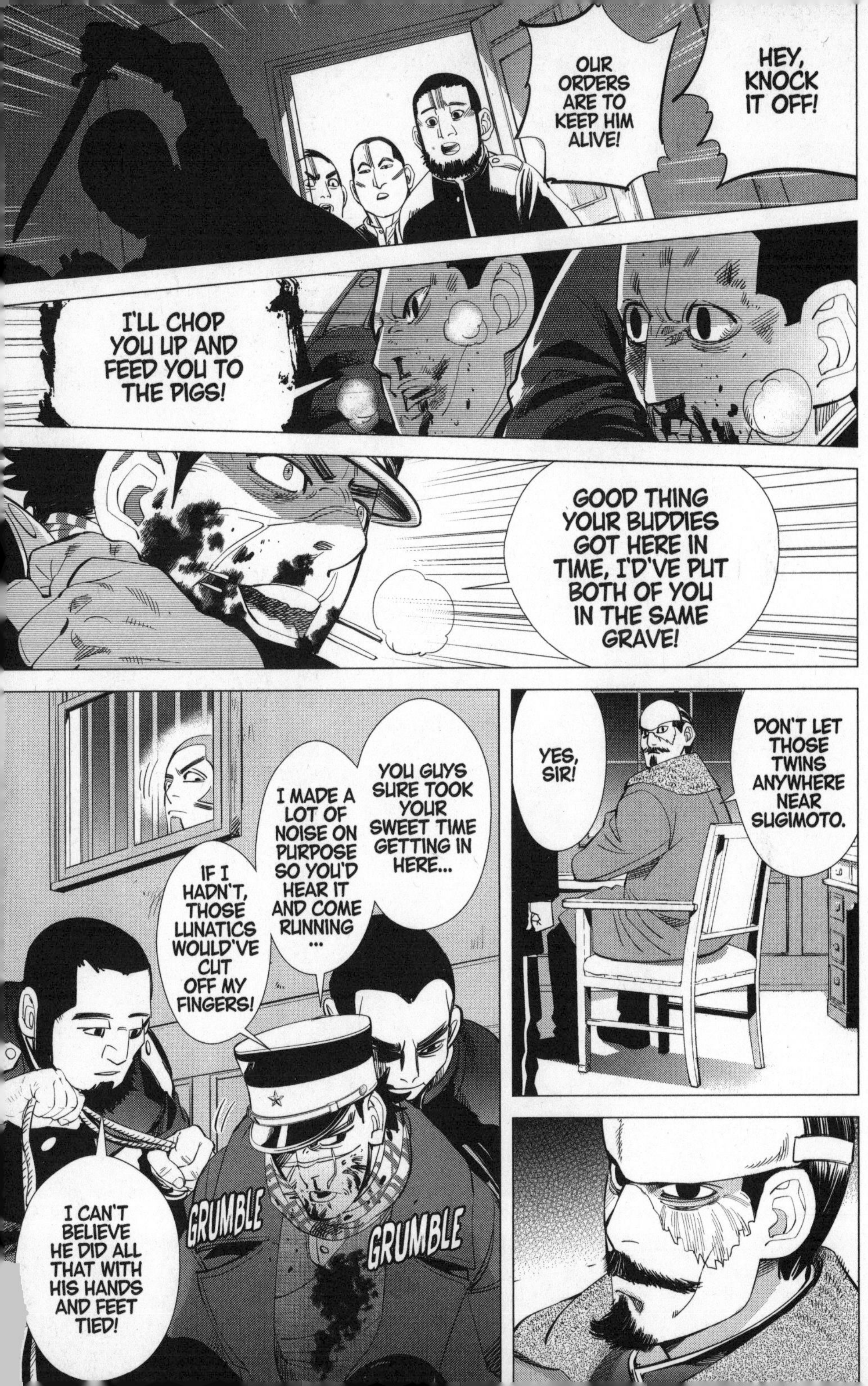
HEY, KNOCK IT OFF!
OUR ORDERS ARE TO KEEP HIM ALIVE!
I'LL CHOP YOU UP AND FEED YOU TO THE PIGS!
GOOD THING YOUR BUDDIES GOT HERE IN TIME, I'D'VE PUT BOTH OF YOU IN THE SAME GRAVE!
DON'T LET THOSE TWINS ANYWHERE NEAR SUGIMOTO.
YES, SIR!
YOU GUYS SURE TOOK YOUR SWEET TIME GETTING IN HERE...
I MADE A LOT OF NOISE ON PURPOSE SO YOU'D HEAR IT AND COME RUNNING...
IF I HADN'T, THOSE LUNATICS WOULD'VE CUT OFF MY FINGERS!
GRUMBLE
GRUMBLE
I CAN'T BELIEVE HE DID ALL THAT WITH HIS HANDS AND FEET TIED!

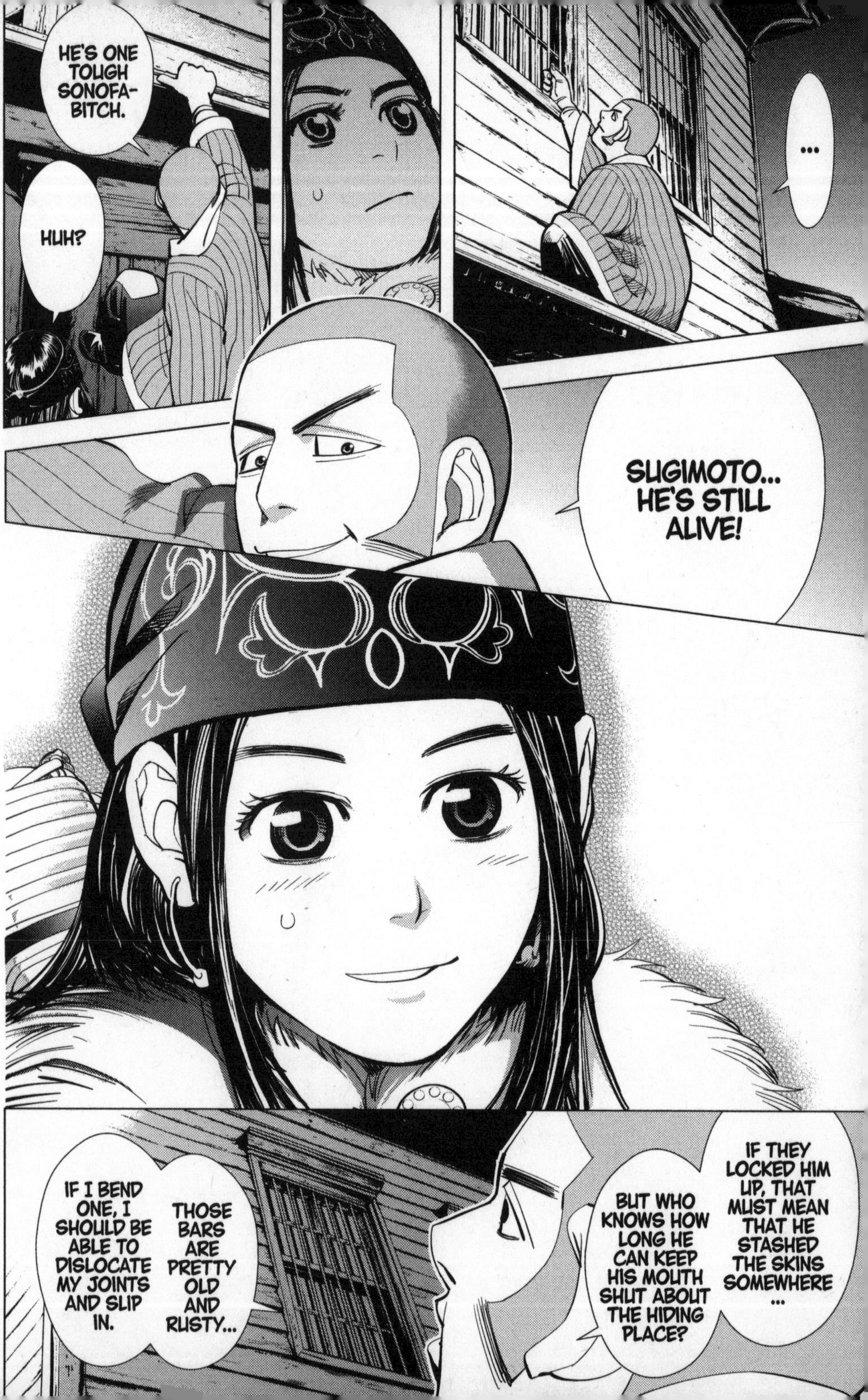
...
HE'S ONE TOUGH SONOFA-BITCH.
HUH?
SUGIMOTO... HE'S STILL ALIVE!
IF THEY LOCKED HIM UP, THAT MUST MEAN THAT HE STASHED THE SKINS SOMEWHERE...
BUT WHO KNOWS HOW LONG HE CAN KEEP HIS MOUTH SHUT ABOUT THE HIDING PLACE?
THOSE BARS ARE PRETTY OLD AND RUSTY...
IF I BEND ONE, I SHOULD BE ABLE TO DISLOCATE MY JOINTS AND SLIP IN.

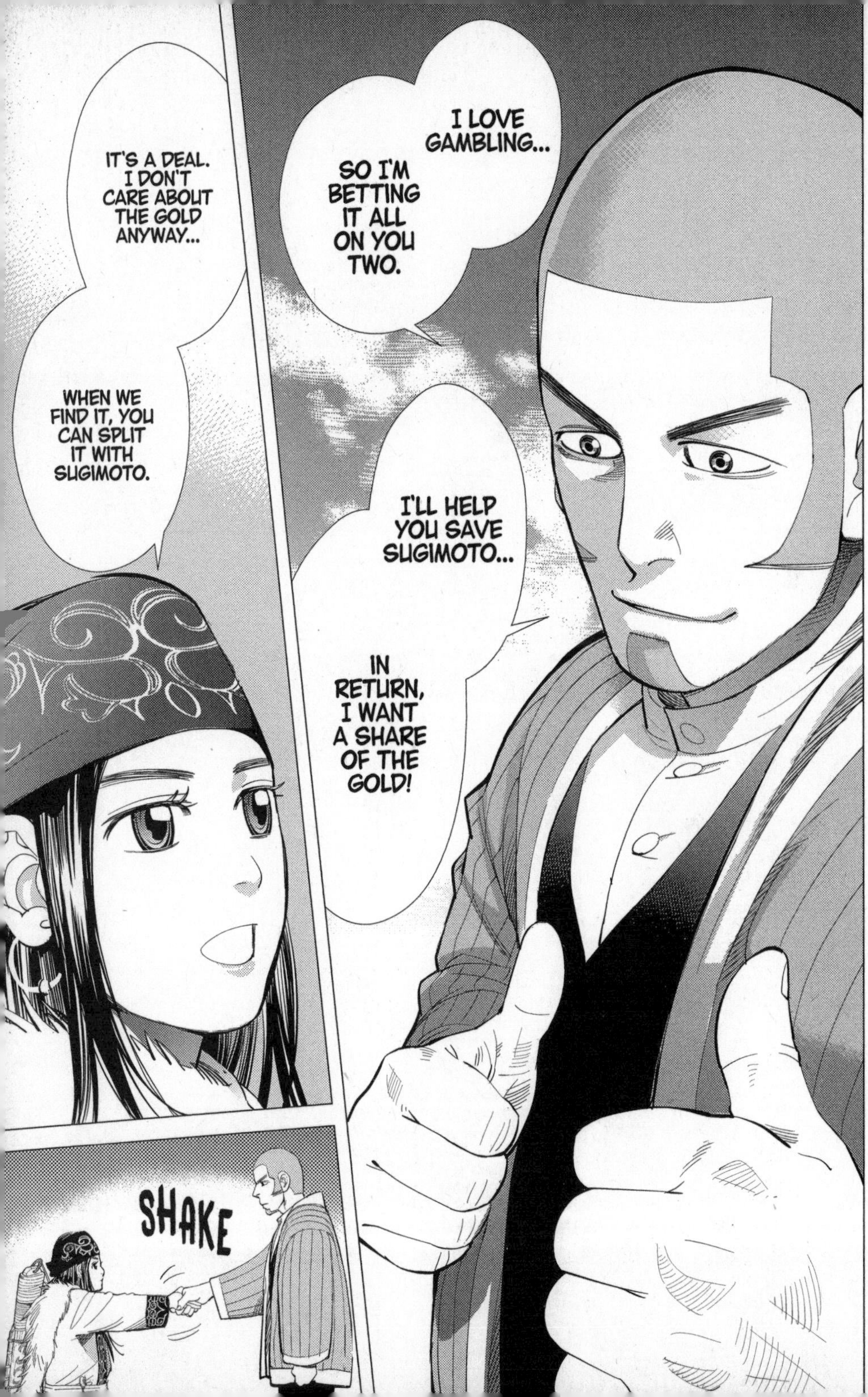
I LOVE GAMBLING...
SO I'M BETTING IT ALL ON YOU TWO.
I'LL HELP YOU SAVE SUGIMOTO...
IN RETURN, I WANT A SHARE OF THE GOLD!
IT'S A DEAL. I DON'T CARE ABOUT THE GOLD ANYWAY...
WHEN WE FIND IT, YOU CAN SPLIT IT WITH SUGIMOTO.
SHAKE

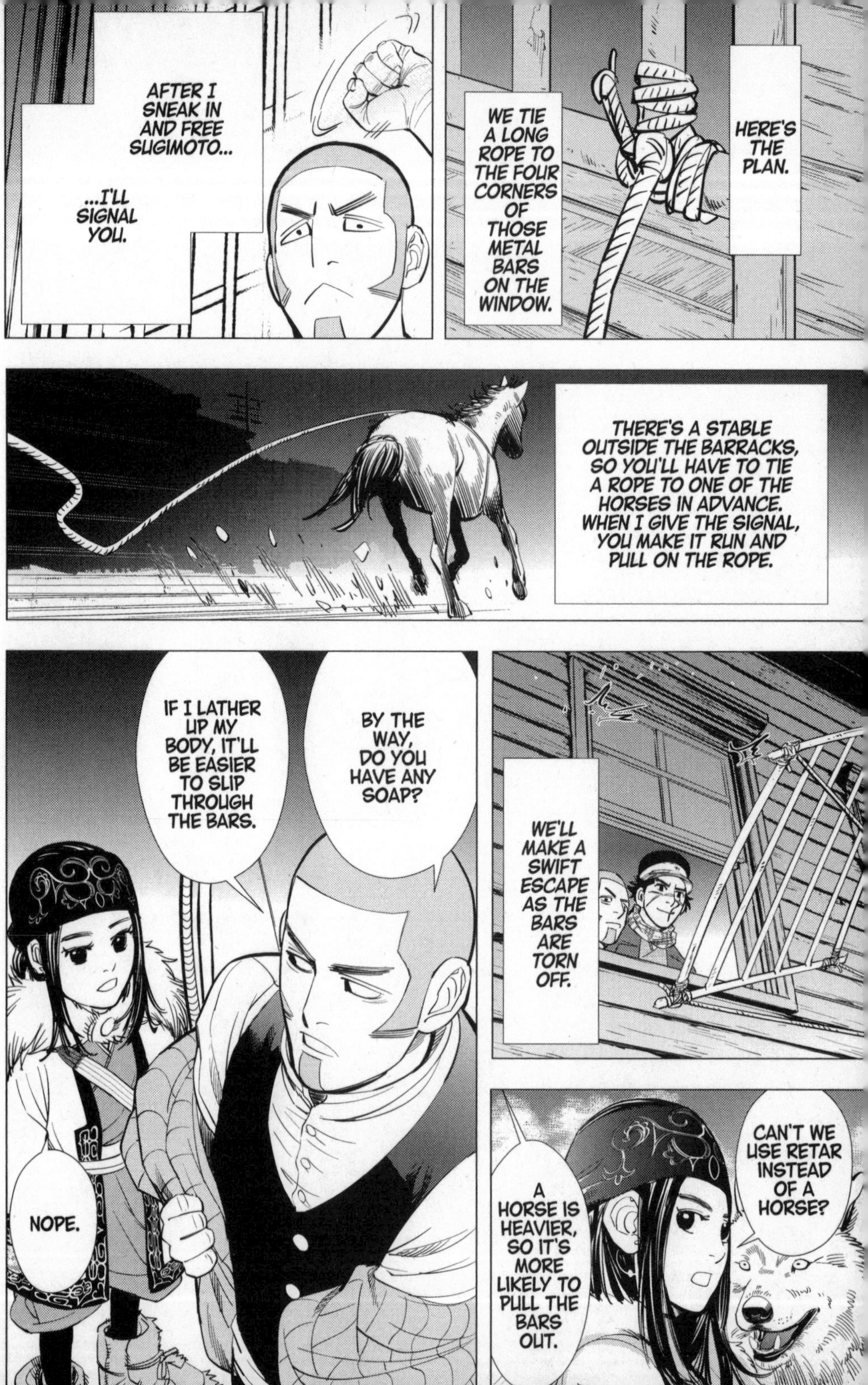
HERE'S THE PLAN.
WE TIE A LONG ROPE TO THE FOUR CORNERS OF THOSE METAL BARS ON THE WINDOW.
AFTER I SNEAK IN AND FREE SUGIMOTO...
...I'LL SIGNAL YOU.
THERE'S A STABLE OUTSIDE THE BARRACKS, SO YOU'LL HAVE TO TIE A ROPE TO ONE OF THE HORSES IN ADVANCE. WHEN I GIVE THE SIGNAL, YOU MAKE IT RUN AND PULL ON THE ROPE.
WE'LL MAKE A SWIFT ESCAPE AS THE BARS ARE TORN OFF.
CAN'T WE USE RETAR INSTEAD OF A HORSE?
A HORSE IS HEAVIER, SO IT'S MORE LIKELY TO PULL THE BARS OUT.
BY THE WAY, DO YOU HAVE ANY SOAP?
IF I LATHER UP MY BODY, IT'LL BE EASIER TO SLIP THROUGH THE BARS.
NOPE.

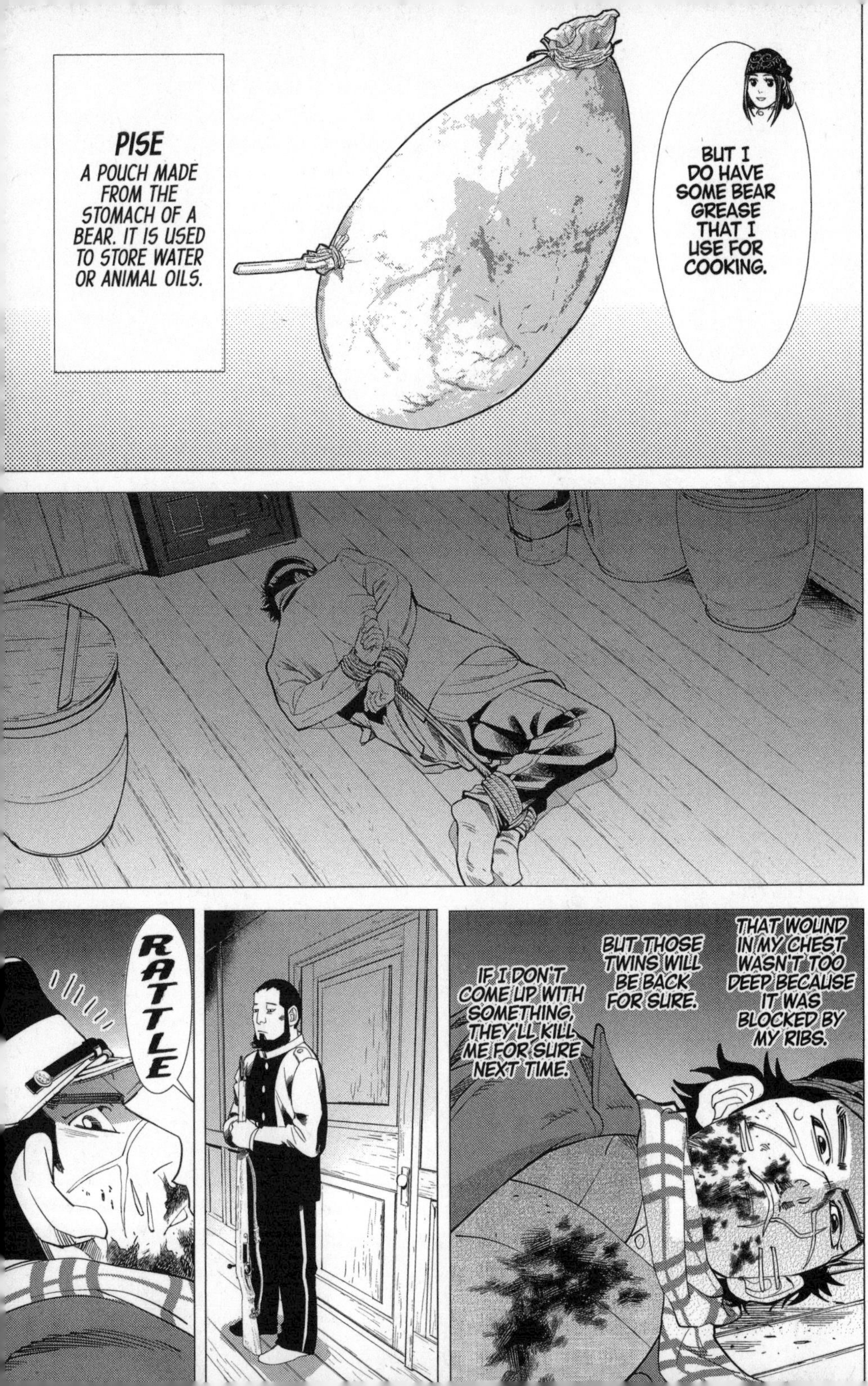
BUT I DO HAVE SOME BEAR GREASE THAT I USE FOR COOKING.
PISE
A POUCH MADE FROM THE STOMACH OF A BEAR. IT IS USED TO STORE WATER OR ANIMAL OILS.
THAT WOUND IN MY CHEST WASN'T TOO DEEP BECAUSE IT WAS BLOCKED BY MY RIBS.
BUT THOSE TWINS WILL BE BACK FOR SURE.
IF I DON'T COME UP WITH SOMETHING, THEY'LL KILL ME FOR SURE NEXT TIME.
RATTLE

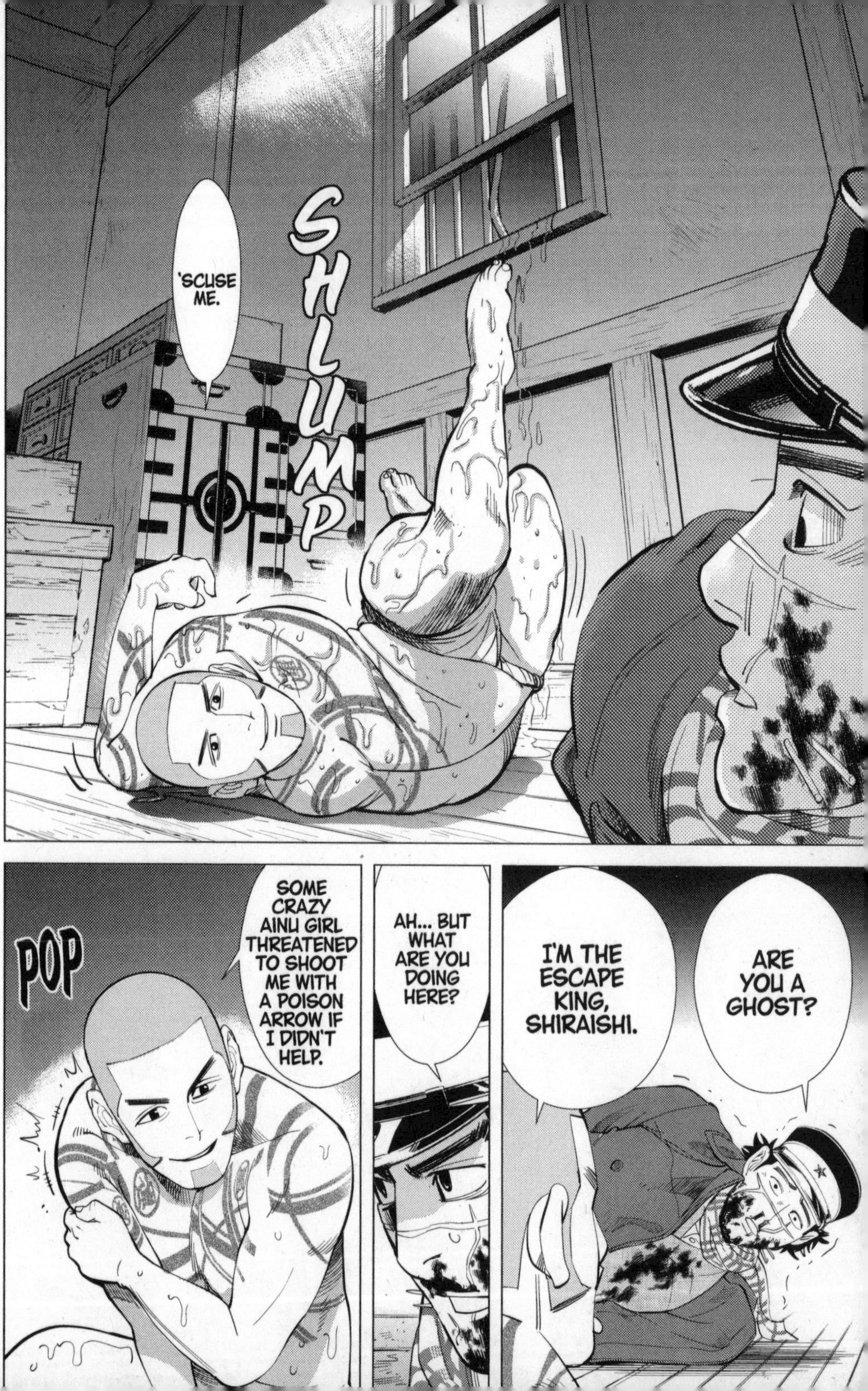
SHLUMP
'SCUSE ME.
ARE YOU A GHOST?
I'M THE ESCAPE KING, SHIRAISHI.
AH... BUT WHAT ARE YOU DOING HERE?
SOME CRAZY AINU GIRL THREATENED TO SHOOT ME WITH A POISON ARROW IF I DIDN'T HELP.
POP

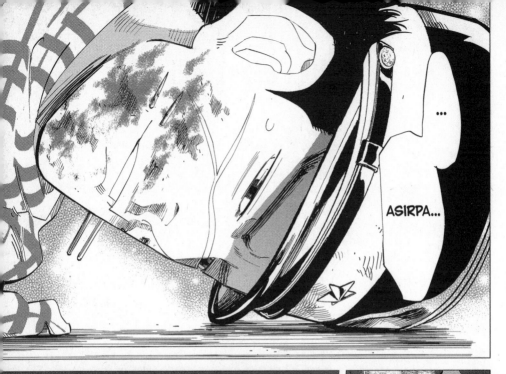

...

ASIRPA...

THOK

WHREE

THUMP

NEEEE

THWUP

NOW WHAT?

SOMETHING SPOOKED THE HORSES.

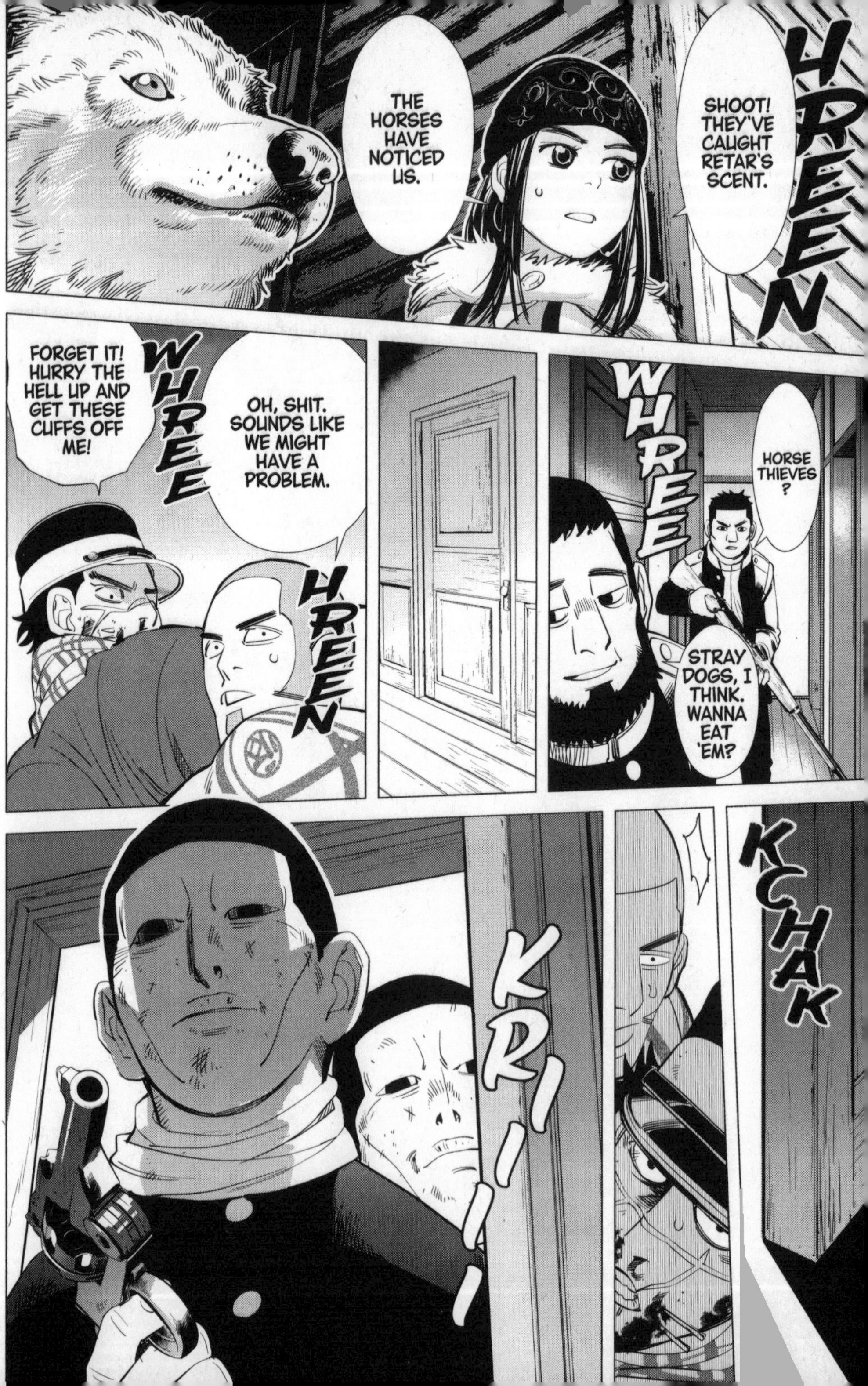
HREEEN
SHOOT! THEY'VE CAUGHT RETAR'S SCENT.
THE HORSES HAVE NOTICED US.
WHREE
HORSE THIEVES?
STRAY DOGS, I THINK. WANNA EAT 'EM?
OH, SHIT. SOUNDS LIKE WE MIGHT HAVE A PROBLEM.
WHREE
FORGET IT! HURRY THE HELL UP AND GET THESE CUFFS OFF ME!
HREEEN
KCHAK
KRI-

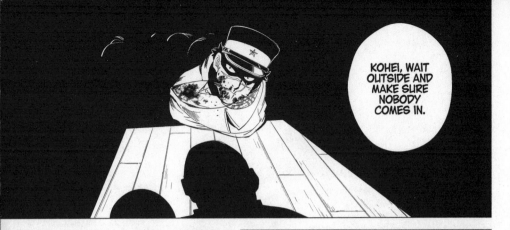

KOHEI, WAIT OUTSIDE AND MAKE SURE NOBODY COMES IN.

AFTER I KILL HIM, I'LL UNDO HIS RESTRAINTS. THEN WE JUST SAY "HE WAS TRYING TO ESCAPE, SO WE HAD NO CHOICE."

HUH?

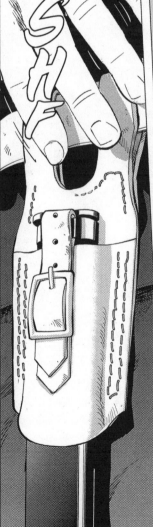

SHF

KLNK

WAIT, YOHEI. DON'T USE YOUR GUN. HAND IT OVER...

USE YOUR BAYONET INSTEAD.

IF YOU SHOOT HIM, EVERYONE WILL COME BEFORE YOU CAN CUT HIM LOOSE...

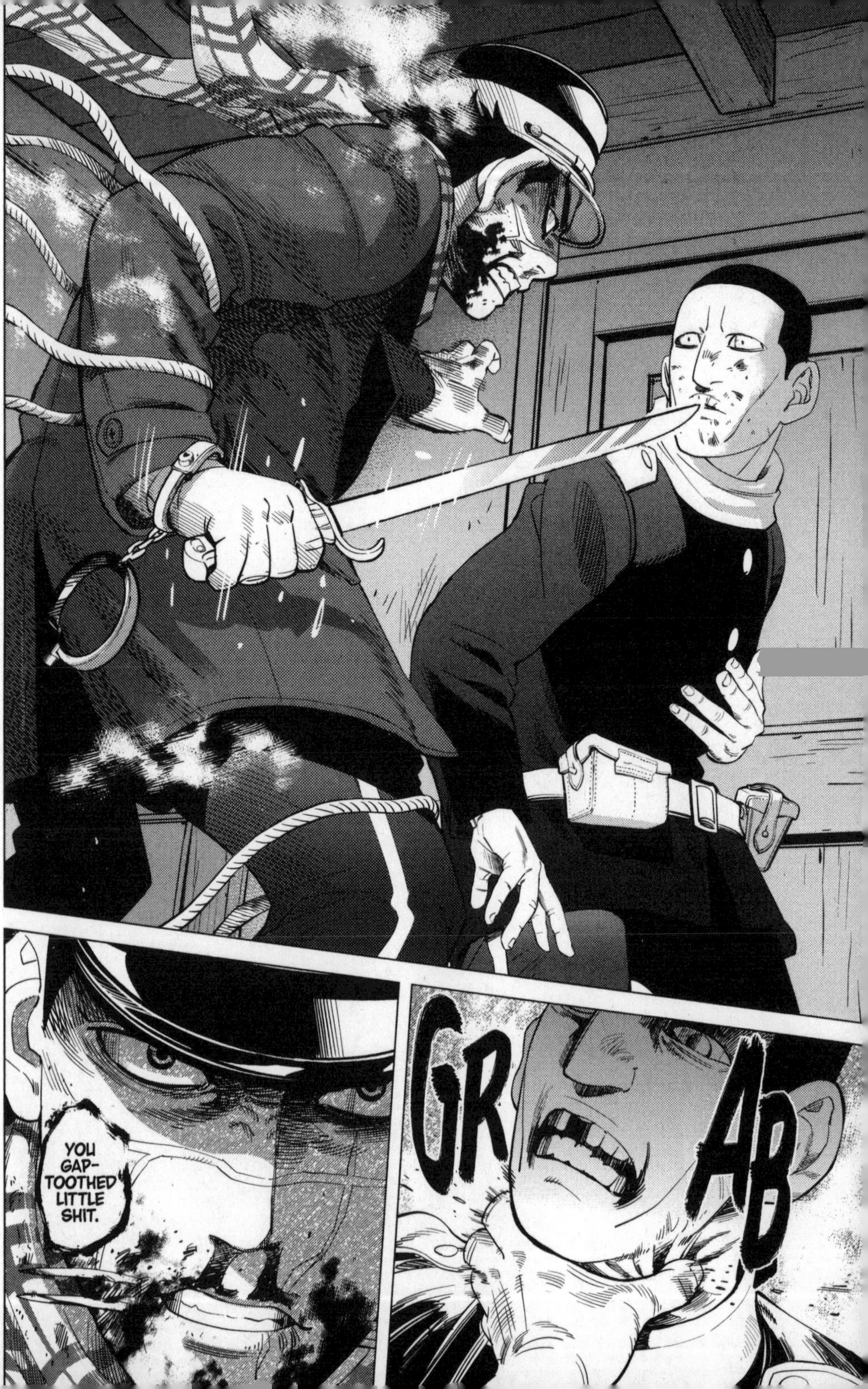
GRAB
YOU GAP-TOOTHED LITTLE SHIT.

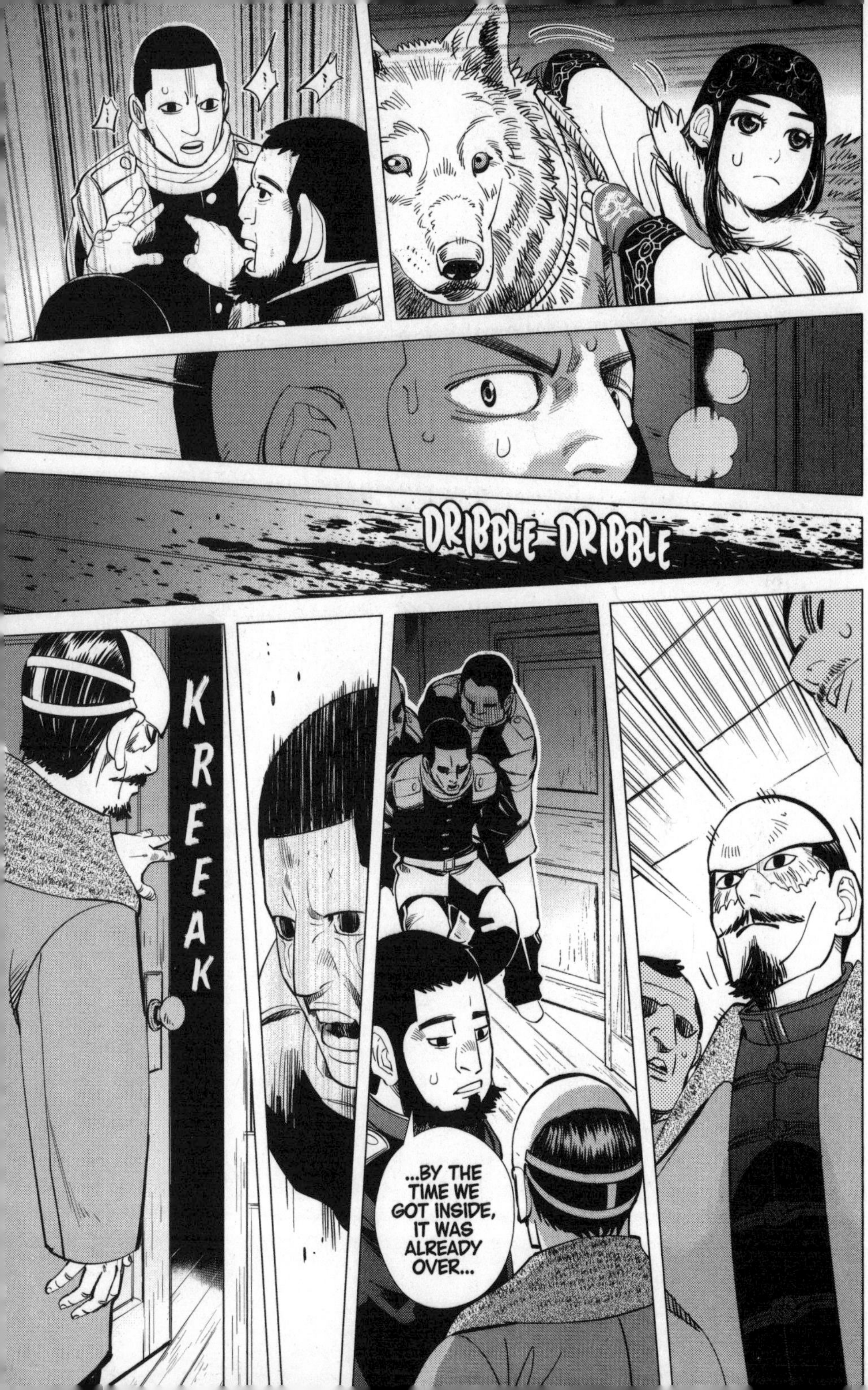
DRIBBLE DRIBBLE
KREEAK
...BY THE TIME WE GOT INSIDE, IT WAS ALREADY OVER...

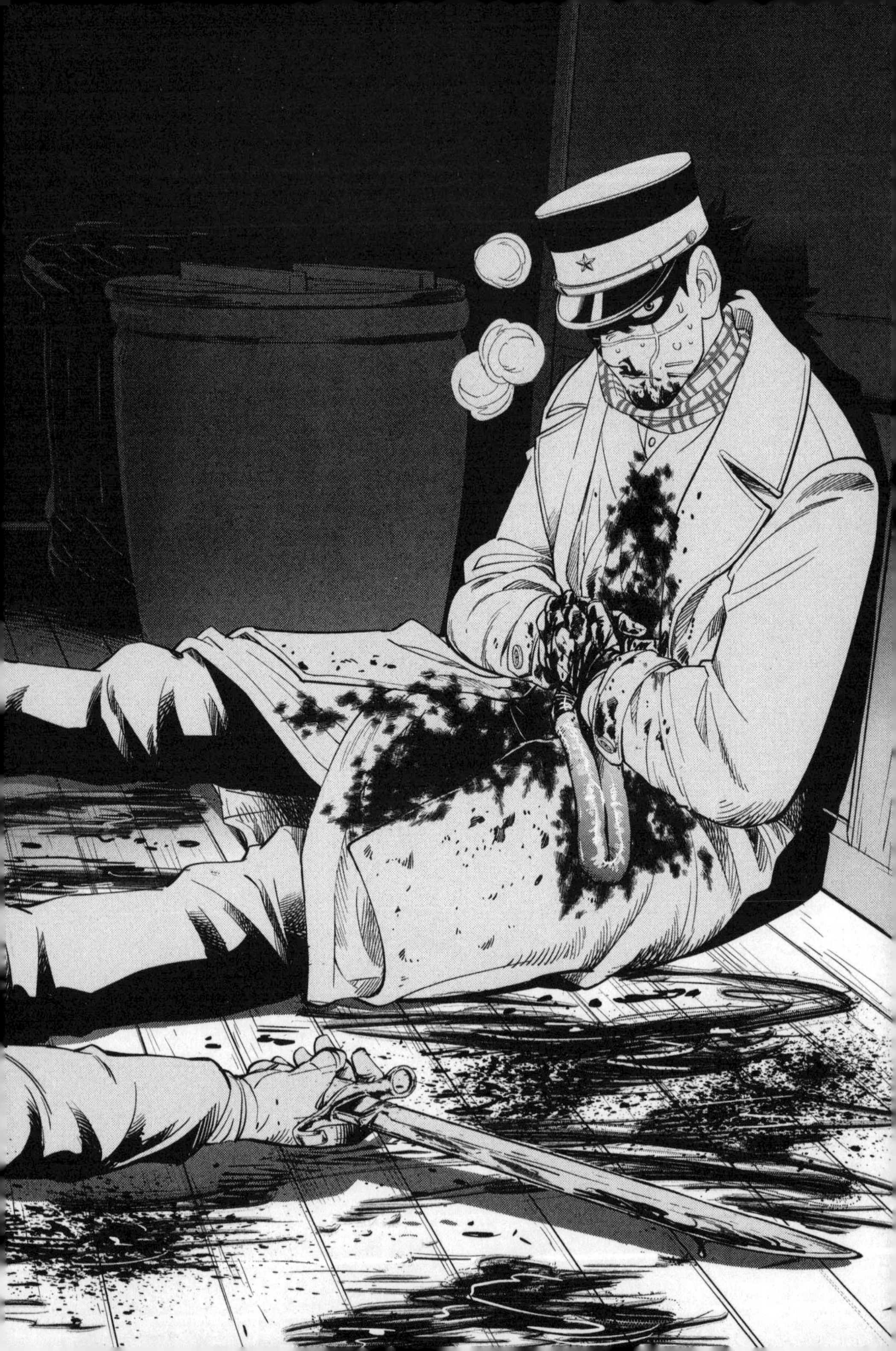

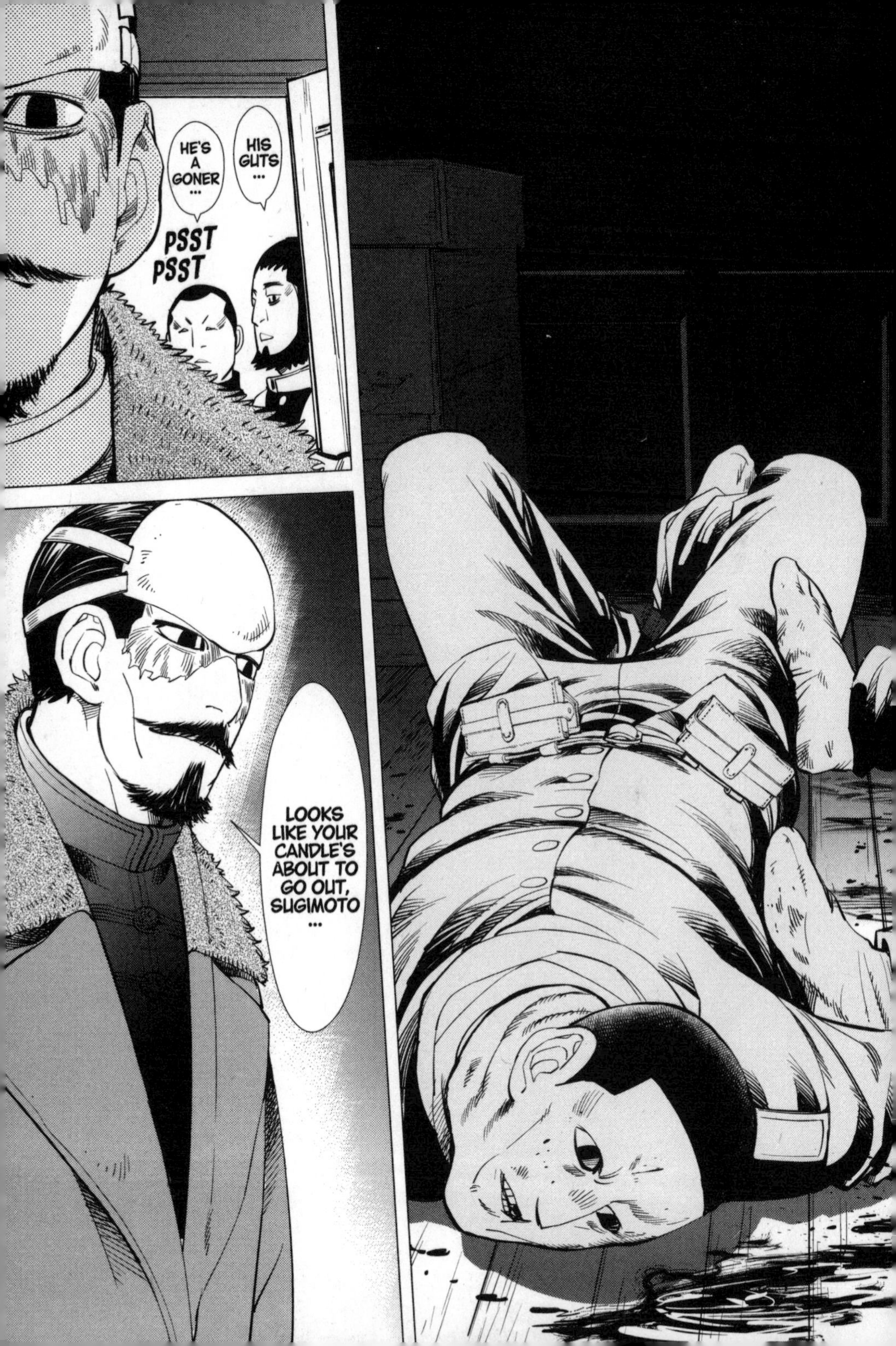
HIS GUTS...
HE'S A GONER...
PSST PSST
LOOKS LIKE YOUR CANDLE'S ABOUT TO GO OUT, SUGIMOTO...

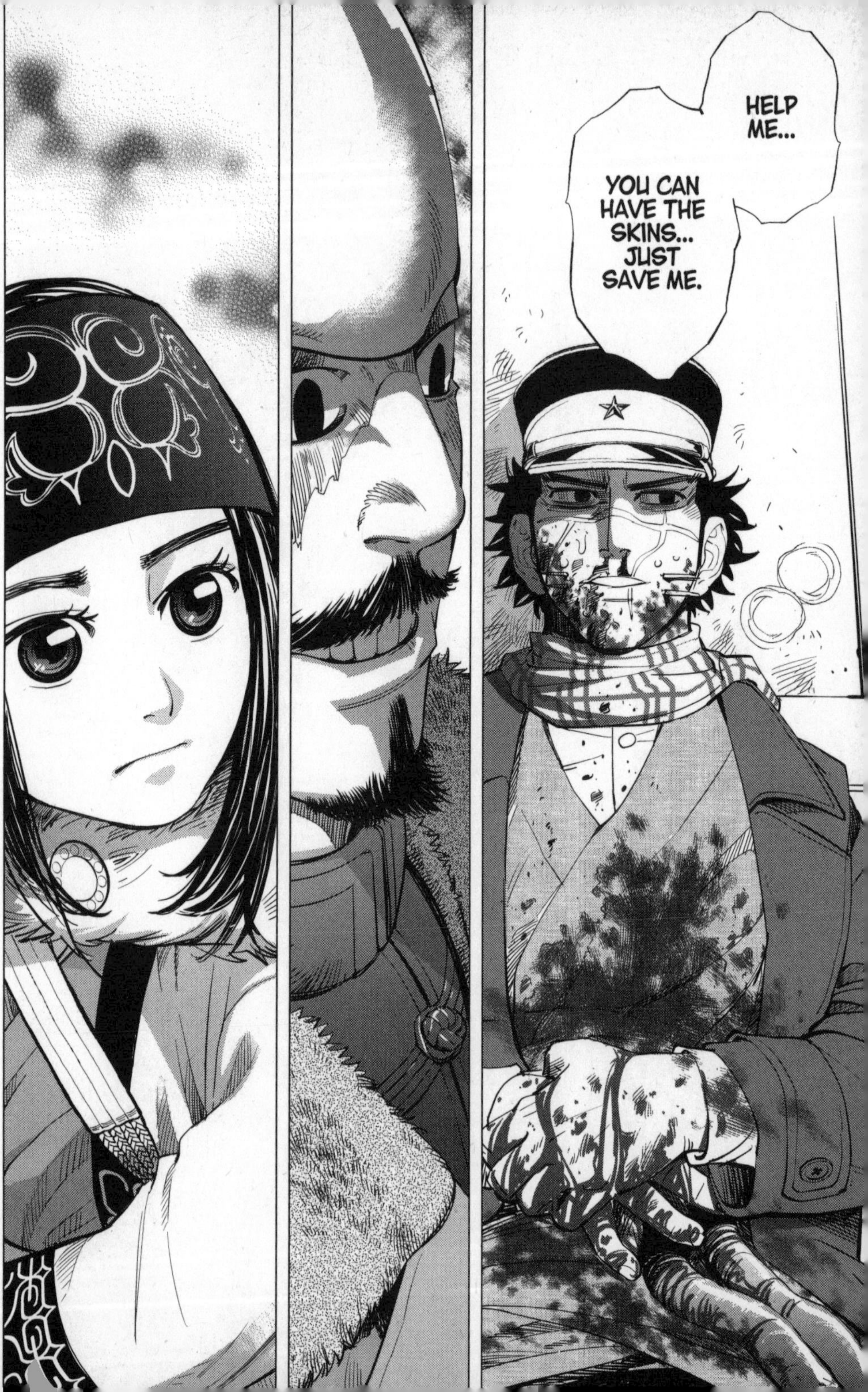
HELP ME...
YOU CAN HAVE THE SKINS... JUST SAVE ME.

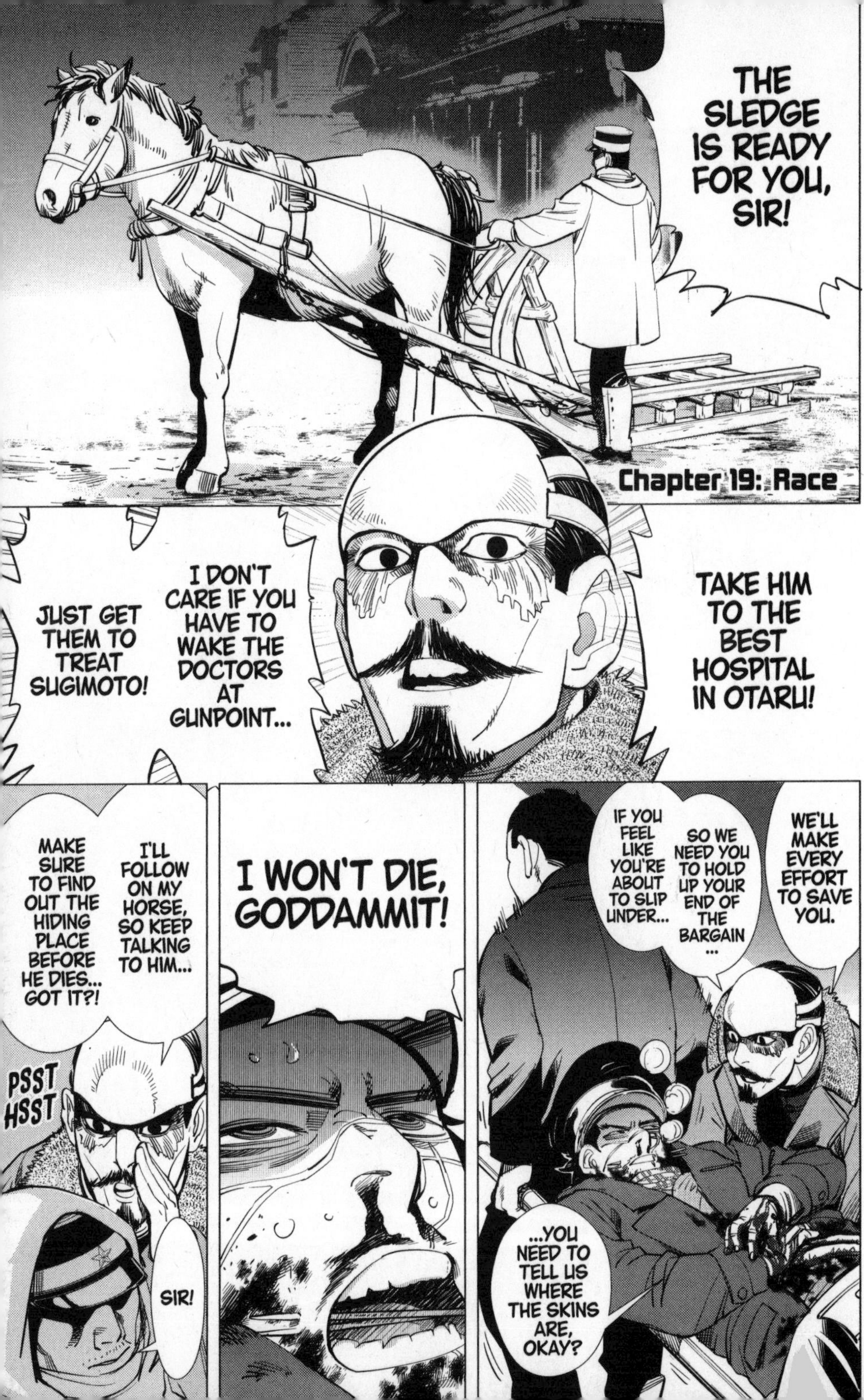
THE SLEDGE IS READY FOR YOU, SIR!
Chapter 19: Race
TAKE HIM TO THE BEST HOSPITAL IN OTARU!
I DON'T CARE IF YOU HAVE TO WAKE THE DOCTORS AT GUNPOINT...
JUST GET THEM TO TREAT SUGIMOTO!
WE'LL MAKE EVERY EFFORT TO SAVE YOU.
SO WE NEED YOU TO HOLD UP YOUR END OF THE BARGAIN...
IF YOU FEEL LIKE YOU'RE ABOUT TO SLIP UNDER...
...YOU NEED TO TELL US WHERE THE SKINS ARE, OKAY?
I WON'T DIE, GODDAMMIT!
I'LL FOLLOW ON MY HORSE, SO KEEP TALKING TO HIM...
MAKE SURE TO FIND OUT THE HIDING PLACE BEFORE HE DIES... GOT IT?!
PSST HSST
SIR!

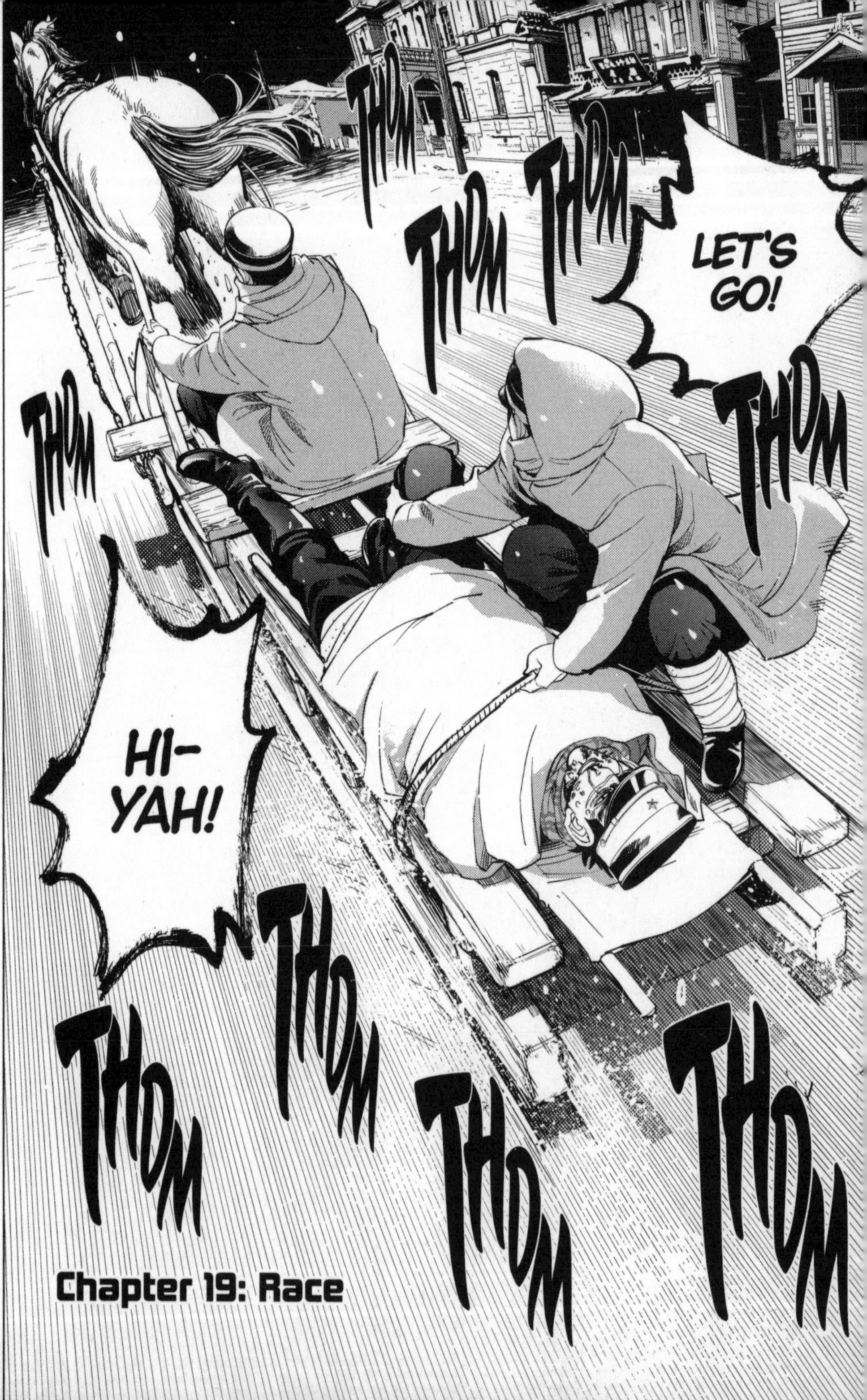
THOM THOM THOM
LET'S GO!
THOM
THOM
HI-YAH!
THOM THOM THOM THOM

Chapter 19: Race

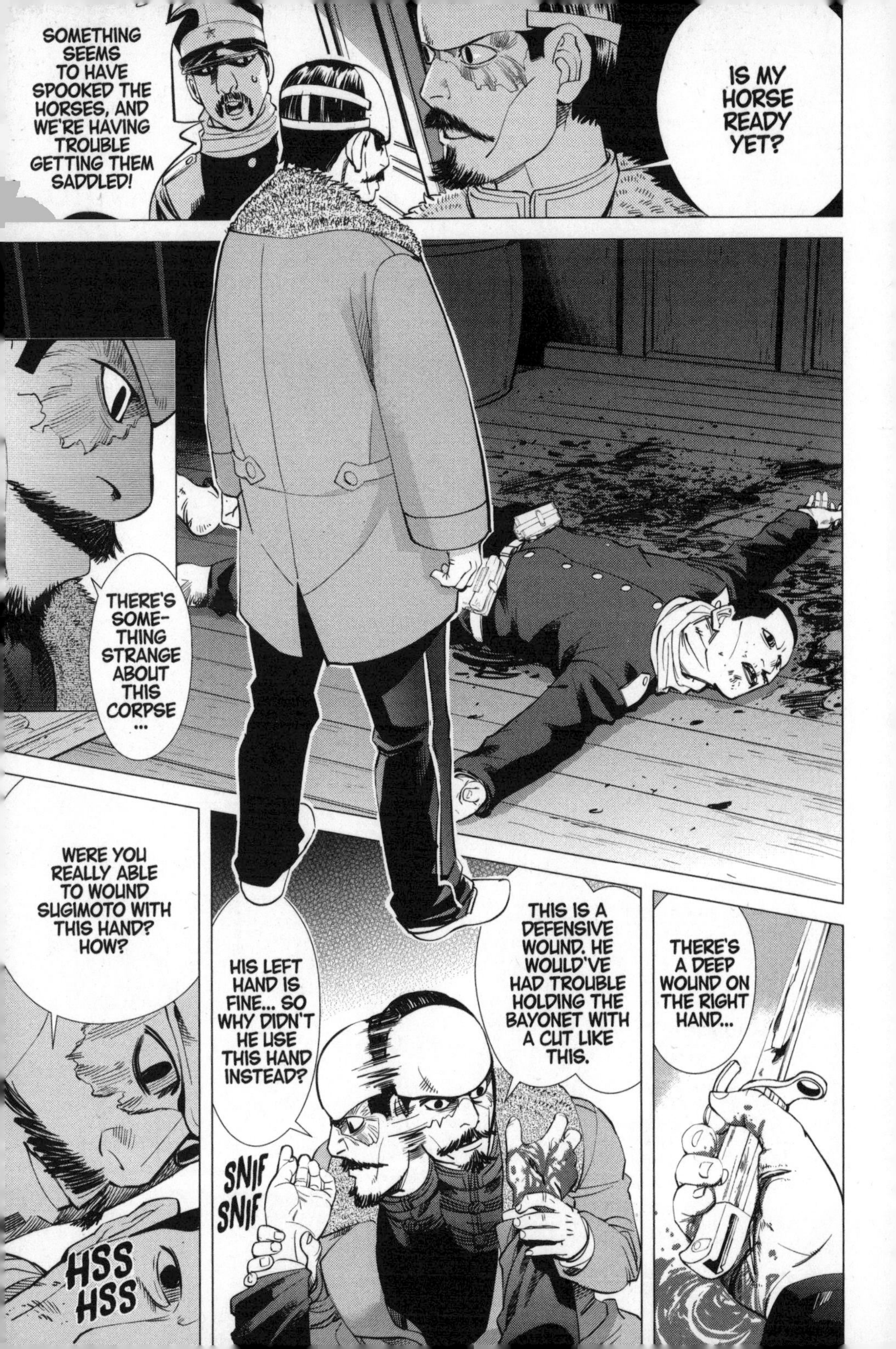
IS MY HORSE READY YET?
SOMETHING SEEMS TO HAVE SPOOKED THE HORSES, AND WE'RE HAVING TROUBLE GETTING THEM SADDLED!
THERE'S SOME-THING STRANGE ABOUT THIS CORPSE ...
THERE'S A DEEP WOUND ON THE RIGHT HAND...
THIS IS A DEFENSIVE WOUND. HE WOULD'VE HAD TROUBLE HOLDING THE BAYONET WITH A CUT LIKE THIS.
HIS LEFT HAND IS FINE... SO WHY DIDN'T HE USE THIS HAND INSTEAD?
SNIF SNIF
WERE YOU REALLY ABLE TO WOUND SUGIMOTO WITH THIS HAND? HOW?
HSS HSS

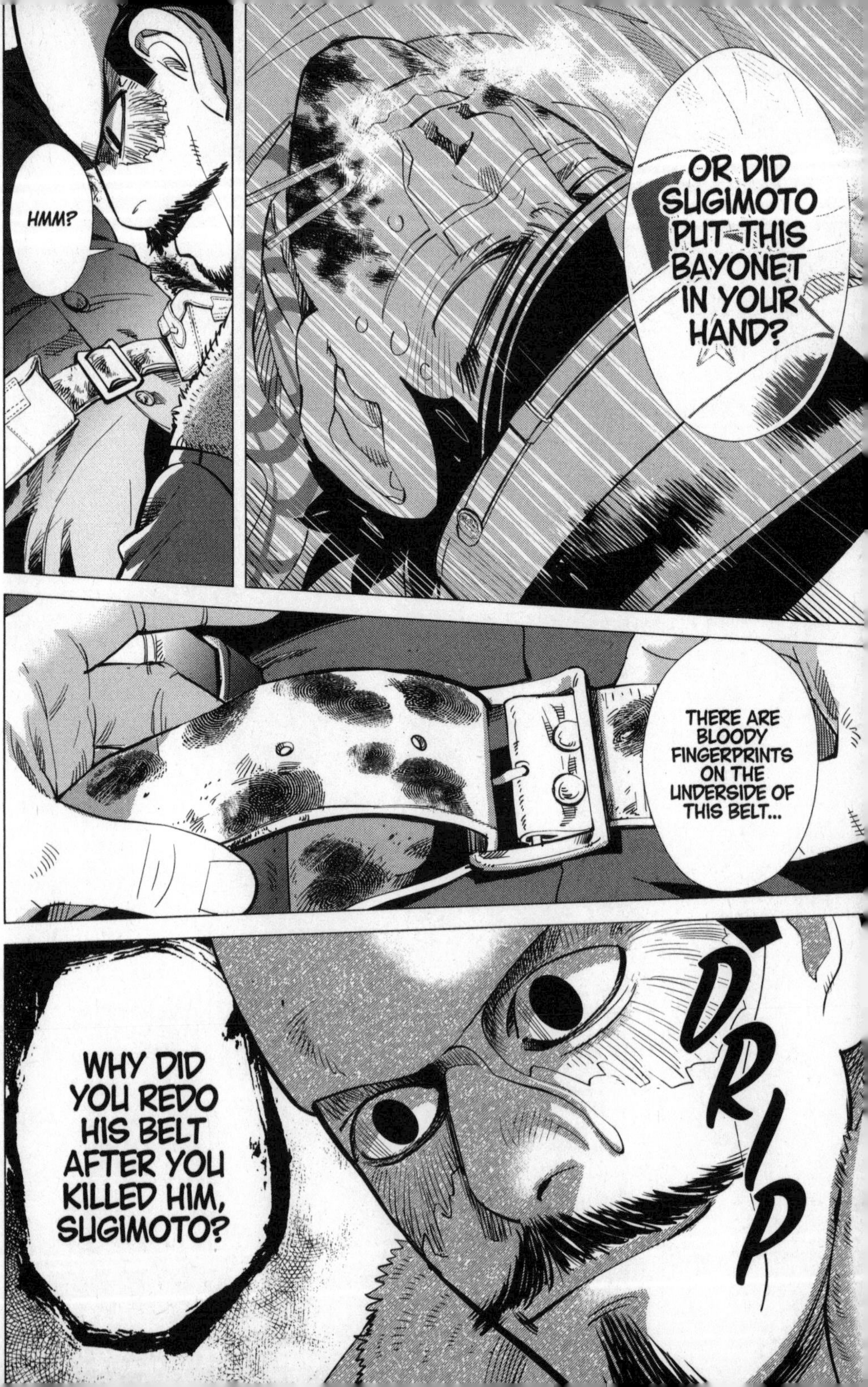
OR DID SUGIMOTO PUT THIS BAYONET IN YOUR HAND?
HMM?
THERE ARE BLOODY FINGERPRINTS ON THE UNDERSIDE OF THIS BELT...
DRIP
WHY DID YOU REDO HIS BELT AFTER YOU KILLED HIM, SUGIMOTO?

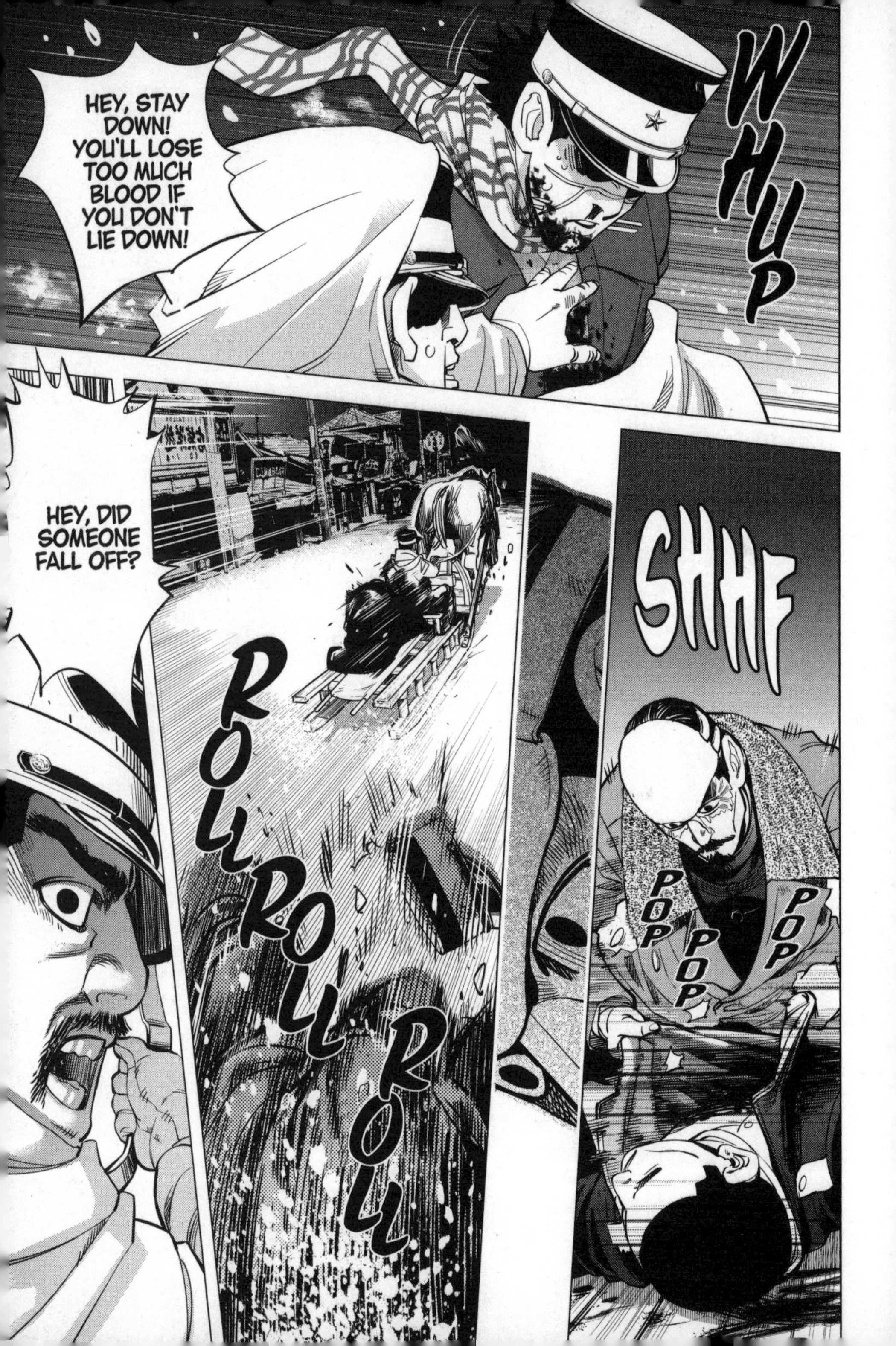
WHUP
HEY, STAY DOWN! YOU'LL LOSE TOO MUCH BLOOD IF YOU DON'T LIE DOWN!
SHHF
POP POP POP POP POP POP
ROLL ROLL ROLL
HEY, DID SOMEONE FALL OFF?

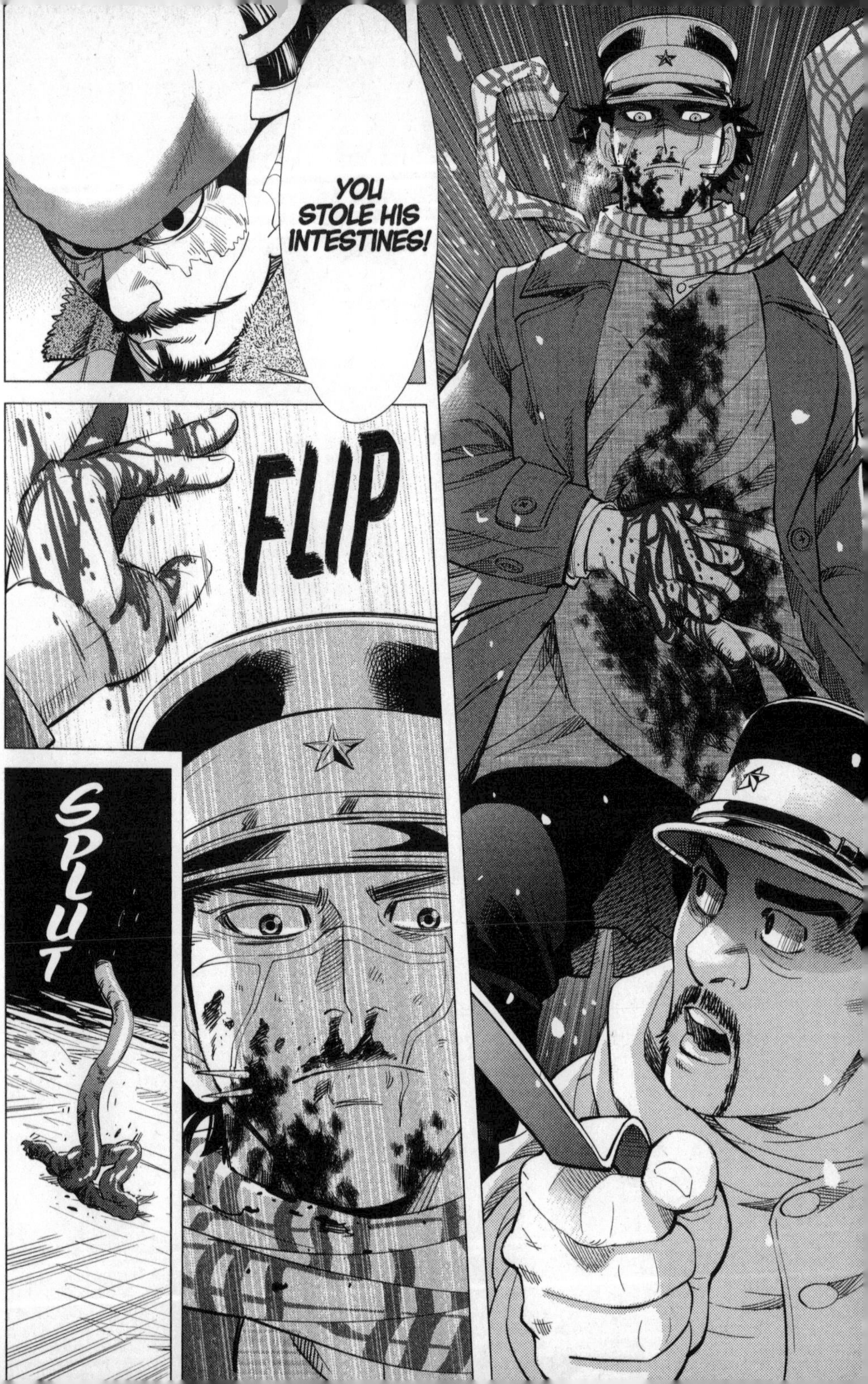
YOU STOLE HIS INTESTINES!
FLIP
SPLUT

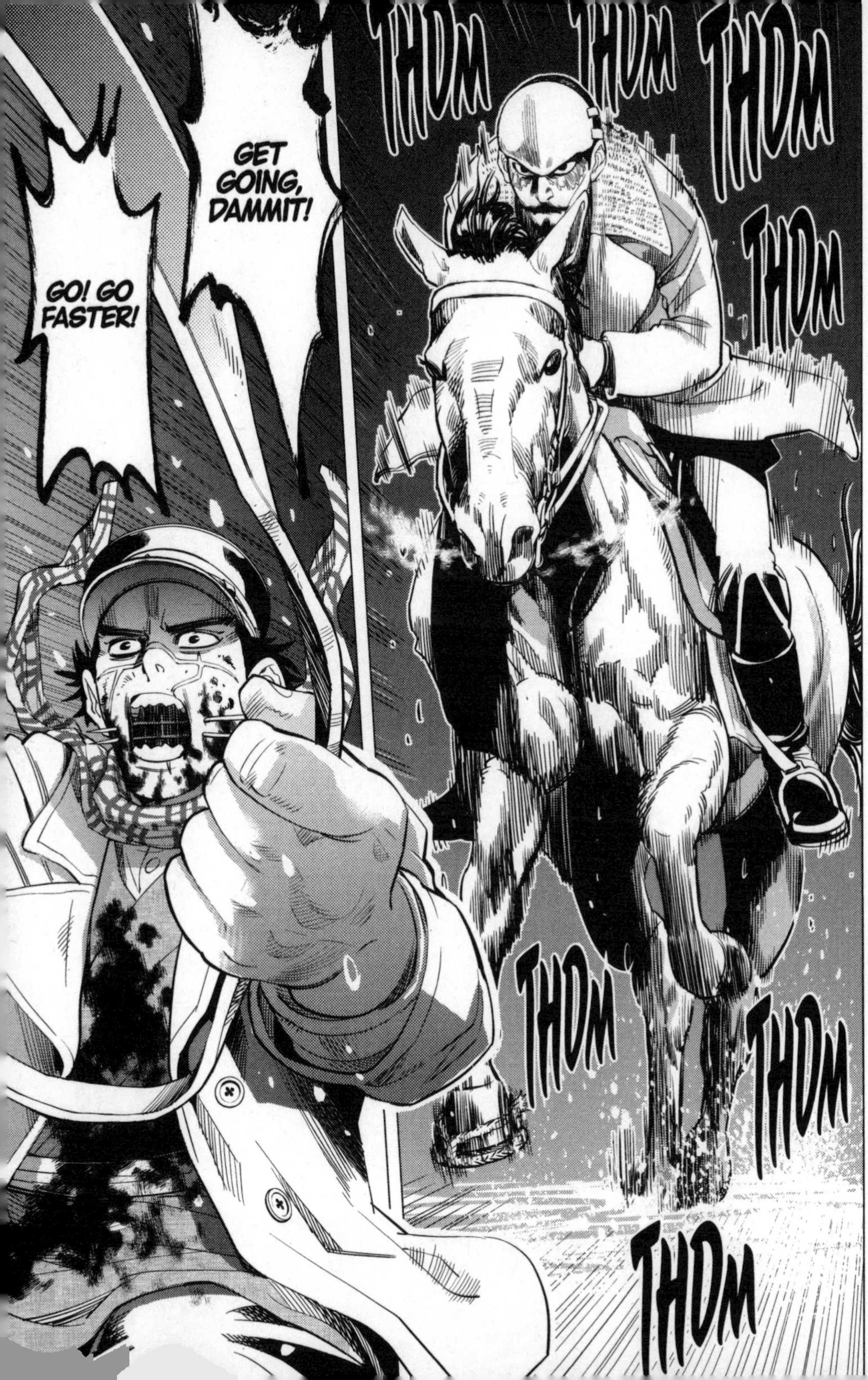
THOM
THOM
THOM
THOM
GET GOING, DAMMIT!
GO! GO FASTER!
THOM
THOM
THOM

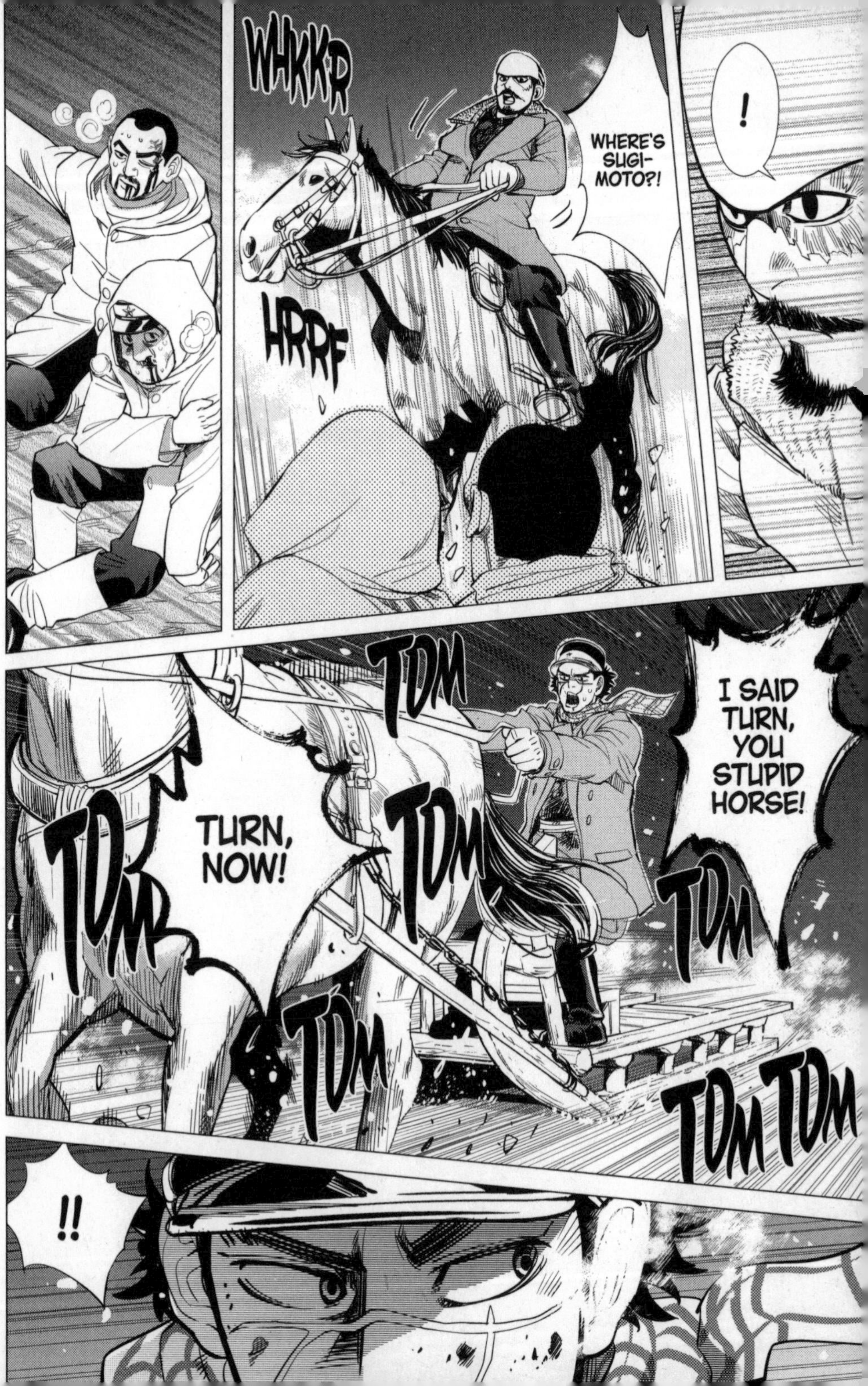

!
WHKKR
WHERE'S SUGI-MOTO?!
HRRF
I SAID TURN, YOU STUPID HORSE!
TOM
TOM
TOM TOM
TOM
TURN, NOW!
TOM
TOM
!!

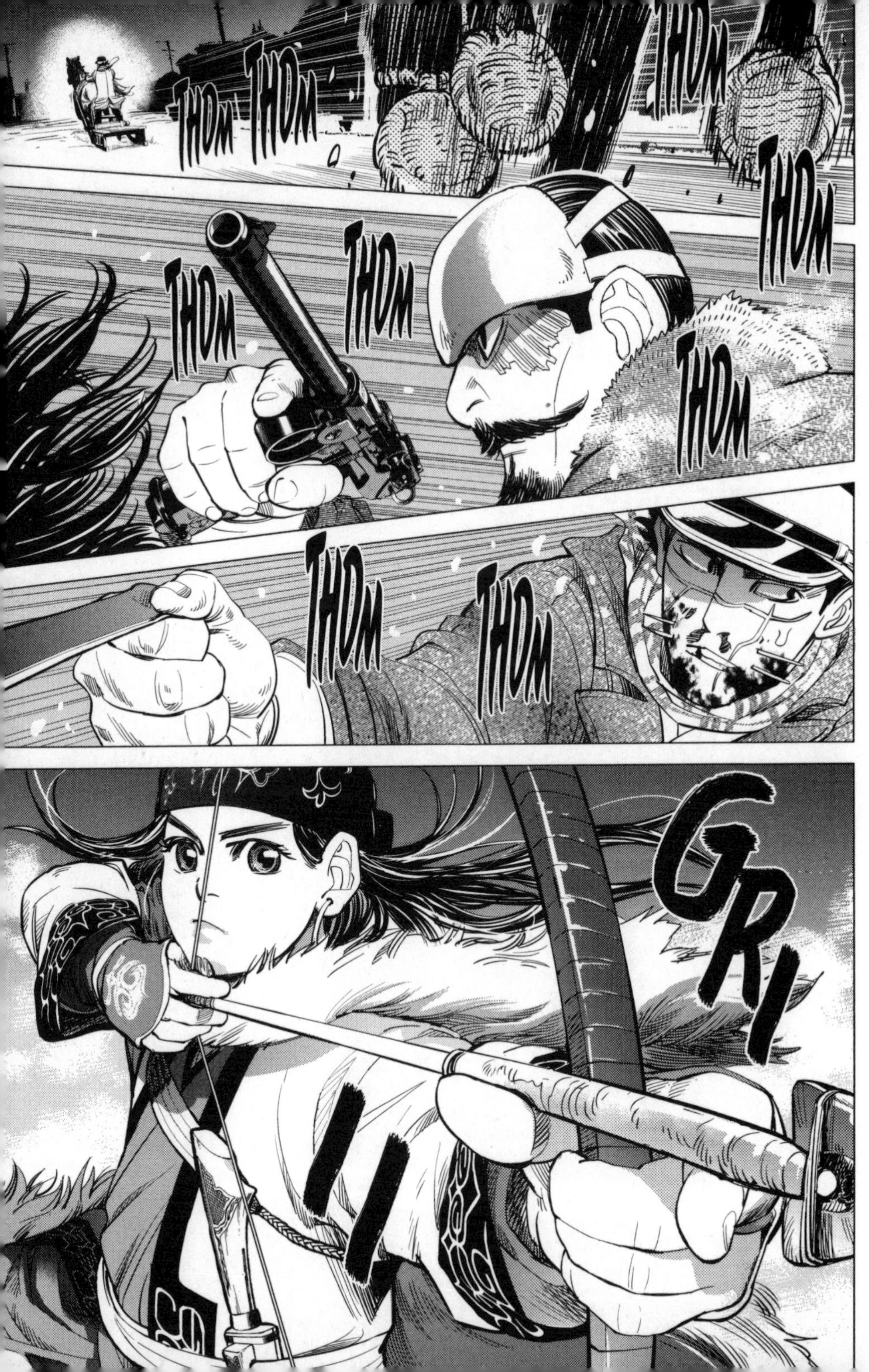
THOM
THOM
THOM
THOM
THOM
THOM
THOM
THOM
THOM
GRIII

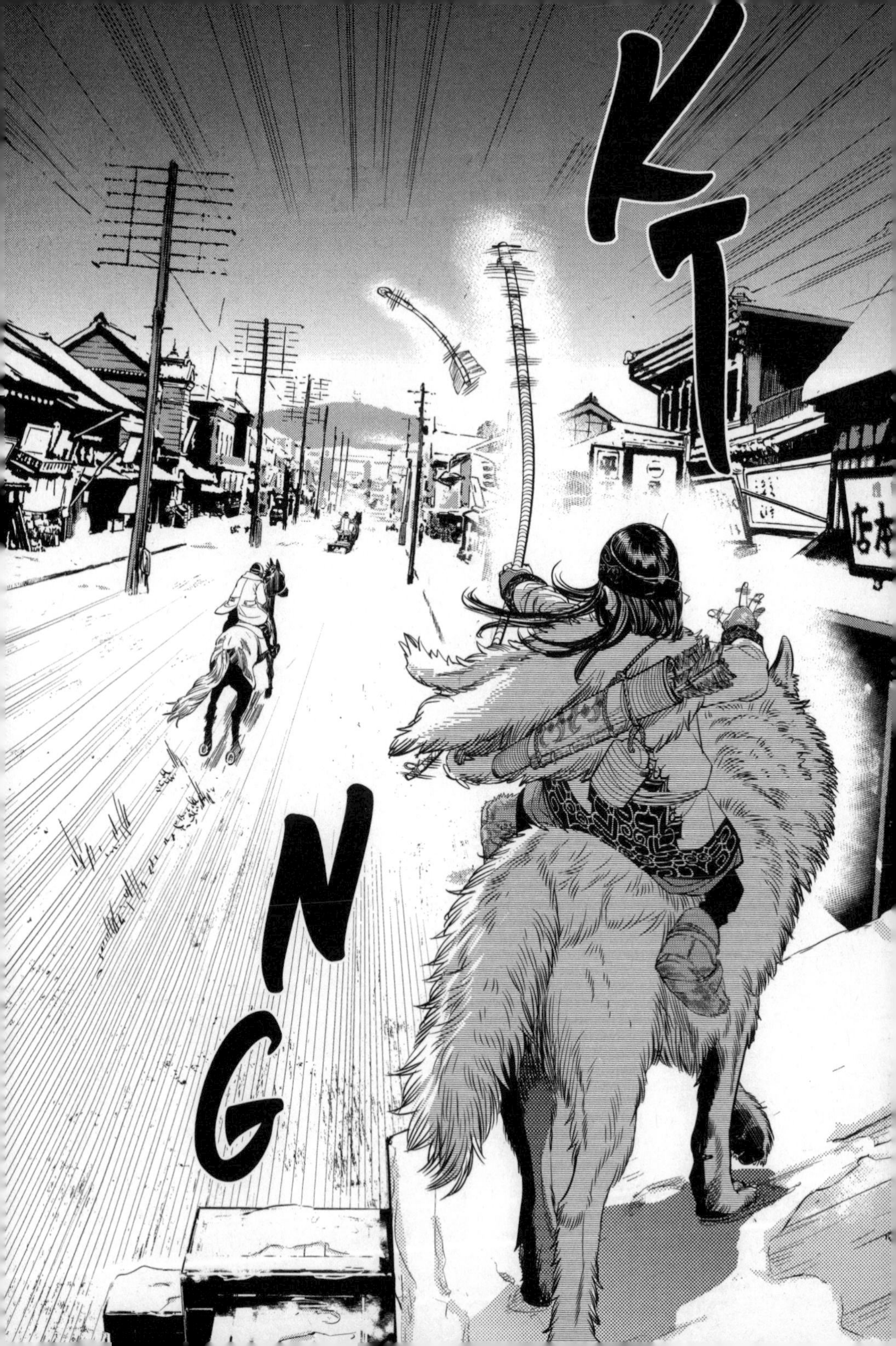
KTNG

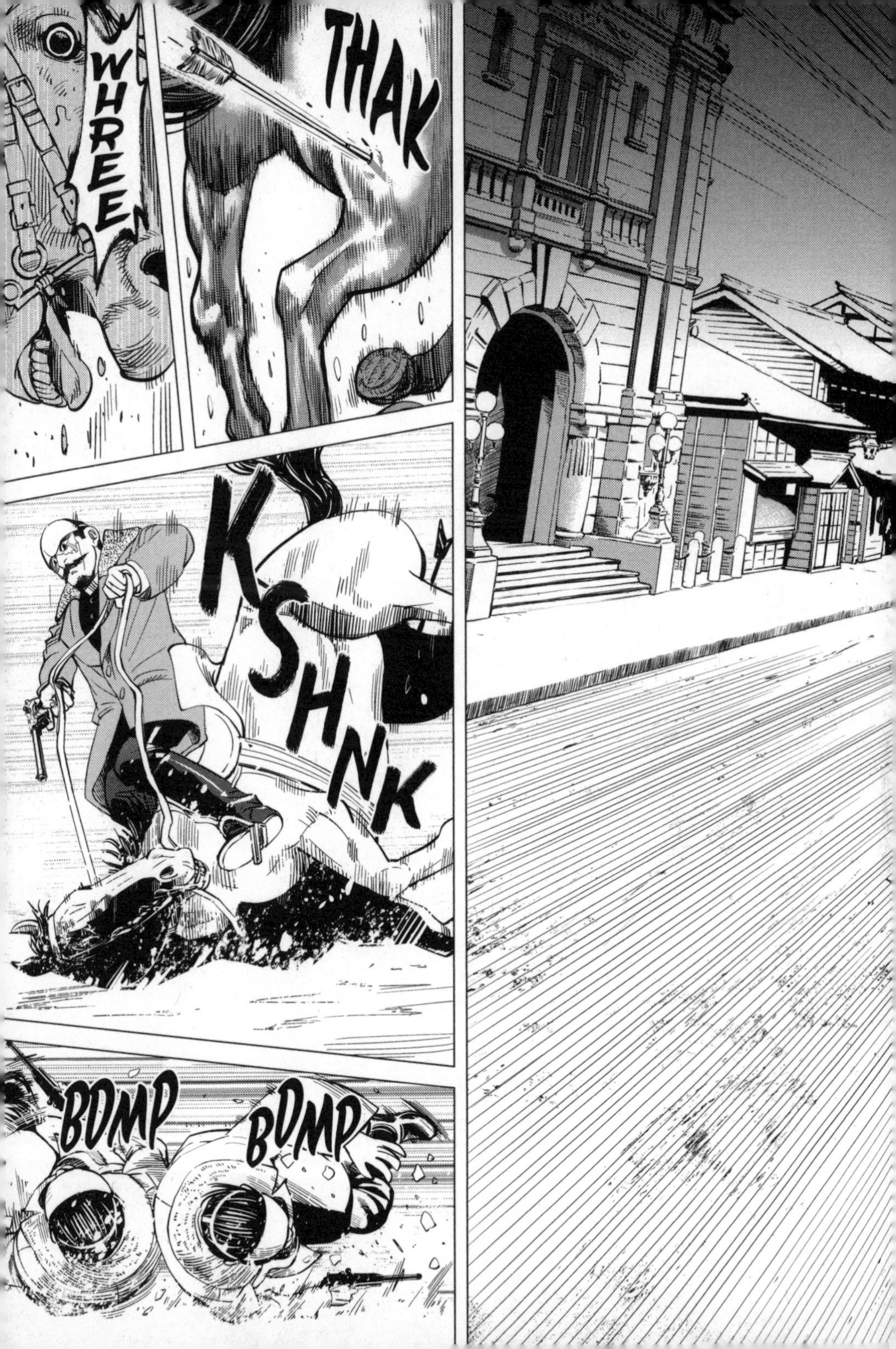
THAK
WHREE
KSHNK
BOMP
BOMP

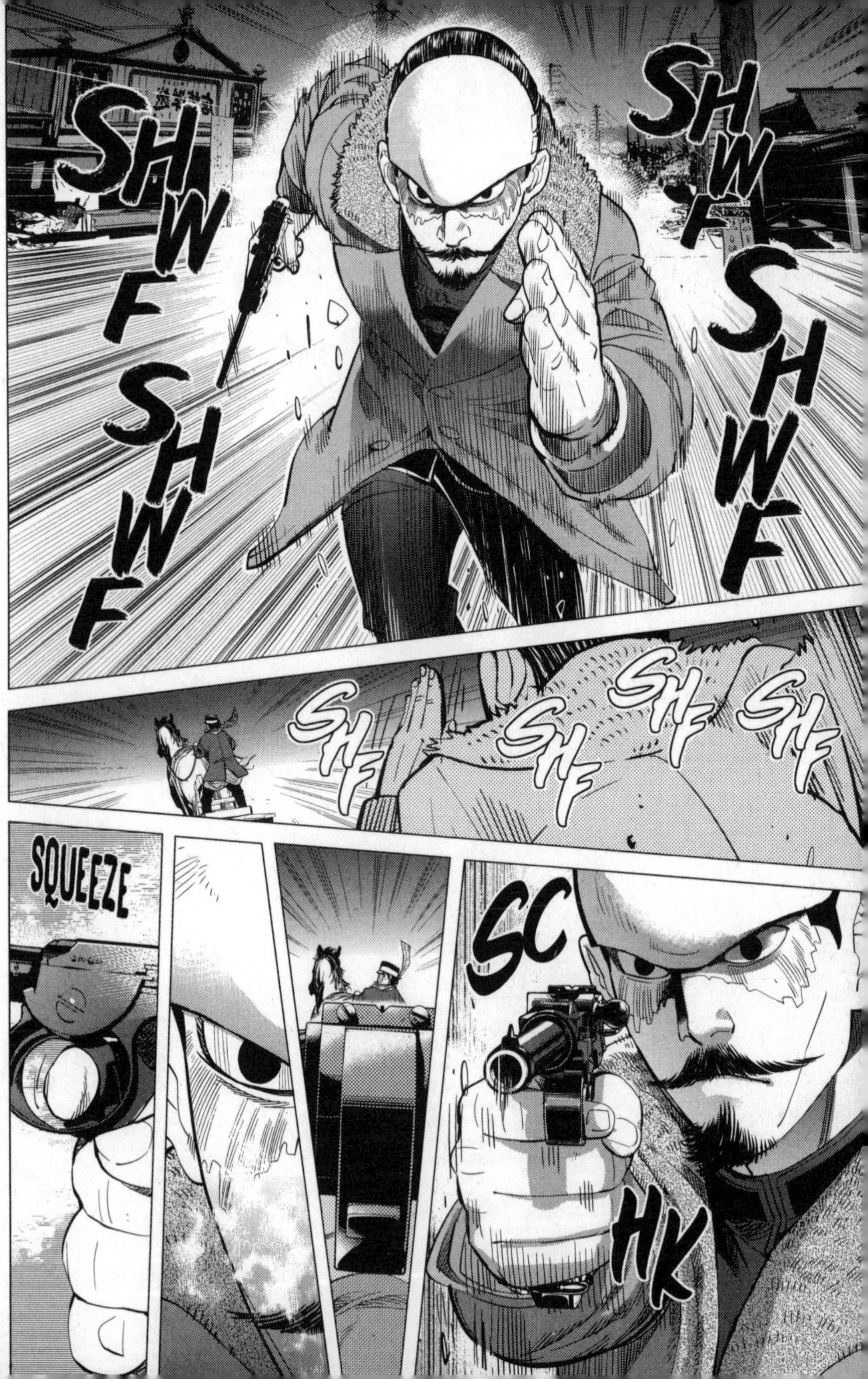
SHWF
SHWF
SHWF
SHWF
SHF
SHF
SHF
SHF
SCHK
SQUEEZE

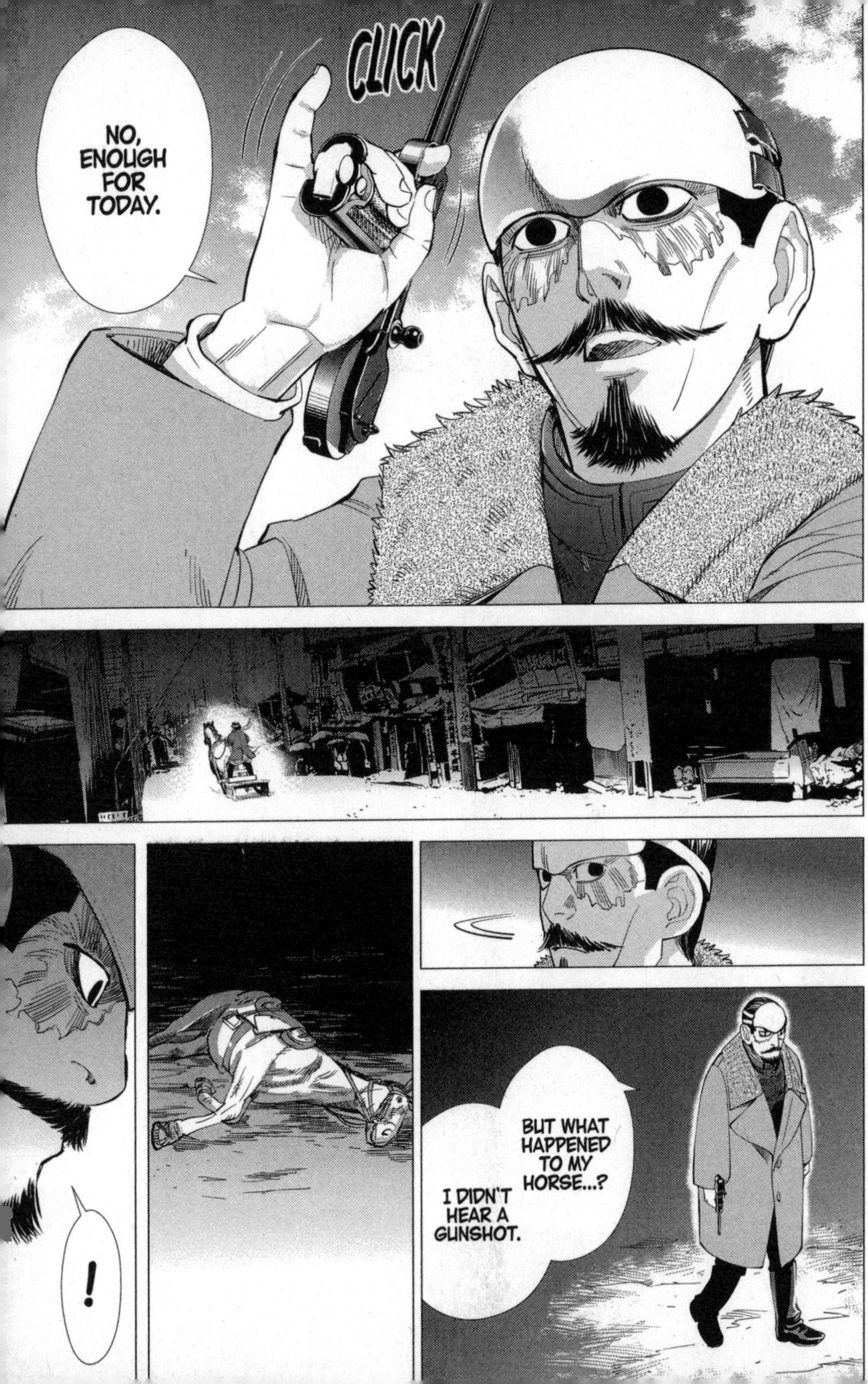
CLICK
NO, ENOUGH FOR TODAY.
BUT WHAT HAPPENED TO MY HORSE...?
I DIDN'T HEAR A GUNSHOT.
!

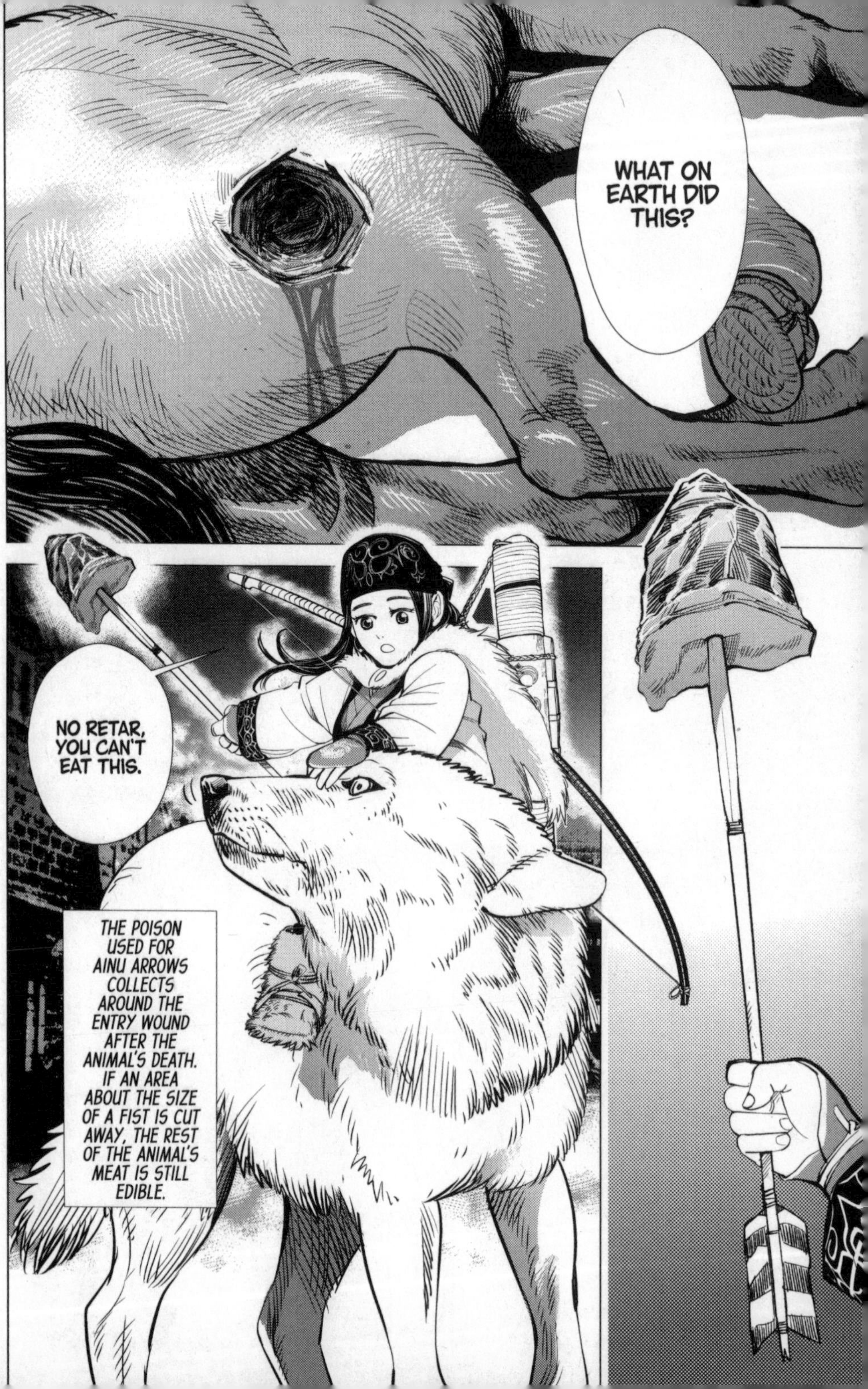
WHAT ON EARTH DID THIS?
NO RETAR, YOU CAN'T EAT THIS.
THE POISON USED FOR AINU ARROWS COLLECTS AROUND THE ENTRY WOUND AFTER THE ANIMAL'S DEATH. IF AN AREA ABOUT THE SIZE OF A FIST IS CUT AWAY, THE REST OF THE ANIMAL'S MEAT IS STILL EDIBLE.

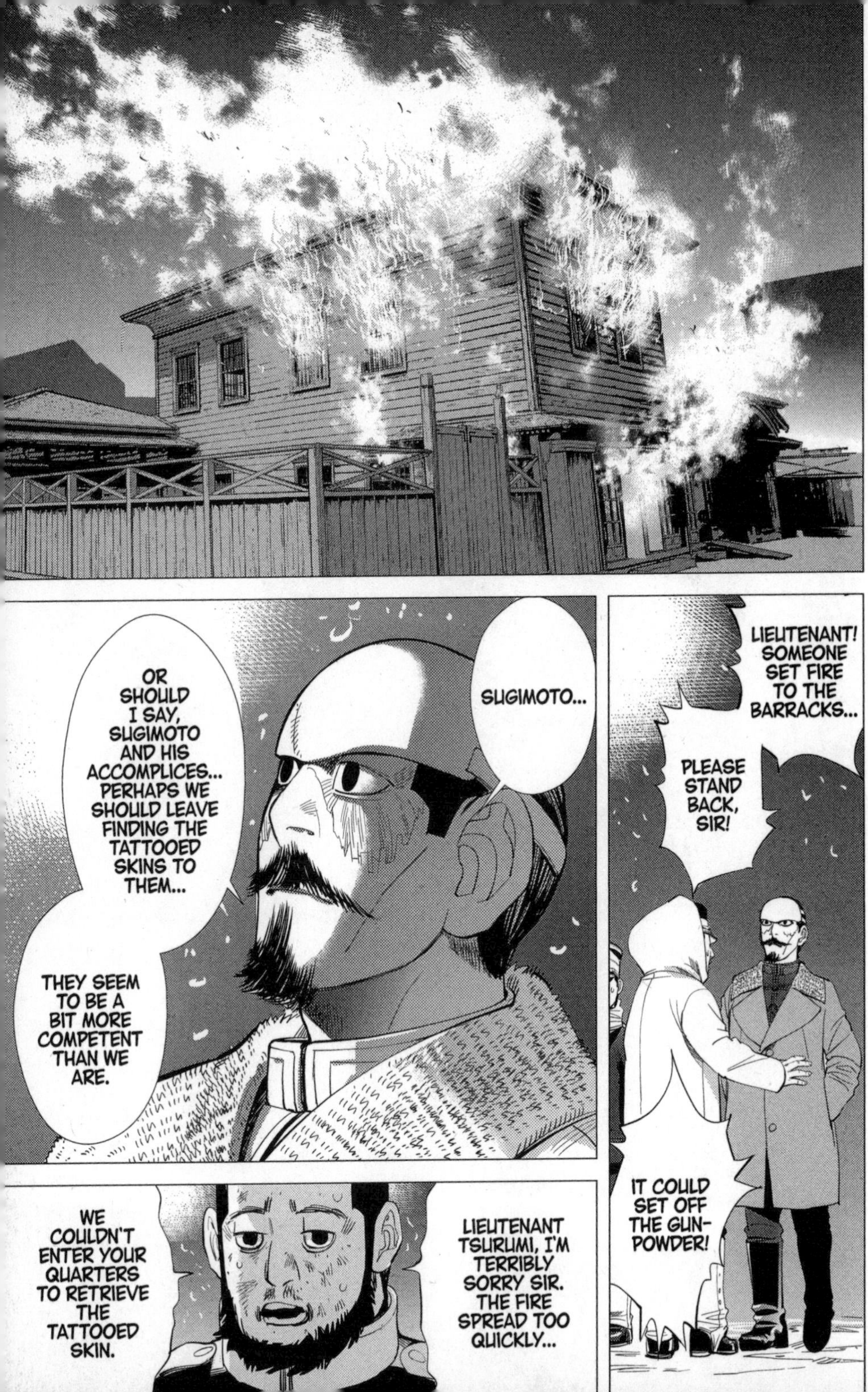
LIEUTENANT! SOMEONE SET FIRE TO THE BARRACKS...
PLEASE STAND BACK, SIR!
IT COULD SET OFF THE GUN-POWDER!
SUGIMOTO...
OR SHOULD I SAY, SUGIMOTO AND HIS ACCOMPLICES... PERHAPS WE SHOULD LEAVE FINDING THE TATTOOED SKINS TO THEM...
THEY SEEM TO BE A BIT MORE COMPETENT THAN WE ARE.
LIEUTENANT TSURUMI, I'M TERRIBLY SORRY SIR. THE FIRE SPREAD TOO QUICKLY...
WE COULDN'T ENTER YOUR QUARTERS TO RETRIEVE THE TATTOOED SKIN.

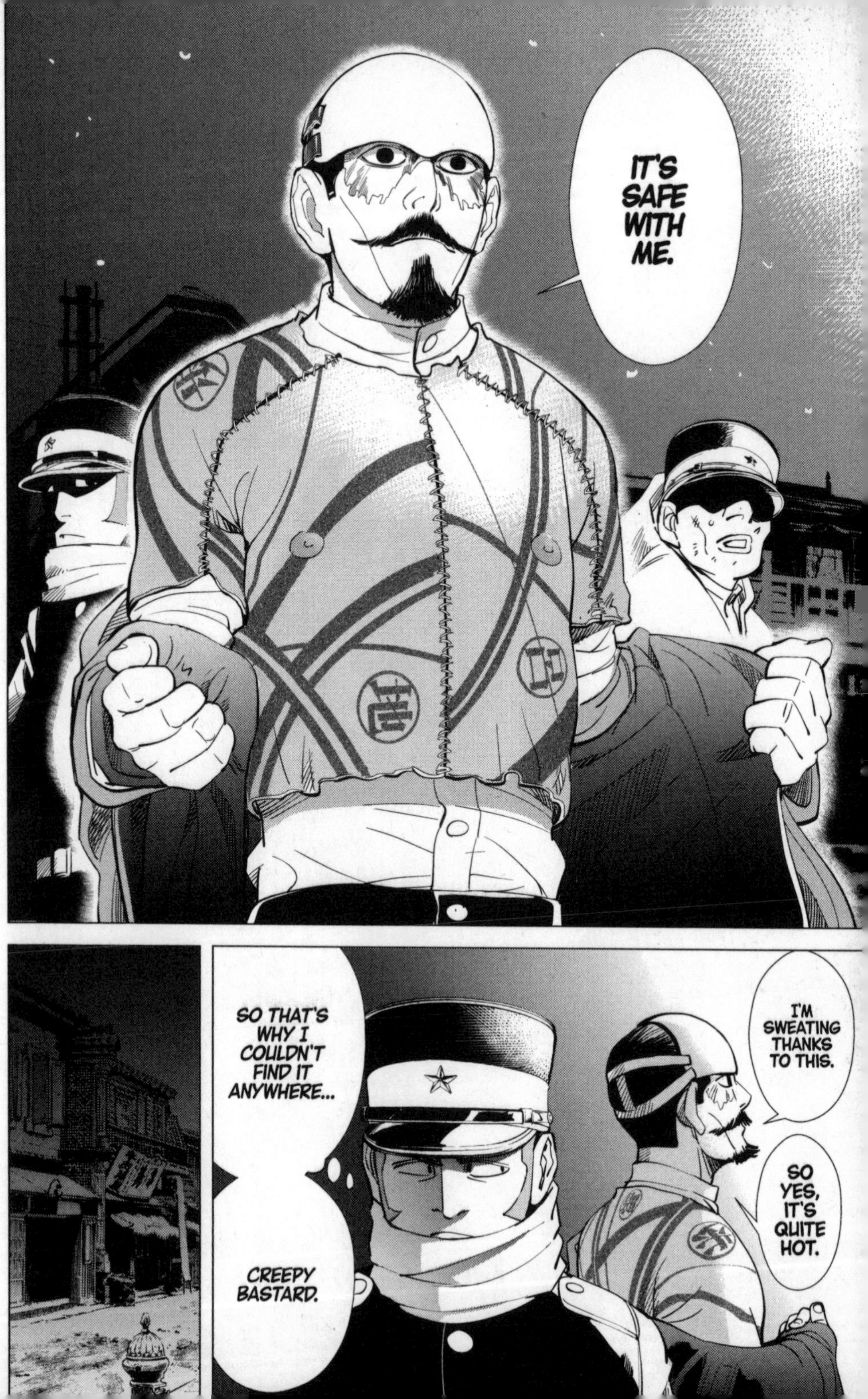
IT'S SAFE WITH ME.
I'M SWEATING THANKS TO THIS.
SO YES, IT'S QUITE HOT.
SO THAT'S WHY I COULDN'T FIND IT ANYWHERE...
CREEPY BASTARD.

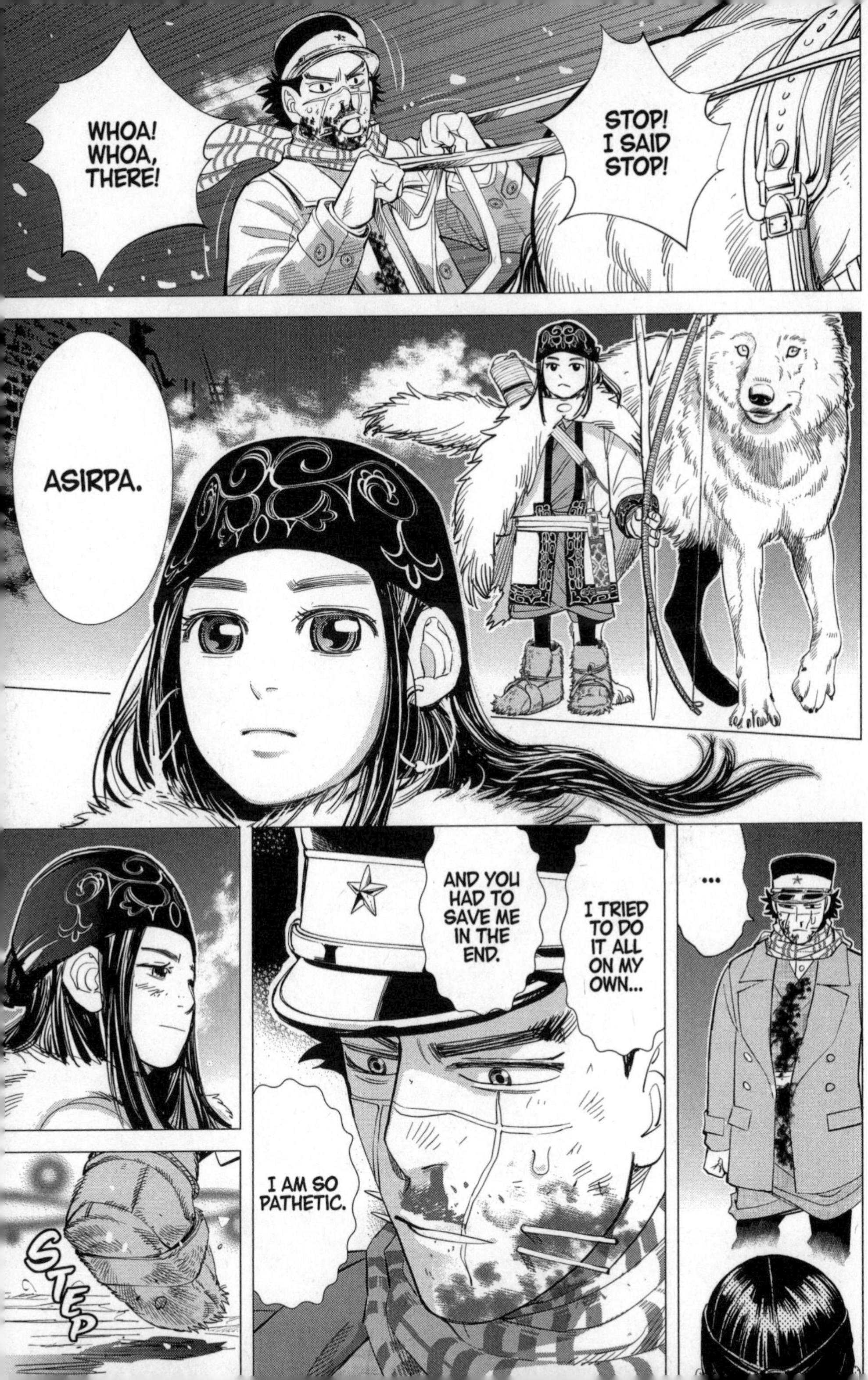
STOP! I SAID STOP!
WHOA! WHOA, THERE!
ASIRPA.
...
I TRIED TO DO IT ALL ON MY OWN...
AND YOU HAD TO SAVE ME IN THE END.
I AM SO PATHETIC.
STEP

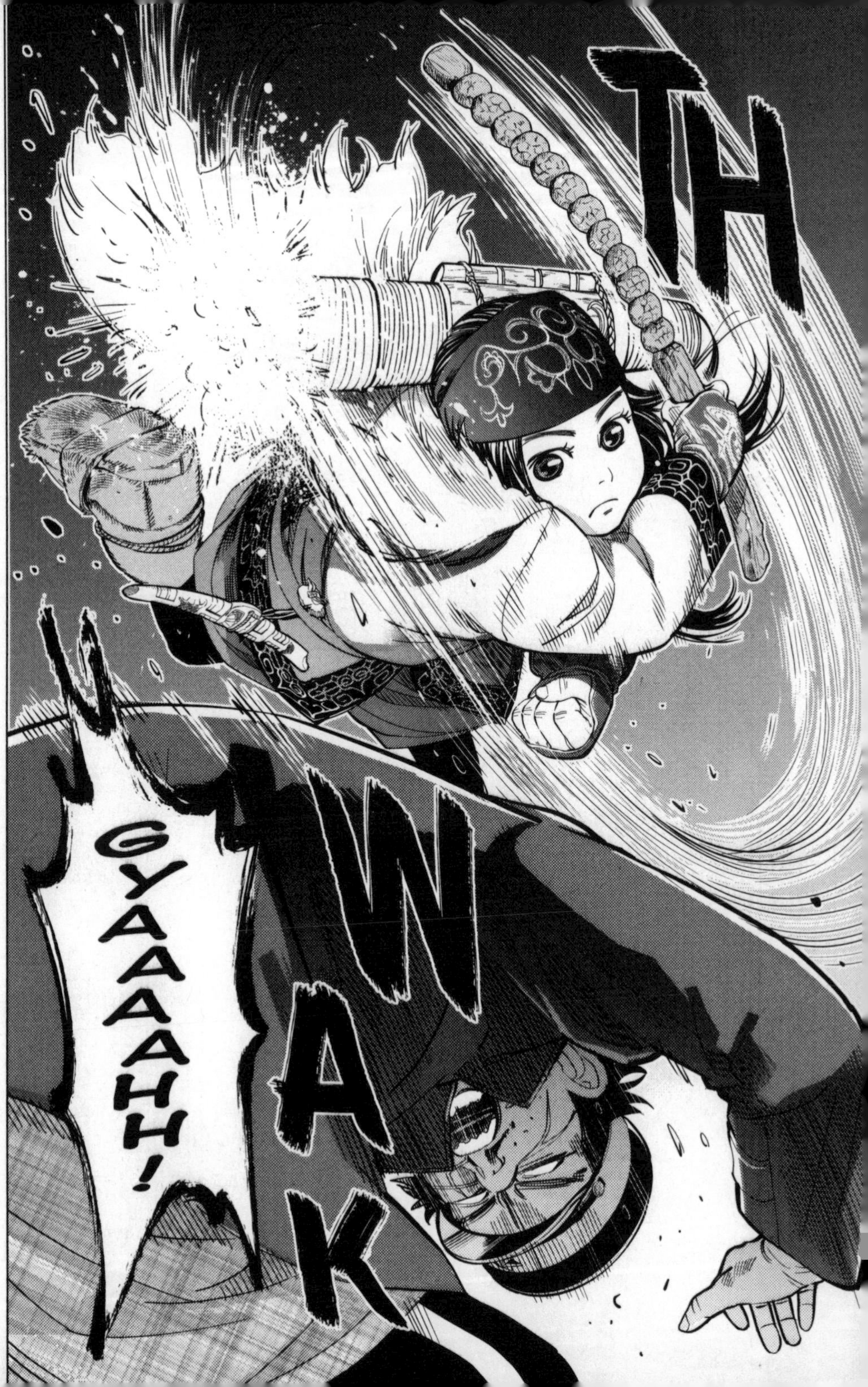
THWAK
GYAAAAAH!

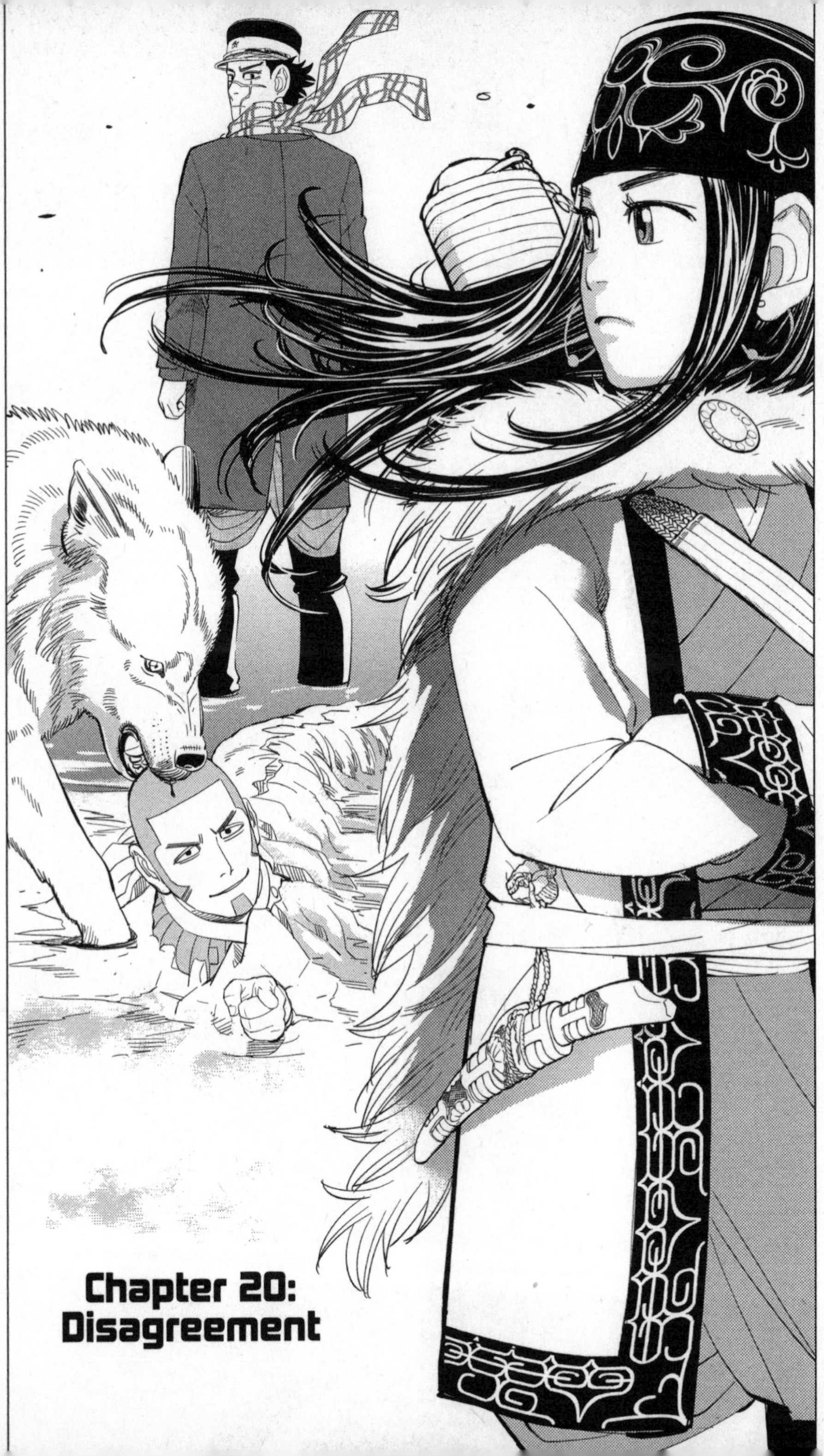
Chapter 20:
Disagreement

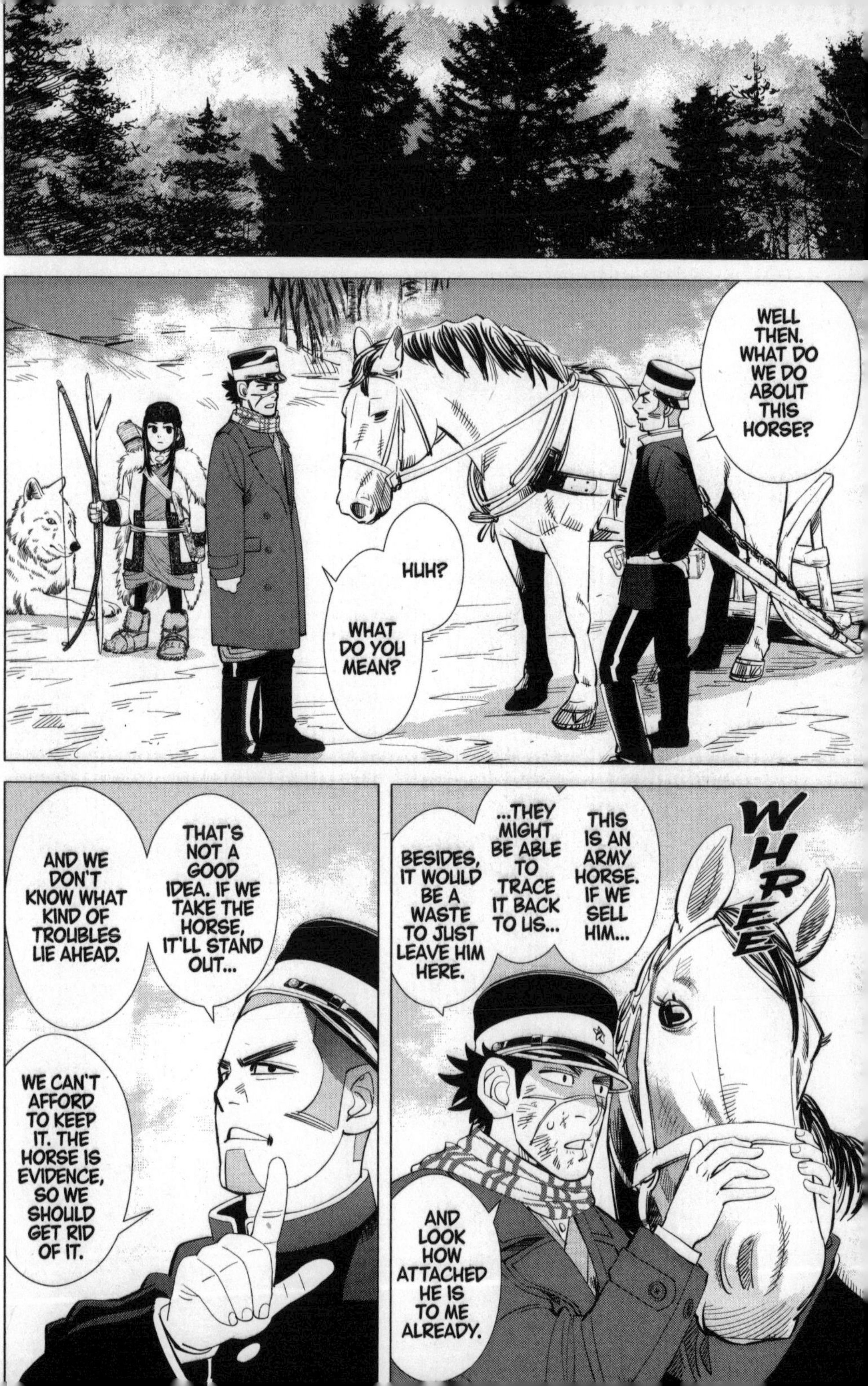
WELL THEN. WHAT DO WE DO ABOUT THIS HORSE?
HUH?
WHAT DO YOU MEAN?
WHREE
THIS IS AN ARMY HORSE. IF WE SELL HIM...
...THEY MIGHT BE ABLE TO TRACE IT BACK TO US...
BESIDES, IT WOULD BE A WASTE TO JUST LEAVE HIM HERE.
AND LOOK HOW ATTACHED HE IS TO ME ALREADY.
THAT'S NOT A GOOD IDEA. IF WE TAKE THE HORSE, IT'LL STAND OUT...
AND WE DON'T KNOW WHAT KIND OF TROUBLES LIE AHEAD.
WE CAN'T AFFORD TO KEEP IT. THE HORSE IS EVIDENCE, SO WE SHOULD GET RID OF IT.

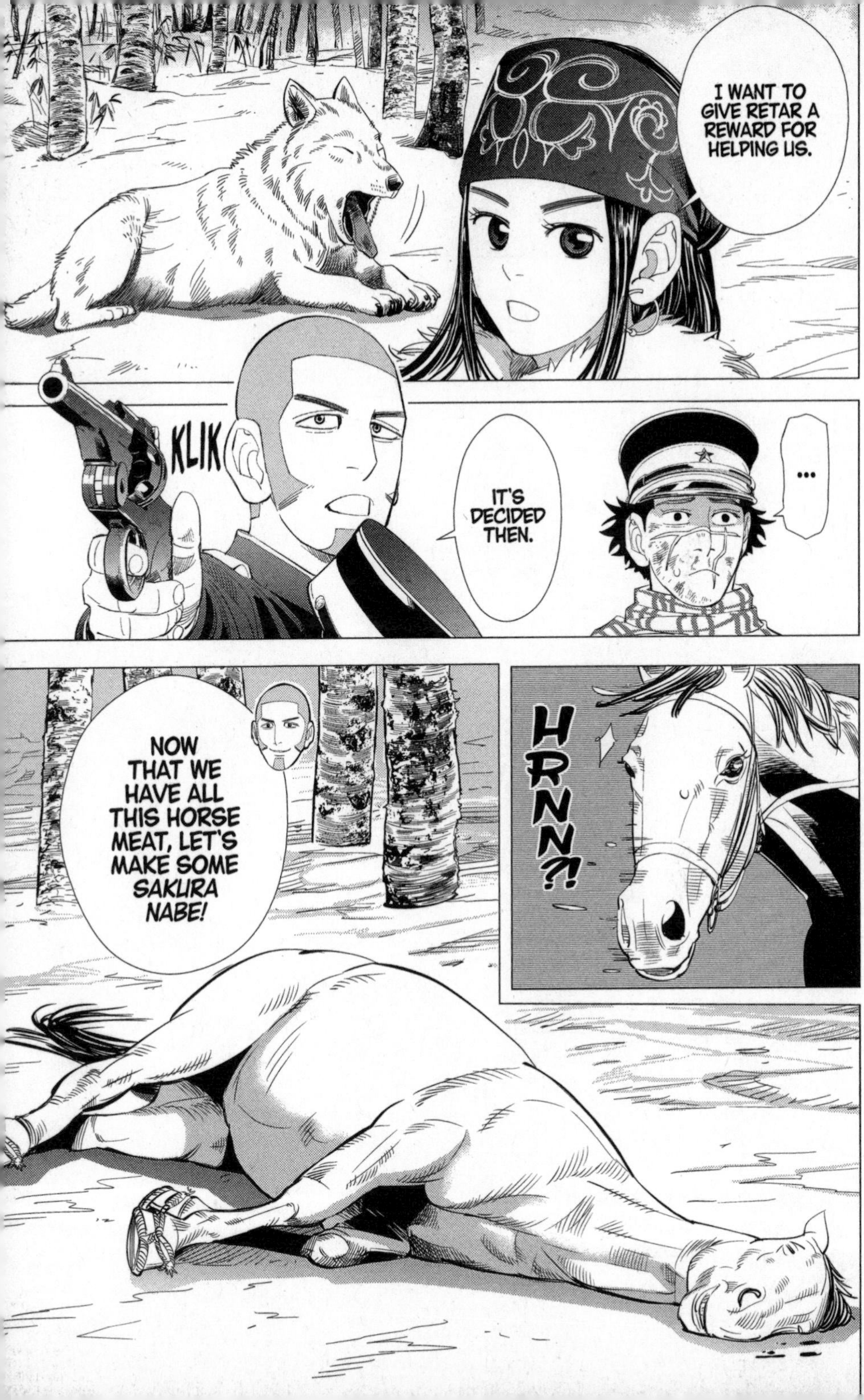
I WANT TO GIVE RETAR A REWARD FOR HELPING US.
...
IT'S DECIDED THEN.
KLIK
HRNN?!
NOW THAT WE HAVE ALL THIS HORSE MEAT, LET'S MAKE SOME SAKURA NABE!

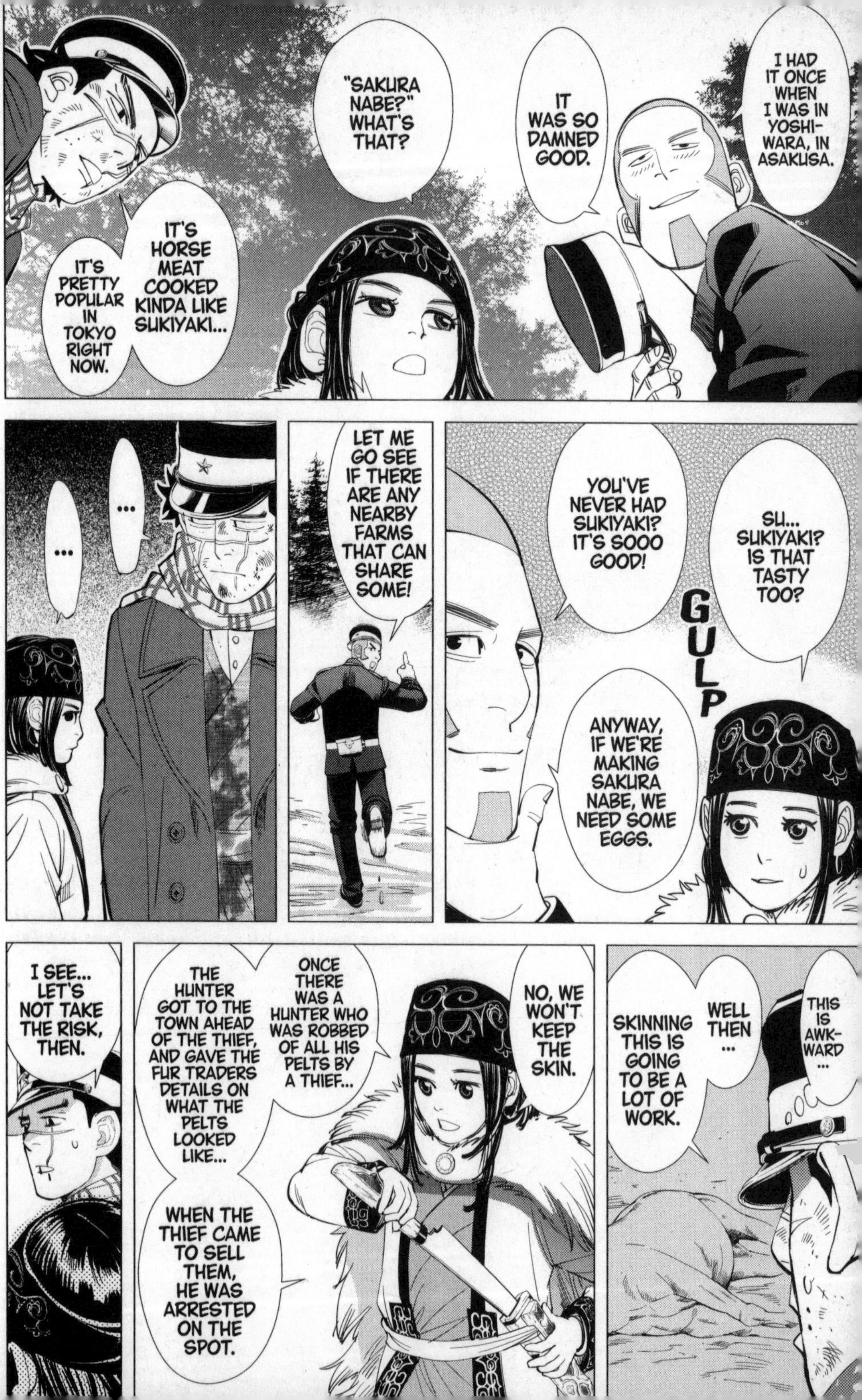
I HAD IT ONCE WHEN I WAS IN YOSHI-WARA, IN ASAKUSA.
IT WAS SO DAMNED GOOD.
"SAKURA NABE?" WHAT'S THAT?
IT'S HORSE MEAT COOKED KINDA LIKE SUKIYAKI...
IT'S PRETTY POPULAR IN TOKYO RIGHT NOW.
SU... SUKIYAKI? IS THAT TASTY TOO?
YOU'VE NEVER HAD SUKIYAKI? IT'S SOOO GOOD!
GULP
ANYWAY, IF WE'RE MAKING SAKURA NABE, WE NEED SOME EGGS.
LET ME GO SEE IF THERE ARE ANY NEARBY FARMS THAT CAN SHARE SOME!
...
...
THIS IS AWK-WARD...
WELL THEN...
SKINNING THIS IS GOING TO BE A LOT OF WORK.
NO, WE WON'T KEEP THE SKIN.
ONCE THERE WAS A HUNTER WHO WAS ROBBED OF ALL HIS PELTS BY A THIEF...
THE HUNTER GOT TO THE TOWN AHEAD OF THE THIEF, AND GAVE THE FUR TRADERS DETAILS ON WHAT THE PELTS LOOKED LIKE...
WHEN THE THIEF CAME TO SELL THEM, HE WAS ARRESTED ON THE SPOT.
I SEE... LET'S NOT TAKE THE RISK, THEN.

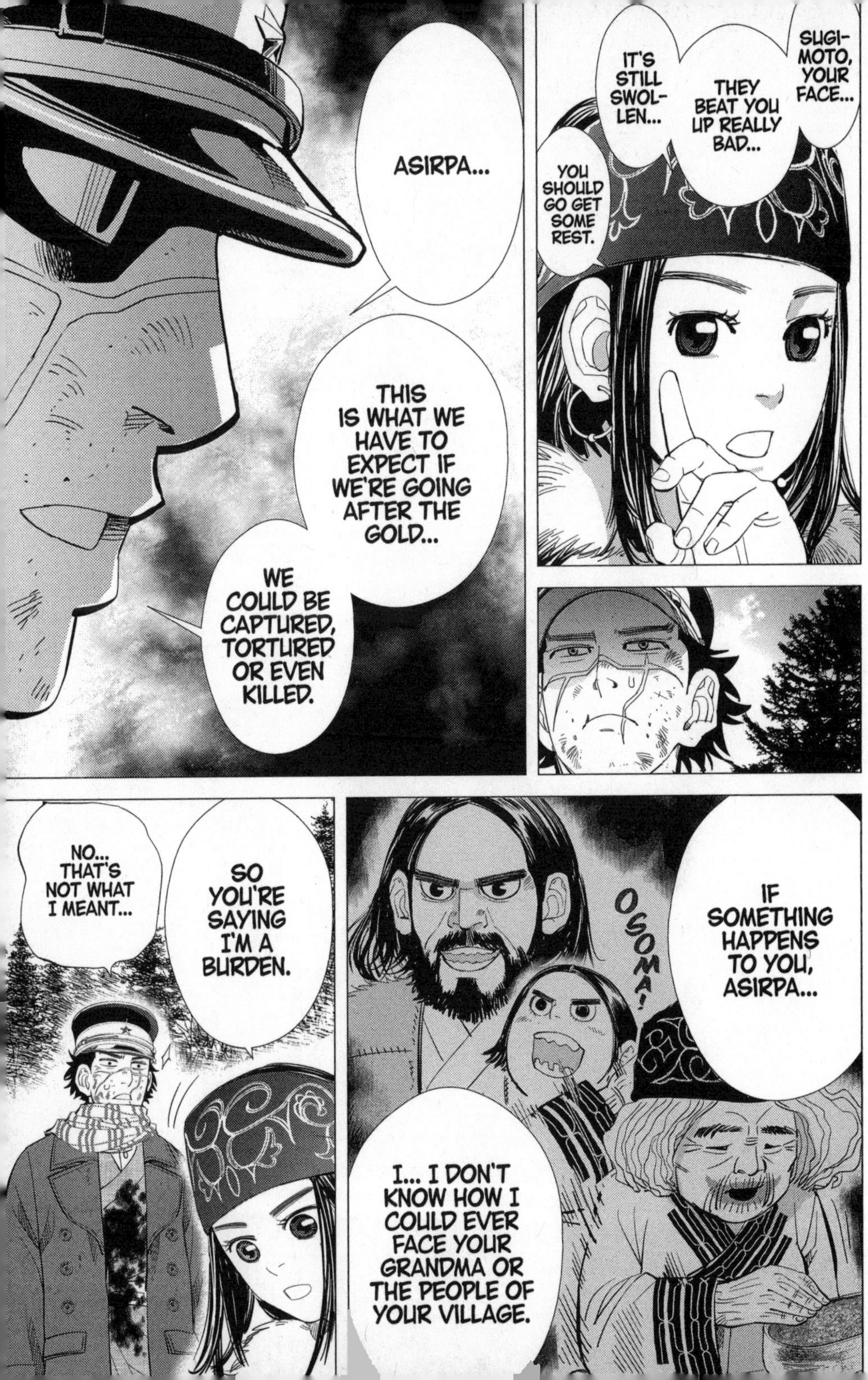
SUGIMOTO, YOUR FACE...
THEY BEAT YOU UP REALLY BAD...
IT'S STILL SWOLLEN...
YOU SHOULD GO GET SOME REST.
ASIRPA...
THIS IS WHAT WE HAVE TO EXPECT IF WE'RE GOING AFTER THE GOLD...
WE COULD BE CAPTURED, TORTURED OR EVEN KILLED.
IF SOMETHING HAPPENS TO YOU, ASIRPA...
OSOMA!
I... I DON'T KNOW HOW I COULD EVER FACE YOUR GRANDMA OR THE PEOPLE OF YOUR VILLAGE.
SO YOU'RE SAYING I'M A BURDEN.
NO... THAT'S NOT WHAT I MEANT...

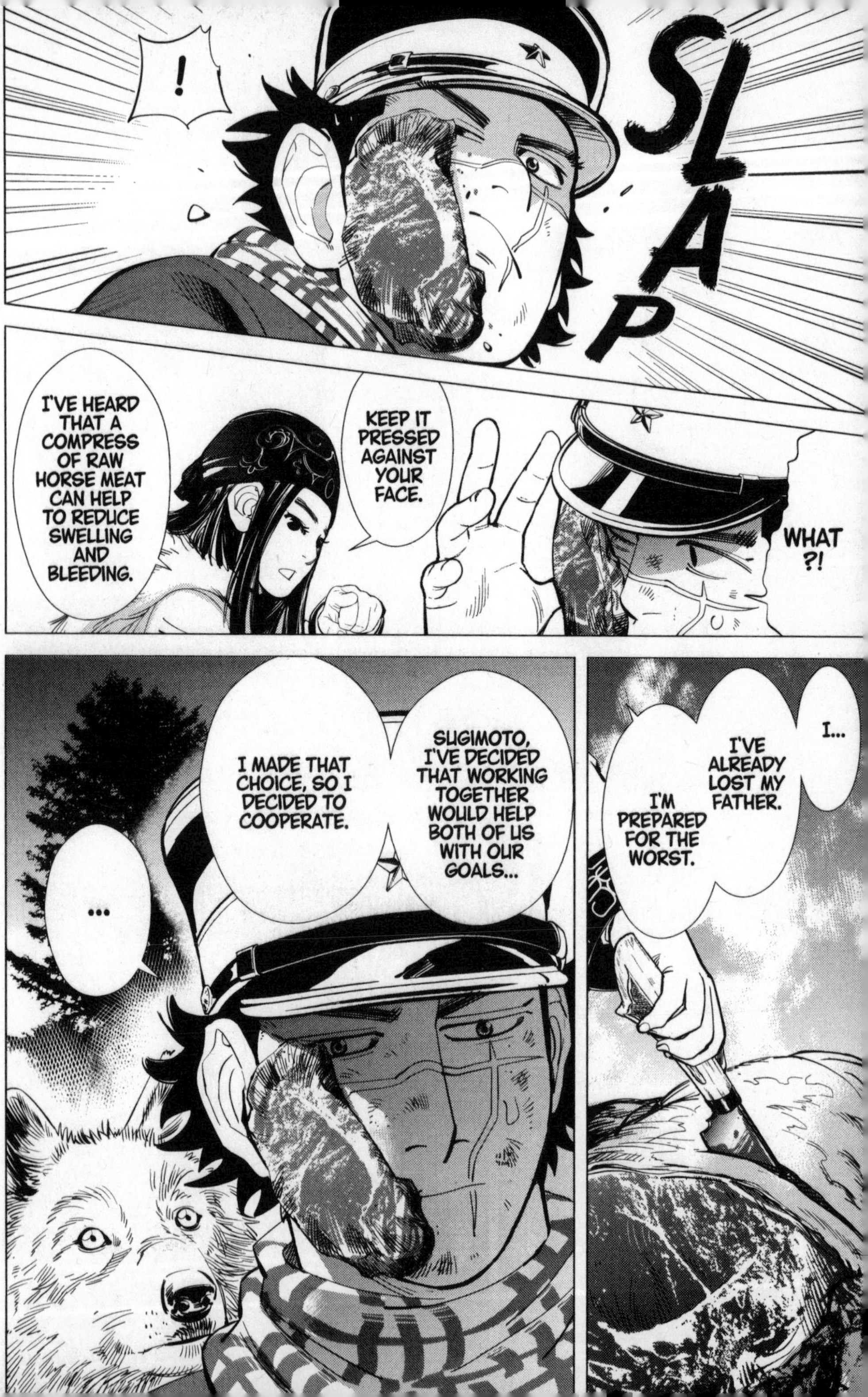
SLAP
!
WHAT ?!
KEEP IT PRESSED AGAINST YOUR FACE.
I'VE HEARD THAT A COMPRESS OF RAW HORSE MEAT CAN HELP TO REDUCE SWELLING AND BLEEDING.
I...
I'VE ALREADY LOST MY FATHER.
I'M PREPARED FOR THE WORST.
SUGIMOTO, I'VE DECIDED THAT WORKING TOGETHER WOULD HELP BOTH OF US WITH OUR GOALS...
I MADE THAT CHOICE, SO I DECIDED TO COOPERATE.
...

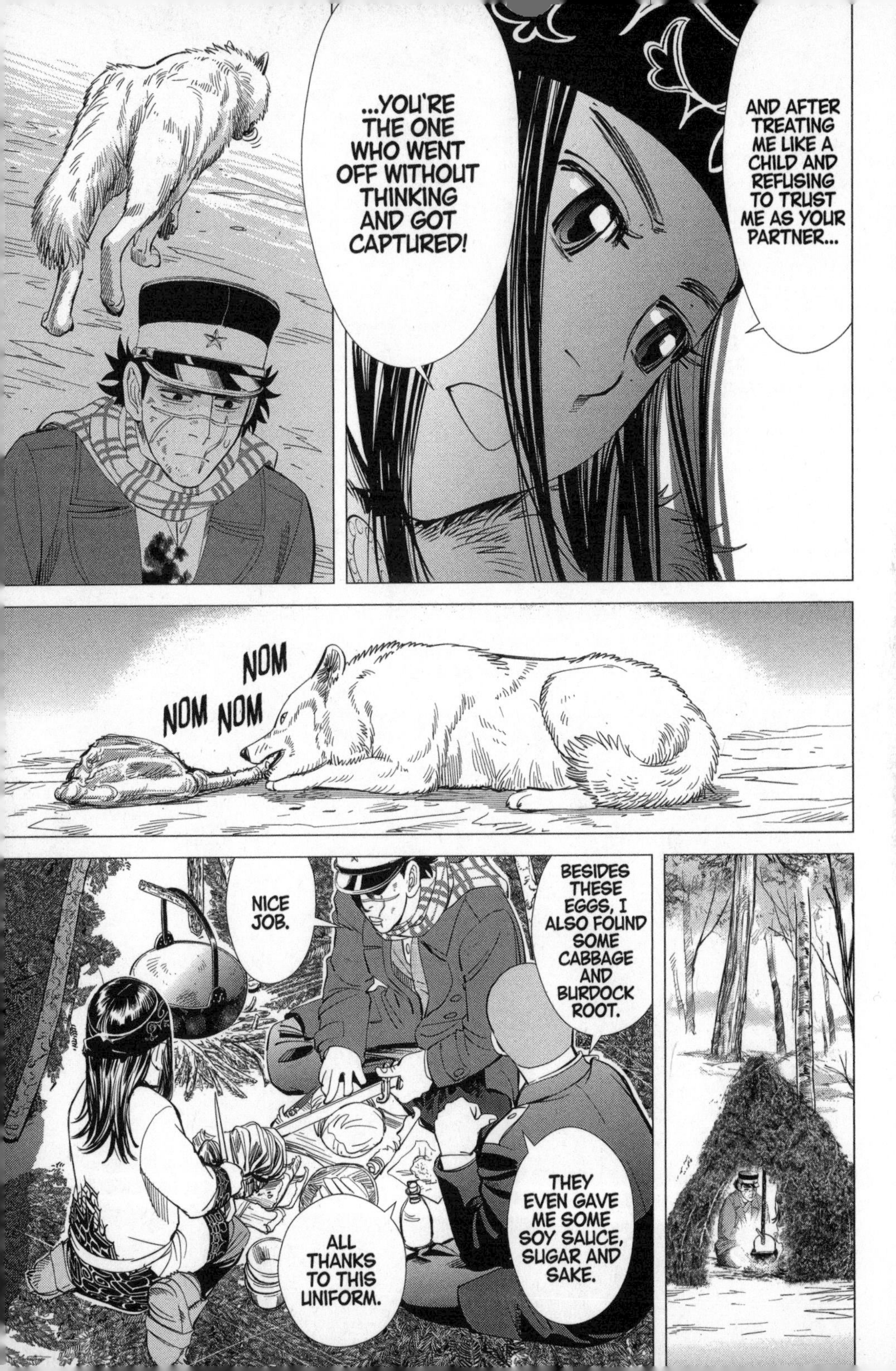
AND AFTER TREATING ME LIKE A CHILD AND REFUSING TO TRUST ME AS YOUR PARTNER...
...YOU'RE THE ONE WHO WENT OFF WITHOUT THINKING AND GOT CAPTURED!
NOM
NOM NOM
BESIDES THESE EGGS, I ALSO FOUND SOME CABBAGE AND BURDOCK ROOT.
NICE JOB.
THEY EVEN GAVE ME SOME SOY SAUCE, SUGAR AND SAKE.
ALL THANKS TO THIS UNIFORM.

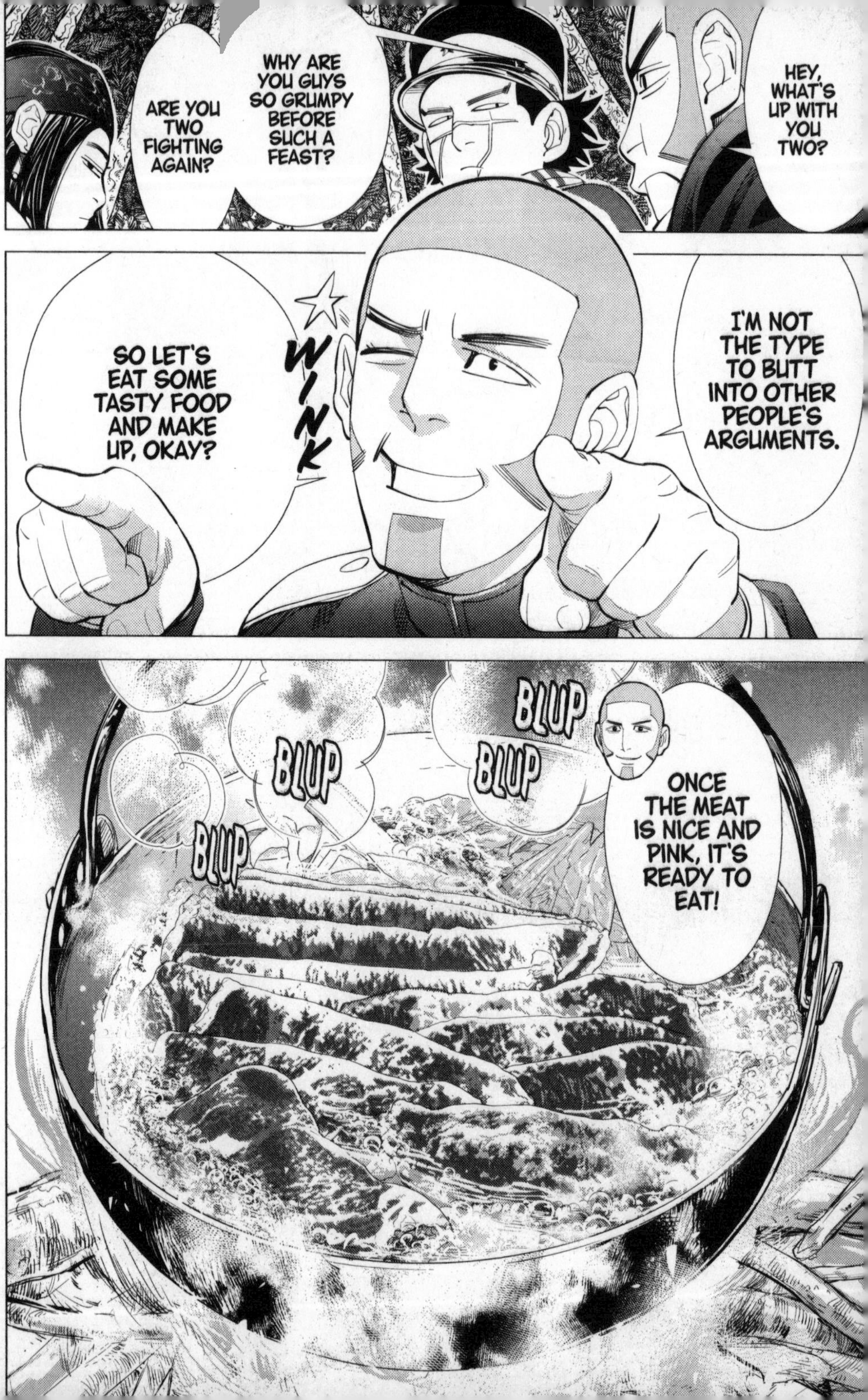
HEY, WHAT'S UP WITH YOU TWO?
WHY ARE YOU GUYS SO GRUMPY BEFORE SUCH A FEAST?
ARE YOU TWO FIGHTING AGAIN?
I'M NOT THE TYPE TO BUTT INTO OTHER PEOPLE'S ARGUMENTS.
WINK
SO LET'S EAT SOME TASTY FOOD AND MAKE UP, OKAY?
ONCE THE MEAT IS NICE AND PINK, IT'S READY TO EAT!
BLUP
BLUP
BLUP
BLUP

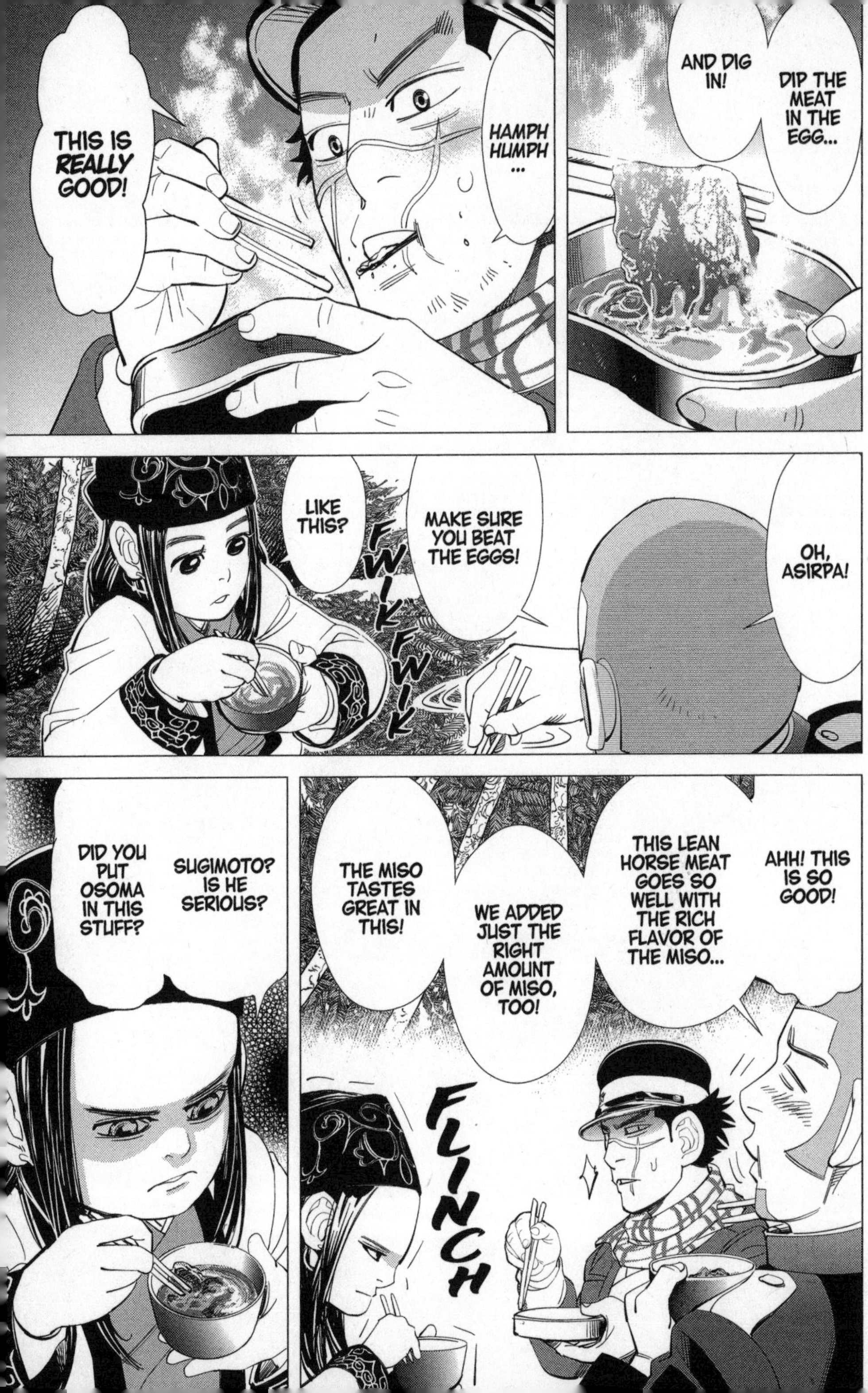
DIP THE MEAT IN THE EGG...
AND DIG IN!
HAMPH HUMPH ...
THIS IS REALLY GOOD!
OH, ASIRPA!
MAKE SURE YOU BEAT THE EGGS!
FWIK FWIK
LIKE THIS?
AHH! THIS IS SO GOOD!
THIS LEAN HORSE MEAT GOES SO WELL WITH THE RICH FLAVOR OF THE MISO...
WE ADDED JUST THE RIGHT AMOUNT OF MISO, TOO!
THE MISO TASTES GREAT IN THIS!
FLINCH
SUGIMOTO? IS HE SERIOUS?
DID YOU PUT OSOMA IN THIS STUFF?

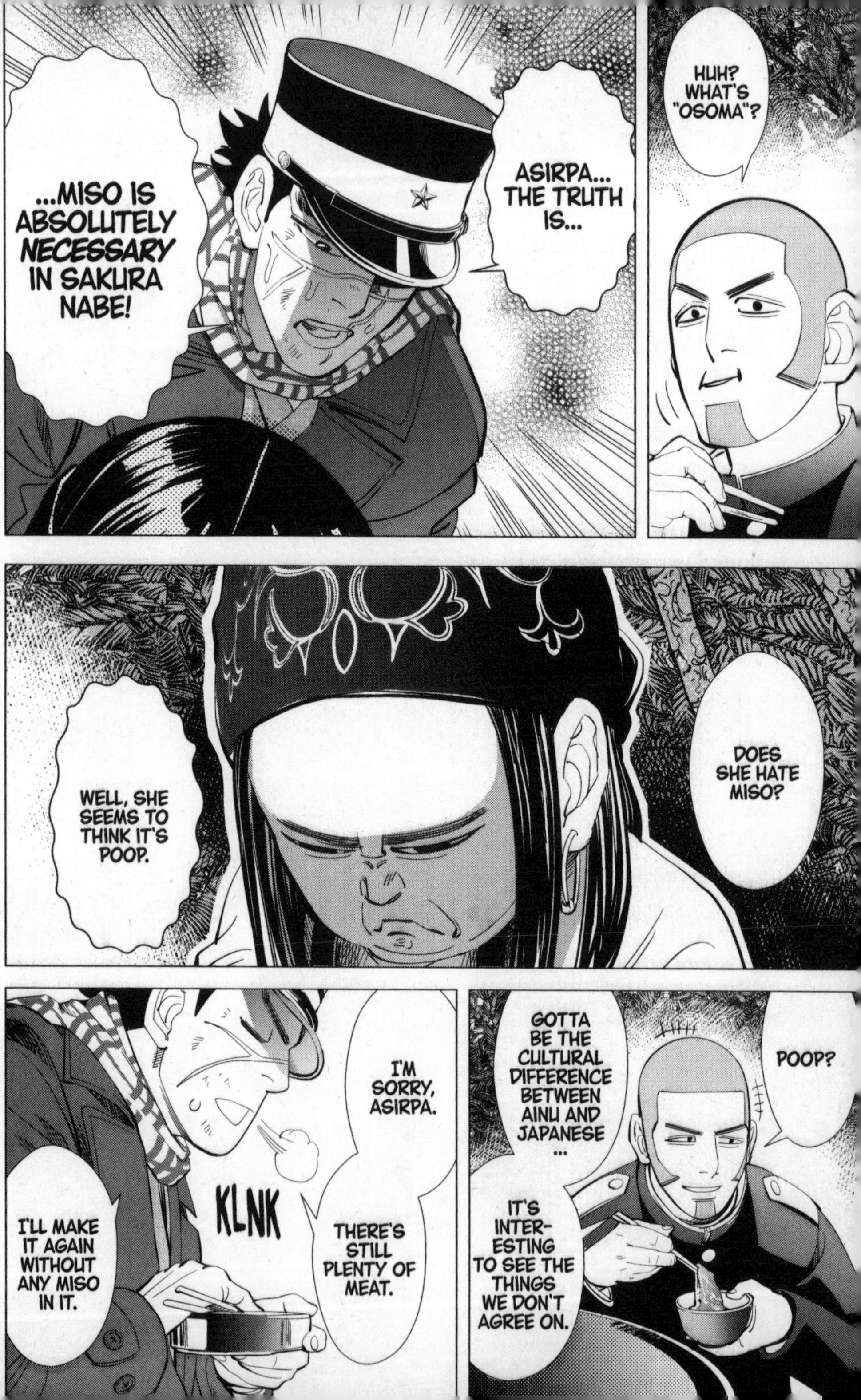
HUH? WHAT'S "OSOMA"?
ASIRPA... THE TRUTH IS...
...MISO IS ABSOLUTELY NECESSARY IN SAKURA NABE!
DOES SHE HATE MISO?
WELL, SHE SEEMS TO THINK IT'S POOP.
POOP?
GOTTA BE THE CULTURAL DIFFERENCE BETWEEN AINU AND JAPANESE...
IT'S INTERESTING TO SEE THE THINGS WE DON'T AGREE ON.
I'M SORRY, ASIRPA.
KLNK
THERE'S STILL PLENTY OF MEAT.
I'LL MAKE IT AGAIN WITHOUT ANY MISO IN IT.

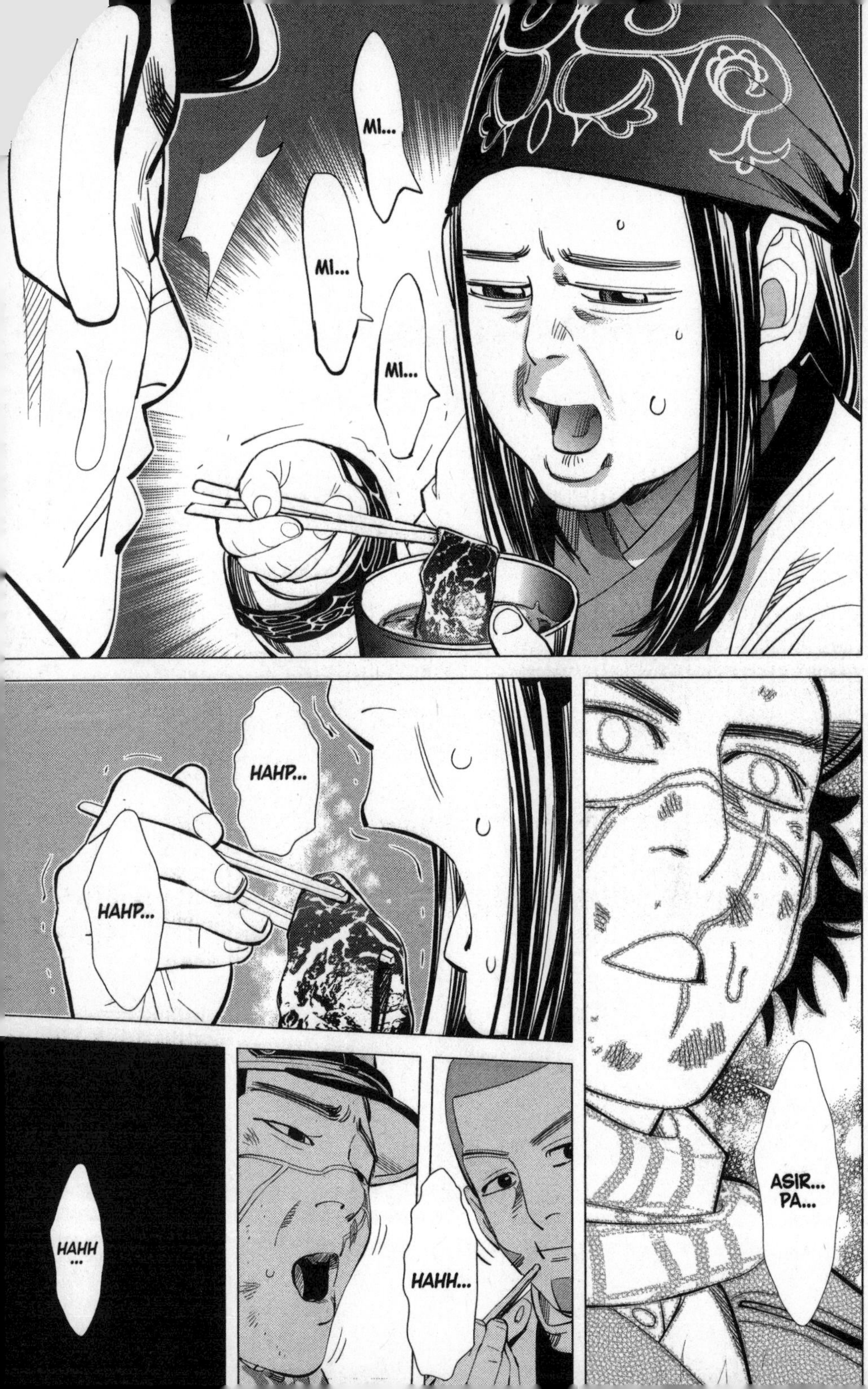

MI...
MI...
MI...
ASIR... PA...
HAHP...
HAHP...
HAHH...
HAHH ...

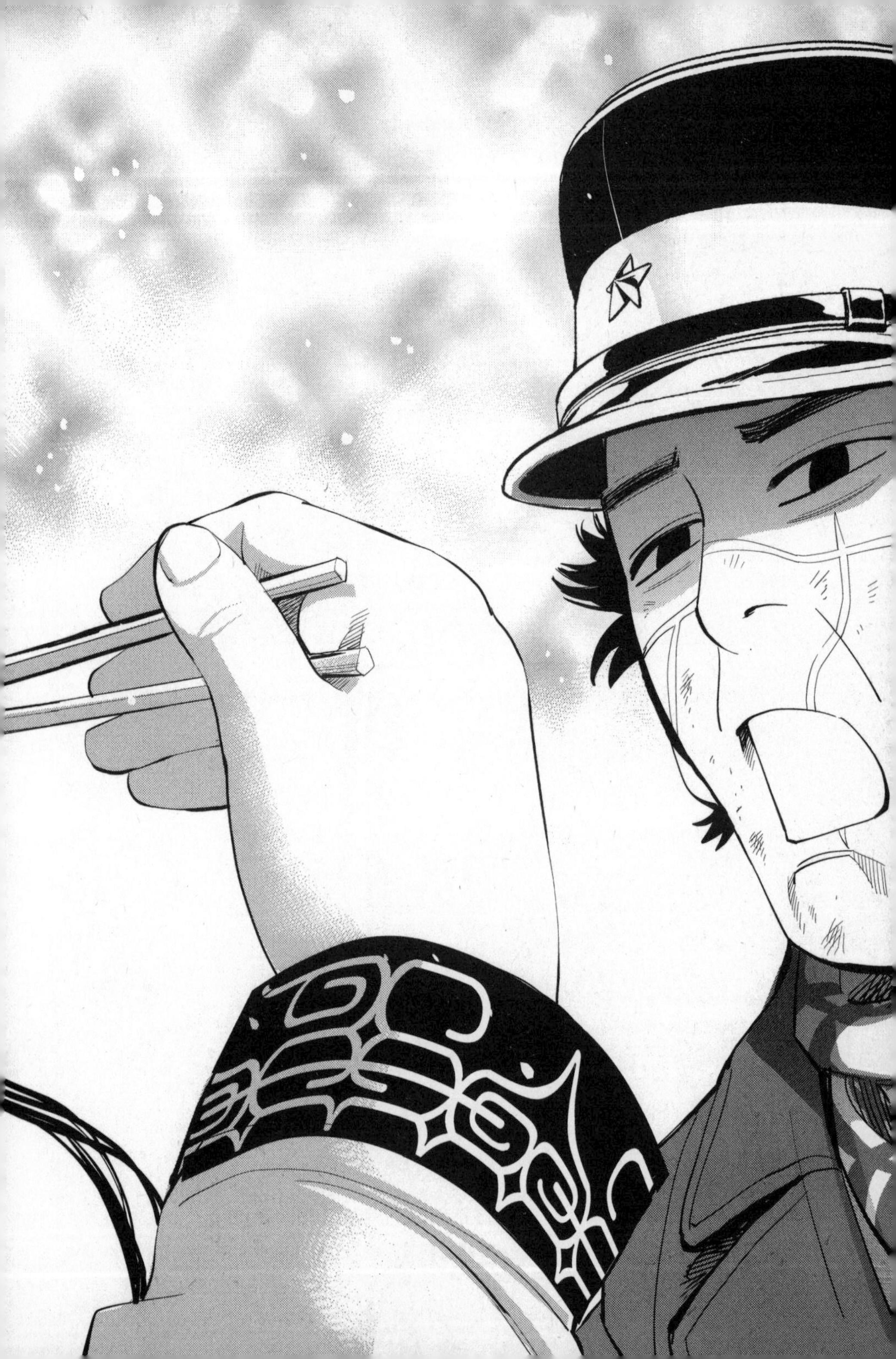

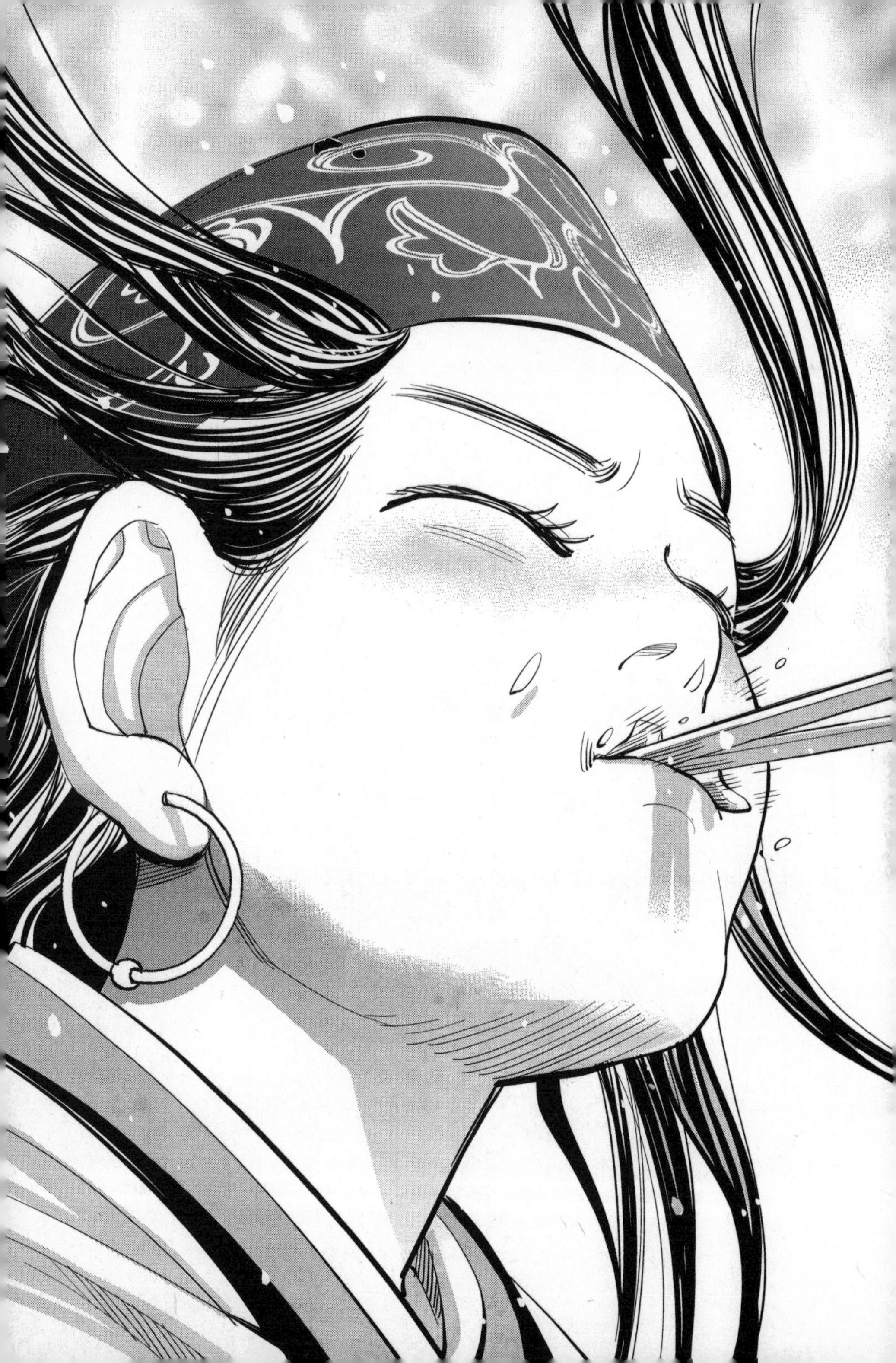

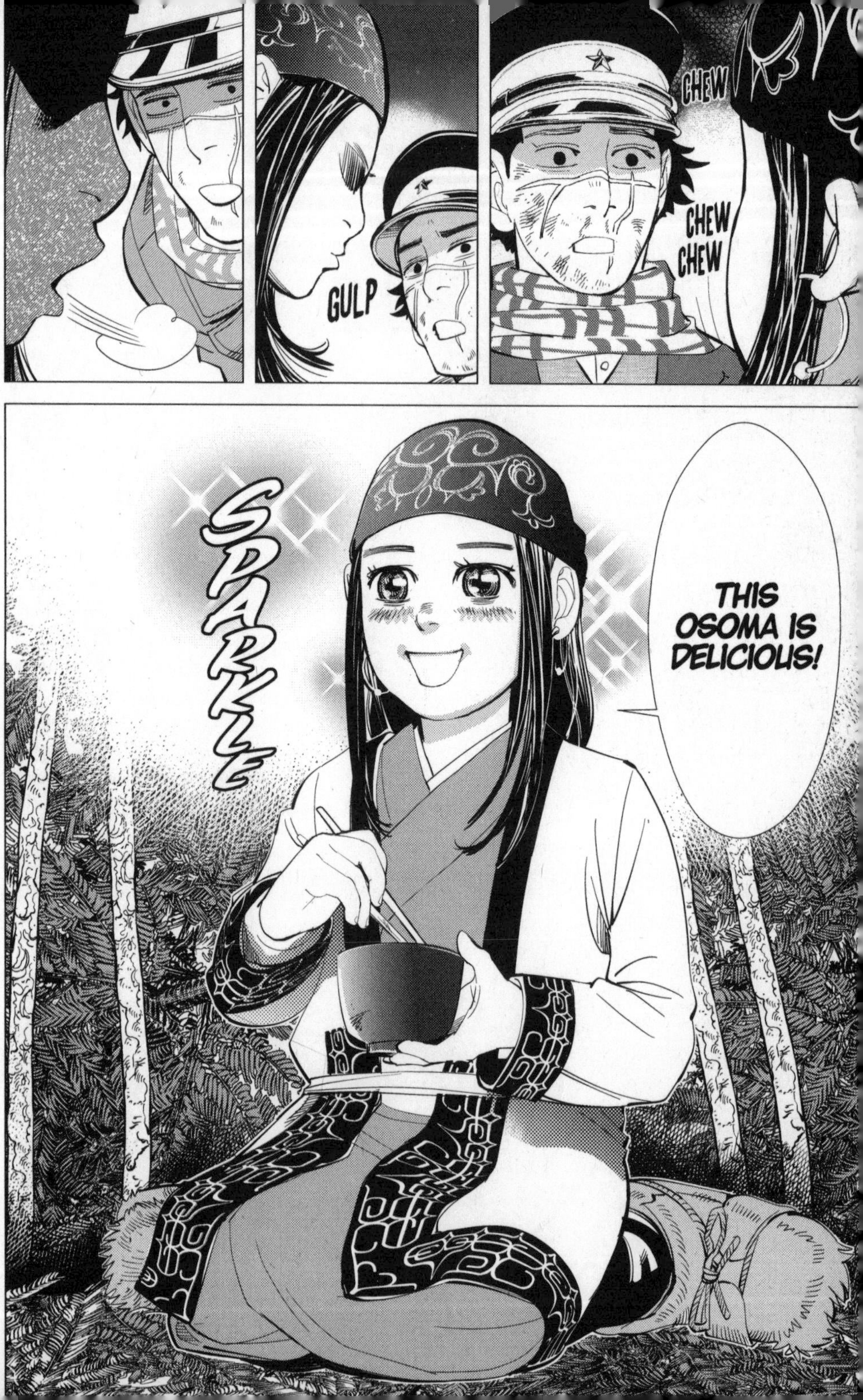
CHEW
CHEW CHEW
GULP
THIS OSOMA IS DELICIOUS!
SPARKLE

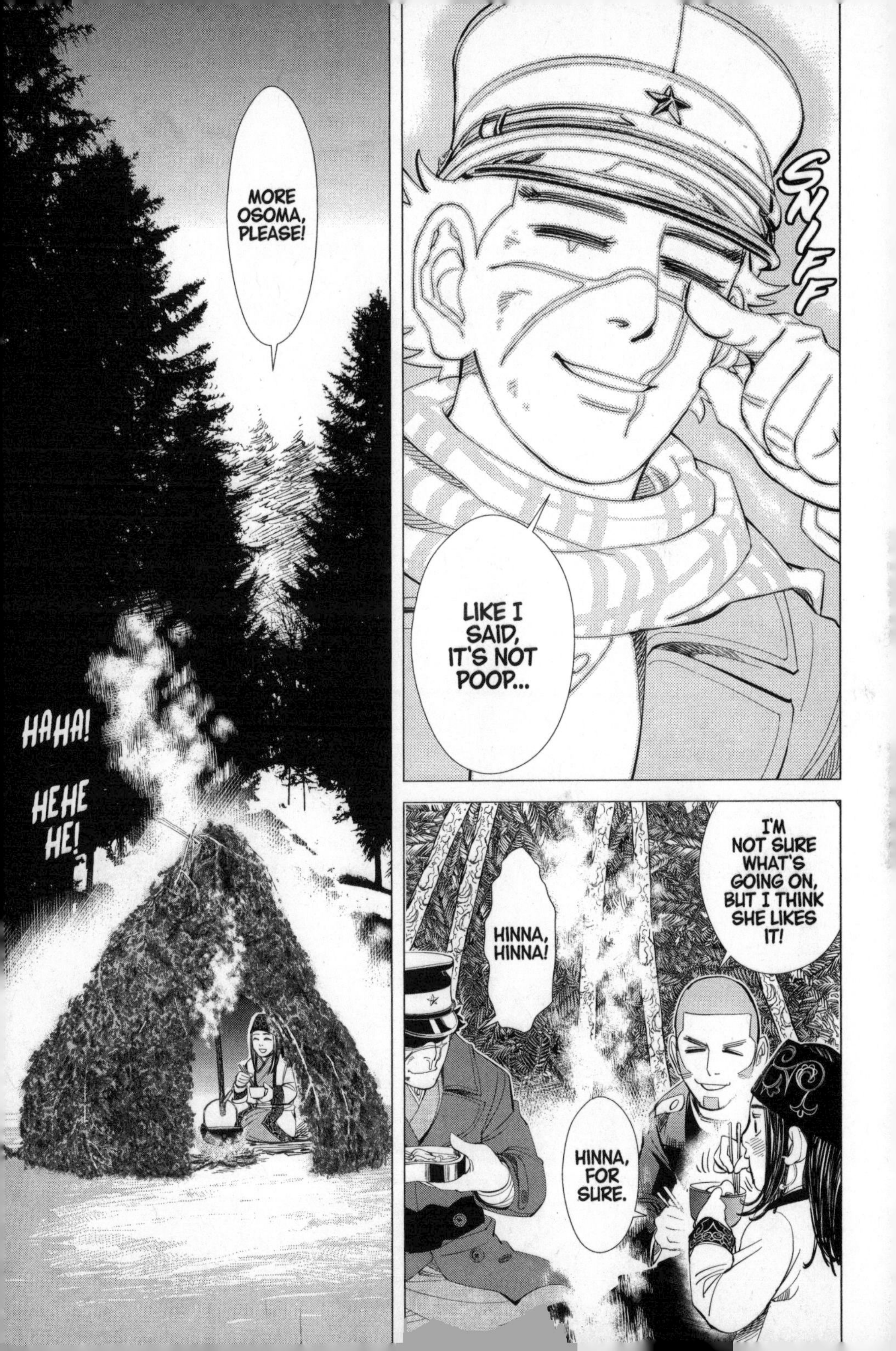
SNIFF
LIKE I SAID, IT'S NOT POOP...
I'M NOT SURE WHAT'S GOING ON, BUT I THINK SHE LIKES IT!
HINNA, HINNA!
HINNA, FOR SURE.
MORE OSOMA, PLEASE!
HAHA!
HEHE HE!

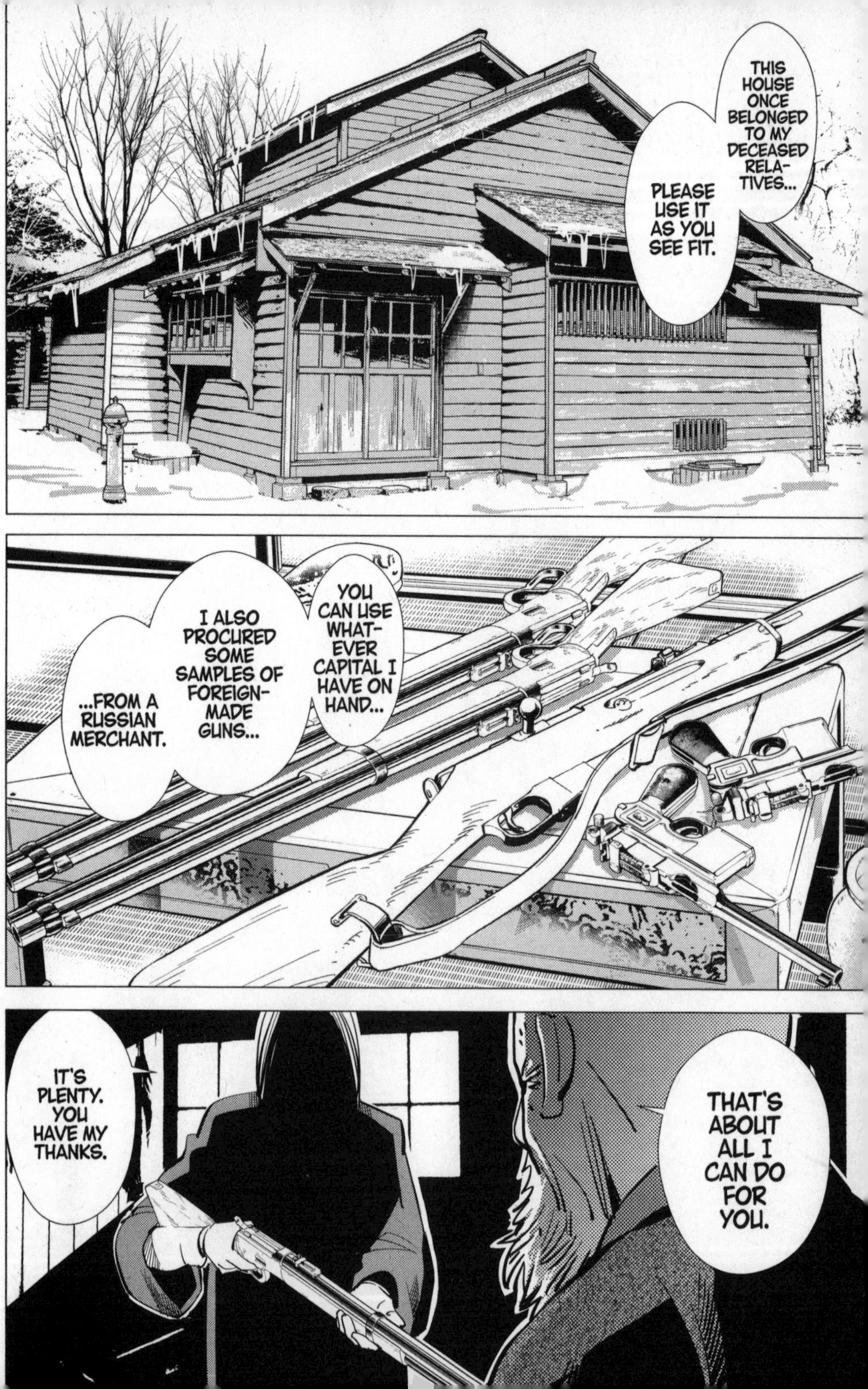
THIS HOUSE ONCE BELONGED TO MY DECEASED RELA-TIVES...
PLEASE USE IT AS YOU SEE FIT.
YOU CAN USE WHAT-EVER CAPITAL I HAVE ON HAND...
I ALSO PROCURED SOME SAMPLES OF FOREIGN-MADE GUNS...
...FROM A RUSSIAN MERCHANT.
THAT'S ABOUT ALL I CAN DO FOR YOU.
IT'S PLENTY. YOU HAVE MY THANKS.

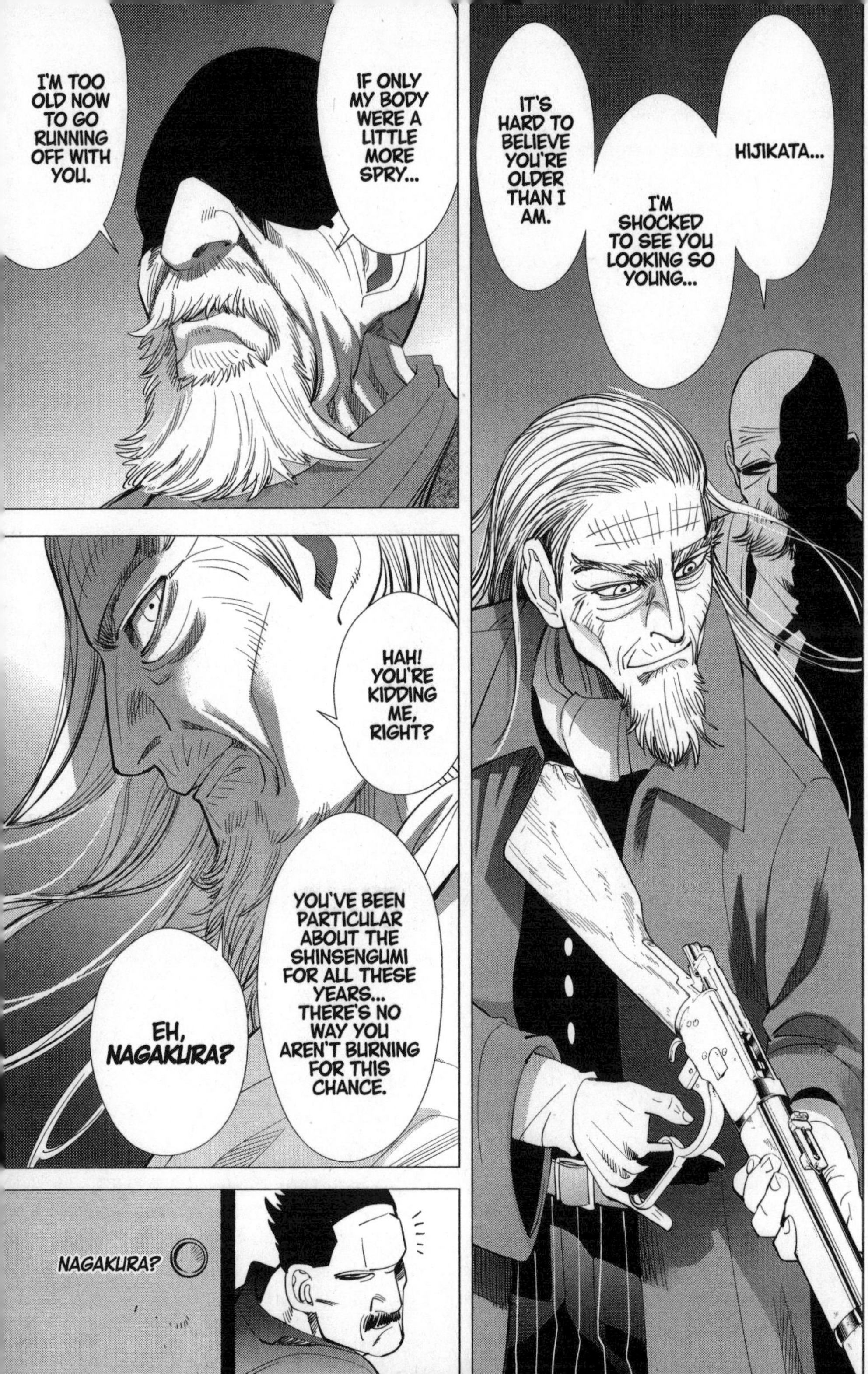
HIJIKATA... I'M SHOCKED TO SEE YOU LOOKING SO YOUNG...
IT'S HARD TO BELIEVE YOU'RE OLDER THAN I AM.
IF ONLY MY BODY WERE A LITTLE MORE SPRY...
I'M TOO OLD NOW TO GO RUNNING OFF WITH YOU.
HAH! YOU'RE KIDDING ME, RIGHT?
YOU'VE BEEN PARTICULAR ABOUT THE SHINSENGUMI FOR ALL THESE YEARS... THERE'S NO WAY YOU AREN'T BURNING FOR THIS CHANCE.
EH, NAGAKURA?
NAGAKURA?

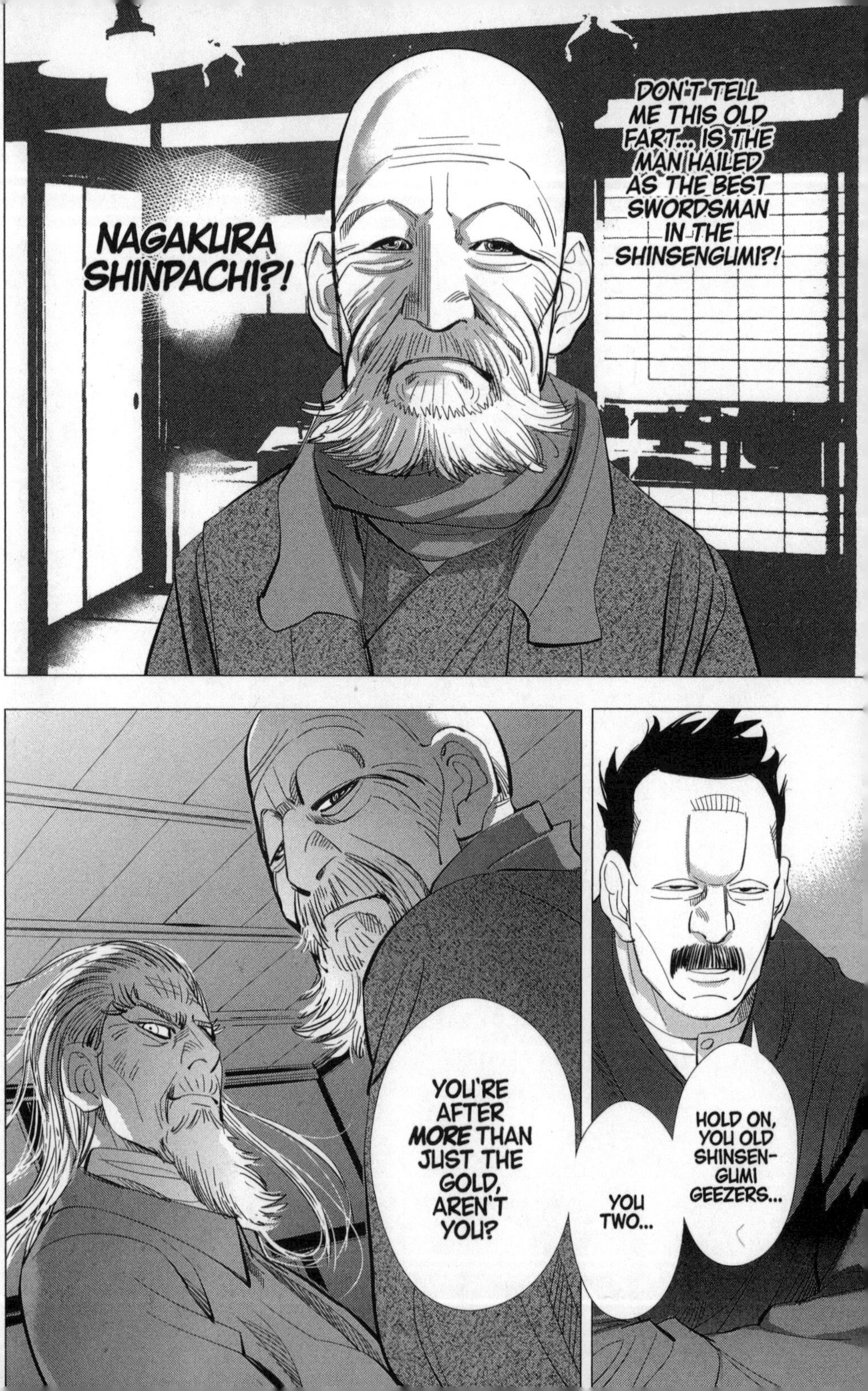
DON'T TELL ME THIS OLD FART... IS THE MAN HAILED AS THE BEST SWORDSMAN IN THE SHINSENGUMI?!
NAGAKURA SHINPACHI?!
HOLD ON, YOU OLD SHINSEN-GUMI GEEZERS...
YOU TWO...
YOU'RE AFTER MORE THAN JUST THE GOLD, AREN'T YOU?

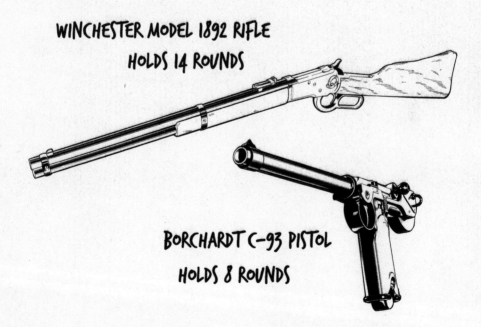

WINCHESTER MODEL 1892 RIFLE
HOLDS 14 ROUNDS

BORCHARDT C-93 PISTOL
HOLDS 8 ROUNDS

Chapter 21: Ghost

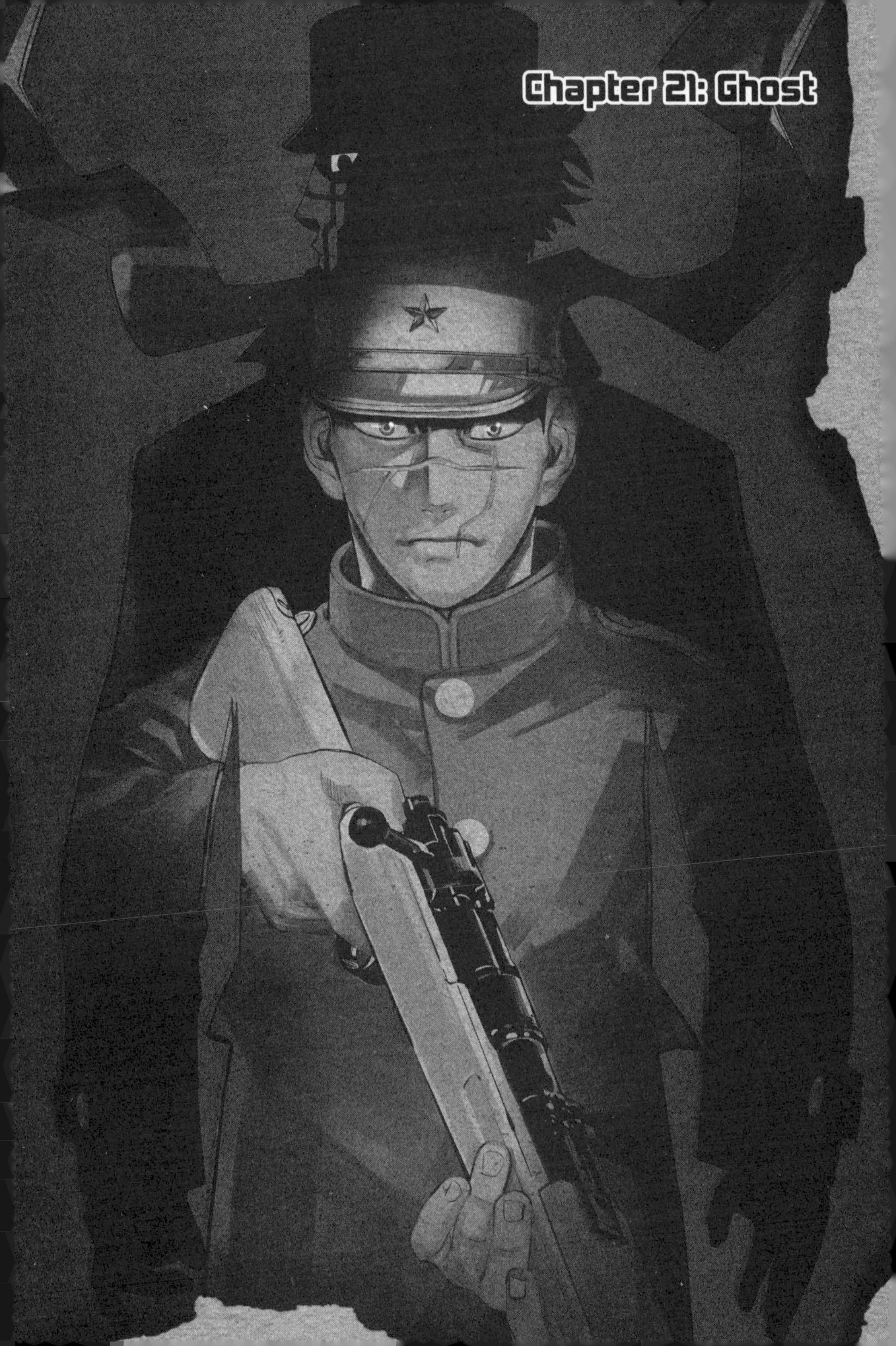

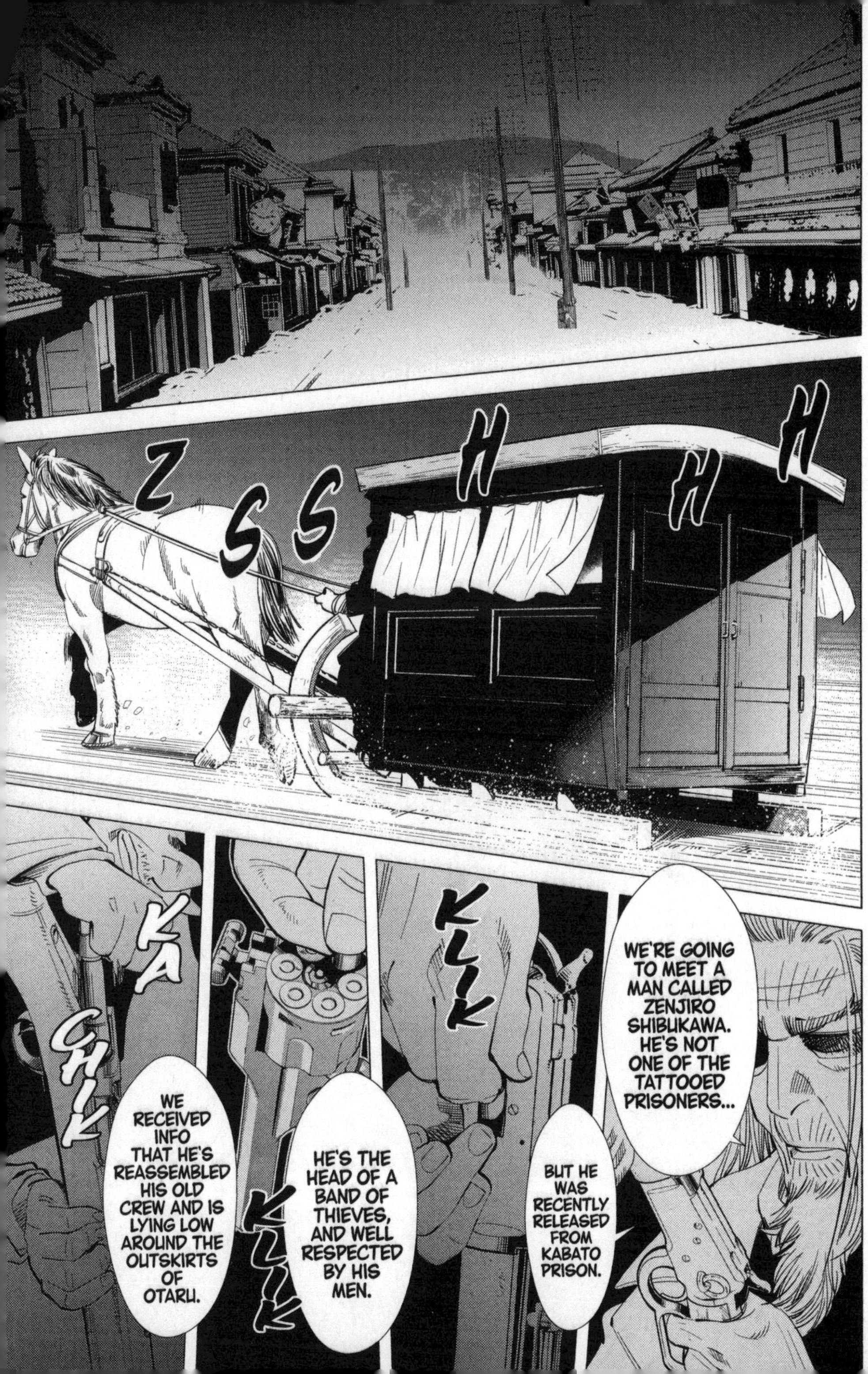
ZSSHHH
WE'RE GOING TO MEET A MAN CALLED ZENJIRO SHIBUKAWA. HE'S NOT ONE OF THE TATTOOED PRISONERS...
BUT HE WAS RECENTLY RELEASED FROM KABATO PRISON.
KLIK
HE'S THE HEAD OF A BAND OF THIEVES, AND WELL RESPECTED BY HIS MEN.
KLIK
KA CHIK
WE RECEIVED INFO THAT HE'S REASSEMBLED HIS OLD CREW AND IS LYING LOW AROUND THE OUTSKIRTS OF OTARU.

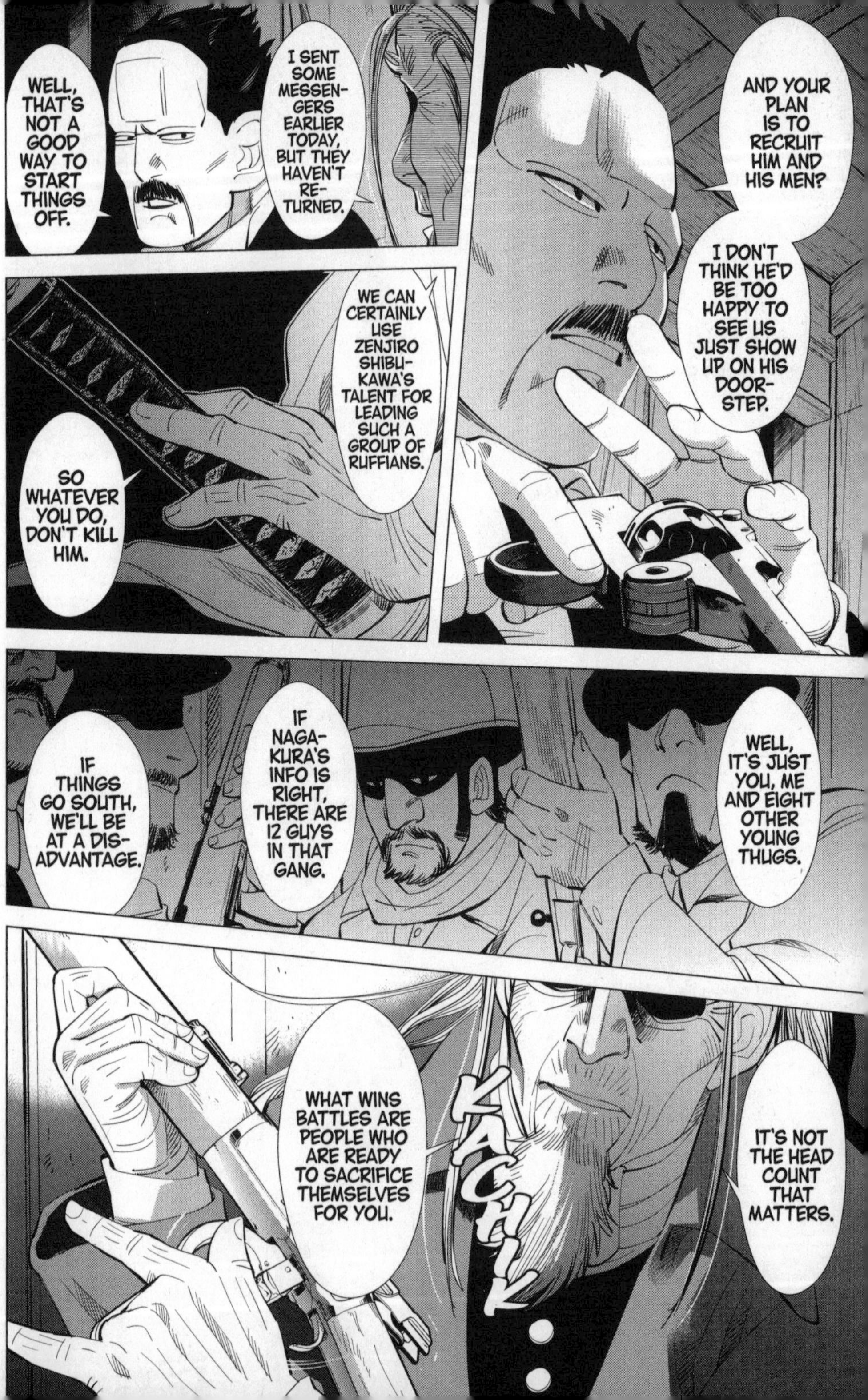
AND YOUR PLAN IS TO RECRUIT HIM AND HIS MEN?
I DON'T THINK HE'D BE TOO HAPPY TO SEE US JUST SHOW UP ON HIS DOOR-STEP.
I SENT SOME MESSEN-GERS EARLIER TODAY, BUT THEY HAVEN'T RE-TURNED.
WELL, THAT'S NOT A GOOD WAY TO START THINGS OFF.
WE CAN CERTAINLY USE ZENJIRO SHIBU-KAWA'S TALENT FOR LEADING SUCH A GROUP OF RUFFIANS.
SO WHATEVER YOU DO, DON'T KILL HIM.
WELL, IT'S JUST YOU, ME AND EIGHT OTHER YOUNG THUGS.
IF NAGA-KURA'S INFO IS RIGHT, THERE ARE 12 GUYS IN THAT GANG.
IF THINGS GO SOUTH, WE'LL BE AT A DIS-ADVANTAGE.
IT'S NOT THE HEAD COUNT THAT MATTERS.
KACHK
WHAT WINS BATTLES ARE PEOPLE WHO ARE READY TO SACRIFICE THEMSELVES FOR YOU.

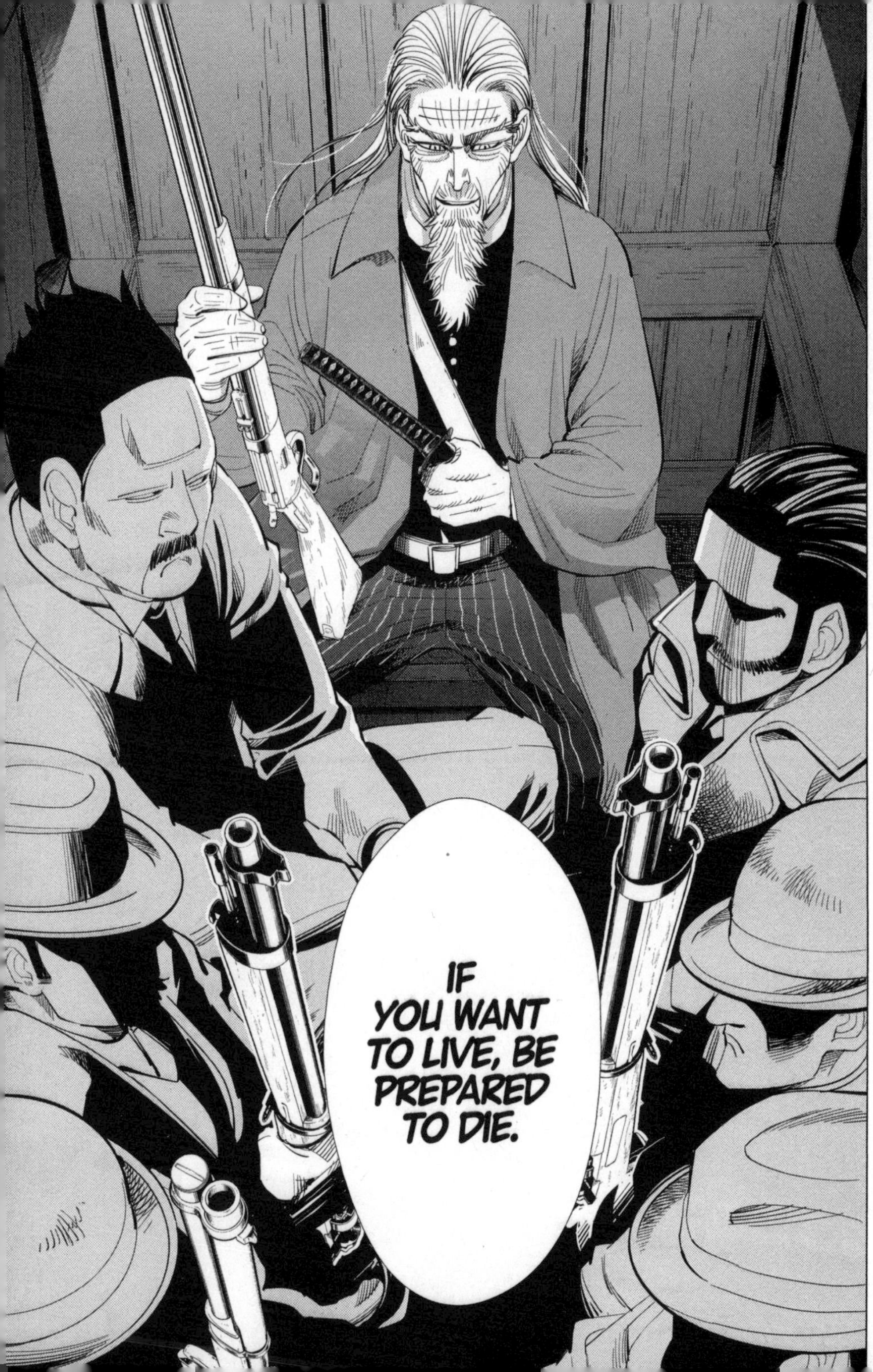
IF YOU WANT TO LIVE, BE PREPARED TO DIE.

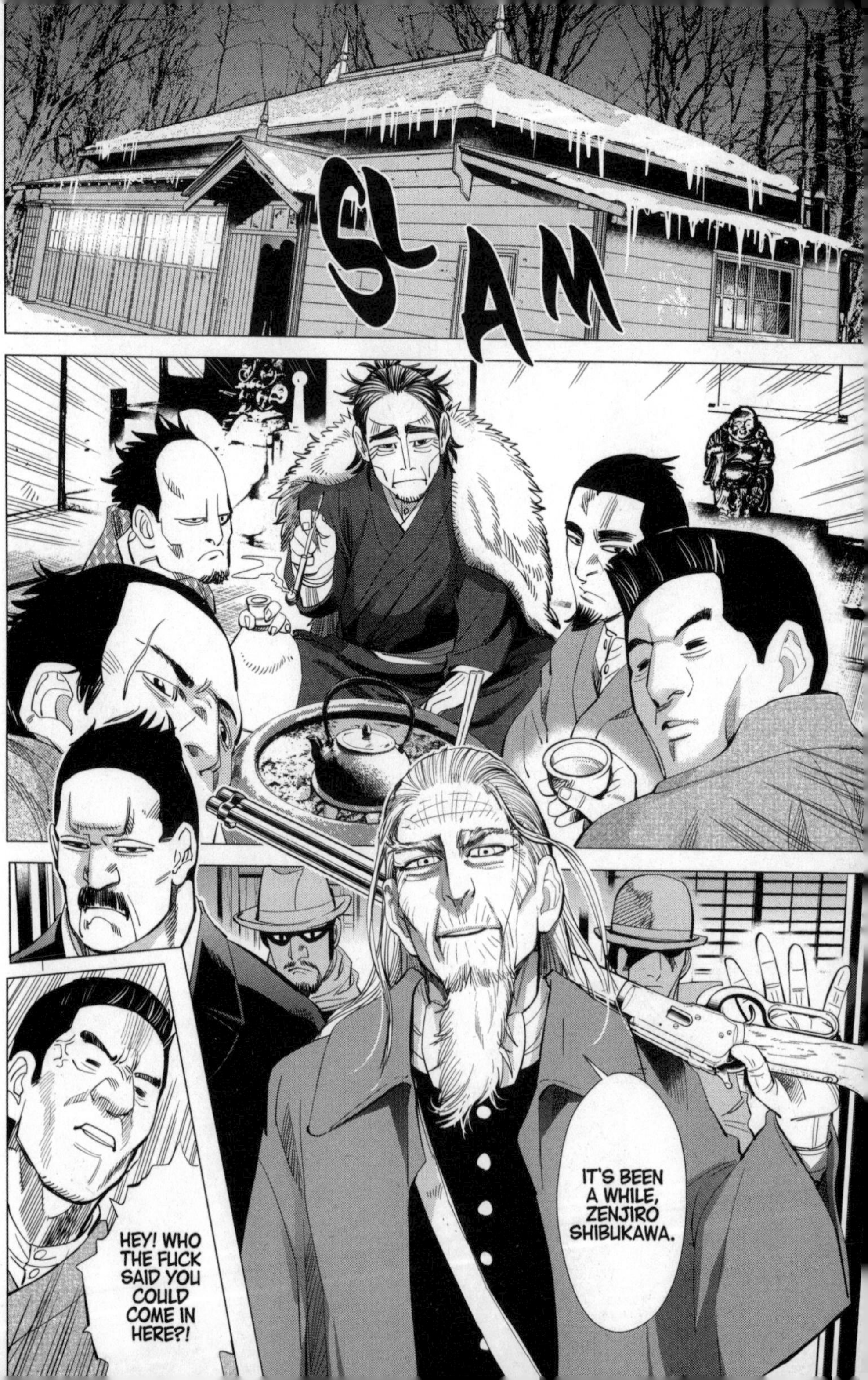
SLAM
IT'S BEEN A WHILE, ZENJIRO SHIBUKAWA.
HEY! WHO THE FUCK SAID YOU COULD COME IN HERE?!

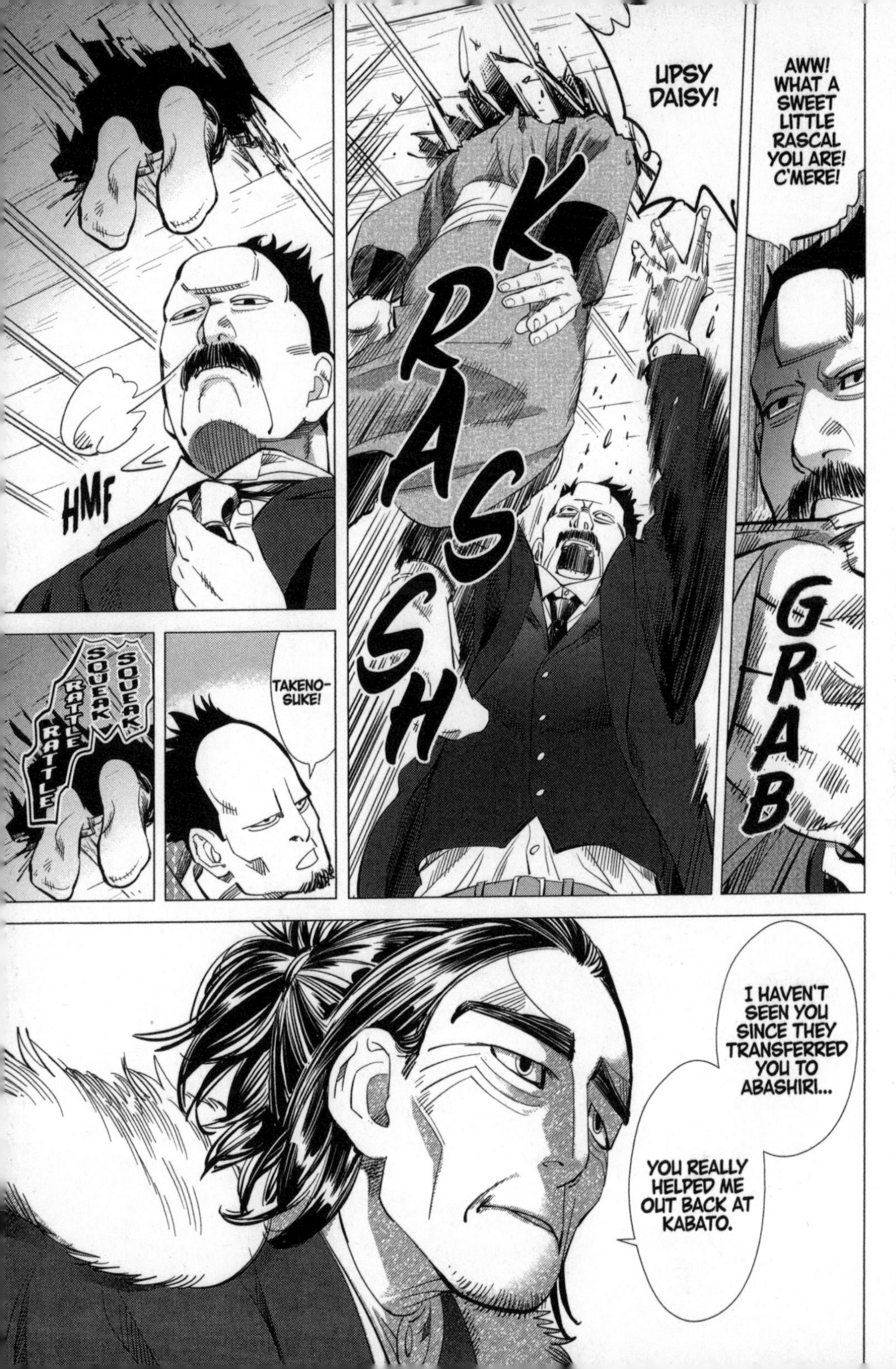
AWW! WHAT A SWEET LITTLE RASCAL YOU ARE! C'MERE!
GRAB
UPSY DAISY!
KRASSH
HMF
TAKENO-SUKE!
SQUEAK SQUEAK
RATTLE RATTLE
I HAVEN'T SEEN YOU SINCE THEY TRANSFERRED YOU TO ABASHIRI...
YOU REALLY HELPED ME OUT BACK AT KABATO.

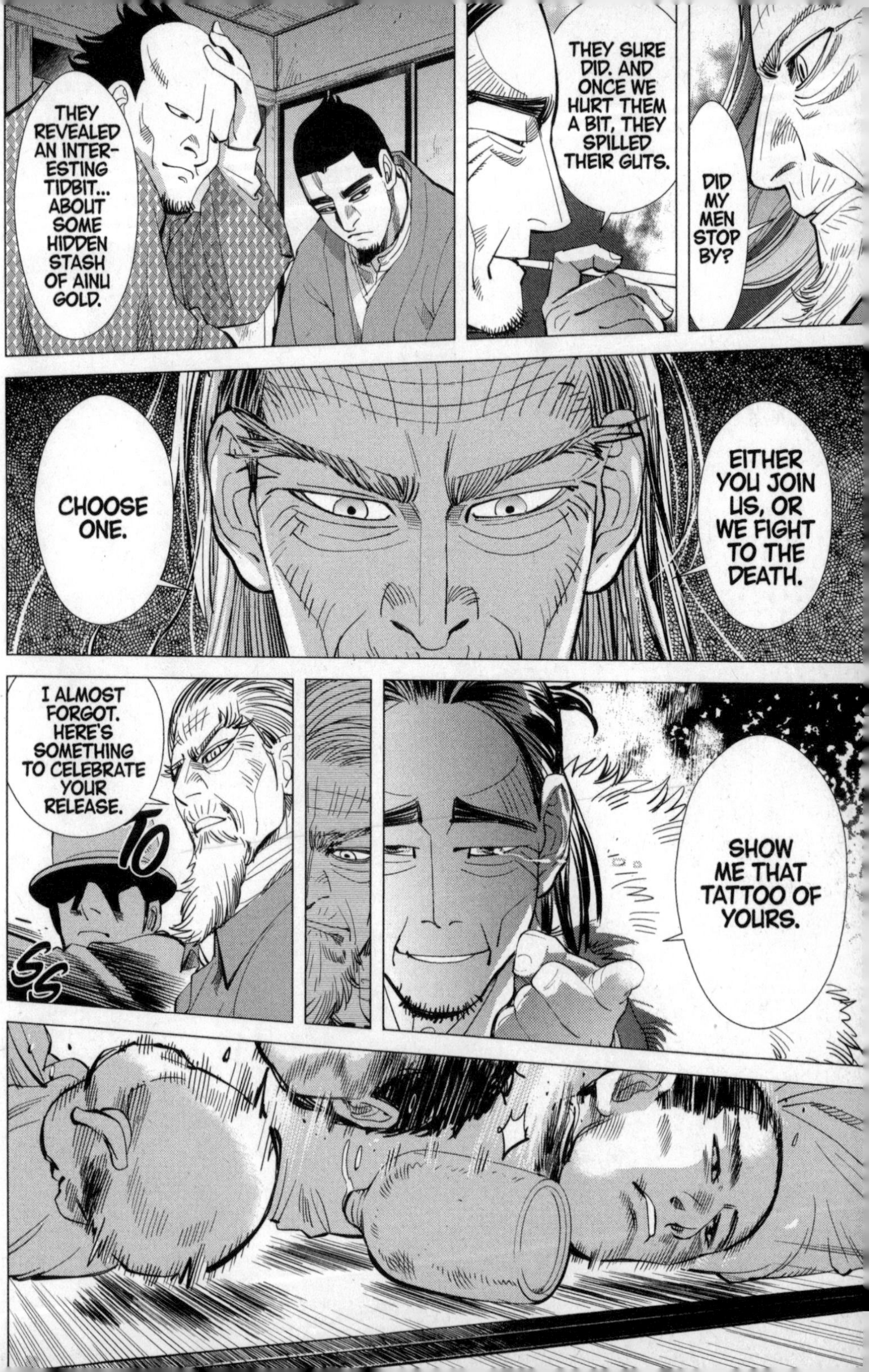
DID MY MEN STOP BY?
THEY SURE DID. AND ONCE WE HURT THEM A BIT, THEY SPILLED THEIR GUTS.
THEY REVEALED AN INTERESTING TIDBIT... ABOUT SOME HIDDEN STASH OF AINU GOLD.
EITHER YOU JOIN US, OR WE FIGHT TO THE DEATH.
CHOOSE ONE.
SHOW ME THAT TATTOO OF YOURS.
I ALMOST FORGOT. HERE'S SOMETHING TO CELEBRATE YOUR RELEASE.
TO
SS

THESE WERE YOUR MEN, RIGHT? YOU HAD THEM WAITING OUTSIDE, READY TO AMBUSH US.

AND TELL YOUR MEN HIDING BEHIND THOSE SLIDING DOORS TO LAY DOWN THEIR WEAPONS.

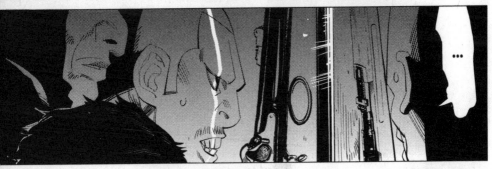

...

FINE, YOU WIN...

YOU MAY HAVE FOOLED EVERYONE AT KABATO BY PRETENDING TO BE JUST A QUIET OLD MAN...

BUT I KNEW YOU WERE A DANGEROUS BASTARD FROM THE MOMENT I SAW YOU.

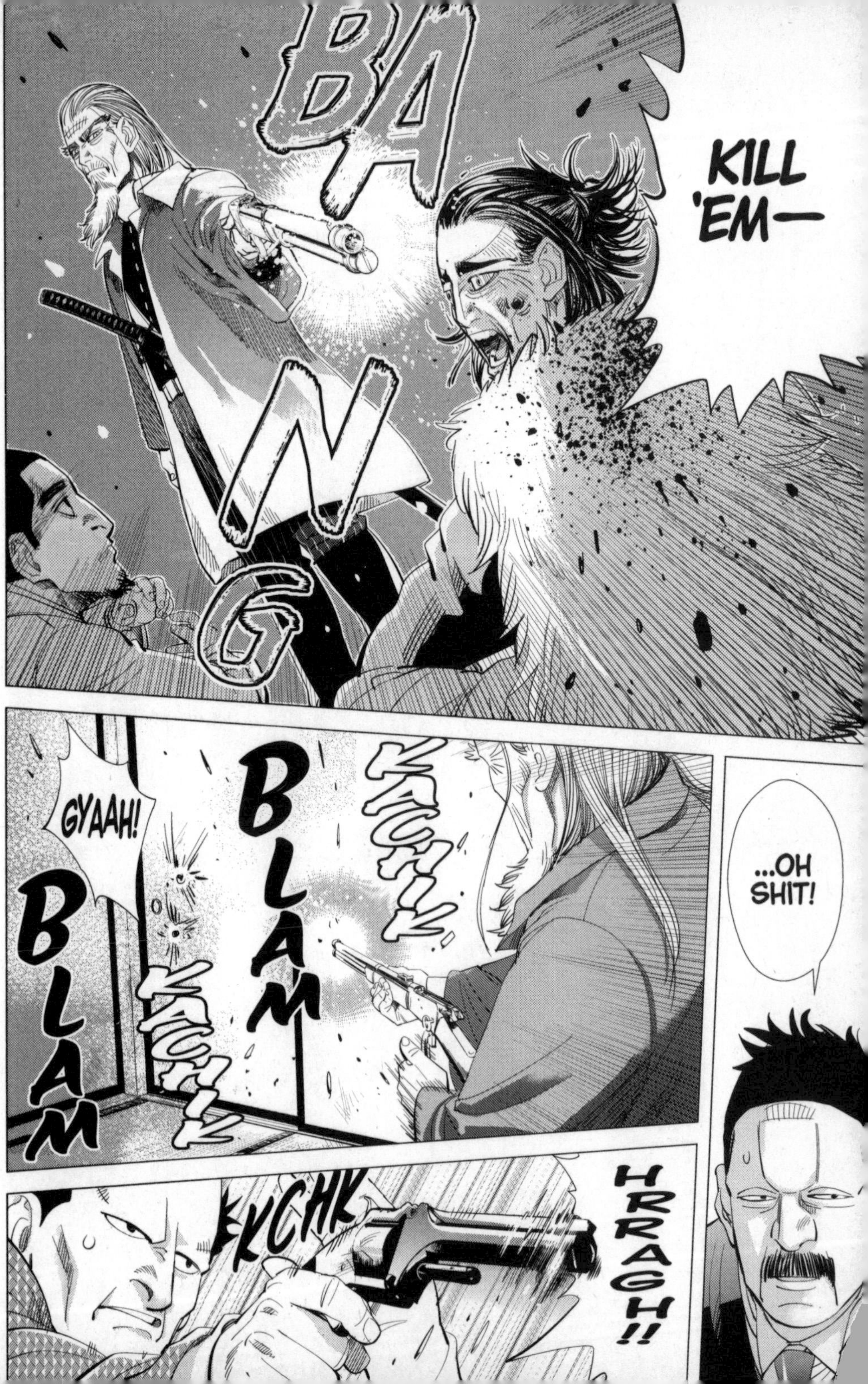
KILL 'EM—
BAWNG
...OH SHIT!
BLAM
GYAAH!
BLAM
HRRAGH!!
KCHK

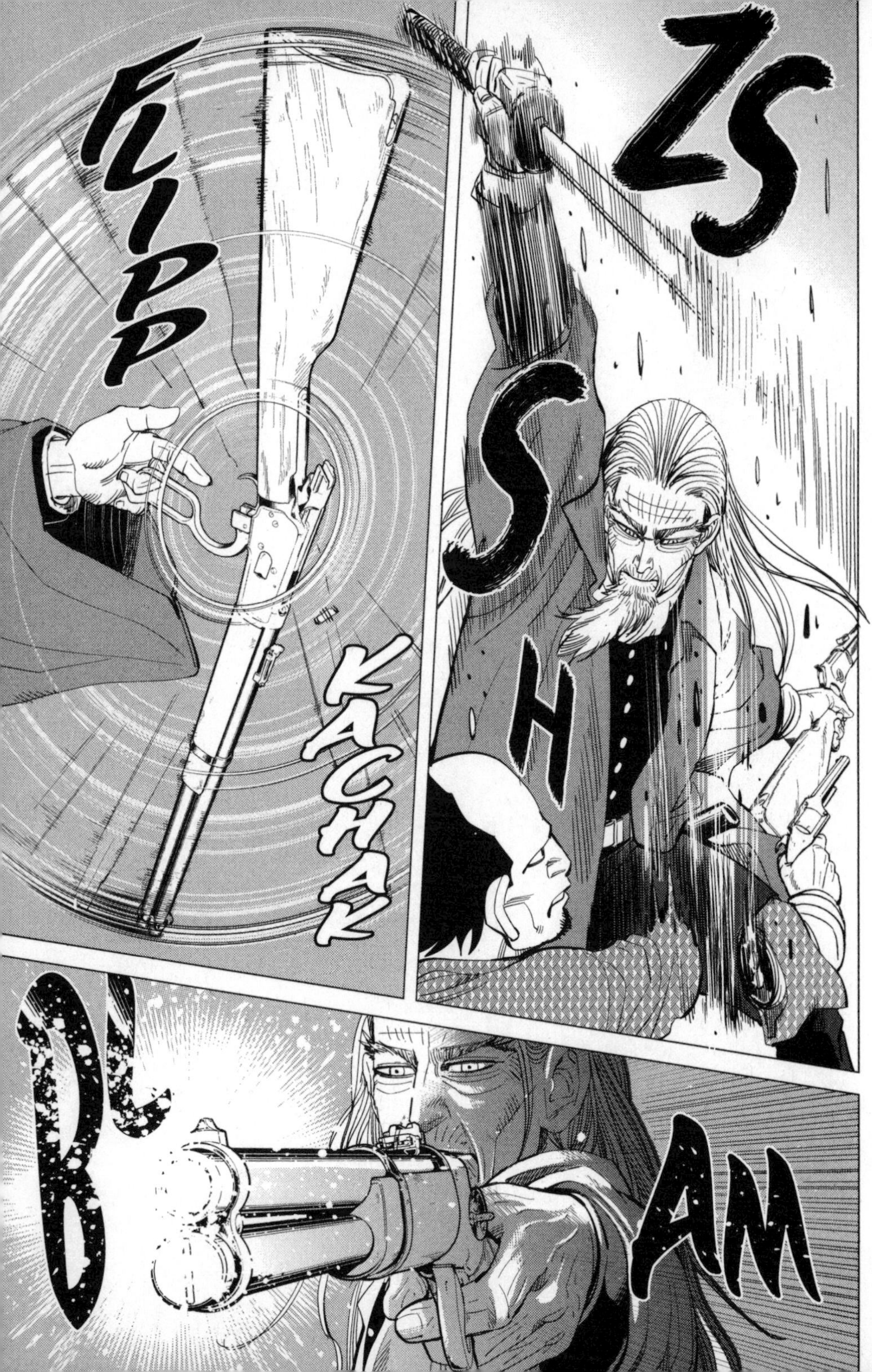
ZS
SH
FLIPP
KACHAK
BLAM

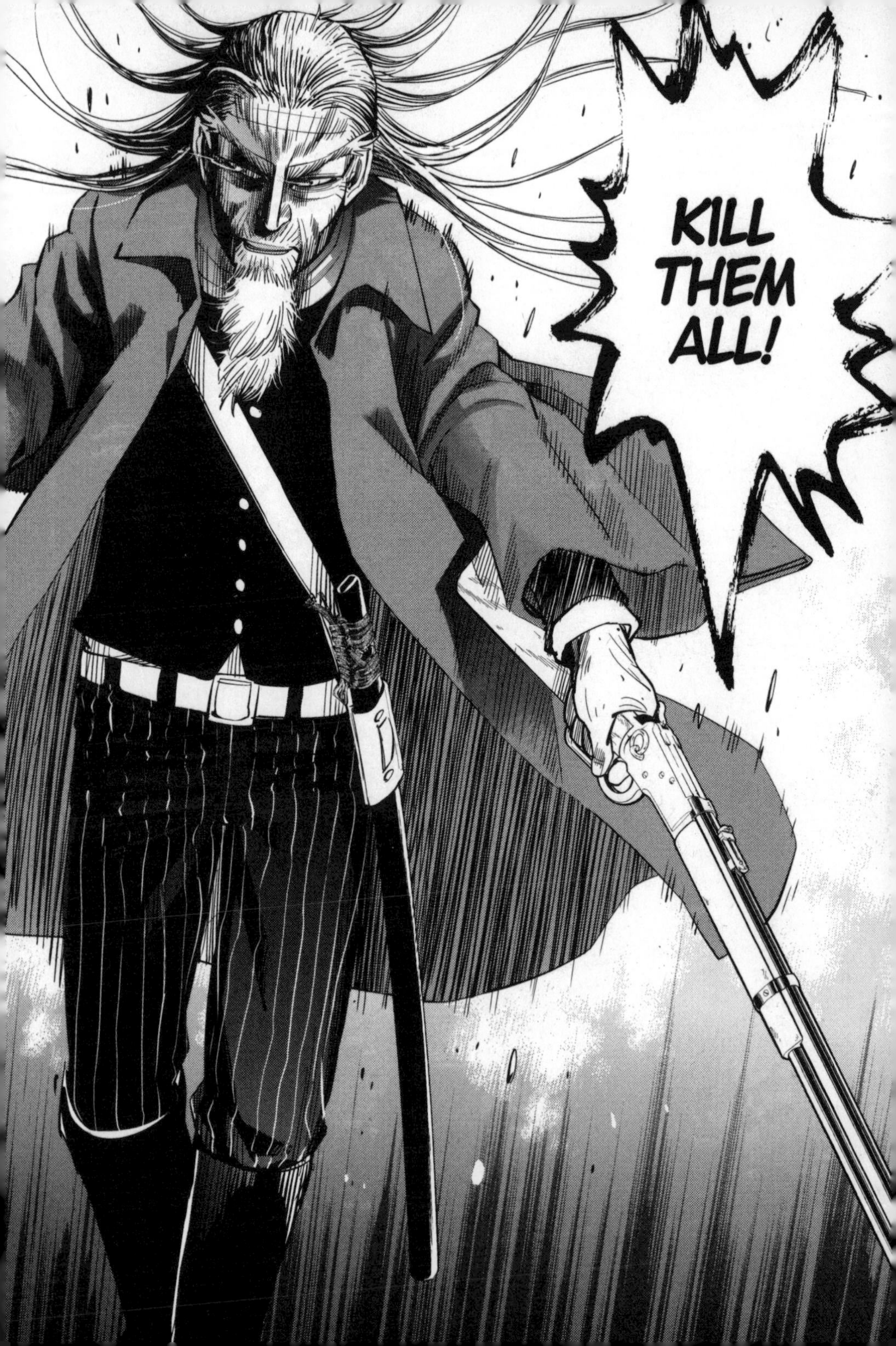
KILL THEM ALL!

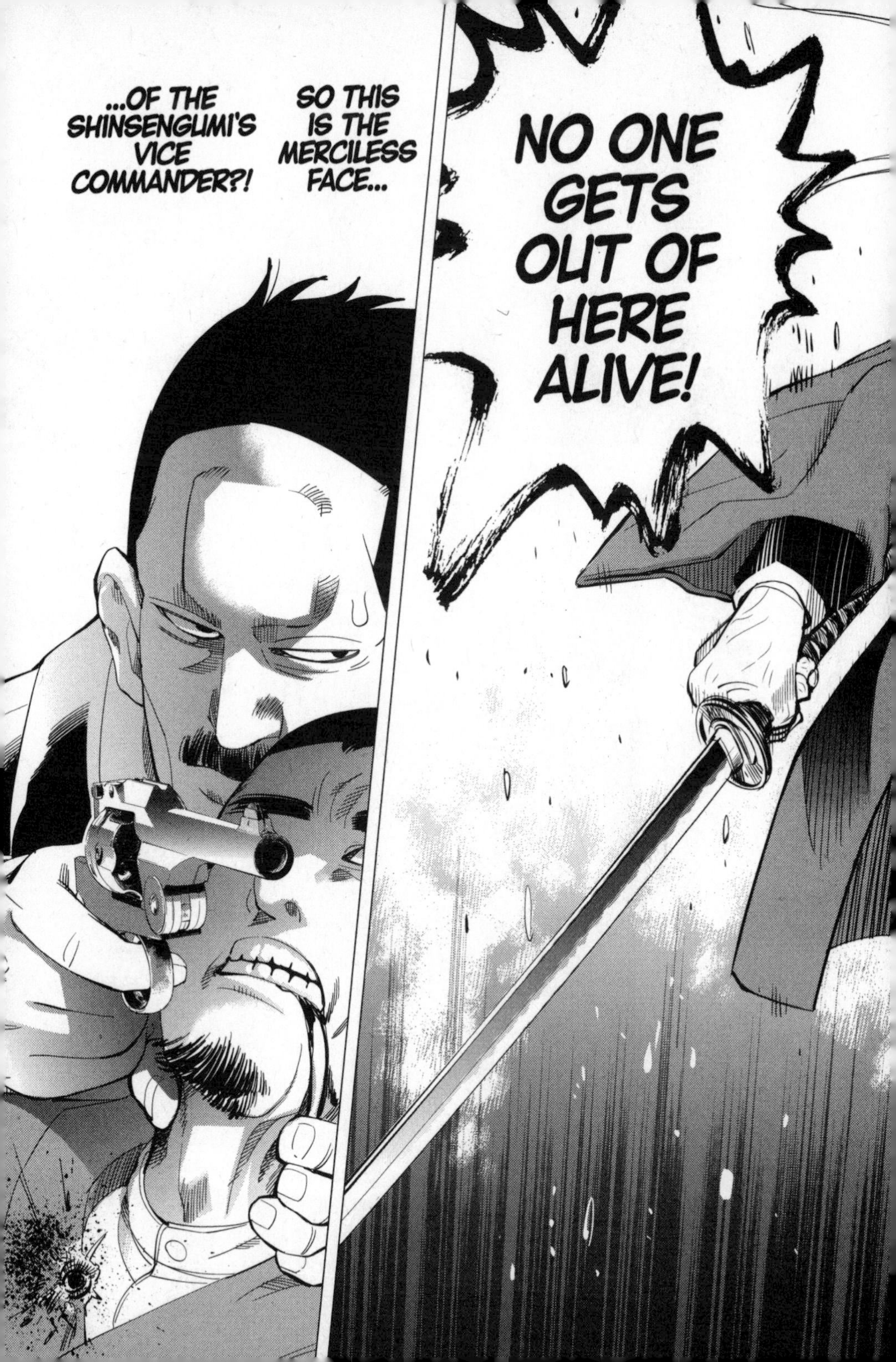
NO ONE GETS OUT OF HERE ALIVE!
SO THIS IS THE MERCILESS FACE...
...OF THE SHINSENGUMI'S VICE COMMANDER?!

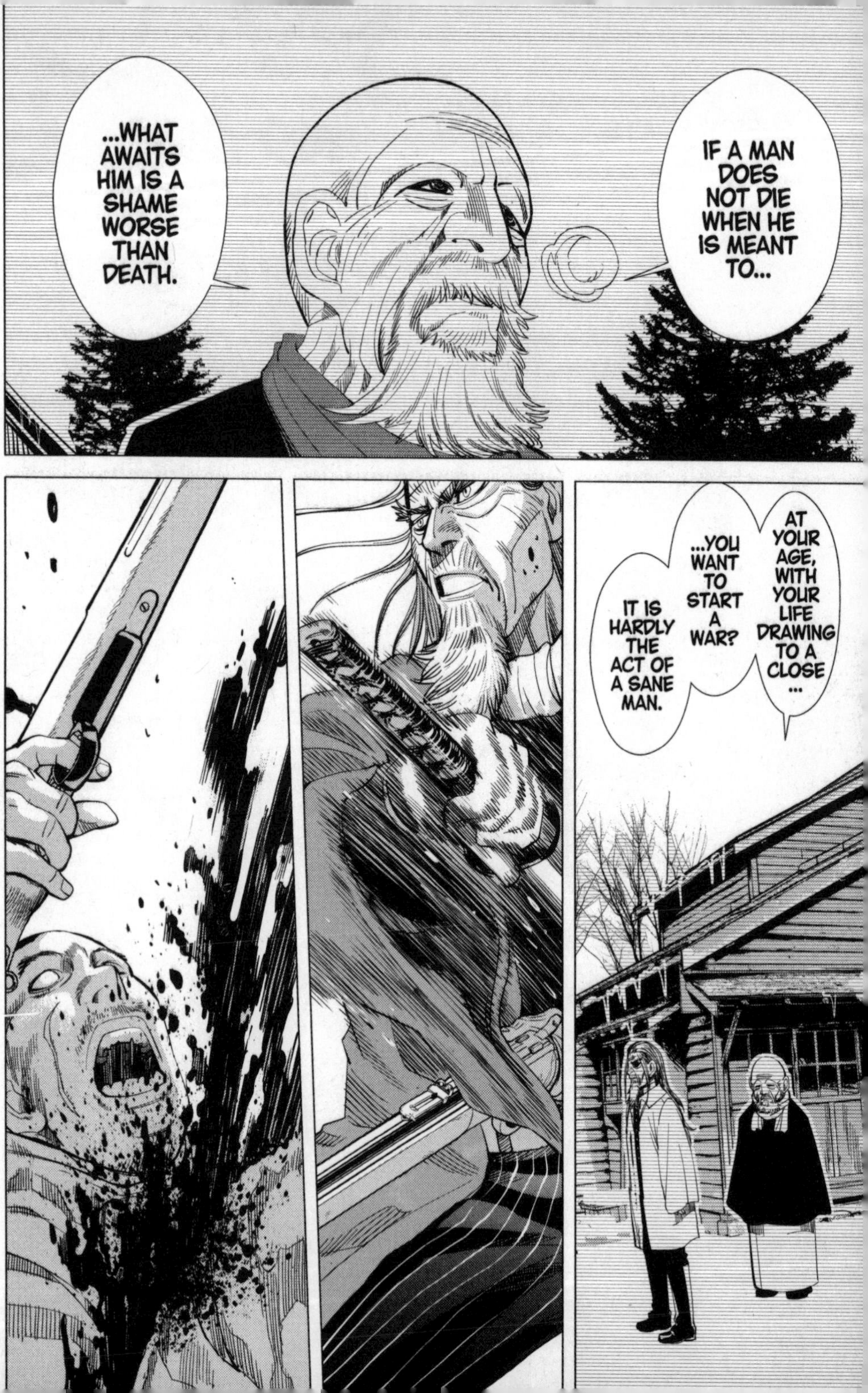
IF A MAN DOES NOT DIE WHEN HE IS MEANT TO...
...WHAT AWAITS HIM IS A SHAME WORSE THAN DEATH.
AT YOUR AGE, WITH YOUR LIFE DRAWING TO A CLOSE...
...YOU WANT TO START A WAR?
IT IS HARDLY THE ACT OF A SANE MAN.

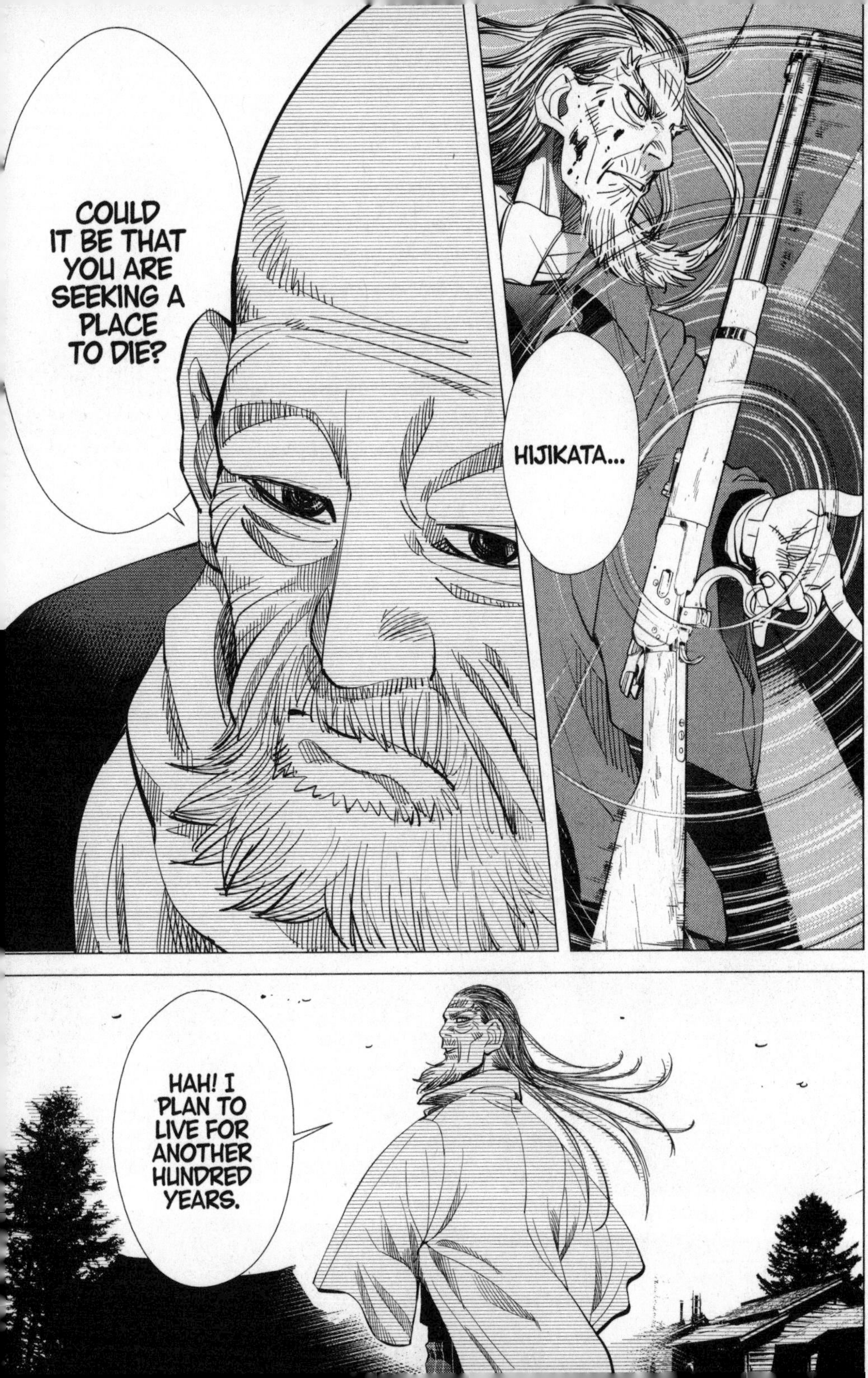
HIJIKATA...
COULD IT BE THAT YOU ARE SEEKING A PLACE TO DIE?
HAH! I PLAN TO LIVE FOR ANOTHER HUNDRED YEARS.

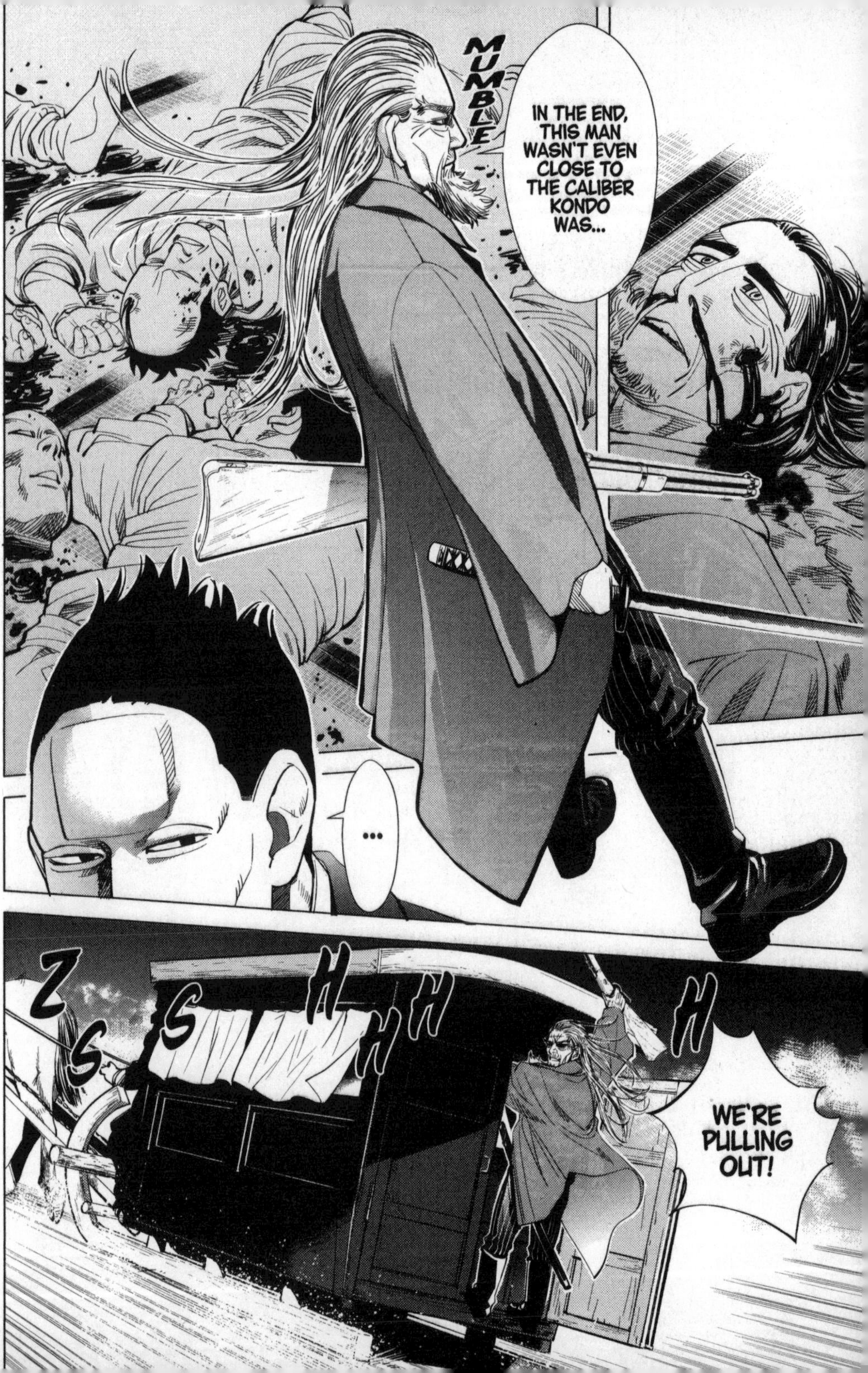
MUMBLE
IN THE END, THIS MAN WASN'T EVEN CLOSE TO THE CALIBER KONDO WAS...
...
WE'RE PULLING OUT!
ZSSHHHHH

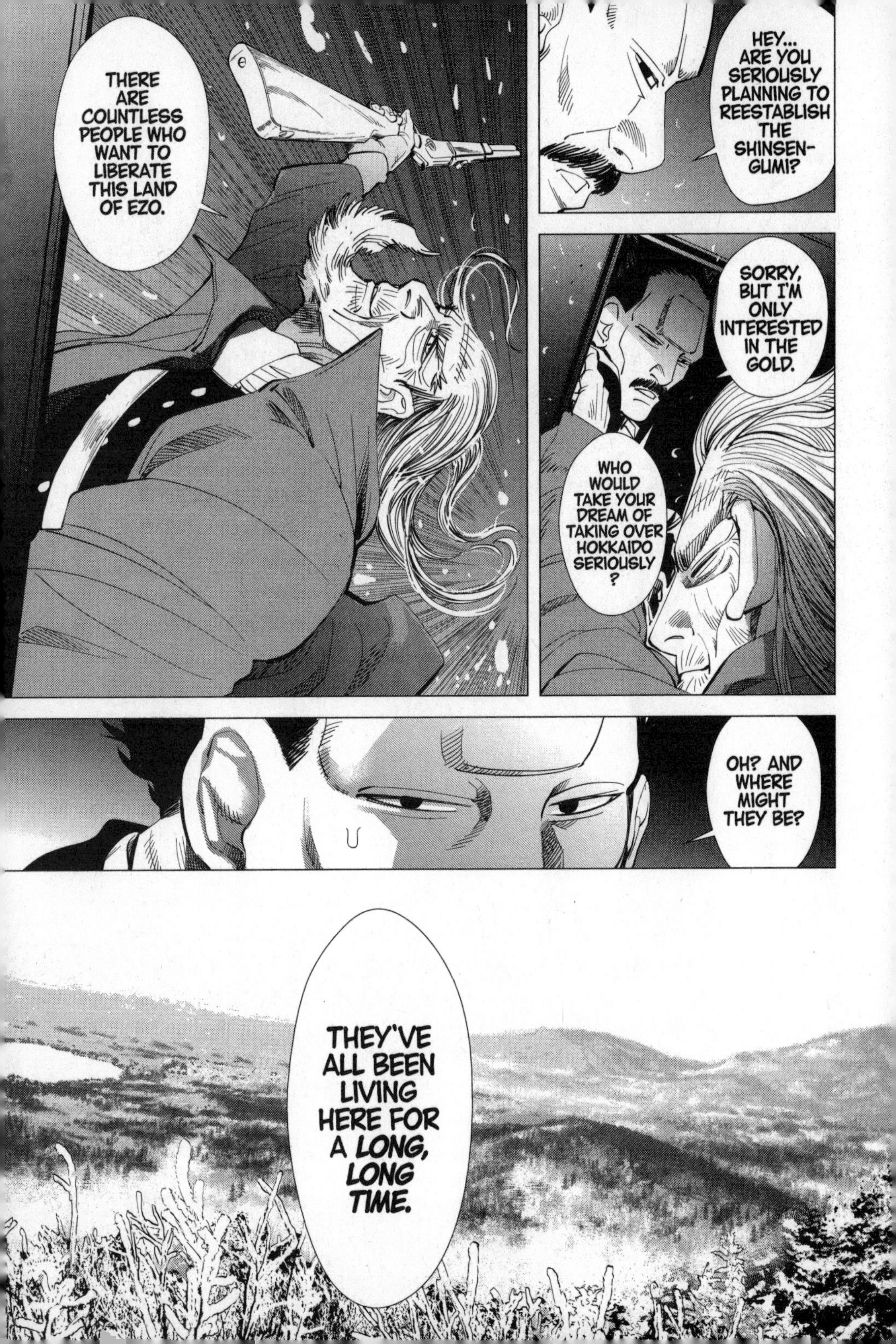
HEY... ARE YOU SERIOUSLY PLANNING TO REESTABLISH THE SHINSEN-GUMI?
SORRY, BUT I'M ONLY INTERESTED IN THE GOLD.
WHO WOULD TAKE YOUR DREAM OF TAKING OVER HOKKAIDO SERIOUSLY?
THERE ARE COUNTLESS PEOPLE WHO WANT TO LIBERATE THIS LAND OF EZO.
OH? AND WHERE MIGHT THEY BE?
THEY'VE ALL BEEN LIVING HERE FOR A *LONG, LONG TIME.*

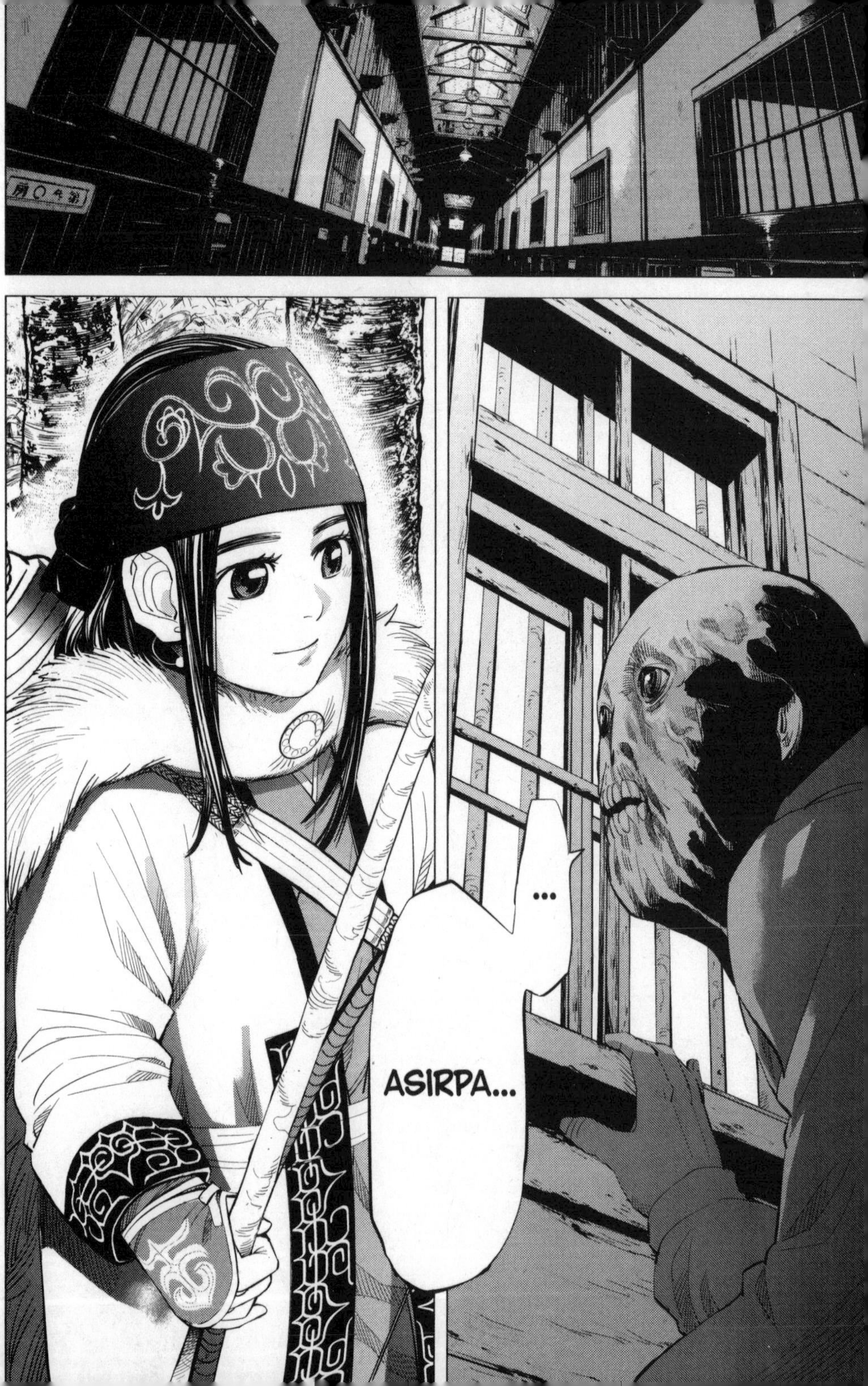
...
ASIRPA...

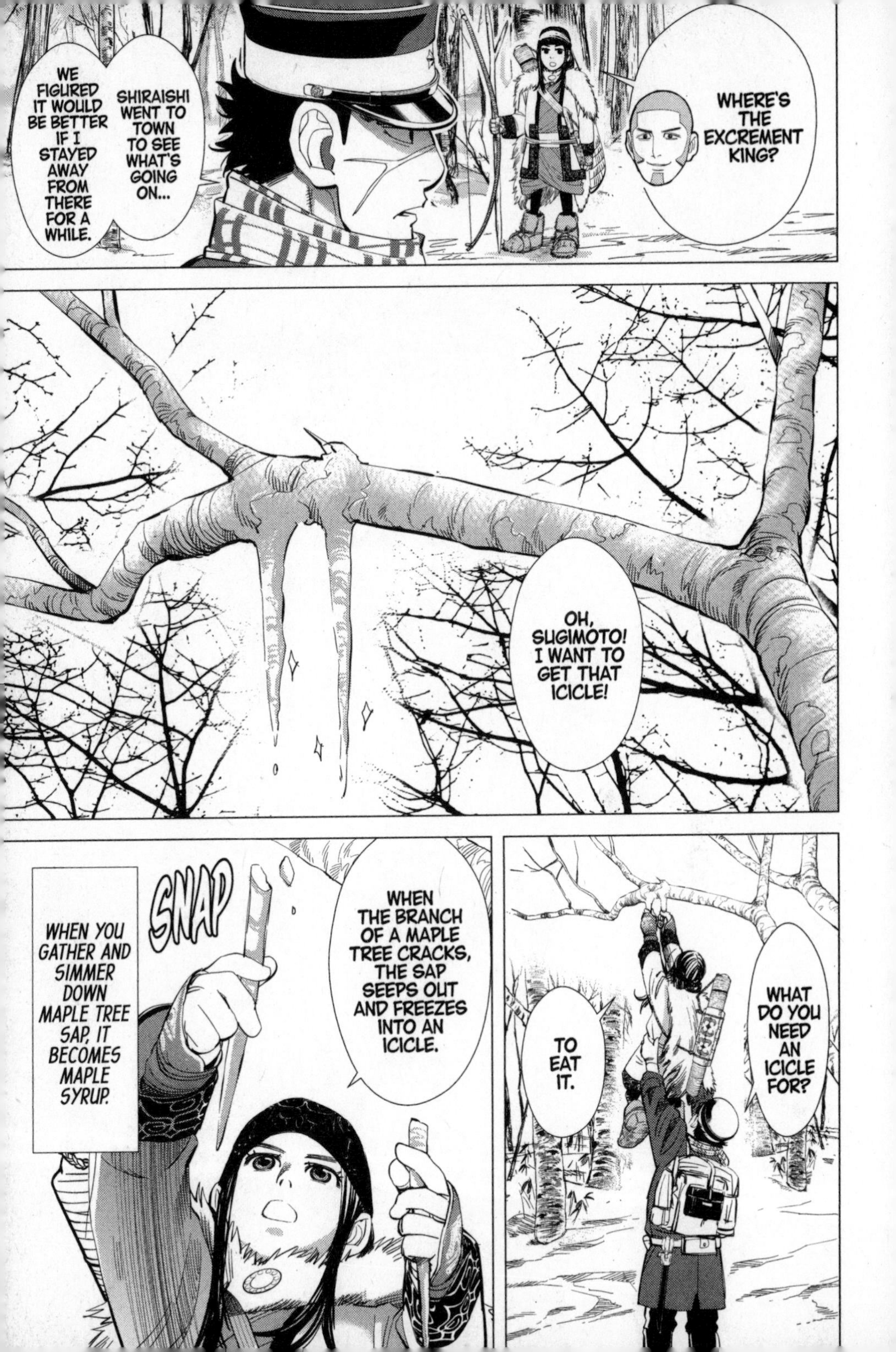
WHERE'S THE EXCREMENT KING?
SHIRAISHI WENT TO TOWN TO SEE WHAT'S GOING ON...
WE FIGURED IT WOULD BE BETTER IF I STAYED AWAY FROM THERE FOR A WHILE.
OH, SUGIMOTO! I WANT TO GET THAT ICICLE!
WHAT DO YOU NEED AN ICICLE FOR?
TO EAT IT.
WHEN THE BRANCH OF A MAPLE TREE CRACKS, THE SAP SEEPS OUT AND FREEZES INTO AN ICICLE.
SNAP
WHEN YOU GATHER AND SIMMER DOWN MAPLE TREE SAP, IT BECOMES MAPLE SYRUP.

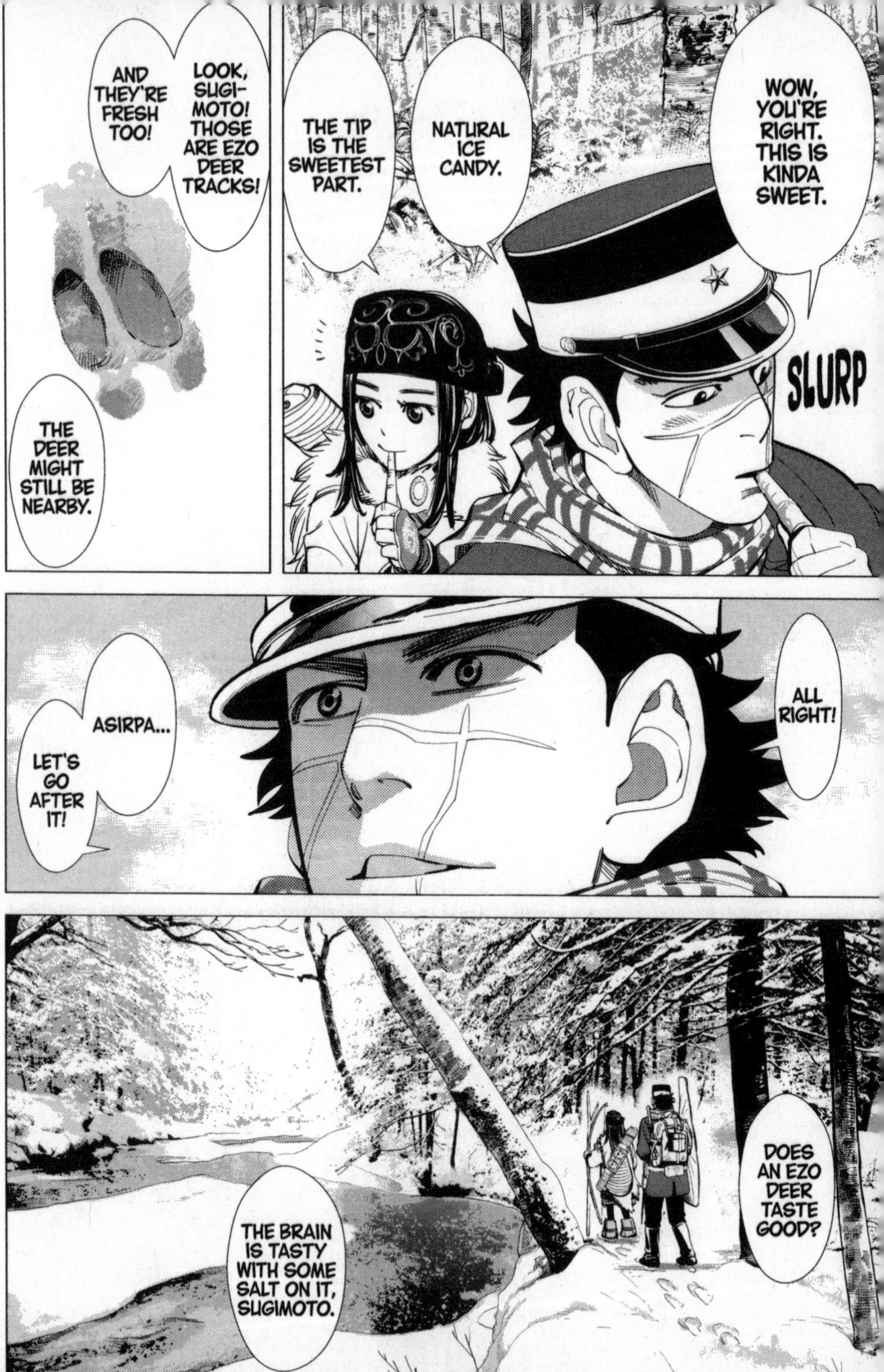
WOW, YOU'RE RIGHT. THIS IS KINDA SWEET.
SLURP
NATURAL ICE CANDY.
THE TIP IS THE SWEETEST PART.
LOOK, SUGI-MOTO! THOSE ARE EZO DEER TRACKS!
AND THEY'RE FRESH TOO!
THE DEER MIGHT STILL BE NEARBY.
ALL RIGHT!
ASIRPA...
LET'S GO AFTER IT!
DOES AN EZO DEER TASTE GOOD?
THE BRAIN IS TASTY WITH SOME SALT ON IT, SUGIMOTO.

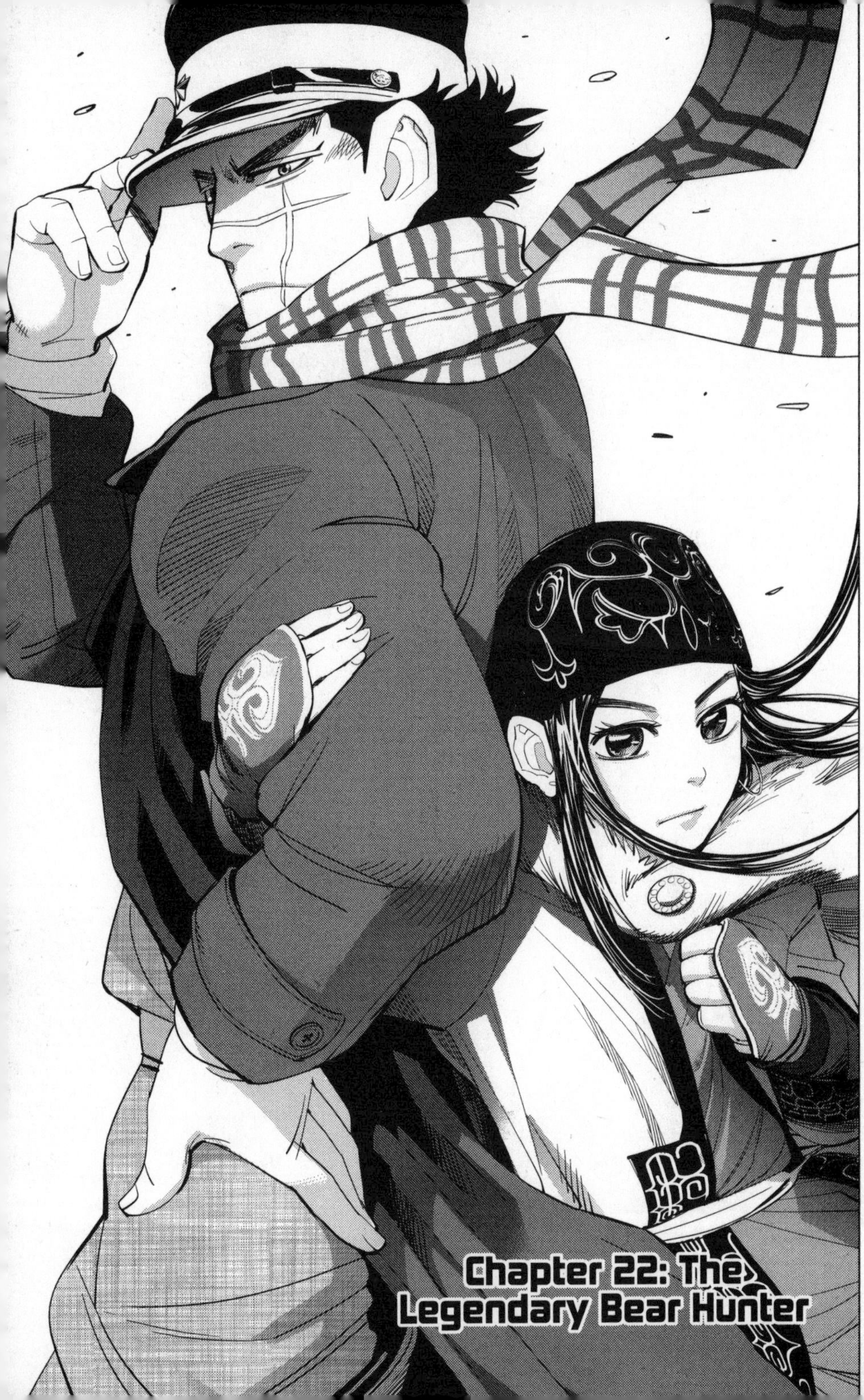
Chapter 22: The Legendary Bear Hunter

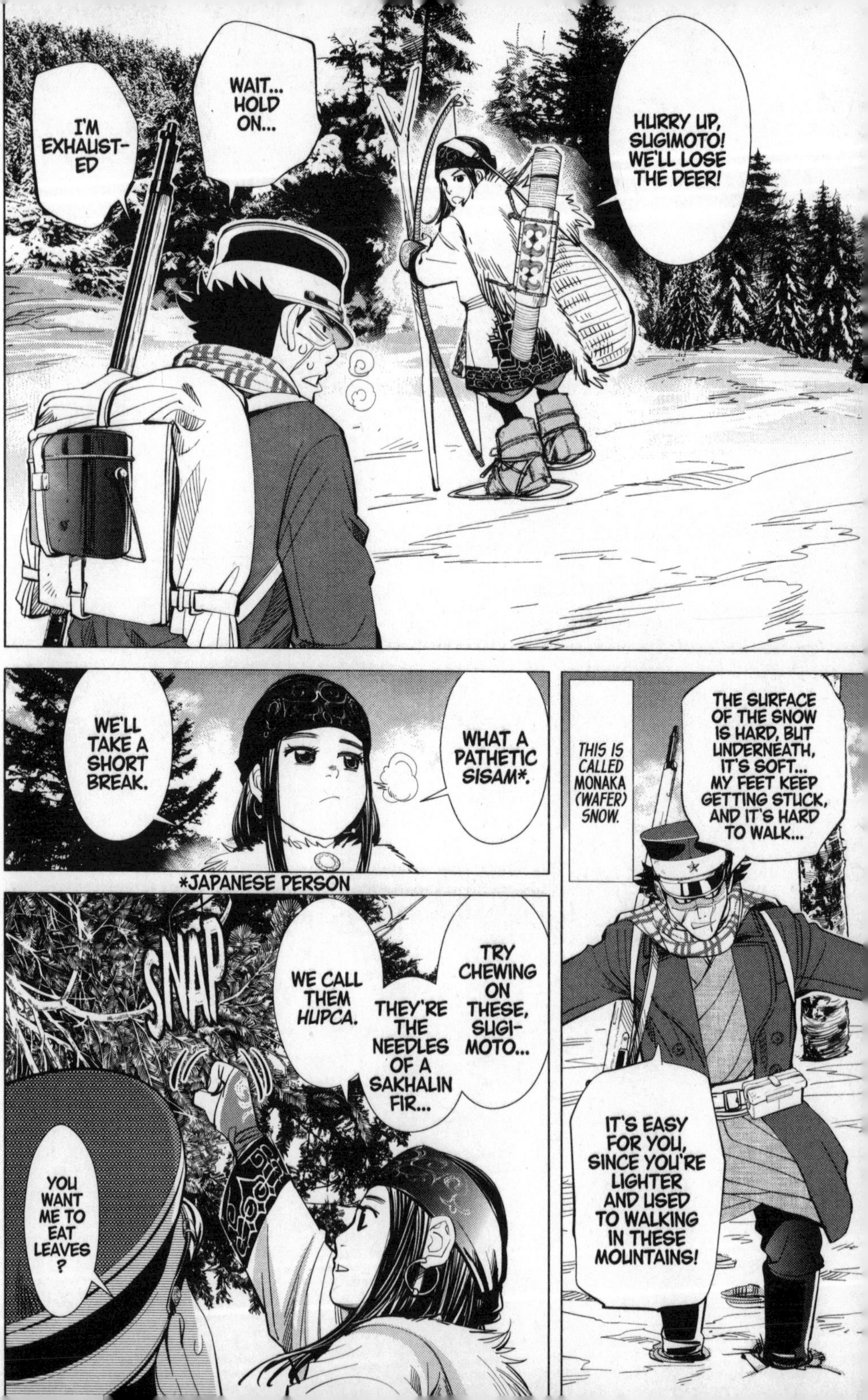
HURRY UP, SUGIMOTO! WE'LL LOSE THE DEER!
WAIT... HOLD ON...
I'M EXHAUST-ED
THE SURFACE OF THE SNOW IS HARD, BUT UNDERNEATH, IT'S SOFT... MY FEET KEEP GETTING STUCK, AND IT'S HARD TO WALK...
THIS IS CALLED MONAKA (WAFER) SNOW.
IT'S EASY FOR YOU, SINCE YOU'RE LIGHTER AND USED TO WALKING IN THESE MOUNTAINS!
WHAT A PATHETIC SISAM*.
WE'LL TAKE A SHORT BREAK.
*JAPANESE PERSON
TRY CHEWING ON THESE, SUGI-MOTO...
THEY'RE THE NEEDLES OF A SAKHALIN FIR...
WE CALL THEM HUPCA.
SNAP
YOU WANT ME TO EAT LEAVES?

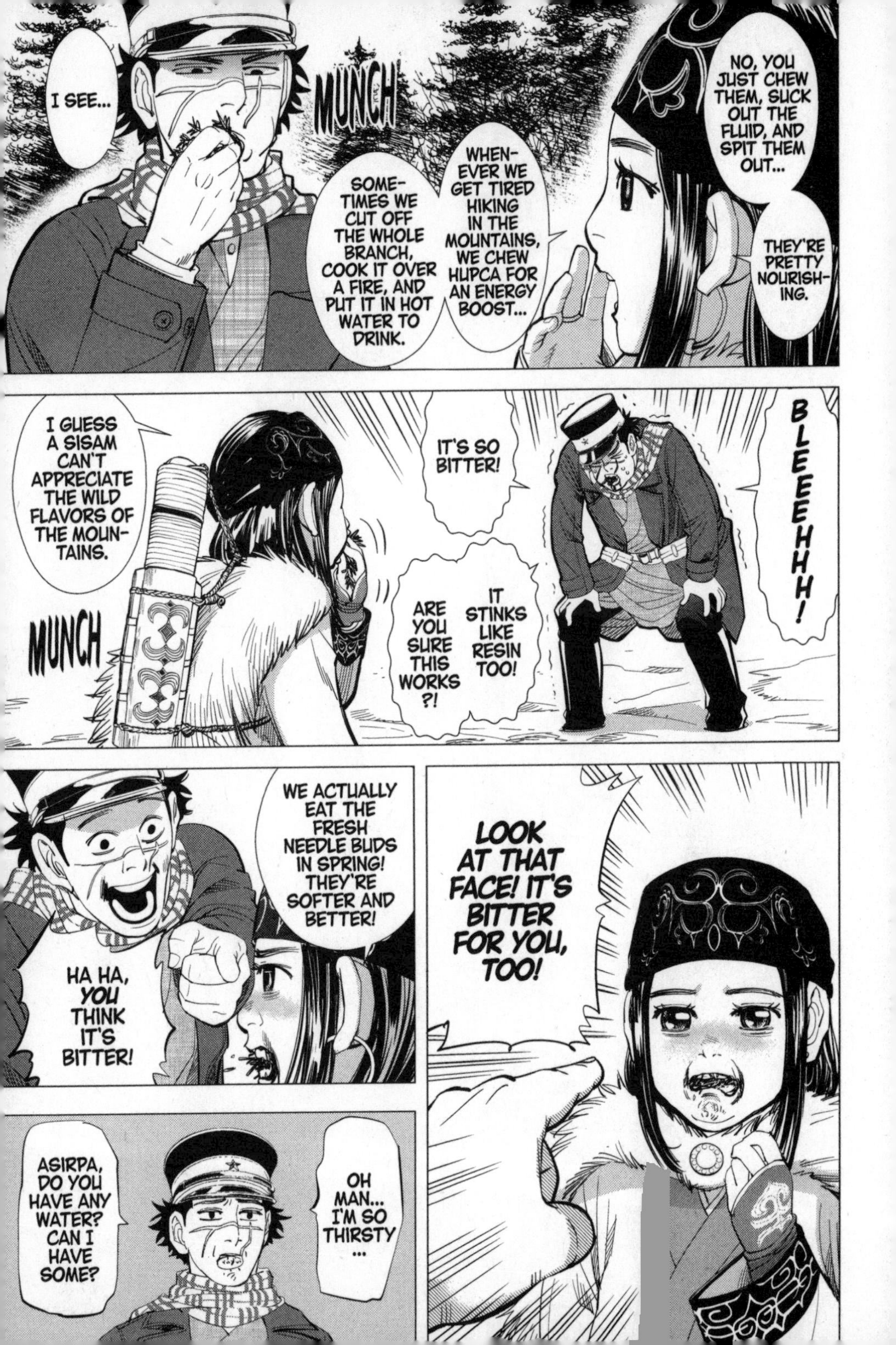
NO, YOU JUST CHEW THEM, SUCK OUT THE FLUID, AND SPIT THEM OUT...
THEY'RE PRETTY NOURISHING.
WHENEVER WE GET TIRED HIKING IN THE MOUNTAINS, WE CHEW HUPCA FOR AN ENERGY BOOST...
SOMETIMES WE CUT OFF THE WHOLE BRANCH, COOK IT OVER A FIRE, AND PUT IT IN HOT WATER TO DRINK.
MUNCH
I SEE...
BLEEEEHHH!
IT'S SO BITTER!
IT STINKS LIKE RESIN TOO!
ARE YOU SURE THIS WORKS?!
I GUESS A SISAM CAN'T APPRECIATE THE WILD FLAVORS OF THE MOUNTAINS.
MUNCH
LOOK AT THAT FACE! IT'S BITTER FOR YOU, TOO!
WE ACTUALLY EAT THE FRESH NEEDLE BUDS IN SPRING! THEY'RE SOFTER AND BETTER!
HA HA, YOU THINK IT'S BITTER!
OH MAN... I'M SO THIRSTY...
ASIRPA, DO YOU HAVE ANY WATER? CAN I HAVE SOME?

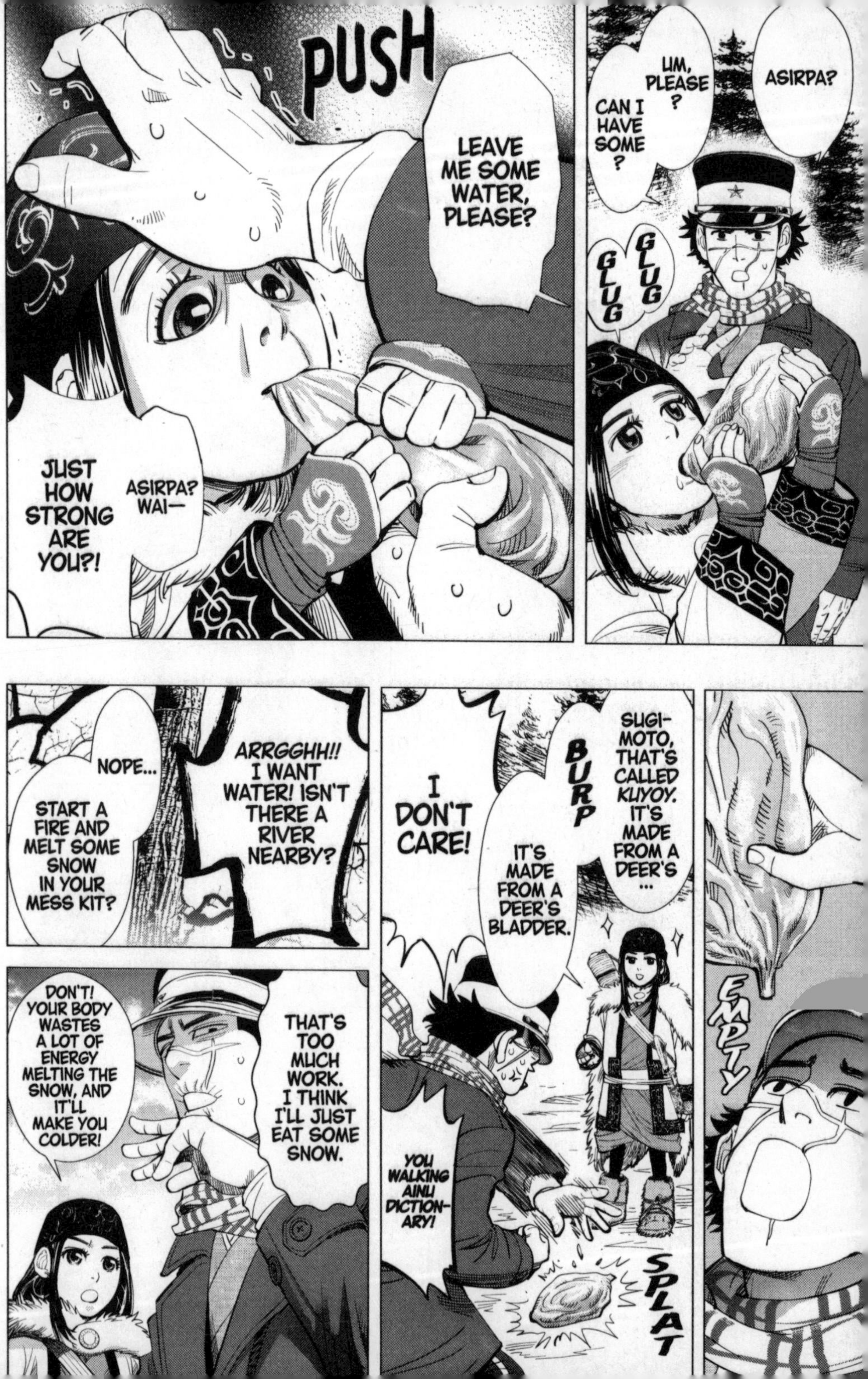
ASIRPA?
UM, PLEASE?
CAN I HAVE SOME?
GLUG GLUG
PUSH
LEAVE ME SOME WATER, PLEASE?
ASIRPA? WAI—
JUST HOW STRONG ARE YOU?!
EMPTY
SPLAT
SUGIMOTO, THAT'S CALLED KUYOY. IT'S MADE FROM A DEER'S ...
BURP
IT'S MADE FROM A DEER'S BLADDER.
I DON'T CARE!
YOU WALKING AINU DICTIONARY!
ARRGGHH!! I WANT WATER! ISN'T THERE A RIVER NEARBY?
NOPE...
START A FIRE AND MELT SOME SNOW IN YOUR MESS KIT?
THAT'S TOO MUCH WORK. I THINK I'LL JUST EAT SOME SNOW.
DON'T! YOUR BODY WASTES A LOT OF ENERGY MELTING THE SNOW, AND IT'LL MAKE YOU COLDER!

CHOP

IF YOU CUT ONE...

OH, SUGIMOTO! LOOK OVER THERE!

THAT'S A HARDY KIWI VINE.

THOSE VINES ABSORB A LOT OF WATER.

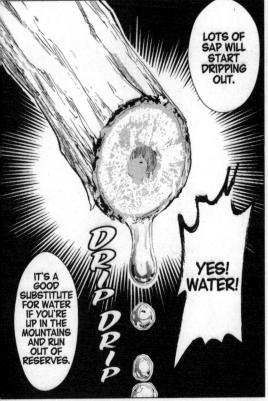

LOTS OF SAP WILL START DRIPPING OUT.

DRIP DRIP

YES! WATER!

IT'S A GOOD SUBSTITUTE FOR WATER IF YOU'RE UP IN THE MOUNTAINS AND RUN OUT OF RESERVES.

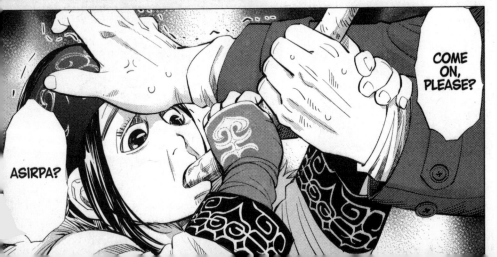

COME ON, PLEASE?

ASIRPA?

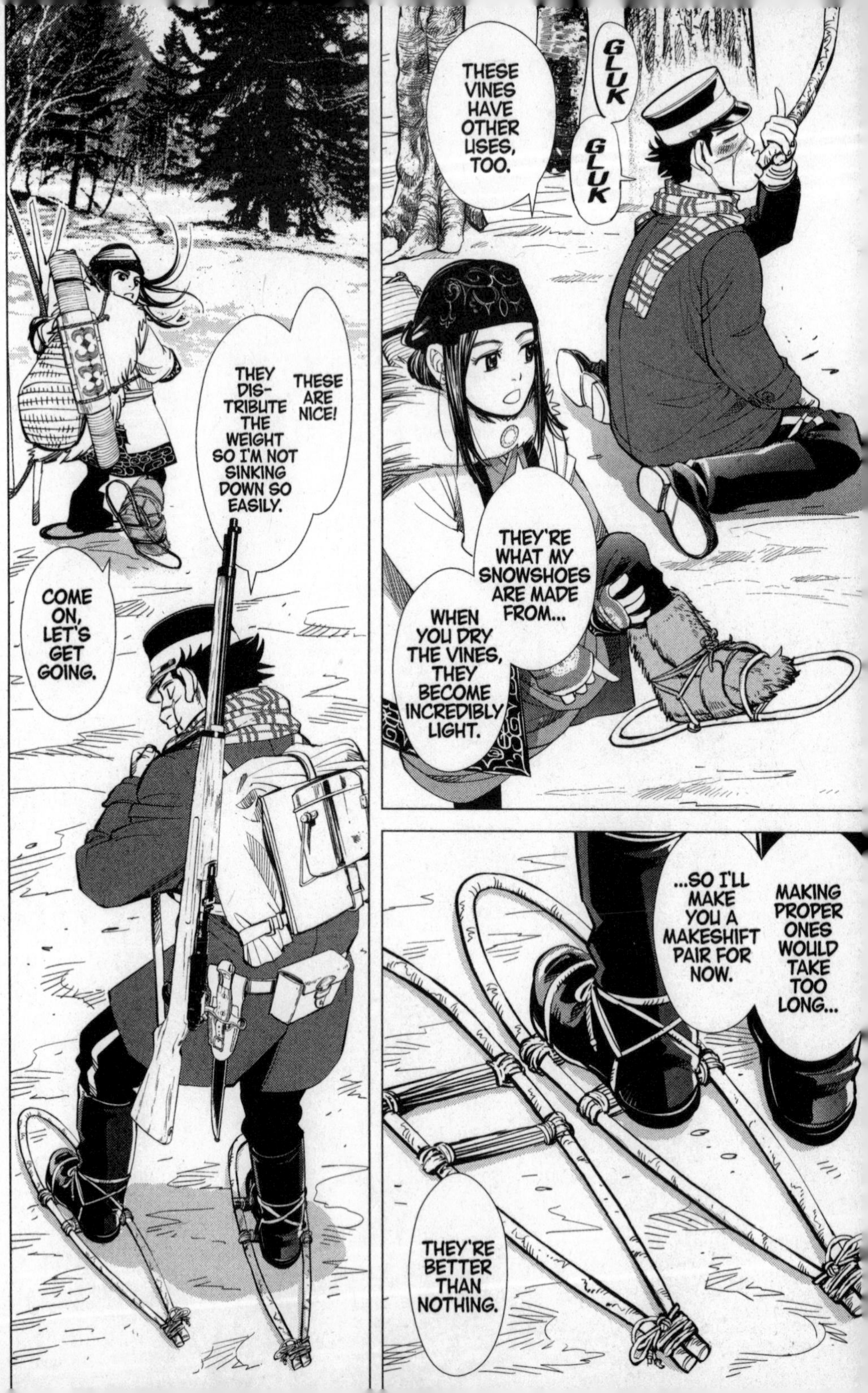
GLUK
GLUK
THESE VINES HAVE OTHER USES, TOO.
THEY'RE WHAT MY SNOWSHOES ARE MADE FROM...
WHEN YOU DRY THE VINES, THEY BECOME INCREDIBLY LIGHT.
MAKING PROPER ONES WOULD TAKE TOO LONG...
...SO I'LL MAKE YOU A MAKESHIFT PAIR FOR NOW.
THEY'RE BETTER THAN NOTHING.
THESE ARE NICE!
THEY DIS-TRIBUTE THE WEIGHT SO I'M NOT SINKING DOWN SO EASILY.
COME ON, LET'S GET GOING.

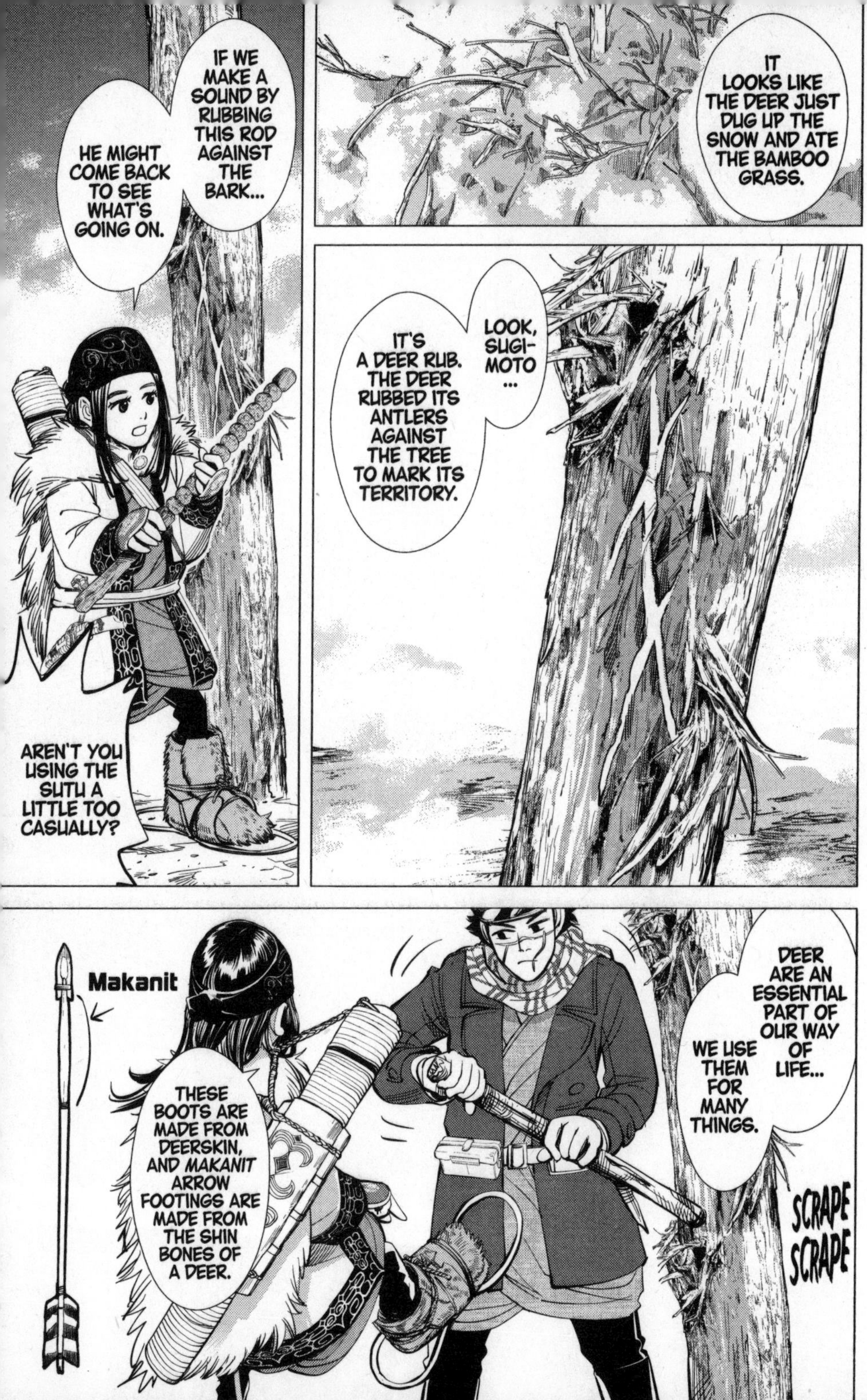
IT LOOKS LIKE THE DEER JUST DUG UP THE SNOW AND ATE THE BAMBOO GRASS.
LOOK, SUGIMOTO...
IT'S A DEER RUB. THE DEER RUBBED ITS ANTLERS AGAINST THE TREE TO MARK ITS TERRITORY.
IF WE MAKE A SOUND BY RUBBING THIS ROD AGAINST THE BARK...
HE MIGHT COME BACK TO SEE WHAT'S GOING ON.
AREN'T YOU USING THE SUTU A LITTLE TOO CASUALLY?
DEER ARE AN ESSENTIAL PART OF OUR WAY OF LIFE...
WE USE THEM FOR MANY THINGS.
SCRAPE SCRAPE
THESE BOOTS ARE MADE FROM DEERSKIN, AND MAKANIT ARROW FOOTINGS ARE MADE FROM THE SHIN BONES OF A DEER.
Makanit

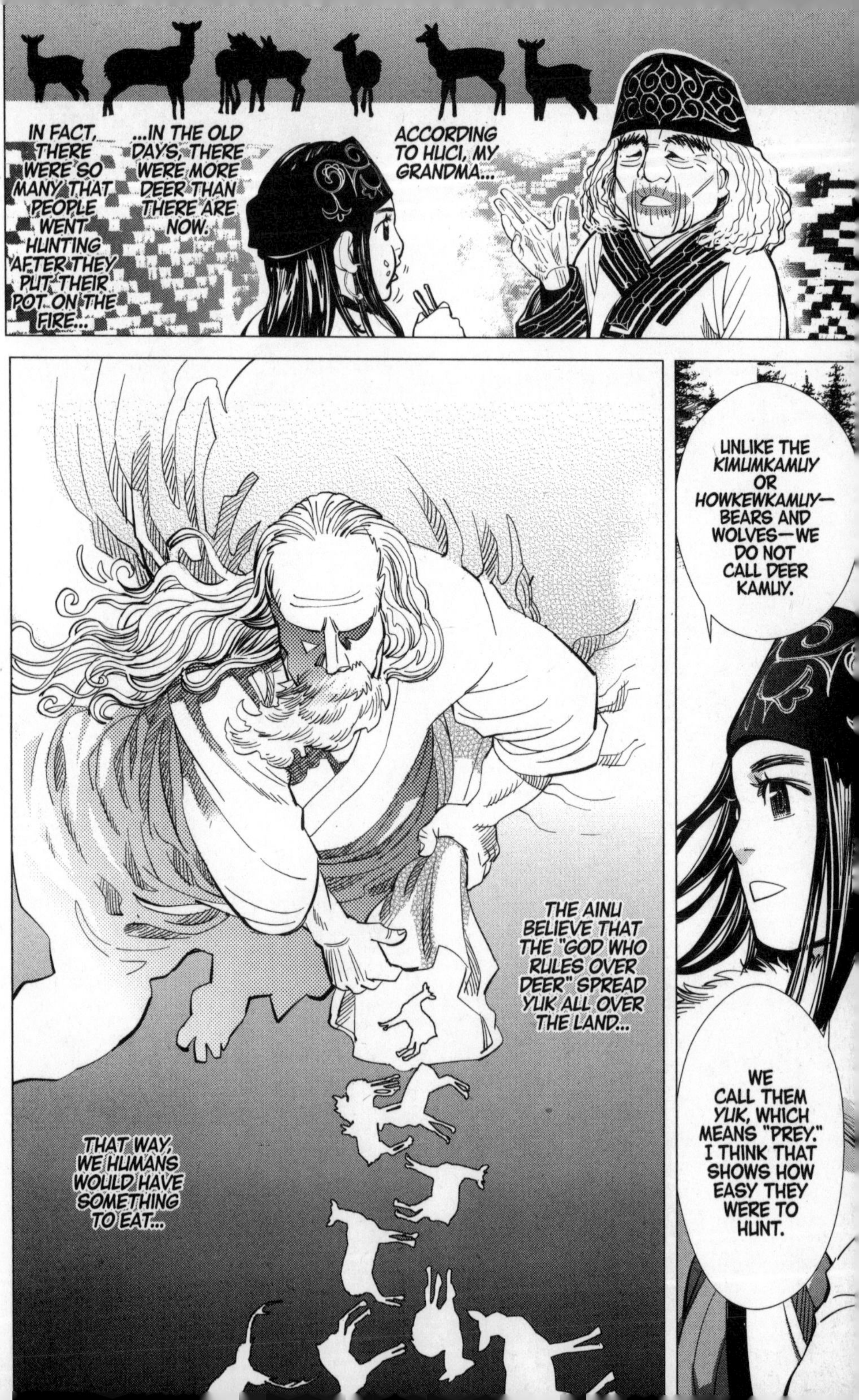
ACCORDING TO HUCI, MY GRANDMA...
...IN THE OLD DAYS, THERE WERE MORE DEER THAN THERE ARE NOW.
IN FACT, THERE WERE SO MANY THAT PEOPLE WENT HUNTING AFTER THEY PUT THEIR POT ON THE FIRE...
UNLIKE THE KIMUMKAMUY OR HOWKEWKAMUY—BEARS AND WOLVES—WE DO NOT CALL DEER KAMUY.
WE CALL THEM YUK, WHICH MEANS "PREY." I THINK THAT SHOWS HOW EASY THEY WERE TO HUNT.
THE AINU BELIEVE THAT THE "GOD WHO RULES OVER DEER" SPREAD YUK ALL OVER THE LAND...
THAT WAY, WE HUMANS WOULD HAVE SOMETHING TO EAT...

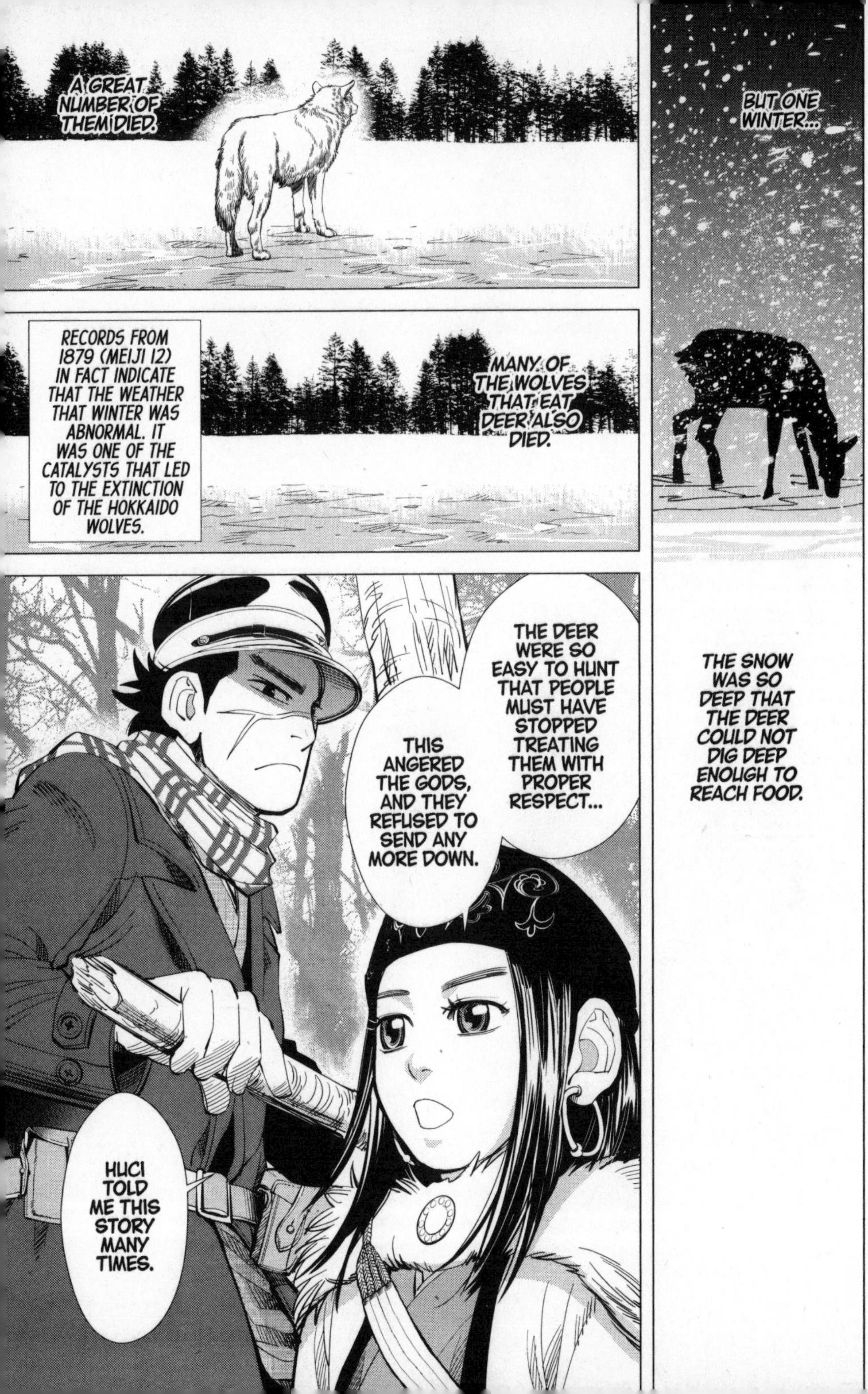
BUT ONE WINTER...
THE SNOW WAS SO DEEP THAT THE DEER COULD NOT DIG DEEP ENOUGH TO REACH FOOD.
A GREAT NUMBER OF THEM DIED.
MANY OF THE WOLVES THAT EAT DEER ALSO DIED.
RECORDS FROM 1879 (MEIJI 12) IN FACT INDICATE THAT THE WEATHER THAT WINTER WAS ABNORMAL. IT WAS ONE OF THE CATALYSTS THAT LED TO THE EXTINCTION OF THE HOKKAIDO WOLVES.
THE DEER WERE SO EASY TO HUNT THAT PEOPLE MUST HAVE STOPPED TREATING THEM WITH PROPER RESPECT...
THIS ANGERED THE GODS, AND THEY REFUSED TO SEND ANY MORE DOWN.
HUCI TOLD ME THIS STORY MANY TIMES.

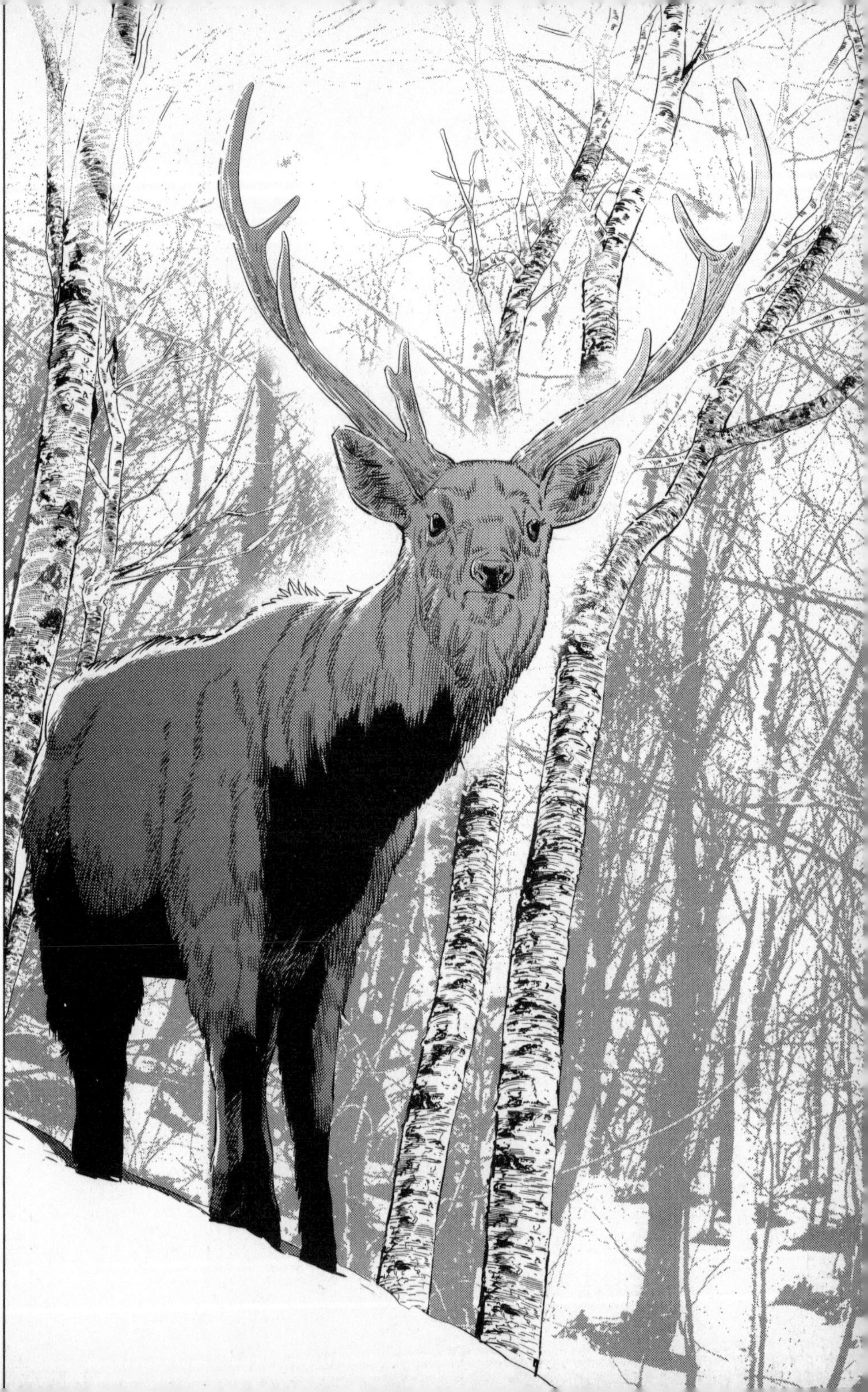

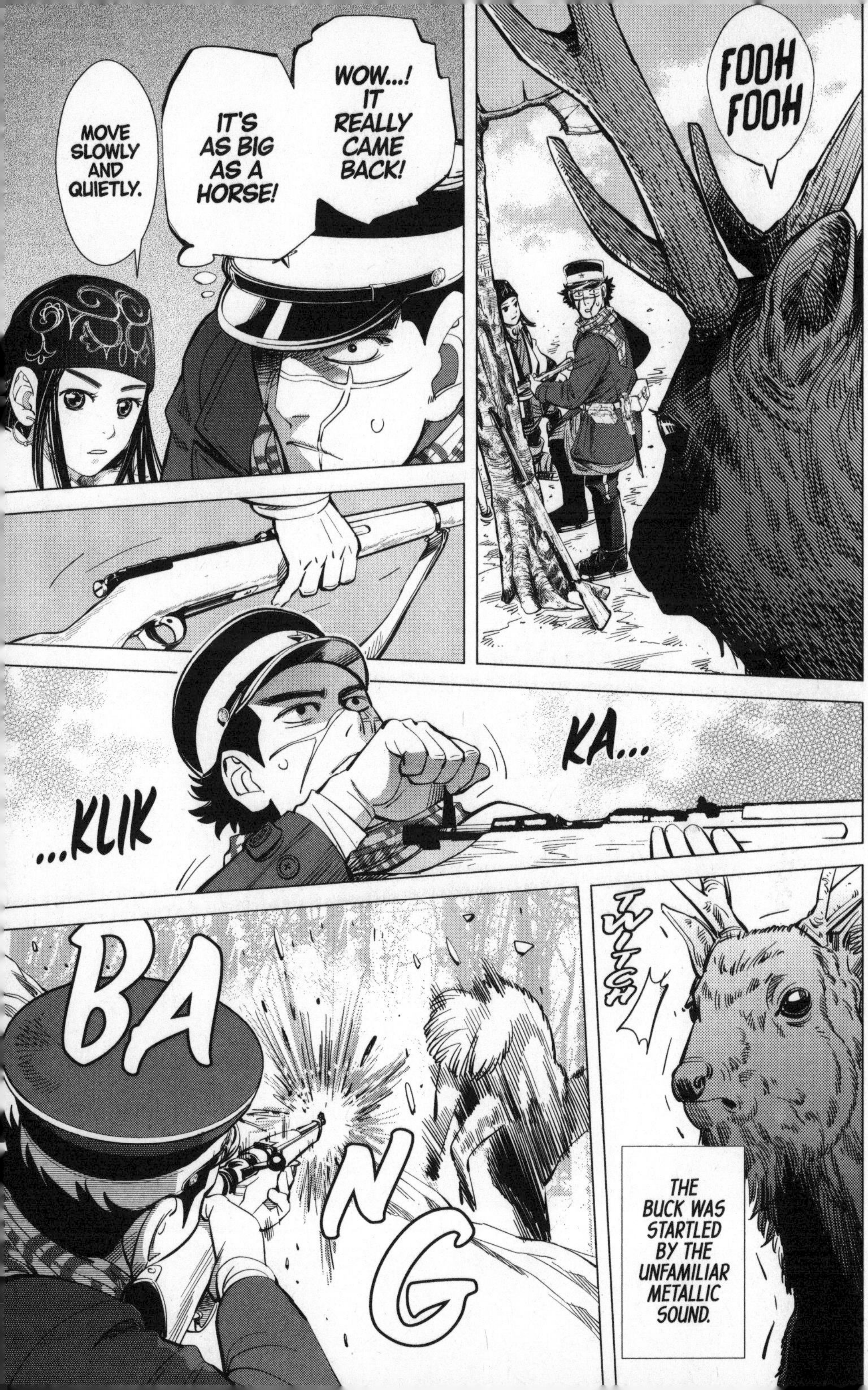
FOOH FOOH
WOW...! IT REALLY CAME BACK!
IT'S AS BIG AS A HORSE!
MOVE SLOWLY AND QUIETLY.
KA...
...KLIK
TWITCH
THE BUCK WAS STARTLED BY THE UNFAMILIAR METALLIC SOUND.
BANG

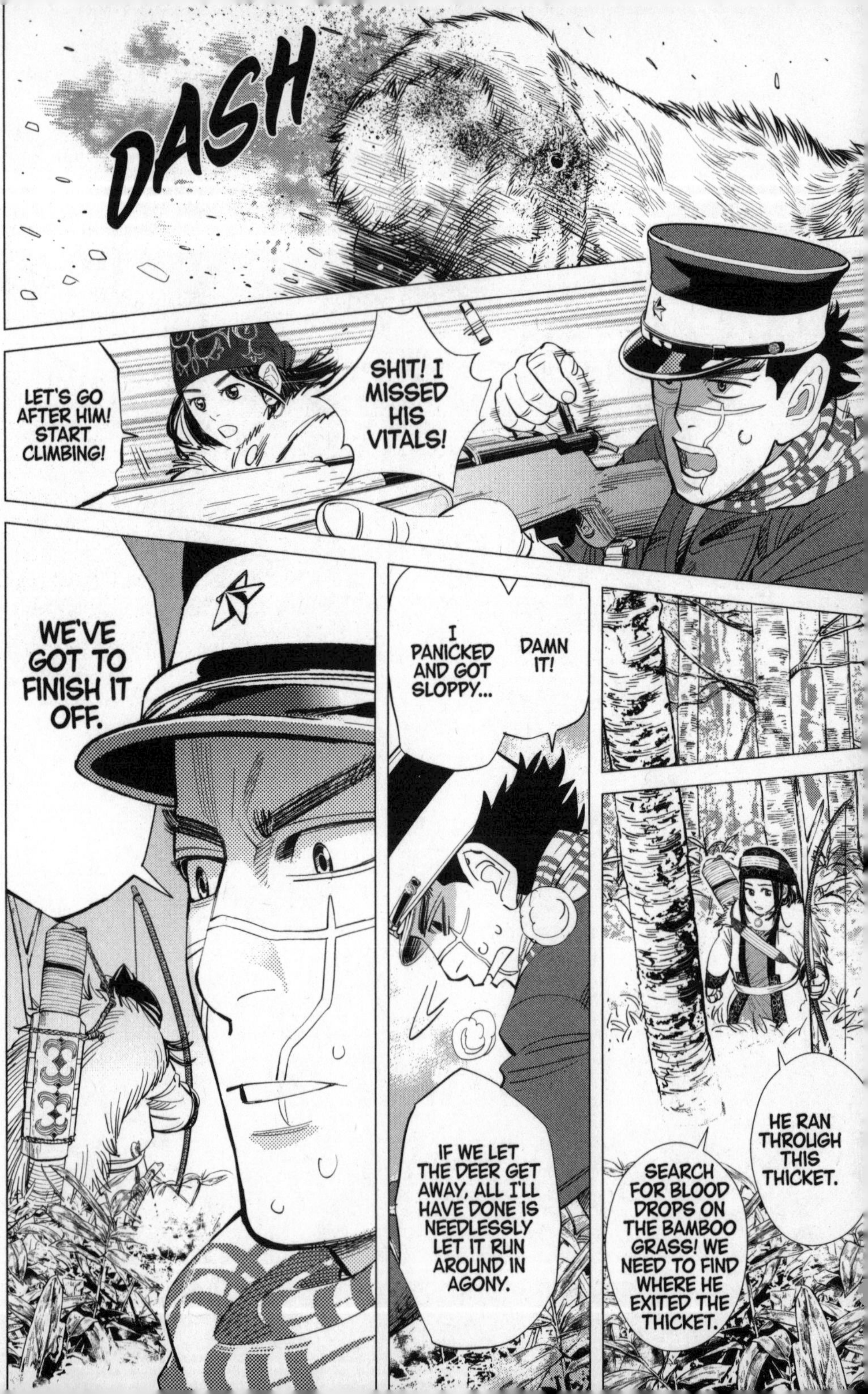
DASH
SHIT! I MISSED HIS VITALS!
LET'S GO AFTER HIM! START CLIMBING!
HE RAN THROUGH THIS THICKET.
SEARCH FOR BLOOD DROPS ON THE BAMBOO GRASS! WE NEED TO FIND WHERE HE EXITED THE THICKET.
DAMN IT!
I PANICKED AND GOT SLOPPY...
IF WE LET THE DEER GET AWAY, ALL I'LL HAVE DONE IS NEEDLESSLY LET IT RUN AROUND IN AGONY.
WE'VE GOT TO FINISH IT OFF.

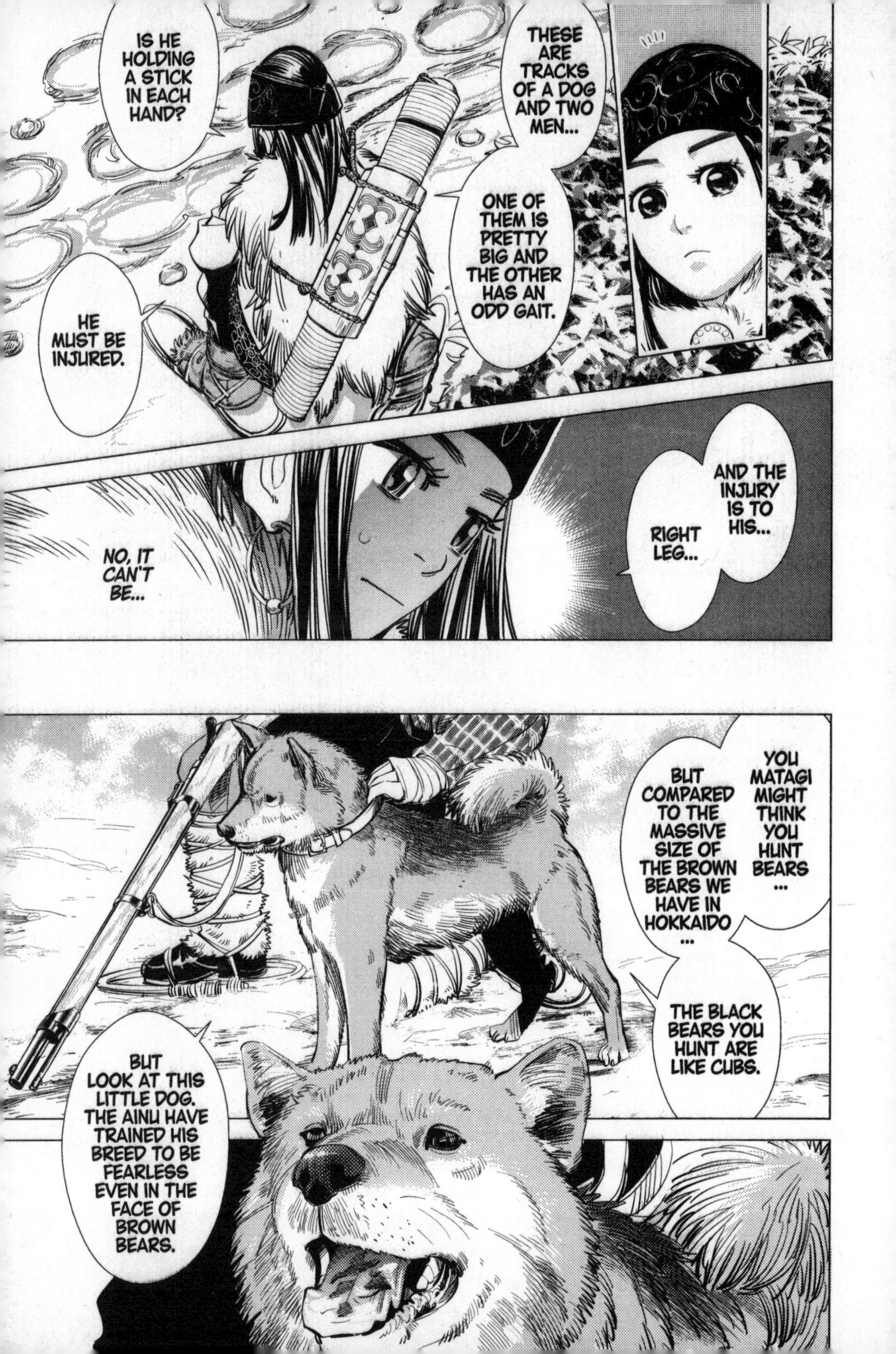

THESE ARE TRACKS OF A DOG AND TWO MEN...
ONE OF THEM IS PRETTY BIG AND THE OTHER HAS AN ODD GAIT.
IS HE HOLDING A STICK IN EACH HAND?
HE MUST BE INJURED.
AND THE INJURY IS TO HIS...
RIGHT LEG...
NO, IT CAN'T BE...
YOU MATAGI MIGHT THINK YOU HUNT BEARS...
BUT COMPARED TO THE MASSIVE SIZE OF THE BROWN BEARS WE HAVE IN HOKKAIDO...
THE BLACK BEARS YOU HUNT ARE LIKE CUBS.
BUT LOOK AT THIS LITTLE DOG. THE AINU HAVE TRAINED HIS BREED TO BE FEARLESS EVEN IN THE FACE OF BROWN BEARS.

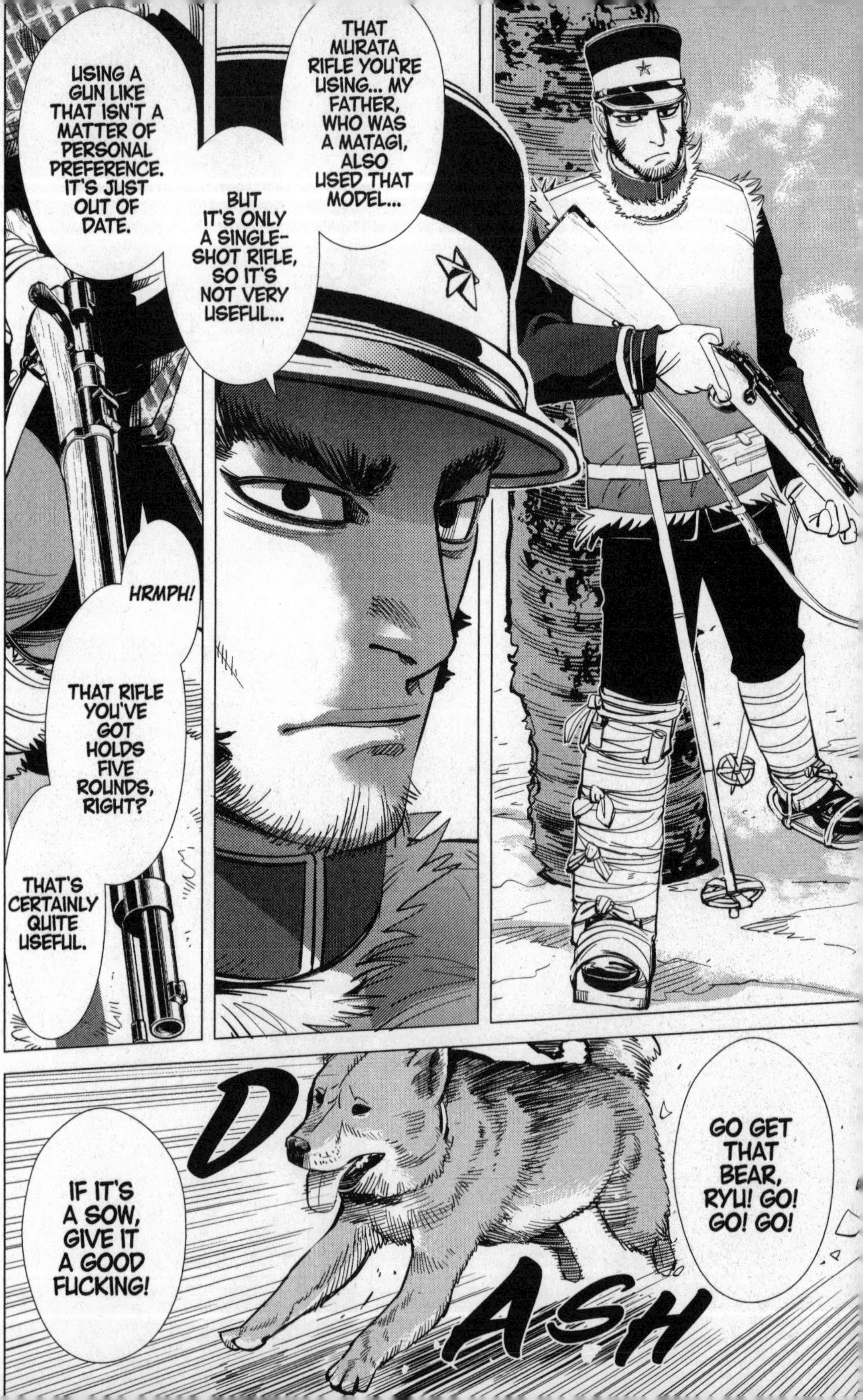
THAT MURATA RIFLE YOU'RE USING... MY FATHER, WHO WAS A MATAGI, ALSO USED THAT MODEL...
BUT IT'S ONLY A SINGLE-SHOT RIFLE, SO IT'S NOT VERY USEFUL...
USING A GUN LIKE THAT ISN'T A MATTER OF PERSONAL PREFERENCE. IT'S JUST OUT OF DATE.
HRMPH!
THAT RIFLE YOU'VE GOT HOLDS FIVE ROUNDS, RIGHT?
THAT'S CERTAINLY QUITE USEFUL.
GO GET THAT BEAR, RYU! GO! GO! GO!
D
ASH
IF IT'S A SOW, GIVE IT A GOOD FUCKING!

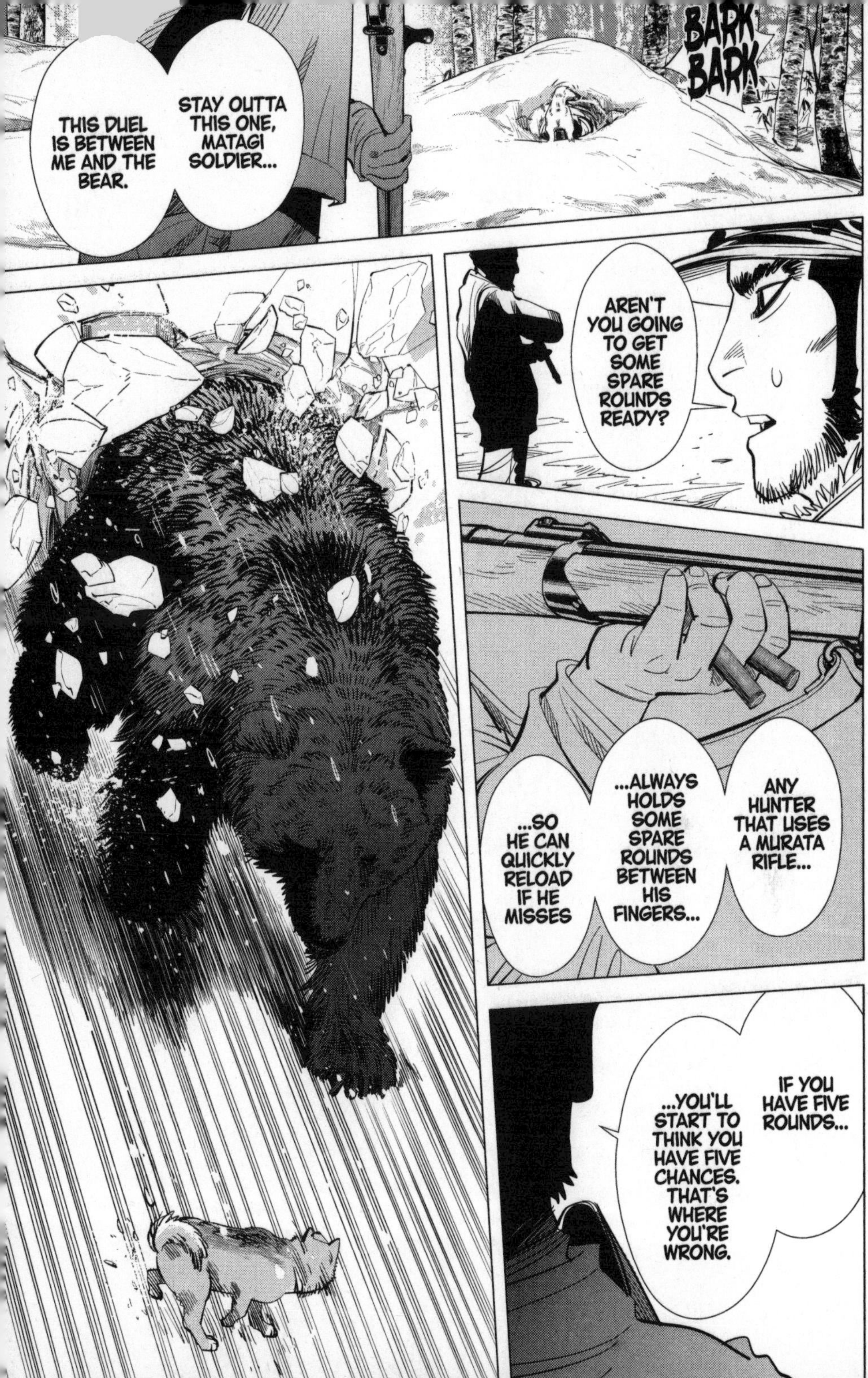
BARK BARK
STAY OUTTA THIS ONE, MATAGI SOLDIER...
THIS DUEL IS BETWEEN ME AND THE BEAR.
AREN'T YOU GOING TO GET SOME SPARE ROUNDS READY?
ANY HUNTER THAT USES A MURATA RIFLE...
...ALWAYS HOLDS SOME SPARE ROUNDS BETWEEN HIS FINGERS...
...SO HE CAN QUICKLY RELOAD IF HE MISSES
IF YOU HAVE FIVE ROUNDS...
...YOU'LL START TO THINK YOU HAVE FIVE CHANCES. THAT'S WHERE YOU'RE WRONG.

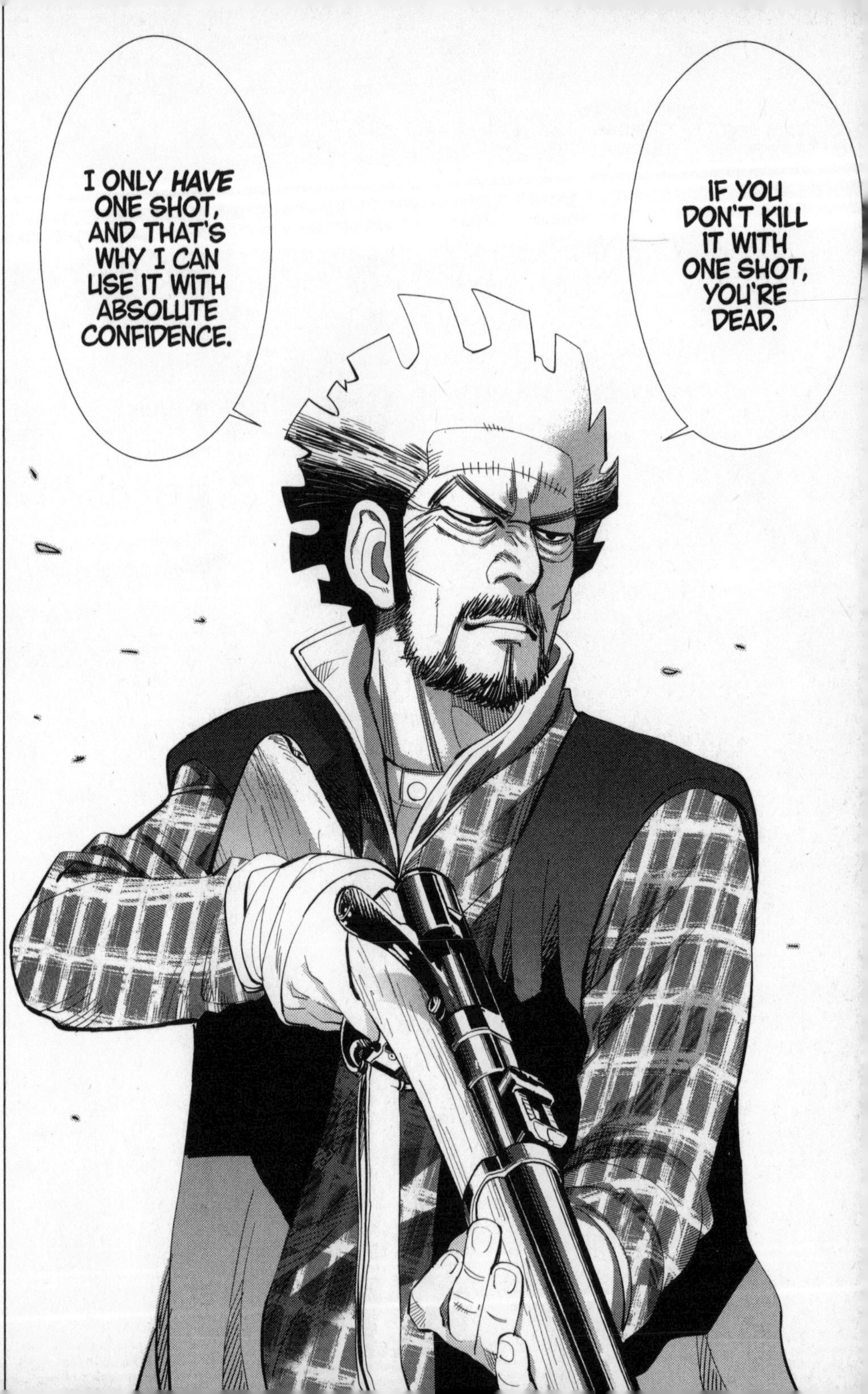
IF YOU DON'T KILL IT WITH ONE SHOT, YOU'RE DEAD.
I ONLY HAVE ONE SHOT, AND THAT'S WHY I CAN USE IT WITH ABSOLUTE CONFIDENCE.

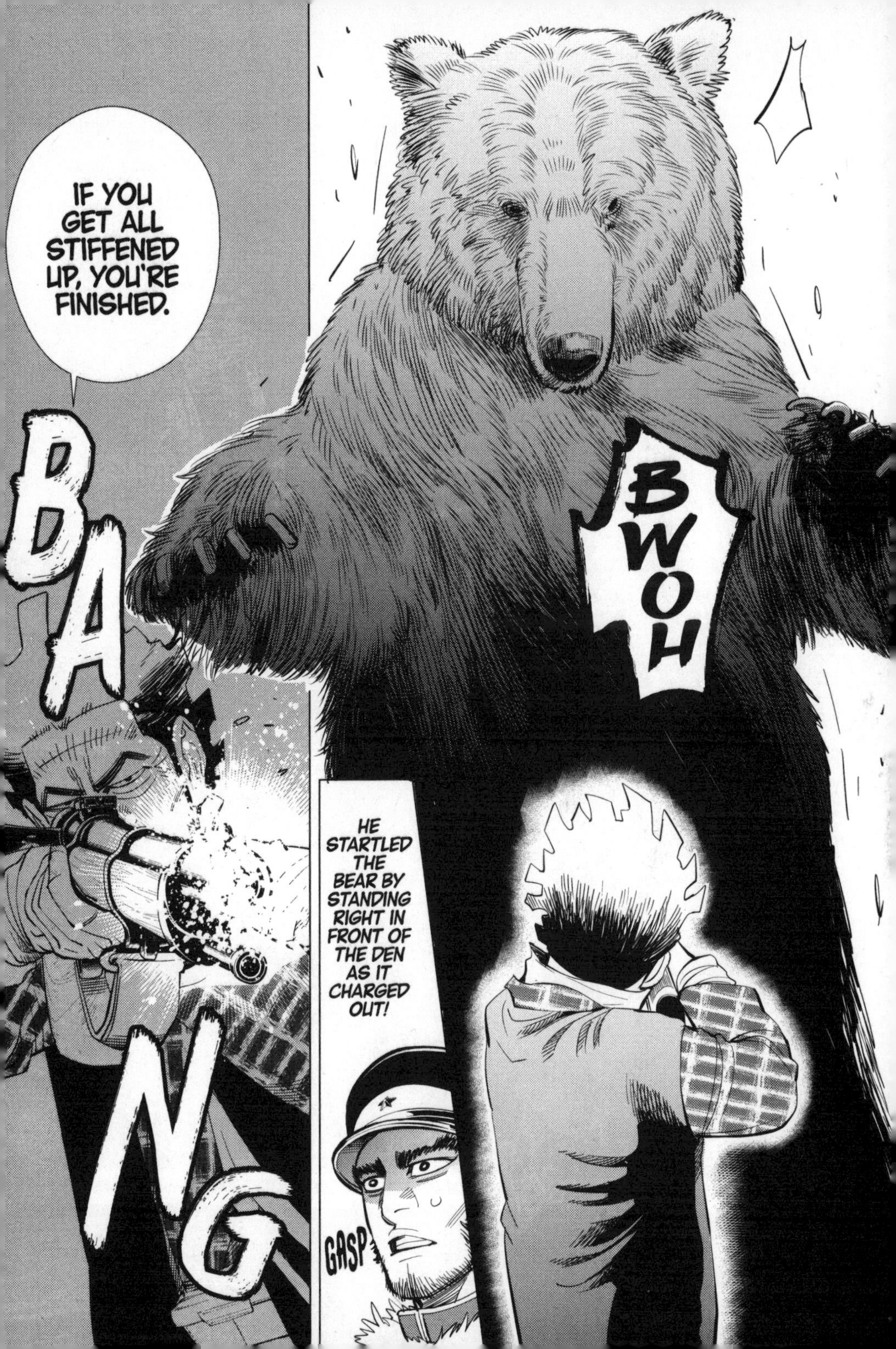
BWOH
HE STARTLED THE BEAR BY STANDING RIGHT IN FRONT OF THE DEN AS IT CHARGED OUT!
GASP
IF YOU GET ALL STIFFENED UP, YOU'RE FINISHED.
BANG

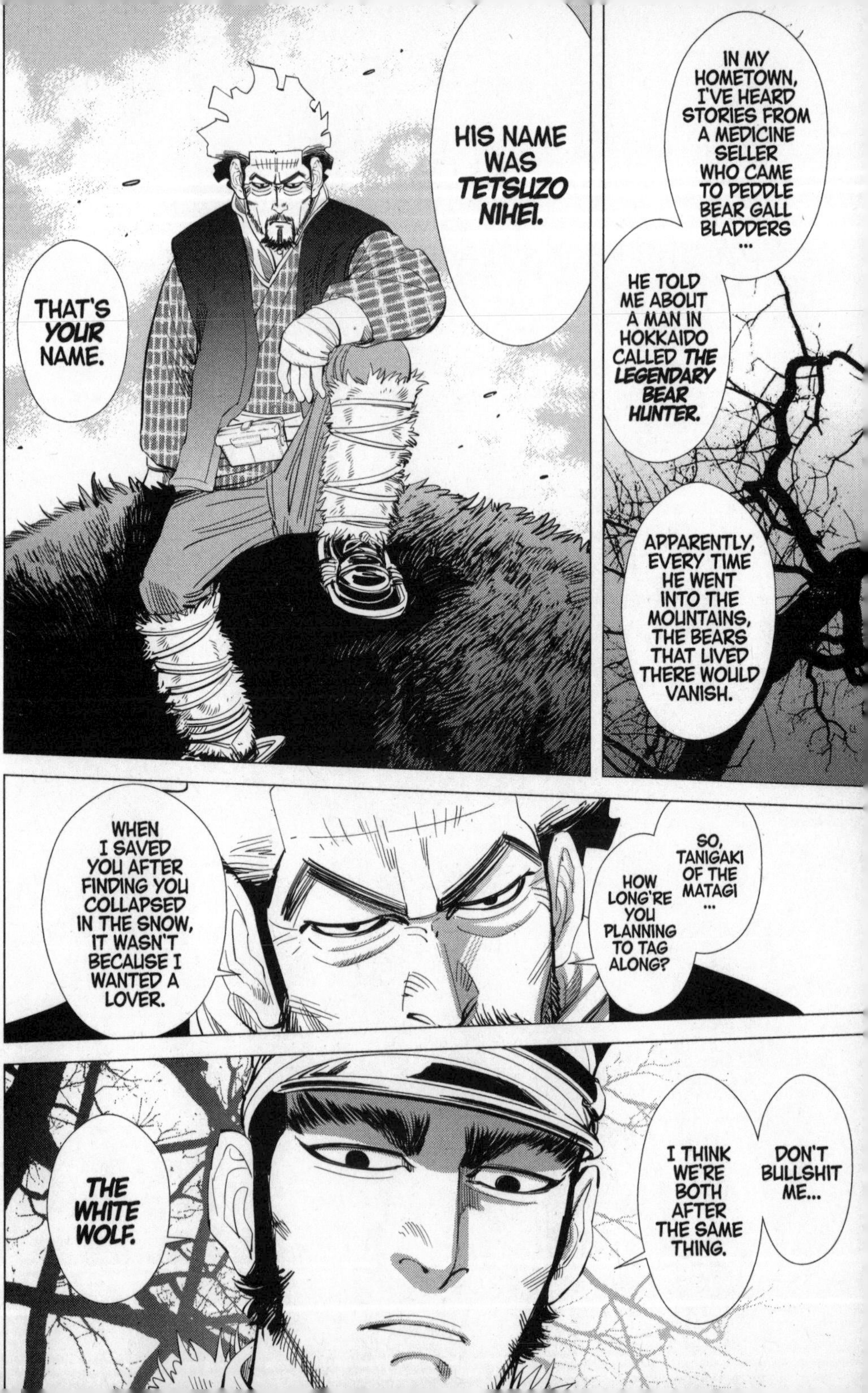
IN MY HOMETOWN, I'VE HEARD STORIES FROM A MEDICINE SELLER WHO CAME TO PEDDLE BEAR GALL BLADDERS ...
HE TOLD ME ABOUT A MAN IN HOKKAIDO CALLED *THE LEGENDARY BEAR HUNTER.*
APPARENTLY, EVERY TIME HE WENT INTO THE MOUNTAINS, THE BEARS THAT LIVED THERE WOULD VANISH.
HIS NAME WAS *TETSUZO NIHEI.*
THAT'S *YOUR* NAME.
SO, TANIGAKI OF THE MATAGI ...
HOW LONG'RE YOU PLANNING TO TAG ALONG?
WHEN I SAVED YOU AFTER FINDING YOU COLLAPSED IN THE SNOW, IT WASN'T BECAUSE I WANTED A LOVER.
DON'T BULLSHIT ME...
I THINK WE'RE BOTH AFTER THE SAME THING.
THE WHITE WOLF.

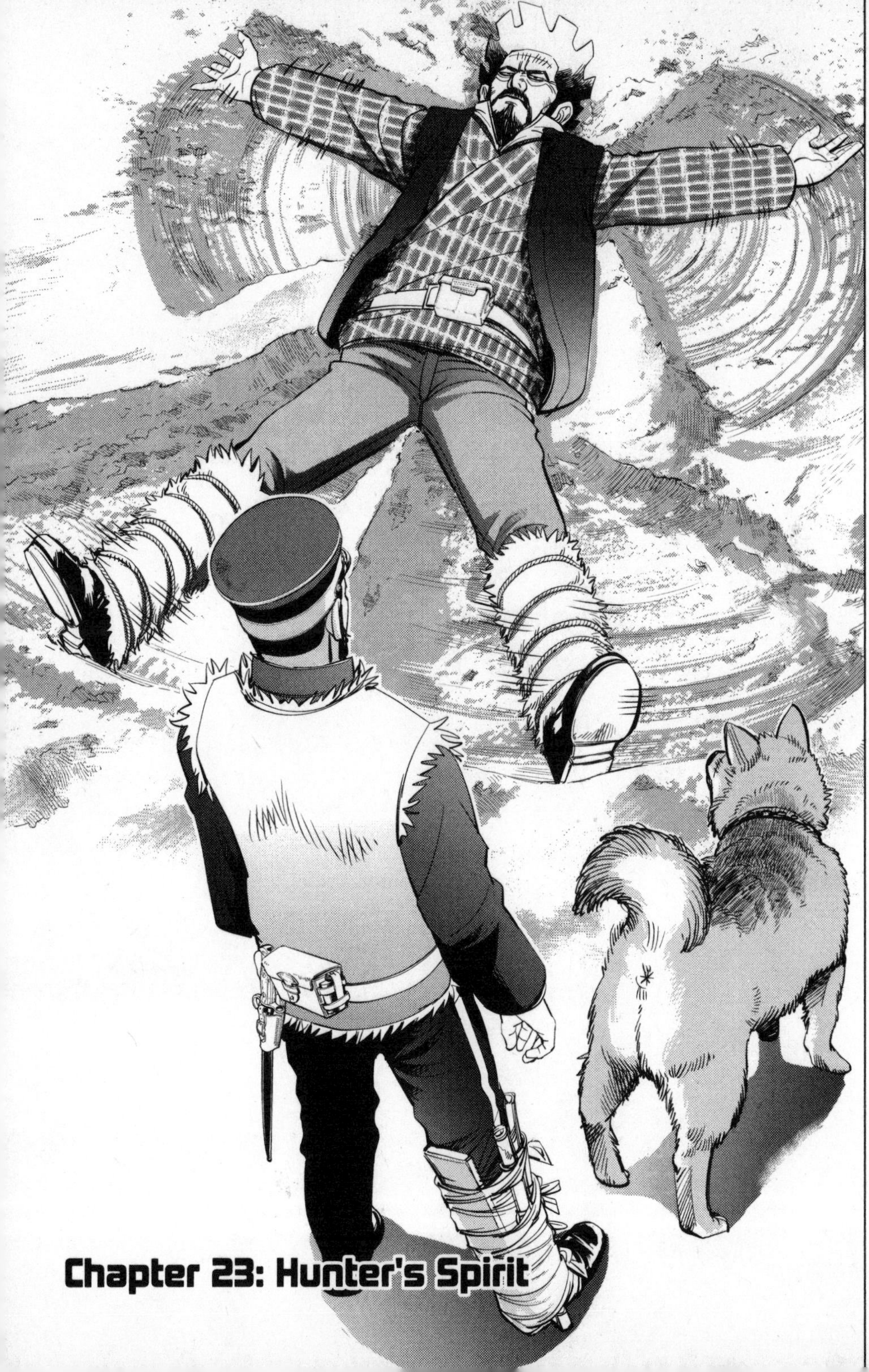
Chapter 23: Hunter's Spirit

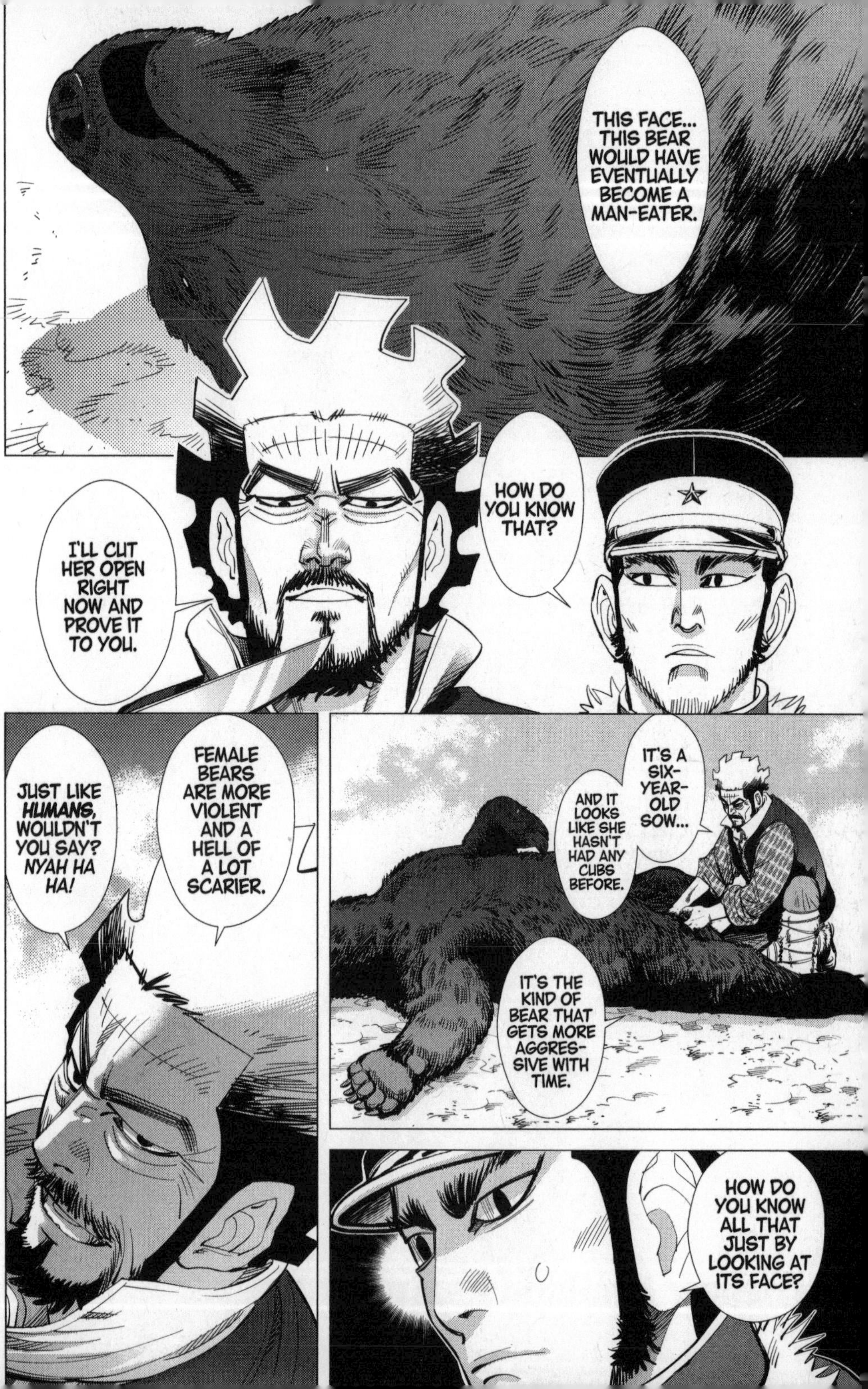
THIS FACE... THIS BEAR WOULD HAVE EVENTUALLY BECOME A MAN-EATER.
HOW DO YOU KNOW THAT?
I'LL CUT HER OPEN RIGHT NOW AND PROVE IT TO YOU.
IT'S A SIX-YEAR-OLD SOW...
AND IT LOOKS LIKE SHE HASN'T HAD ANY CUBS BEFORE.
IT'S THE KIND OF BEAR THAT GETS MORE AGGRES-SIVE WITH TIME.
HOW DO YOU KNOW ALL THAT JUST BY LOOKING AT ITS FACE?
FEMALE BEARS ARE MORE VIOLENT AND A HELL OF A LOT SCARIER.
JUST LIKE *HUMANS*, WOULDN'T YOU SAY? NYAH HA HA!

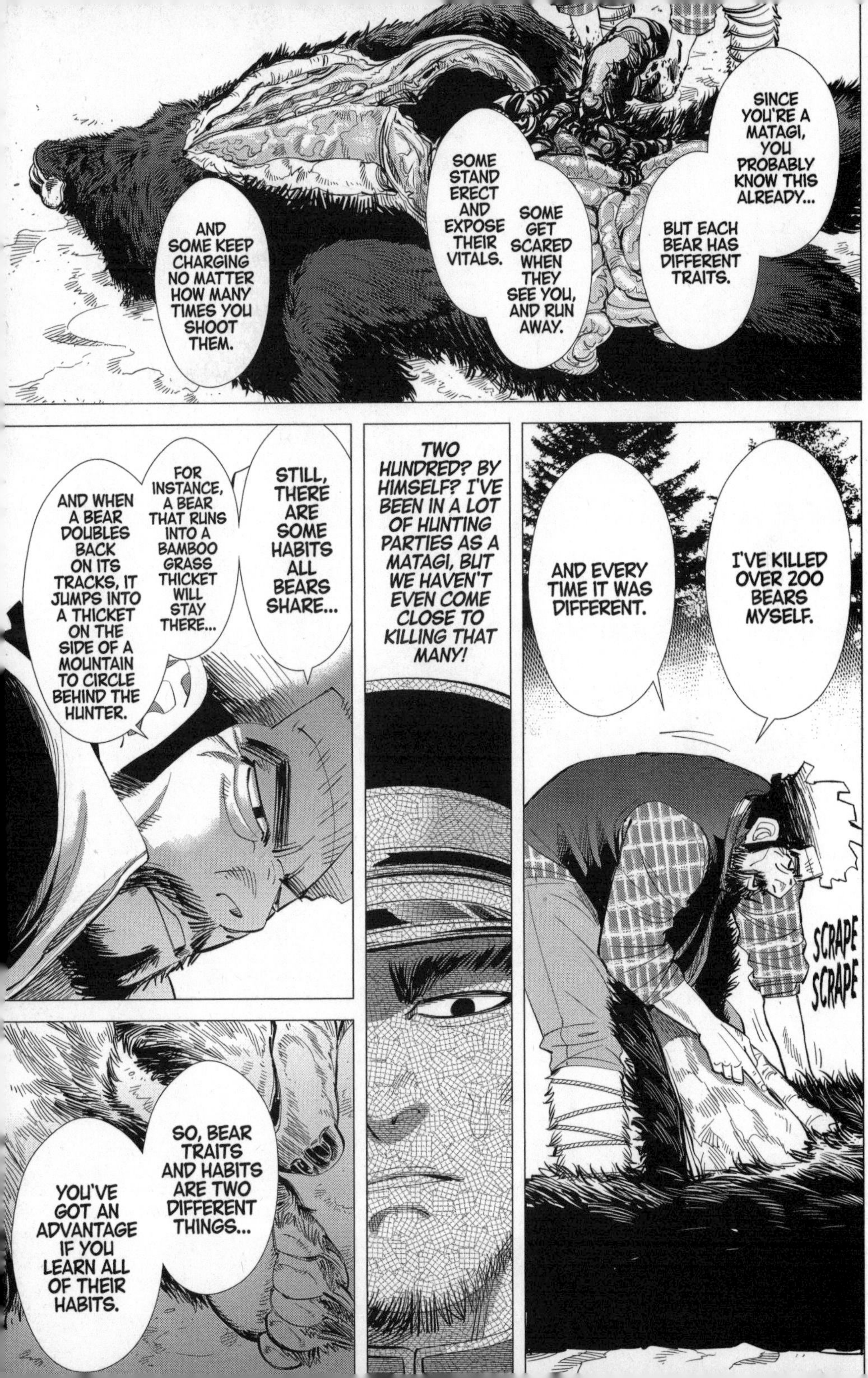

SINCE YOU'RE A MATAGI, YOU PROBABLY KNOW THIS ALREADY...
BUT EACH BEAR HAS DIFFERENT TRAITS.
SOME GET SCARED WHEN THEY SEE YOU, AND RUN AWAY.
SOME STAND ERECT AND EXPOSE THEIR VITALS.
AND SOME KEEP CHARGING NO MATTER HOW MANY TIMES YOU SHOOT THEM.
I'VE KILLED OVER 200 BEARS MYSELF.
AND EVERY TIME IT WAS DIFFERENT.
SCRAPE SCRAPE
TWO HUNDRED? BY HIMSELF? I'VE BEEN IN A LOT OF HUNTING PARTIES AS A MATAGI, BUT WE HAVEN'T EVEN COME CLOSE TO KILLING THAT MANY!
STILL, THERE ARE SOME HABITS ALL BEARS SHARE...
FOR INSTANCE, A BEAR THAT RUNS INTO A BAMBOO GRASS THICKET WILL STAY THERE...
AND WHEN A BEAR DOUBLES BACK ON ITS TRACKS, IT JUMPS INTO A THICKET ON THE SIDE OF A MOUNTAIN TO CIRCLE BEHIND THE HUNTER.
SO, BEAR TRAITS AND HABITS ARE TWO DIFFERENT THINGS...
YOU'VE GOT AN ADVANTAGE IF YOU LEARN ALL OF THEIR HABITS.

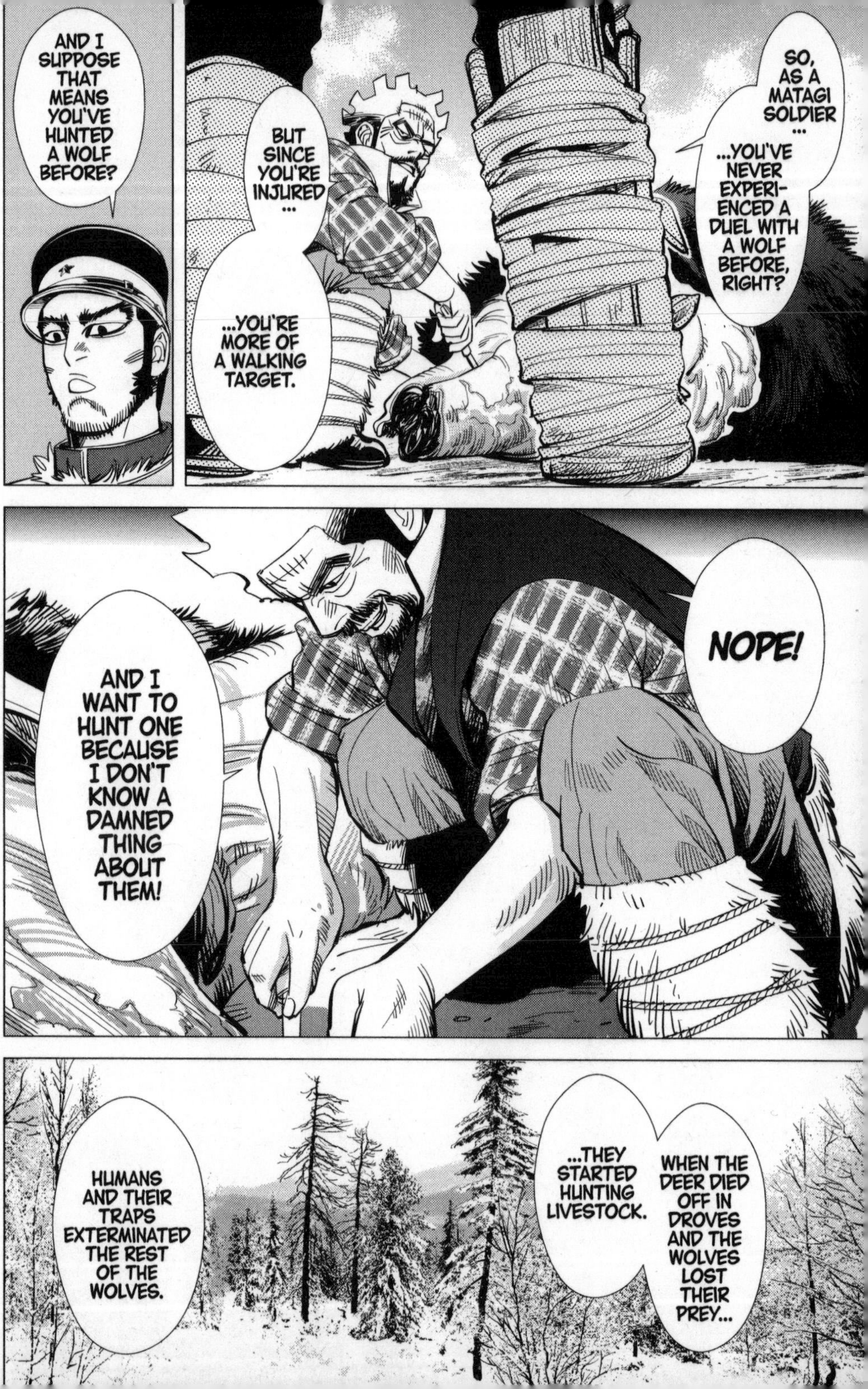
SO, AS A MATAGI SOLDIER...
...YOU'VE NEVER EXPERIENCED A DUEL WITH A WOLF BEFORE, RIGHT?
BUT SINCE YOU'RE INJURED...
...YOU'RE MORE OF A WALKING TARGET.
AND I SUPPOSE THAT MEANS YOU'VE HUNTED A WOLF BEFORE?
NOPE!
AND I WANT TO HUNT ONE BECAUSE I DON'T KNOW A DAMNED THING ABOUT THEM!
WHEN THE DEER DIED OFF IN DROVES AND THE WOLVES LOST THEIR PREY...
...THEY STARTED HUNTING LIVESTOCK.
HUMANS AND THEIR TRAPS EXTERMINATED THE REST OF THE WOLVES.

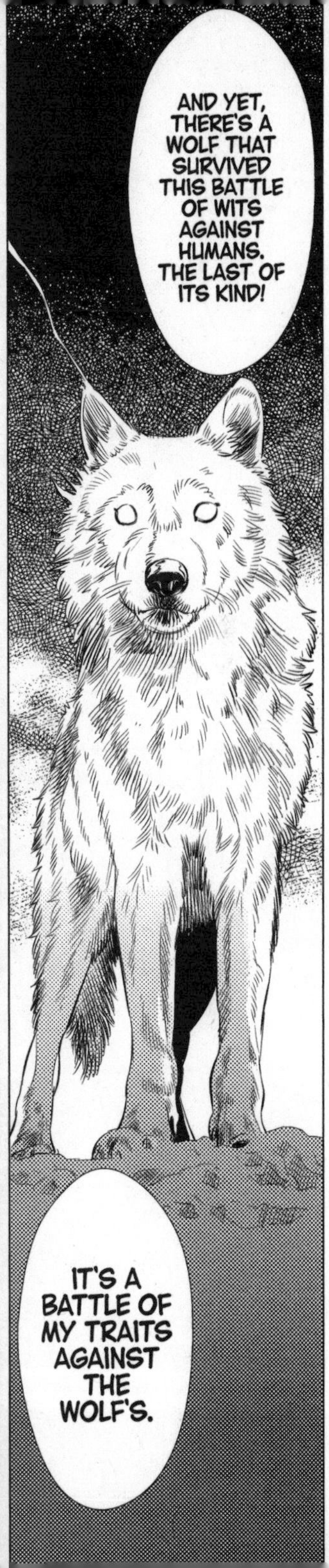
AND YET, THERE'S A WOLF THAT SURVIVED THIS BATTLE OF WITS AGAINST HUMANS. THE LAST OF ITS KIND!
IT'S A BATTLE OF MY TRAITS AGAINST THE WOLF'S.
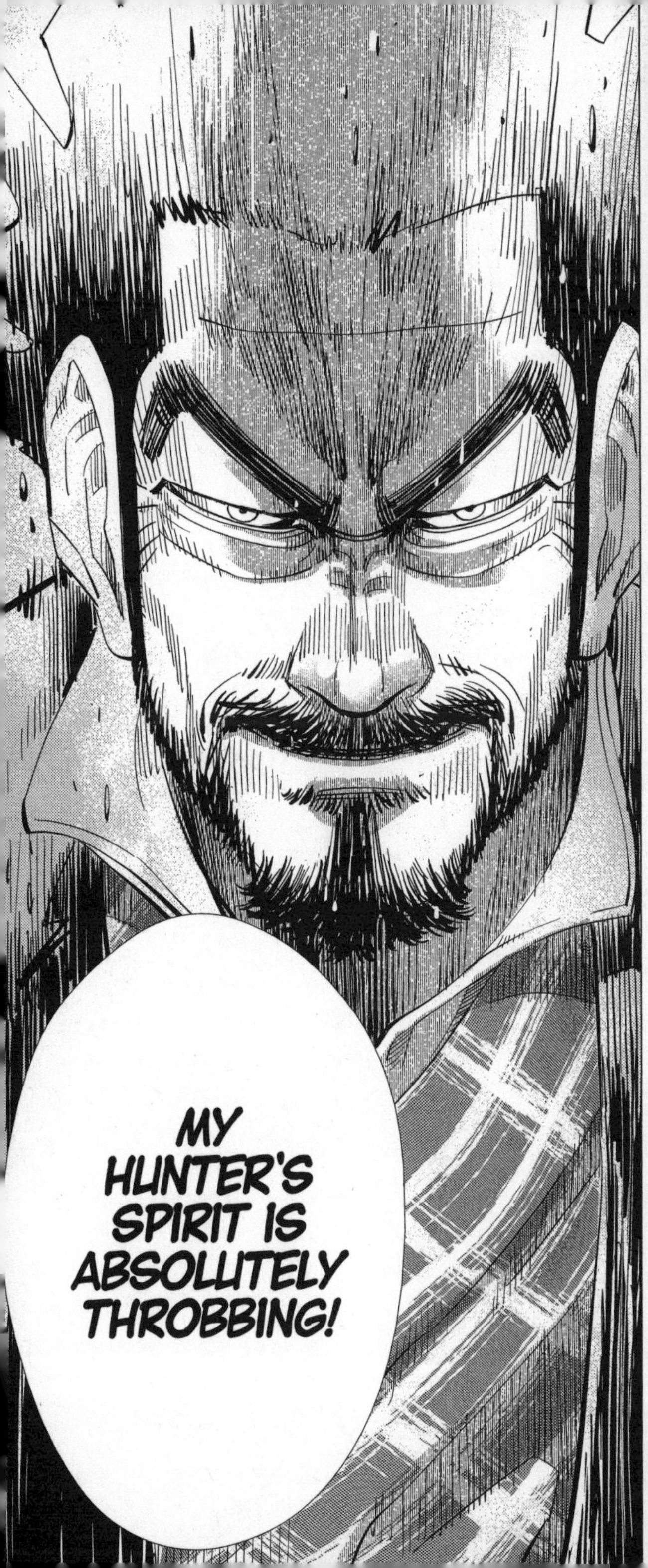
MY HUNTER'S SPIRIT IS ABSOLUTELY THROBBING!

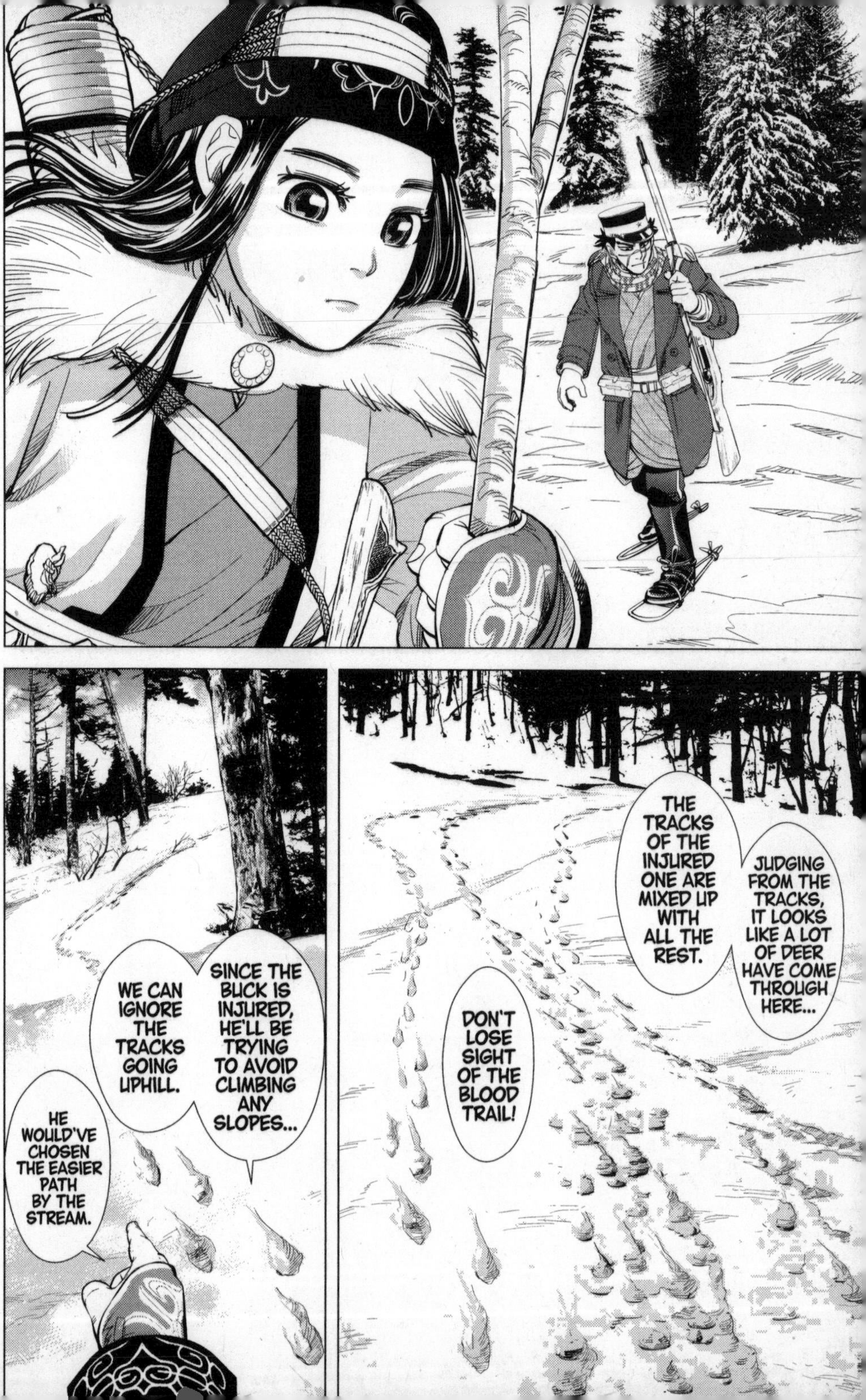
JUDGING FROM THE TRACKS, IT LOOKS LIKE A LOT OF DEER HAVE COME THROUGH HERE...
THE TRACKS OF THE INJURED ONE ARE MIXED UP WITH ALL THE REST.
DON'T LOSE SIGHT OF THE BLOOD TRAIL!
SINCE THE BUCK IS INJURED, HE'LL BE TRYING TO AVOID CLIMBING ANY SLOPES...
WE CAN IGNORE THE TRACKS GOING UPHILL.
HE WOULD'VE CHOSEN THE EASIER PATH BY THE STREAM.

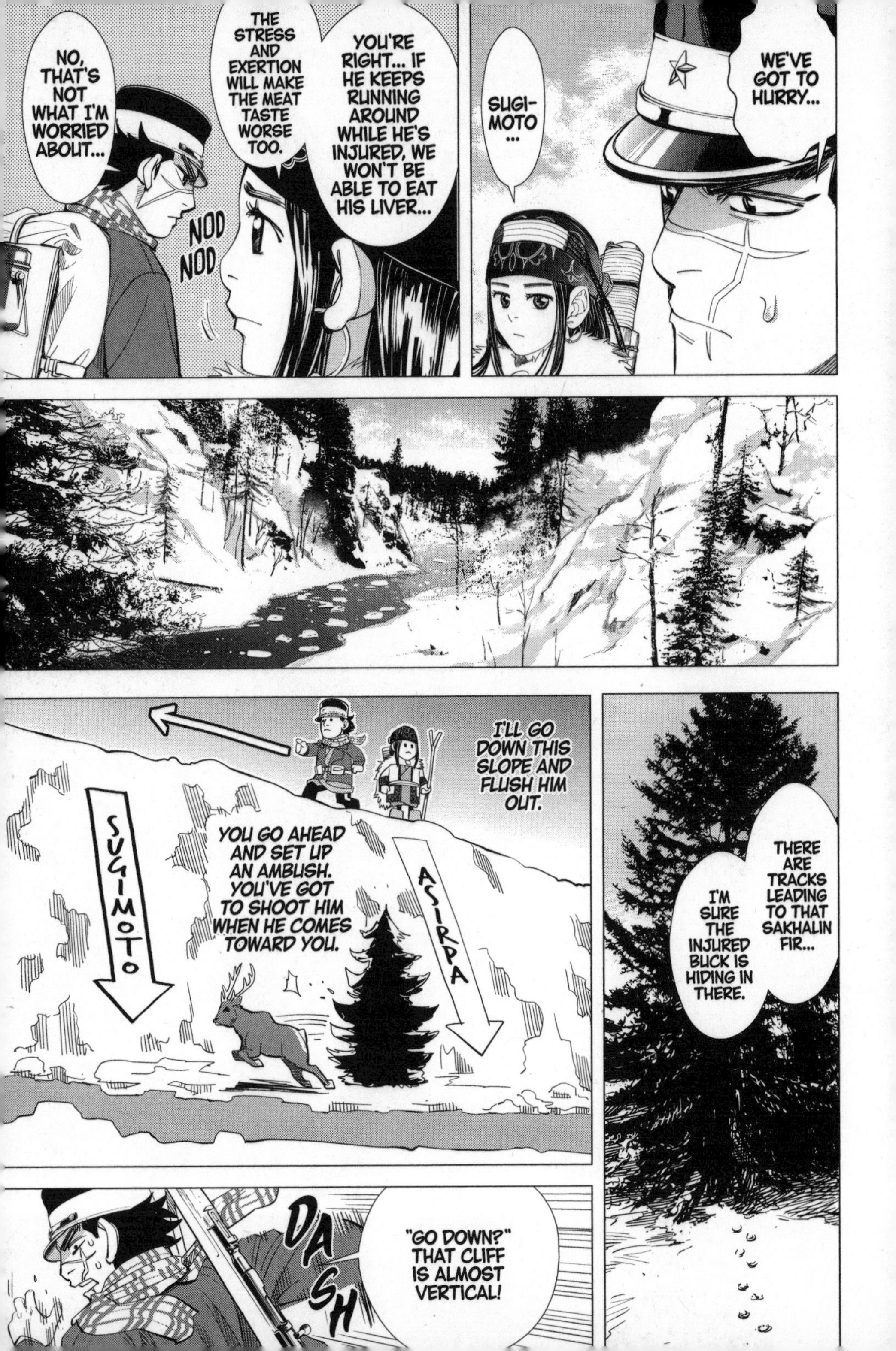

WE'VE GOT TO HURRY...
SUGI-MOTO ...
YOU'RE RIGHT... IF HE KEEPS RUNNING AROUND WHILE HE'S INJURED, WE WON'T BE ABLE TO EAT HIS LIVER...
THE STRESS AND EXERTION WILL MAKE THE MEAT TASTE WORSE TOO.
NOD NOD
NO, THAT'S NOT WHAT I'M WORRIED ABOUT...
THERE ARE TRACKS LEADING TO THAT SAKHALIN FIR...
I'M SURE THE INJURED BUCK IS HIDING IN THERE.
I'LL GO DOWN THIS SLOPE AND FLUSH HIM OUT.
ASIRPA
YOU GO AHEAD AND SET UP AN AMBUSH. YOU'VE GOT TO SHOOT HIM WHEN HE COMES TOWARD YOU.
SUGIMOTO
"GO DOWN?" THAT CLIFF IS ALMOST VERTICAL!
DASH

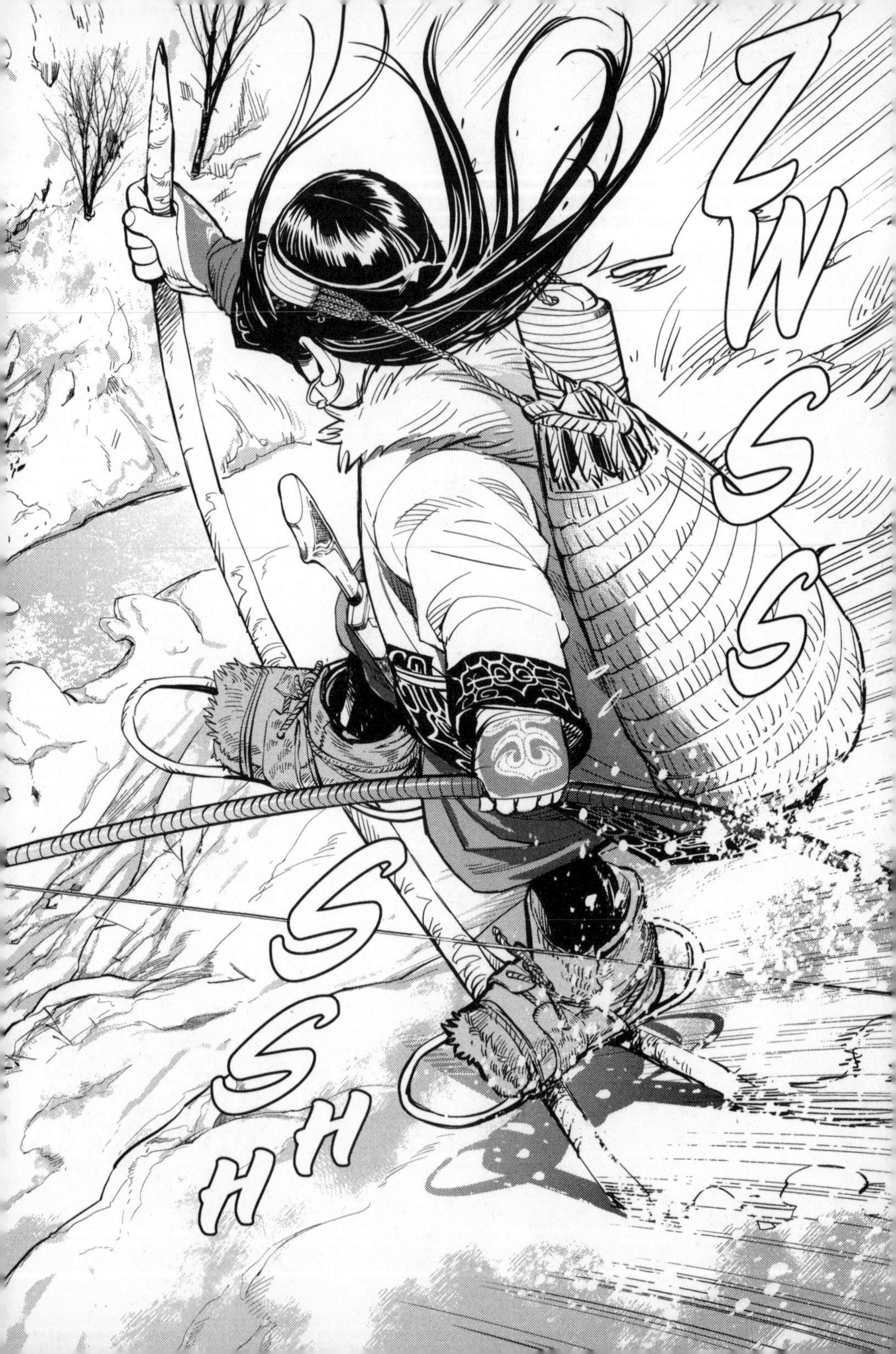
ZWSSSSSHH

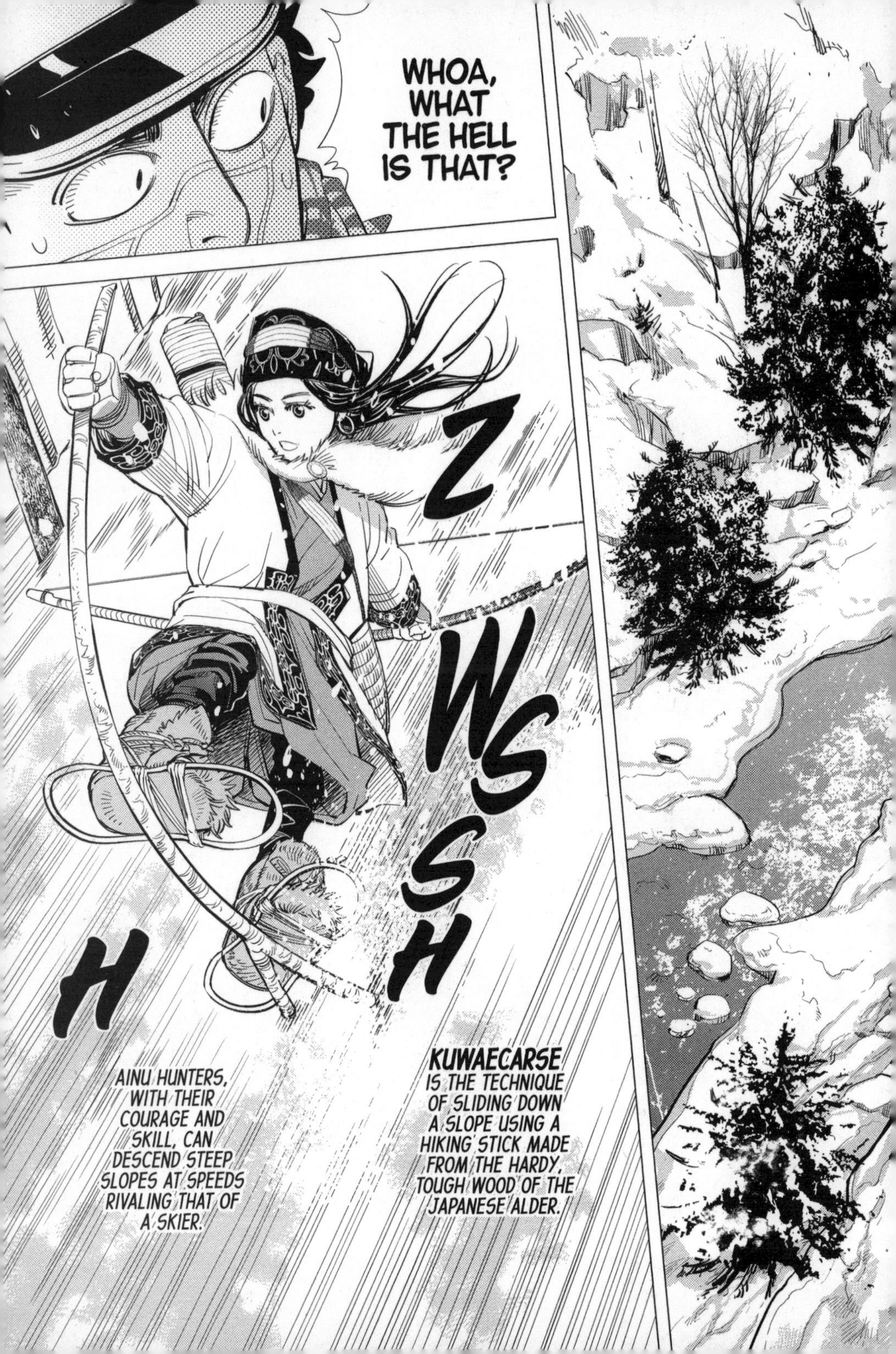
WHOA, WHAT THE HELL IS THAT?
ZWSSHH
KUWAECARSE IS THE TECHNIQUE OF SLIDING DOWN A SLOPE USING A HIKING STICK MADE FROM THE HARDY, TOUGH WOOD OF THE JAPANESE ALDER.
AINU HUNTERS, WITH THEIR COURAGE AND SKILL, CAN DESCEND STEEP SLOPES AT SPEEDS RIVALING THAT OF A SKIER.

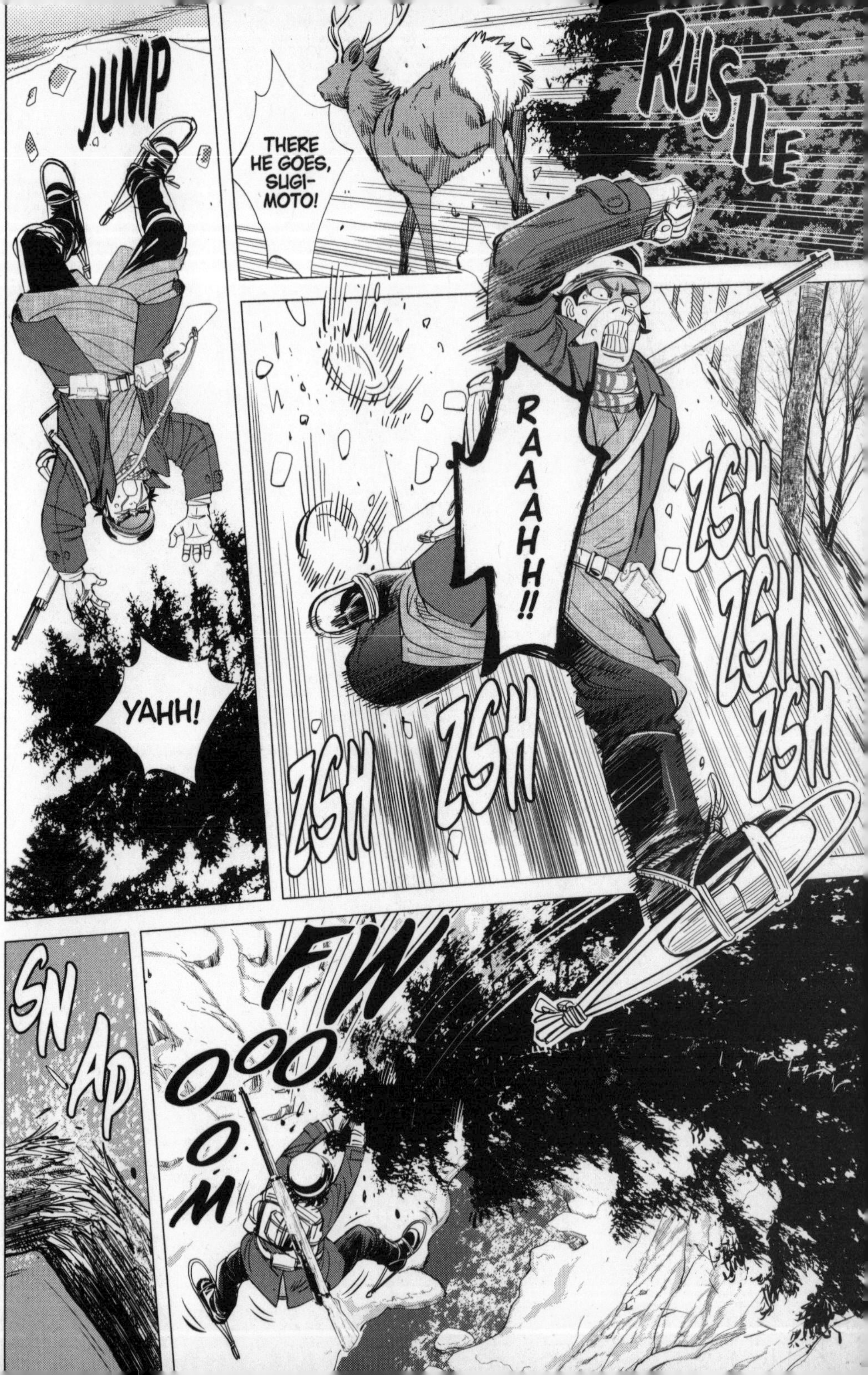

RUSTLE
THERE HE GOES, SUGIMOTO!
RAAAHH!!
ZSH ZSH ZSH
ZSH ZSH
JUMP
YAHH!
FWOOOOM
SNAP

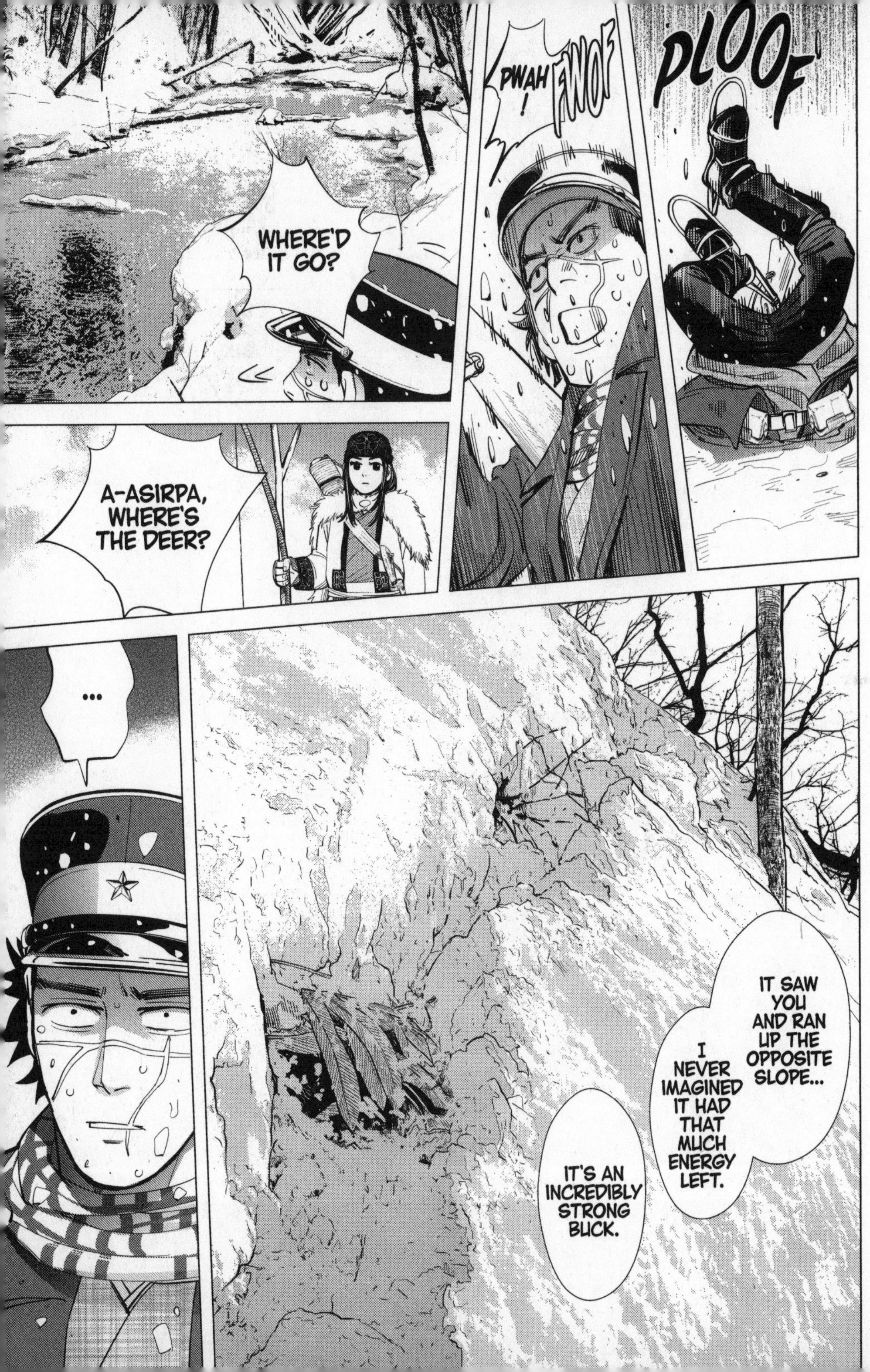
PLOOF
PWAH !
FWOF
WHERE'D IT GO?
A-ASIRPA, WHERE'S THE DEER?
IT SAW YOU AND RAN UP THE OPPOSITE SLOPE...
I NEVER IMAGINED IT HAD THAT MUCH ENERGY LEFT.
IT'S AN INCREDIBLY STRONG BUCK.
...

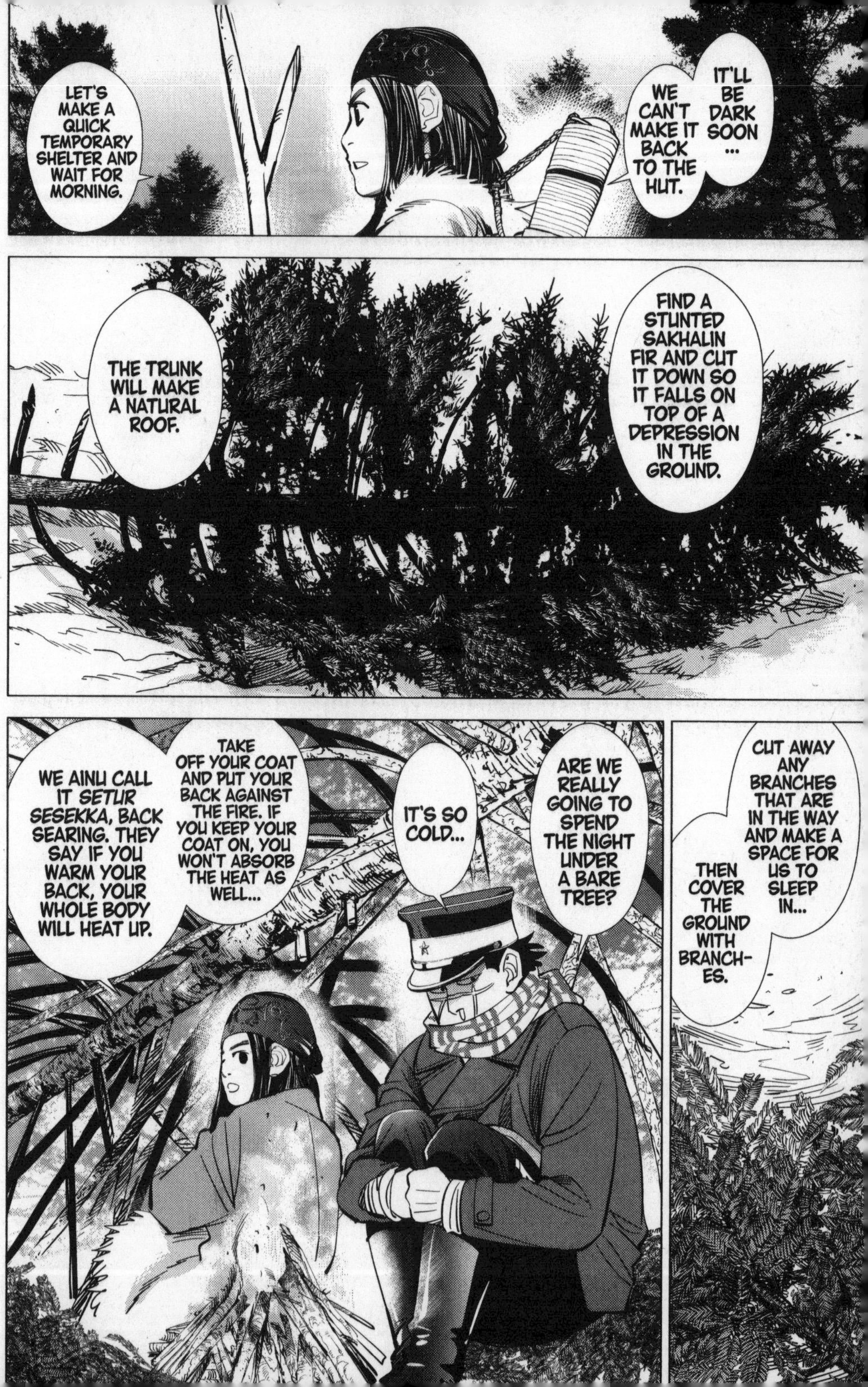
IT'LL BE DARK SOON...
WE CAN'T MAKE IT BACK TO THE HUT.
LET'S MAKE A QUICK TEMPORARY SHELTER AND WAIT FOR MORNING.
FIND A STUNTED SAKHALIN FIR AND CUT IT DOWN SO IT FALLS ON TOP OF A DEPRESSION IN THE GROUND.
THE TRUNK WILL MAKE A NATURAL ROOF.
CUT AWAY ANY BRANCHES THAT ARE IN THE WAY AND MAKE A SPACE FOR US TO SLEEP IN...
THEN COVER THE GROUND WITH BRANCH-ES.
ARE WE REALLY GOING TO SPEND THE NIGHT UNDER A BARE TREE?
IT'S SO COLD...
TAKE OFF YOUR COAT AND PUT YOUR BACK AGAINST THE FIRE. IF YOU KEEP YOUR COAT ON, YOU WON'T ABSORB THE HEAT AS WELL...
WE AINU CALL IT *SETUR SESEKKA*, BACK SEARING. THEY SAY IF YOU WARM YOUR BACK, YOUR WHOLE BODY WILL HEAT UP.

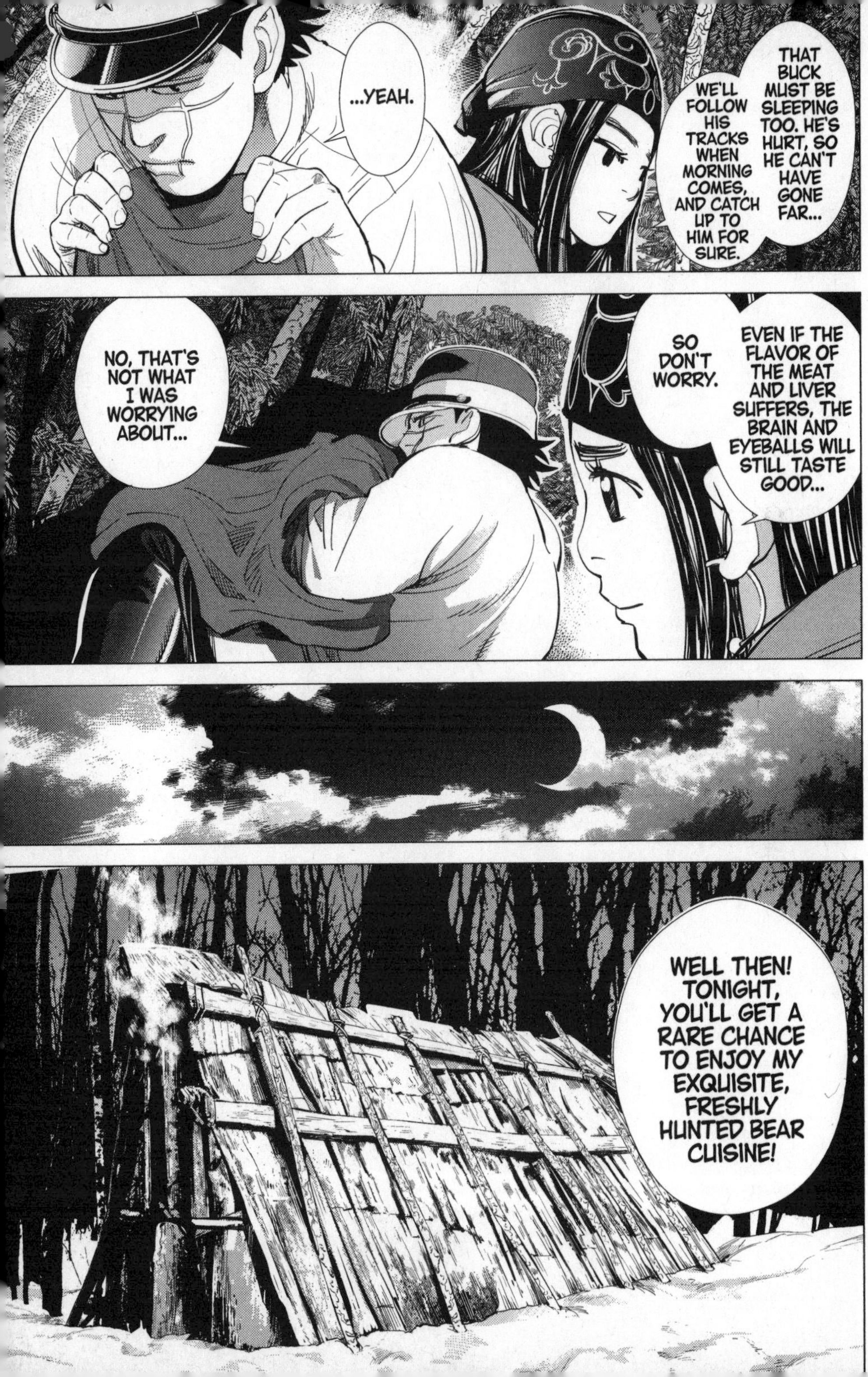
THAT BUCK MUST BE SLEEPING TOO. HE'S HURT, SO HE CAN'T HAVE GONE FAR...
WE'LL FOLLOW HIS TRACKS WHEN MORNING COMES, AND CATCH UP TO HIM FOR SURE.
...YEAH.
EVEN IF THE FLAVOR OF THE MEAT AND LIVER SUFFERS, THE BRAIN AND EYEBALLS WILL STILL TASTE GOOD...
SO DON'T WORRY.
NO, THAT'S NOT WHAT I WAS WORRYING ABOUT...
WELL THEN! TONIGHT, YOU'LL GET A RARE CHANCE TO ENJOY MY EXQUISITE, FRESHLY HUNTED BEAR CUISINE!

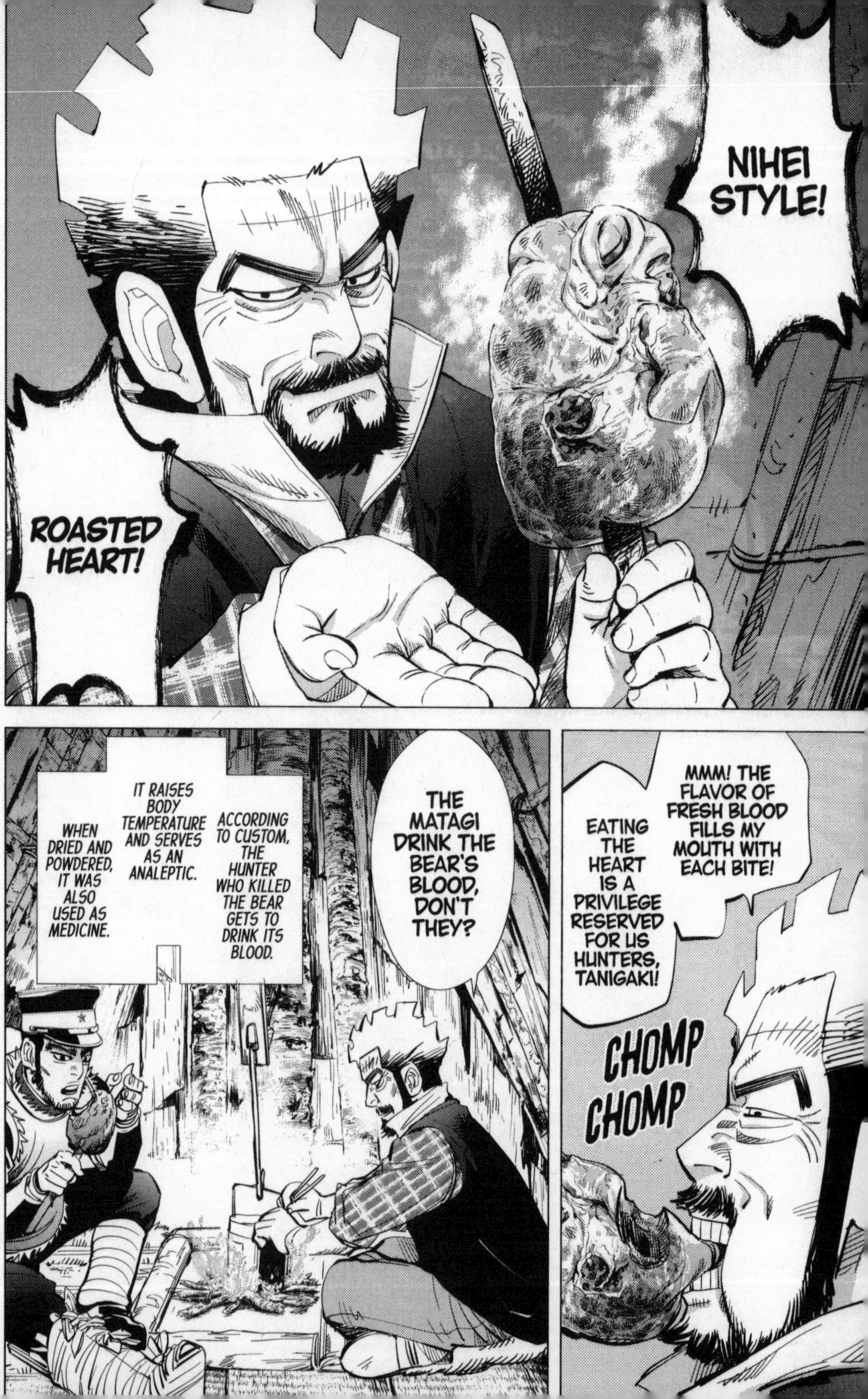
NIHEI STYLE!
ROASTED HEART!
MMM! THE FLAVOR OF FRESH BLOOD FILLS MY MOUTH WITH EACH BITE!
EATING THE HEART IS A PRIVILEGE RESERVED FOR US HUNTERS, TANIGAKI!
CHOMP CHOMP
THE MATAGI DRINK THE BEAR'S BLOOD, DON'T THEY?
ACCORDING TO CUSTOM, THE HUNTER WHO KILLED THE BEAR GETS TO DRINK ITS BLOOD.
IT RAISES BODY TEMPERATURE AND SERVES AS AN ANALEPTIC.
WHEN DRIED AND POWDERED, IT WAS ALSO USED AS MEDICINE.

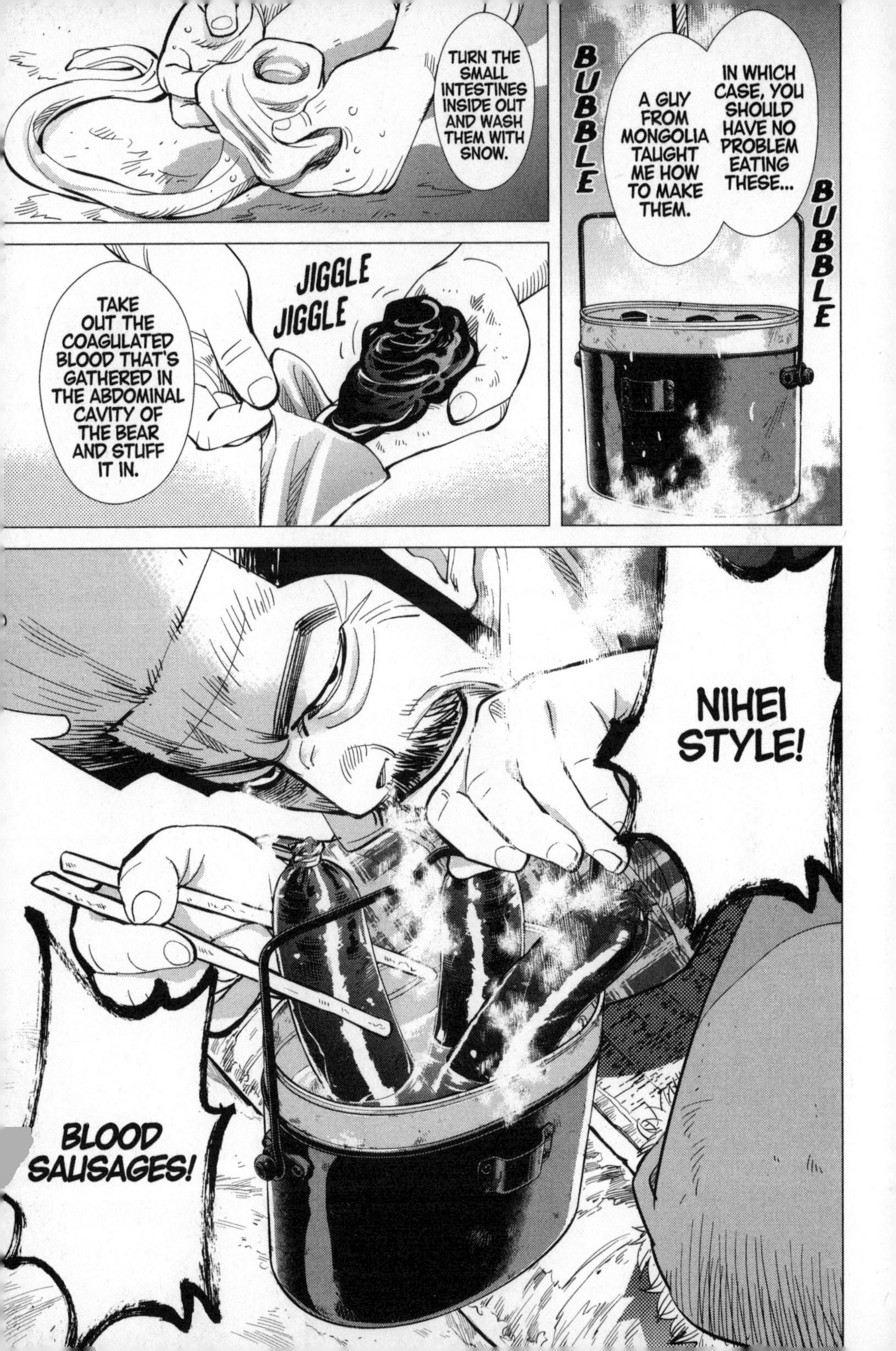
BUBBLE
IN WHICH CASE, YOU SHOULD HAVE NO PROBLEM EATING THESE...
A GUY FROM MONGOLIA TAUGHT ME HOW TO MAKE THEM.
BUBBLE
TURN THE SMALL INTESTINES INSIDE OUT AND WASH THEM WITH SNOW.
JIGGLE JIGGLE
TAKE OUT THE COAGULATED BLOOD THAT'S GATHERED IN THE ABDOMINAL CAVITY OF THE BEAR AND STUFF IT IN.
NIHEI STYLE!
BLOOD SAUSAGES!

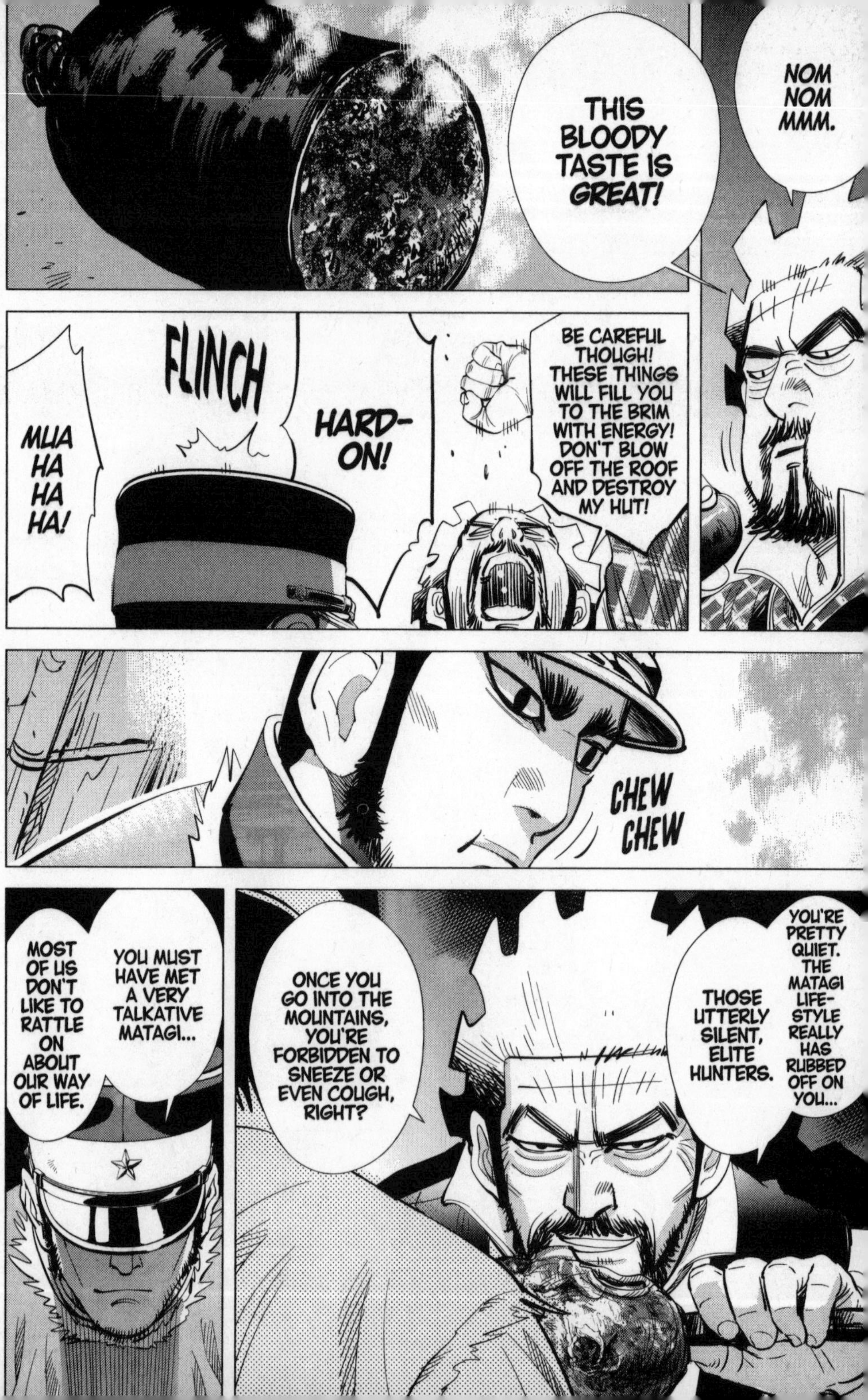
NOM NOM MMM.
THIS BLOODY TASTE IS GREAT!
BE CAREFUL THOUGH! THESE THINGS WILL FILL YOU TO THE BRIM WITH ENERGY! DON'T BLOW OFF THE ROOF AND DESTROY MY HUT!
HARD-ON!
FLINCH
MUA HA HA HA!
CHEW CHEW
YOU'RE PRETTY QUIET. THE MATAGI LIFE-STYLE REALLY HAS RUBBED OFF ON YOU...
THOSE UTTERLY SILENT, ELITE HUNTERS.
ONCE YOU GO INTO THE MOUNTAINS, YOU'RE FORBIDDEN TO SNEEZE OR EVEN COUGH, RIGHT?
YOU MUST HAVE MET A VERY TALKATIVE MATAGI...
MOST OF US DON'T LIKE TO RATTLE ON ABOUT OUR WAY OF LIFE.

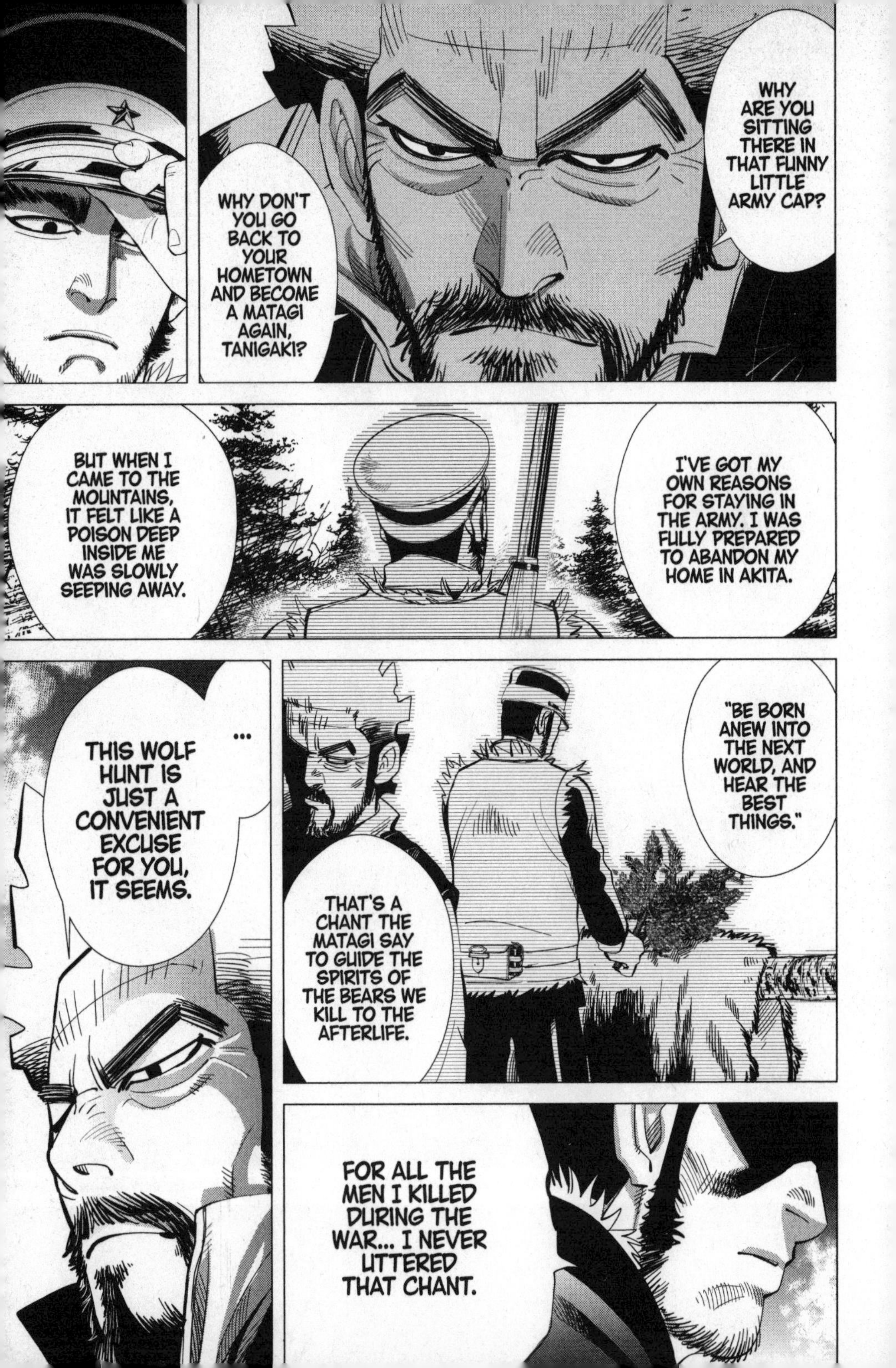
WHY ARE YOU SITTING THERE IN THAT FUNNY LITTLE ARMY CAP?
WHY DON'T YOU GO BACK TO YOUR HOMETOWN AND BECOME A MATAGI AGAIN, TANIGAKI?
I'VE GOT MY OWN REASONS FOR STAYING IN THE ARMY. I WAS FULLY PREPARED TO ABANDON MY HOME IN AKITA.
BUT WHEN I CAME TO THE MOUNTAINS, IT FELT LIKE A POISON DEEP INSIDE ME WAS SLOWLY SEEPING AWAY.
"BE BORN ANEW INTO THE NEXT WORLD, AND HEAR THE BEST THINGS."
THAT'S A CHANT THE MATAGI SAY TO GUIDE THE SPIRITS OF THE BEARS WE KILL TO THE AFTERLIFE.
FOR ALL THE MEN I KILLED DURING THE WAR... I NEVER UTTERED THAT CHANT.
...
THIS WOLF HUNT IS JUST A CONVENIENT EXCUSE FOR YOU, IT SEEMS.

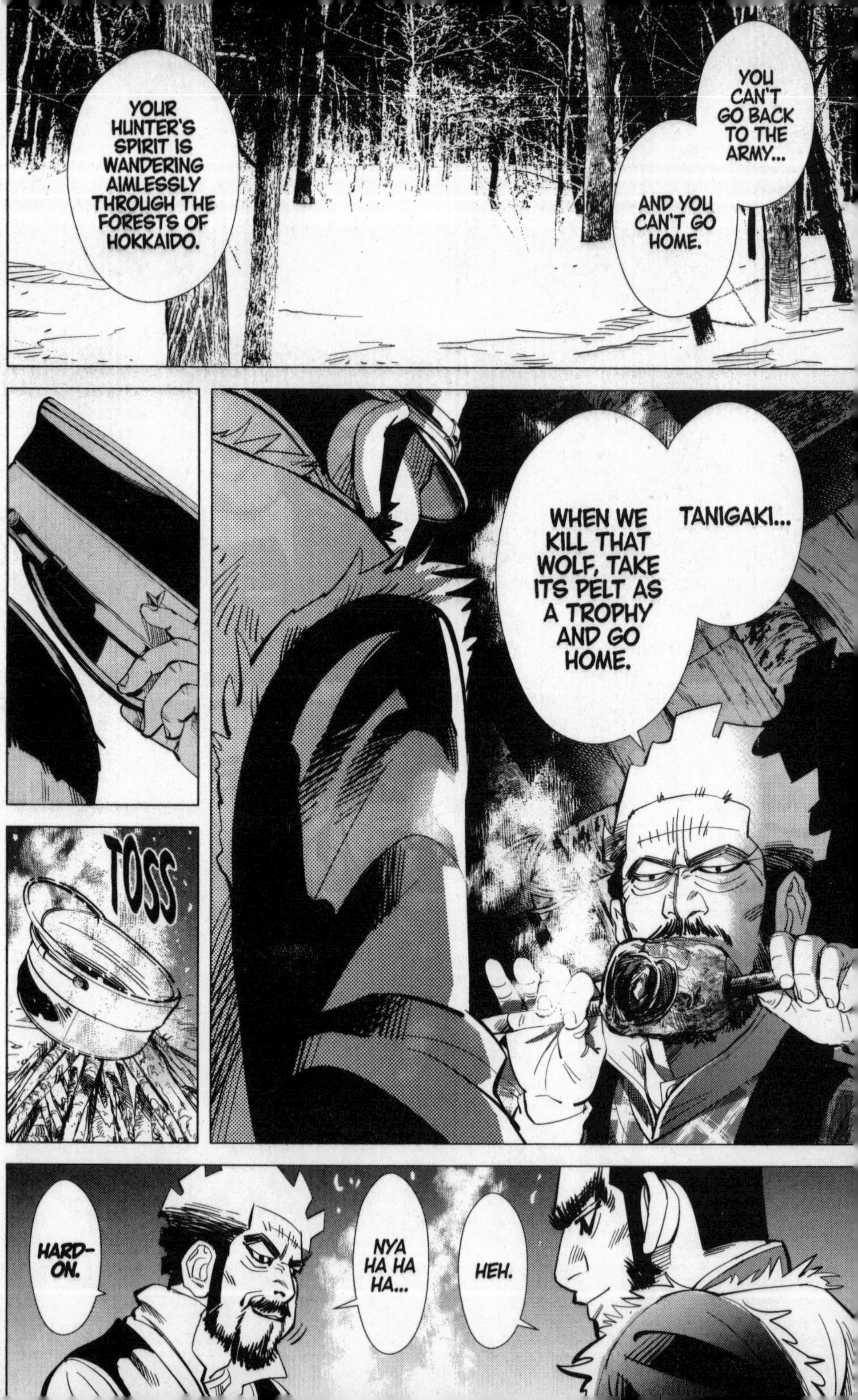

YOU CAN'T GO BACK TO THE ARMY...
AND YOU CAN'T GO HOME.
YOUR HUNTER'S SPIRIT IS WANDERING AIMLESSLY THROUGH THE FORESTS OF HOKKAIDO.
TANIGAKI...
WHEN WE KILL THAT WOLF, TAKE ITS PELT AS A TROPHY AND GO HOME.
TOSS
HEH.
NYA HA HA HA...
HARD-ON.

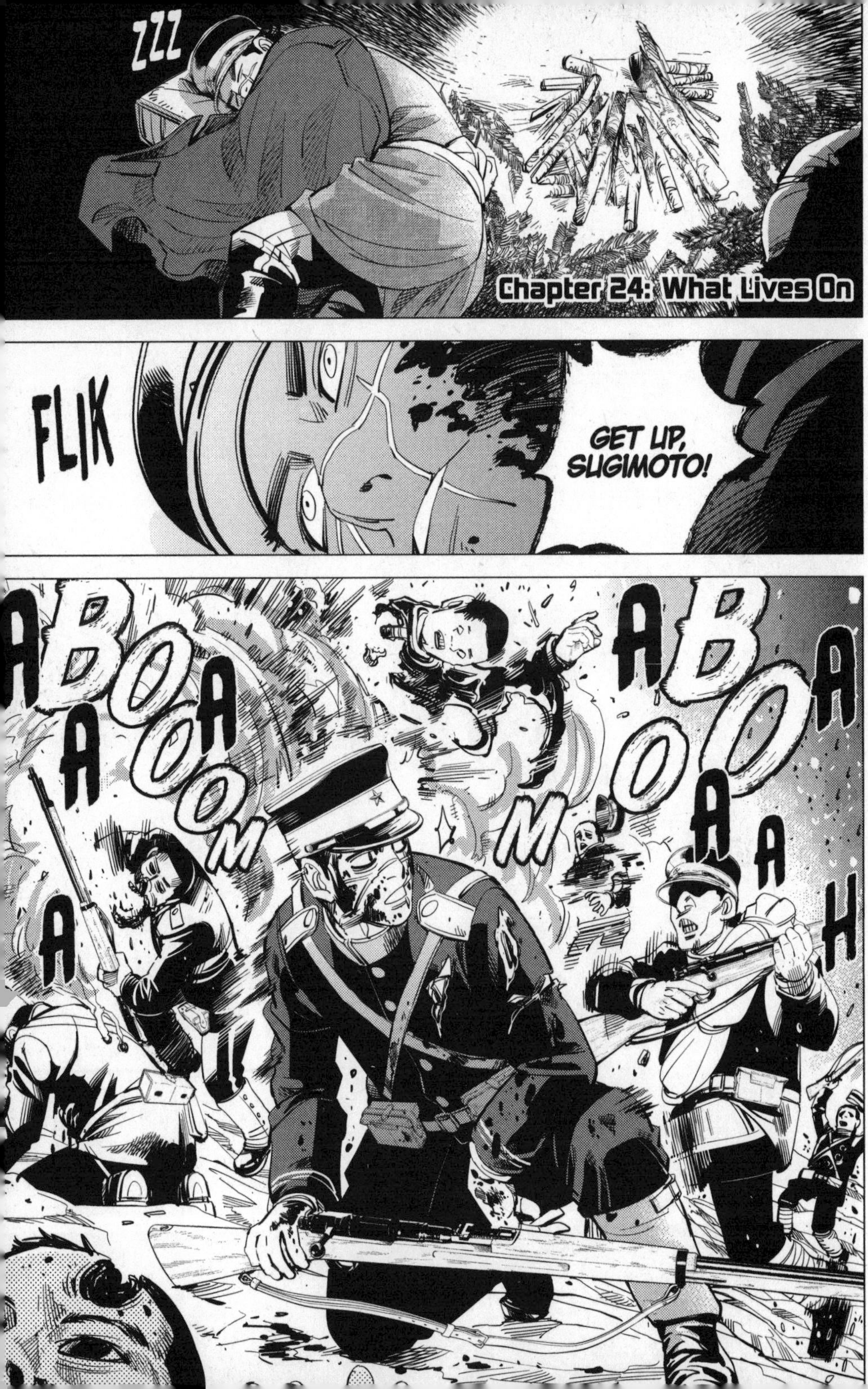
Chapter 24: What Lives On
ZZZ
GET UP, SUGIMOTO!
FLIK
ABOOOM
AAAAH
ABOOOM
AAAA

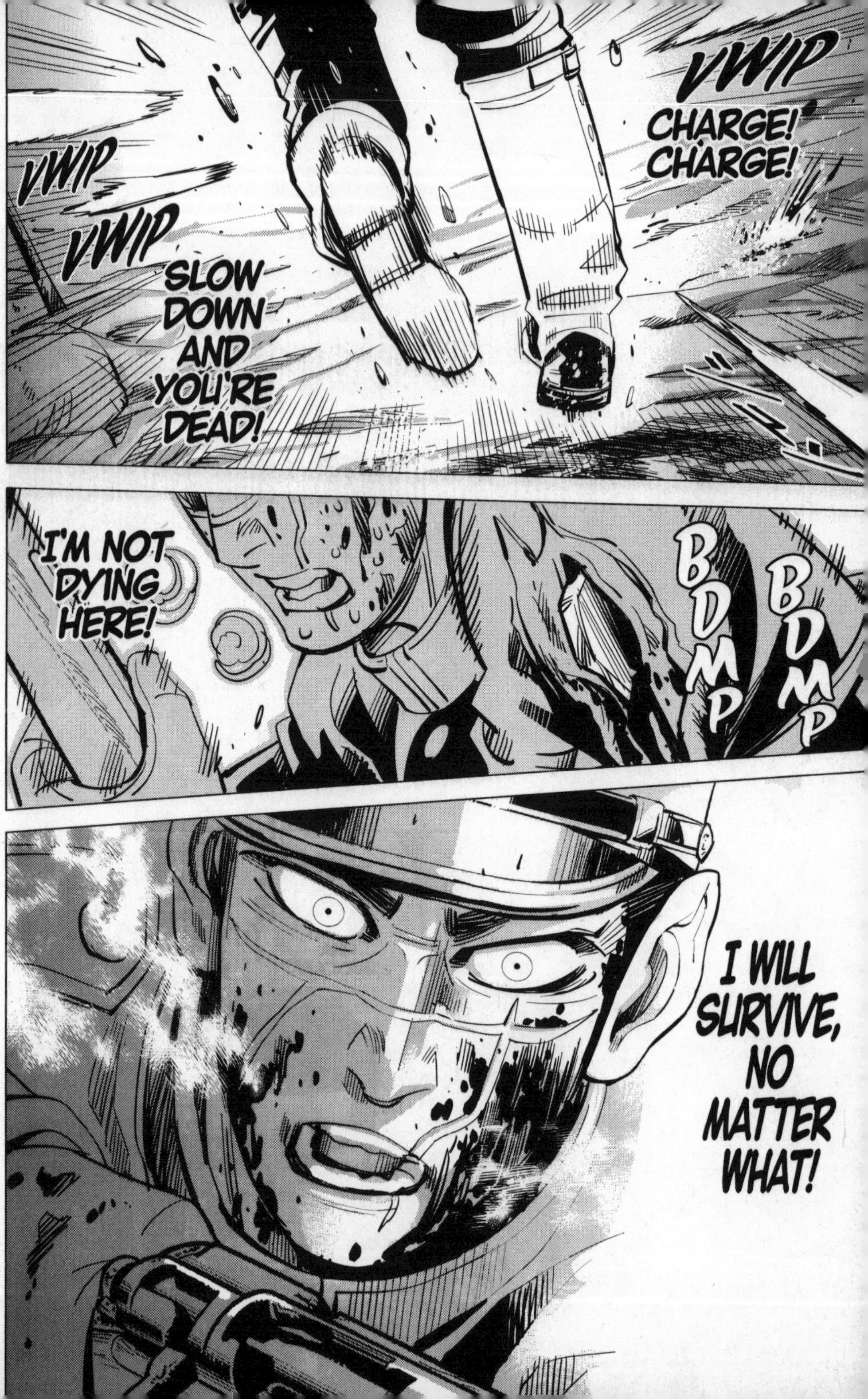
VWIP
CHARGE! CHARGE!
VWIP
VWIP
SLOW DOWN AND YOU'RE DEAD!
BDMP
BDMP
I'M NOT DYING HERE!
I WILL SURVIVE, NO MATTER WHAT!

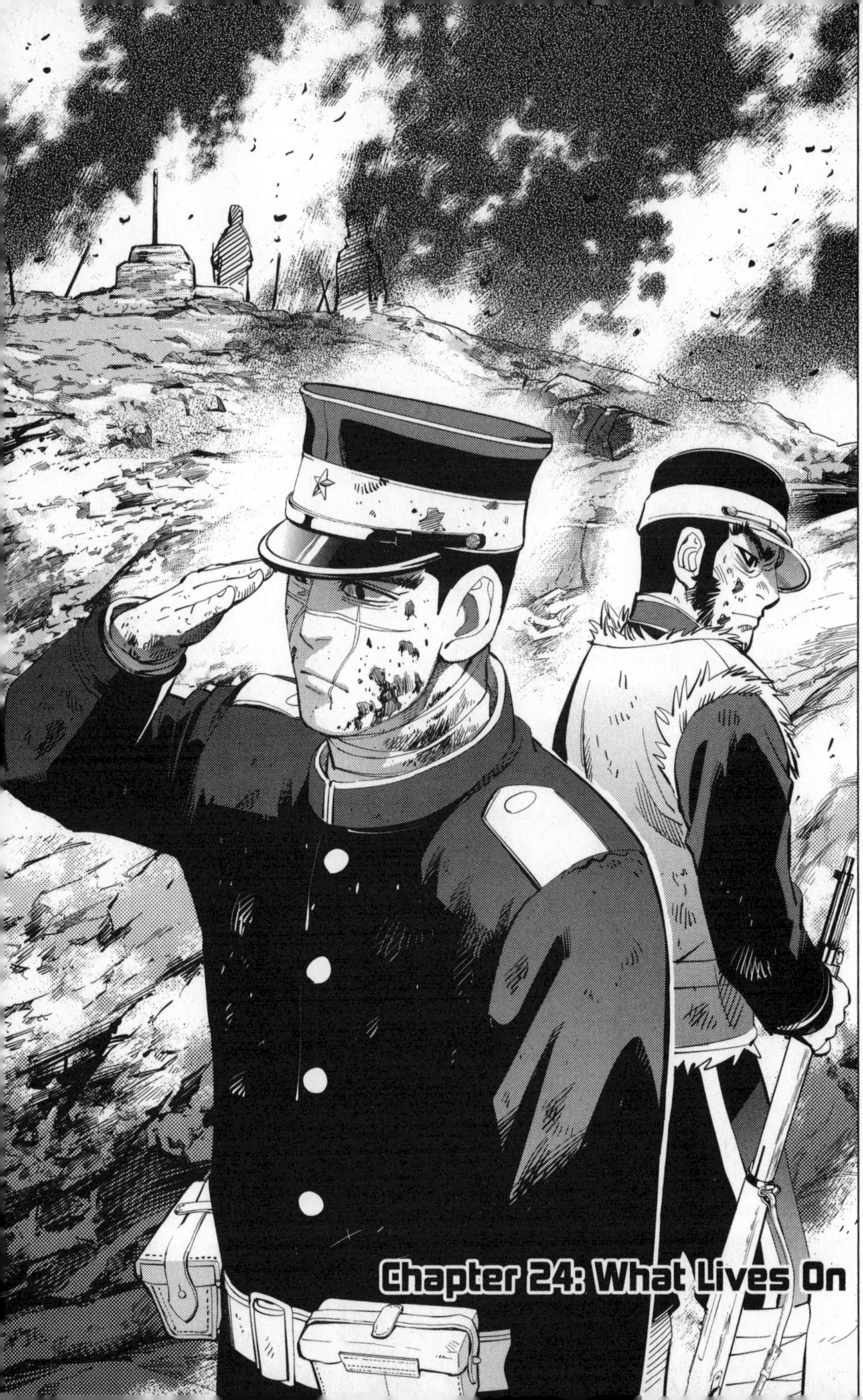

Chapter 24: What Lives On

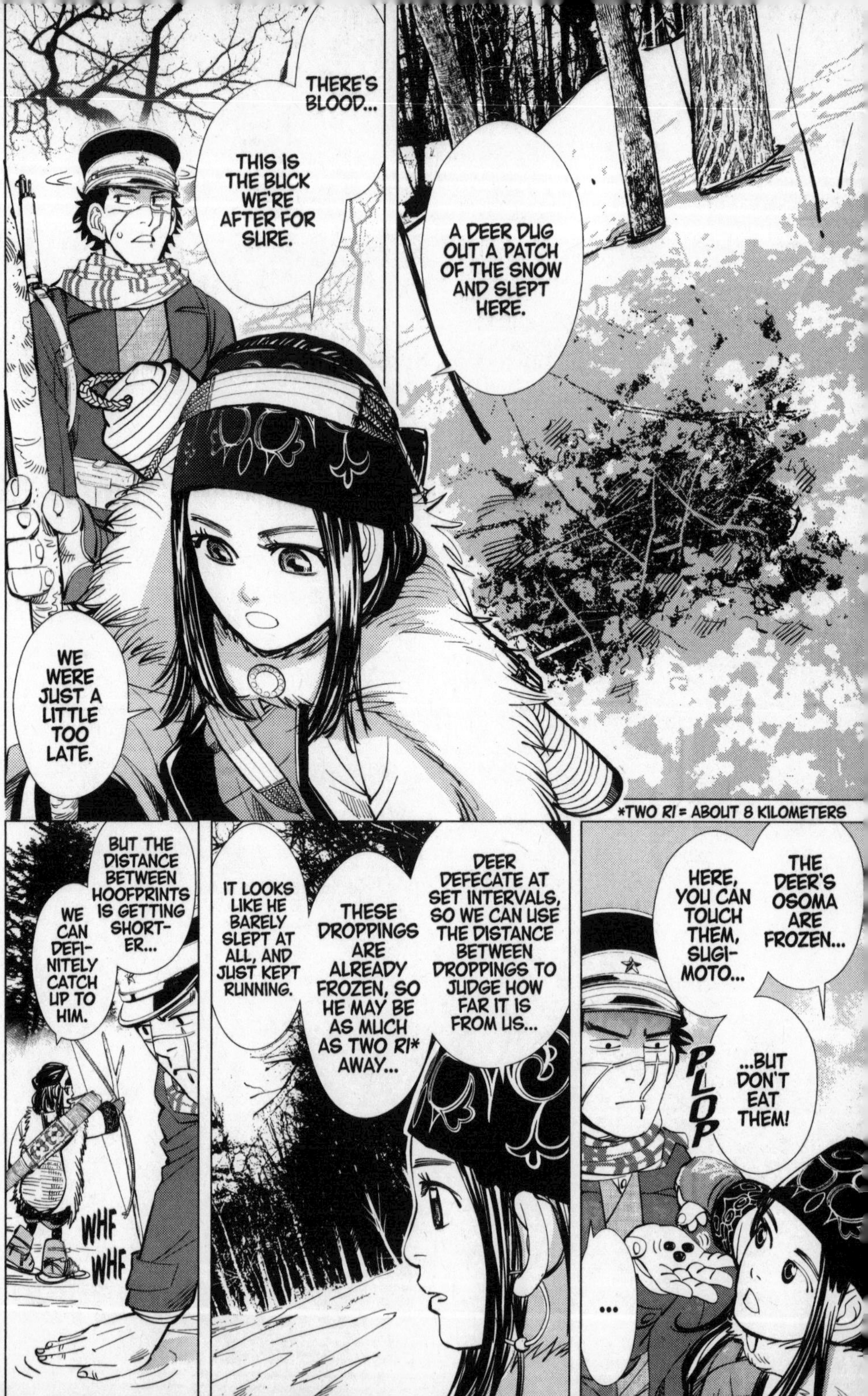
A DEER DUG OUT A PATCH OF THE SNOW AND SLEPT HERE.
THERE'S BLOOD...
THIS IS THE BUCK WE'RE AFTER FOR SURE.
WE WERE JUST A LITTLE TOO LATE.
*TWO RI = ABOUT 8 KILOMETERS
THE DEER'S OSOMA ARE FROZEN...
HERE, YOU CAN TOUCH THEM, SUGI-MOTO...
PLOP
...BUT DON'T EAT THEM!
...
DEER DEFECATE AT SET INTERVALS, SO WE CAN USE THE DISTANCE BETWEEN DROPPINGS TO JUDGE HOW FAR IT IS FROM US...
THESE DROPPINGS ARE ALREADY FROZEN, SO HE MAY BE AS MUCH AS TWO RI* AWAY...
IT LOOKS LIKE HE BARELY SLEPT AT ALL, AND JUST KEPT RUNNING.
BUT THE DISTANCE BETWEEN HOOFPRINTS IS GETTING SHORTER...
WE CAN DEFI-NITELY CATCH UP TO HIM.
WHF
WHF

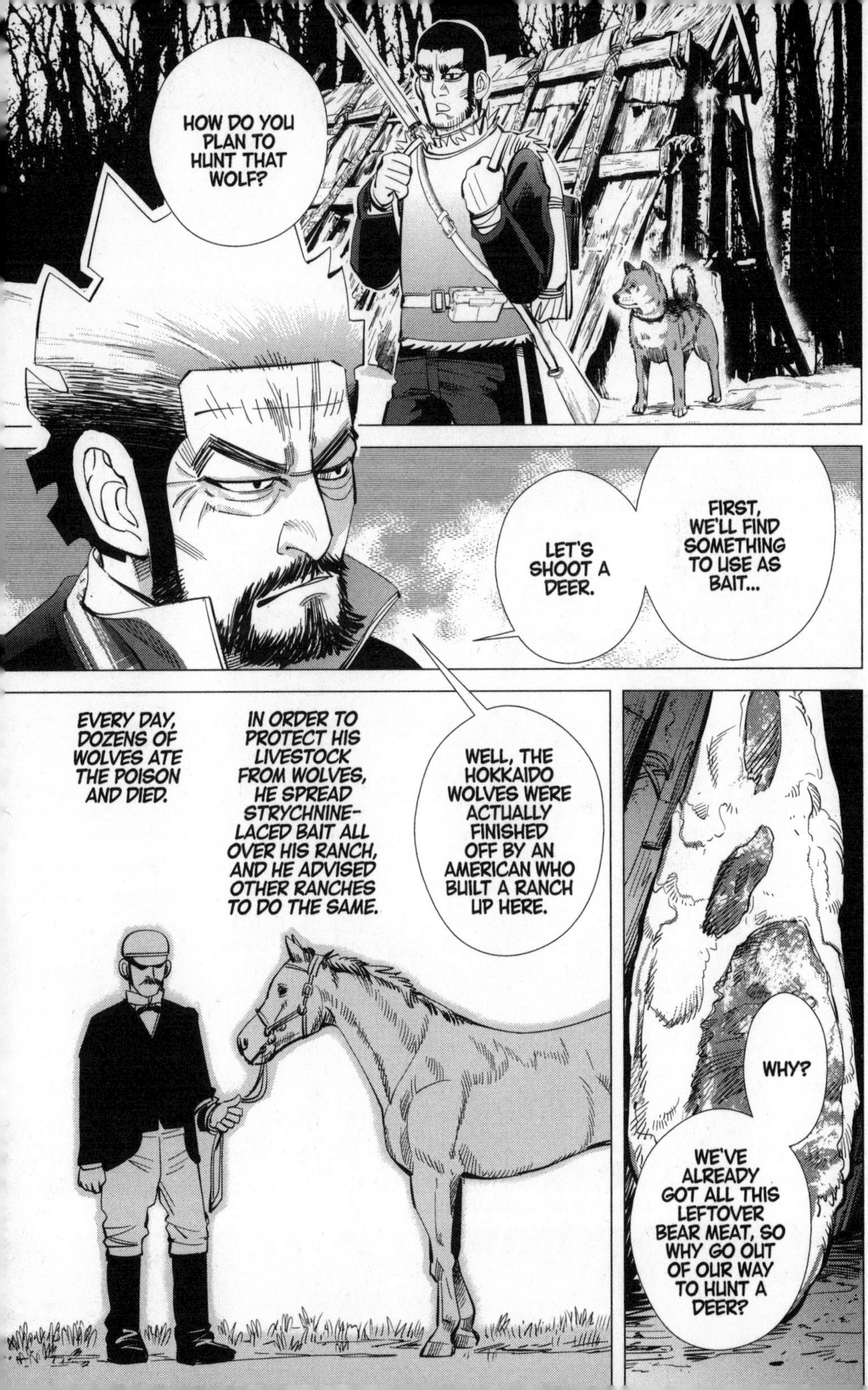
HOW DO YOU PLAN TO HUNT THAT WOLF?
FIRST, WE'LL FIND SOMETHING TO USE AS BAIT...
LET'S SHOOT A DEER.
WHY?
WE'VE ALREADY GOT ALL THIS LEFTOVER BEAR MEAT, SO WHY GO OUT OF OUR WAY TO HUNT A DEER?
WELL, THE HOKKAIDO WOLVES WERE ACTUALLY FINISHED OFF BY AN AMERICAN WHO BUILT A RANCH UP HERE.
IN ORDER TO PROTECT HIS LIVESTOCK FROM WOLVES, HE SPREAD STRYCHNINE-LACED BAIT ALL OVER HIS RANCH, AND HE ADVISED OTHER RANCHES TO DO THE SAME.
EVERY DAY, DOZENS OF WOLVES ATE THE POISON AND DIED.

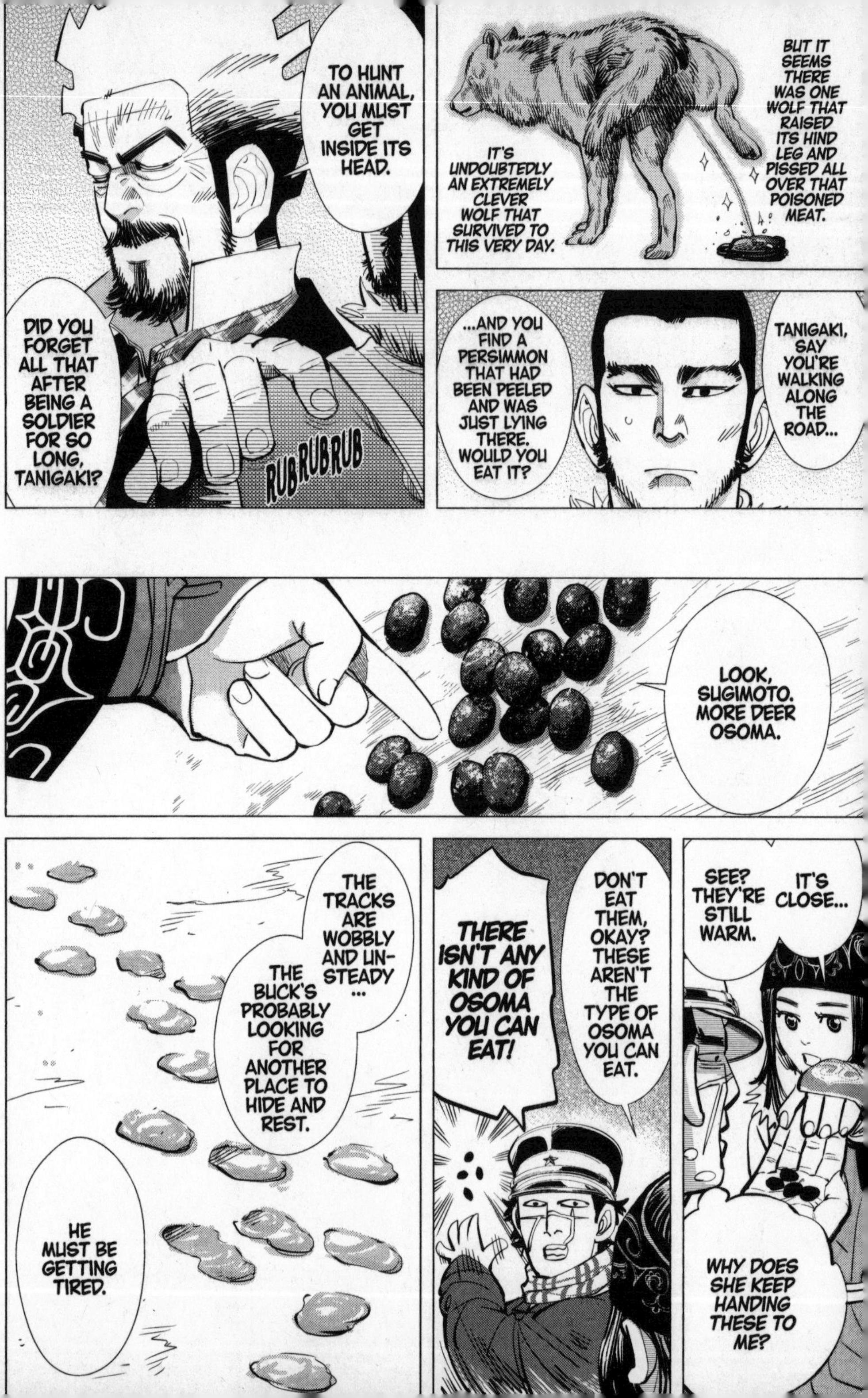
BUT IT SEEMS THERE WAS ONE WOLF THAT RAISED ITS HIND LEG AND PISSED ALL OVER THAT POISONED MEAT.
IT'S UNDOUBTEDLY AN EXTREMELY CLEVER WOLF THAT SURVIVED TO THIS VERY DAY.
TANIGAKI, SAY YOU'RE WALKING ALONG THE ROAD...
...AND YOU FIND A PERSIMMON THAT HAD BEEN PEELED AND WAS JUST LYING THERE. WOULD YOU EAT IT?
TO HUNT AN ANIMAL, YOU MUST GET INSIDE ITS HEAD.
DID YOU FORGET ALL THAT AFTER BEING A SOLDIER FOR SO LONG, TANIGAKI?
RUB RUB RUB
LOOK, SUGIMOTO. MORE DEER OSOMA.
IT'S CLOSE...
SEE? THEY'RE STILL WARM.
WHY DOES SHE KEEP HANDING THESE TO ME?
DON'T EAT THEM, OKAY? THESE AREN'T THE TYPE OF OSOMA YOU CAN EAT.
THERE ISN'T ANY KIND OF OSOMA YOU CAN EAT!
THE TRACKS ARE WOBBLY AND UN-STEADY...
THE BUCK'S PROBABLY LOOKING FOR ANOTHER PLACE TO HIDE AND REST.
HE MUST BE GETTING TIRED.

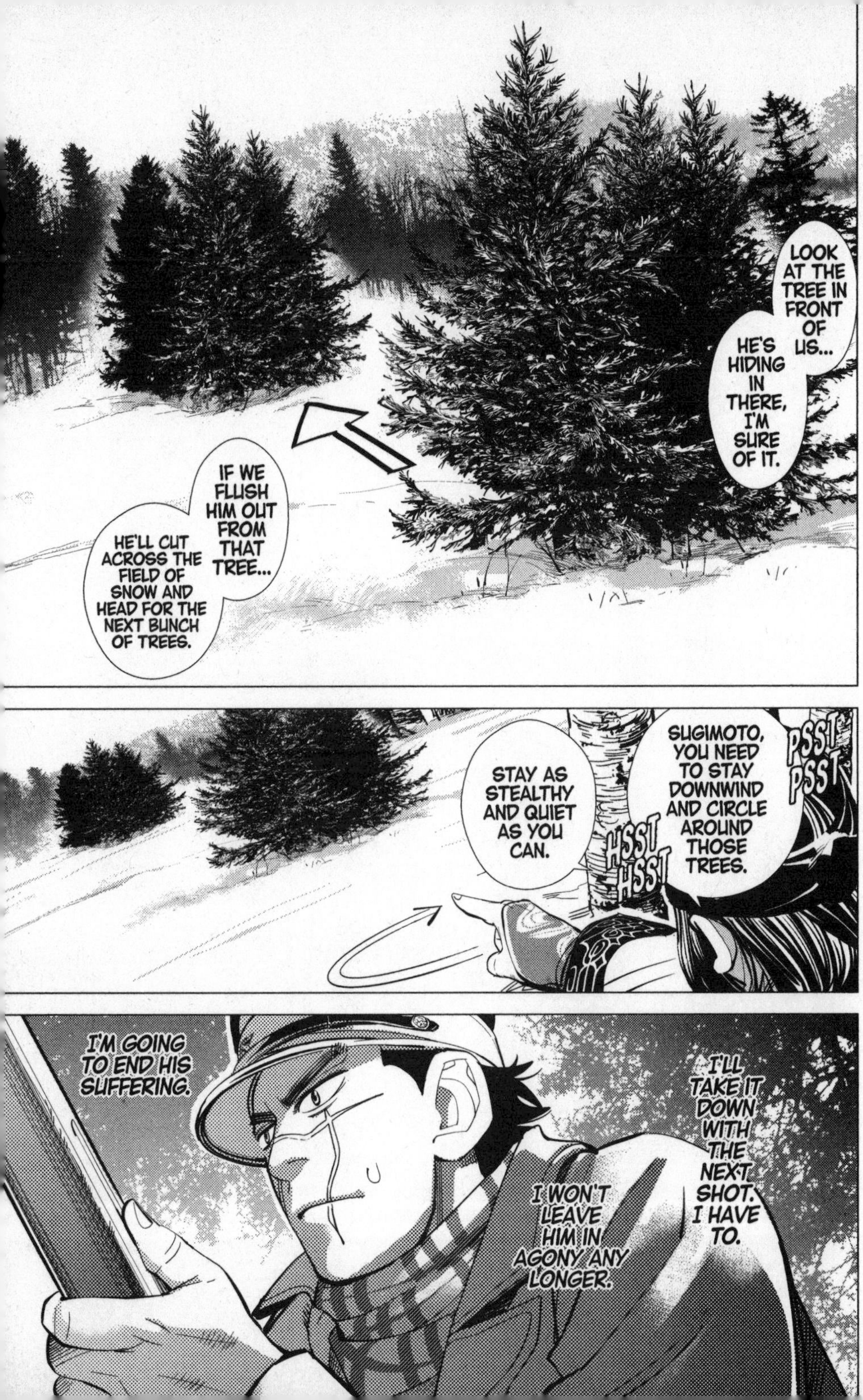
LOOK AT THE TREE IN FRONT OF US...
HE'S HIDING IN THERE, I'M SURE OF IT.
IF WE FLUSH HIM OUT FROM THAT TREE...
HE'LL CUT ACROSS THE FIELD OF SNOW AND HEAD FOR THE NEXT BUNCH OF TREES.
PSST PSST
SUGIMOTO, YOU NEED TO STAY DOWNWIND AND CIRCLE AROUND THOSE TREES.
HSST HSST
STAY AS STEALTHY AND QUIET AS YOU CAN.
I'LL TAKE IT DOWN WITH THE NEXT SHOT. I HAVE TO.
I WON'T LEAVE HIM IN AGONY ANY LONGER.
I'M GOING TO END HIS SUFFERING.

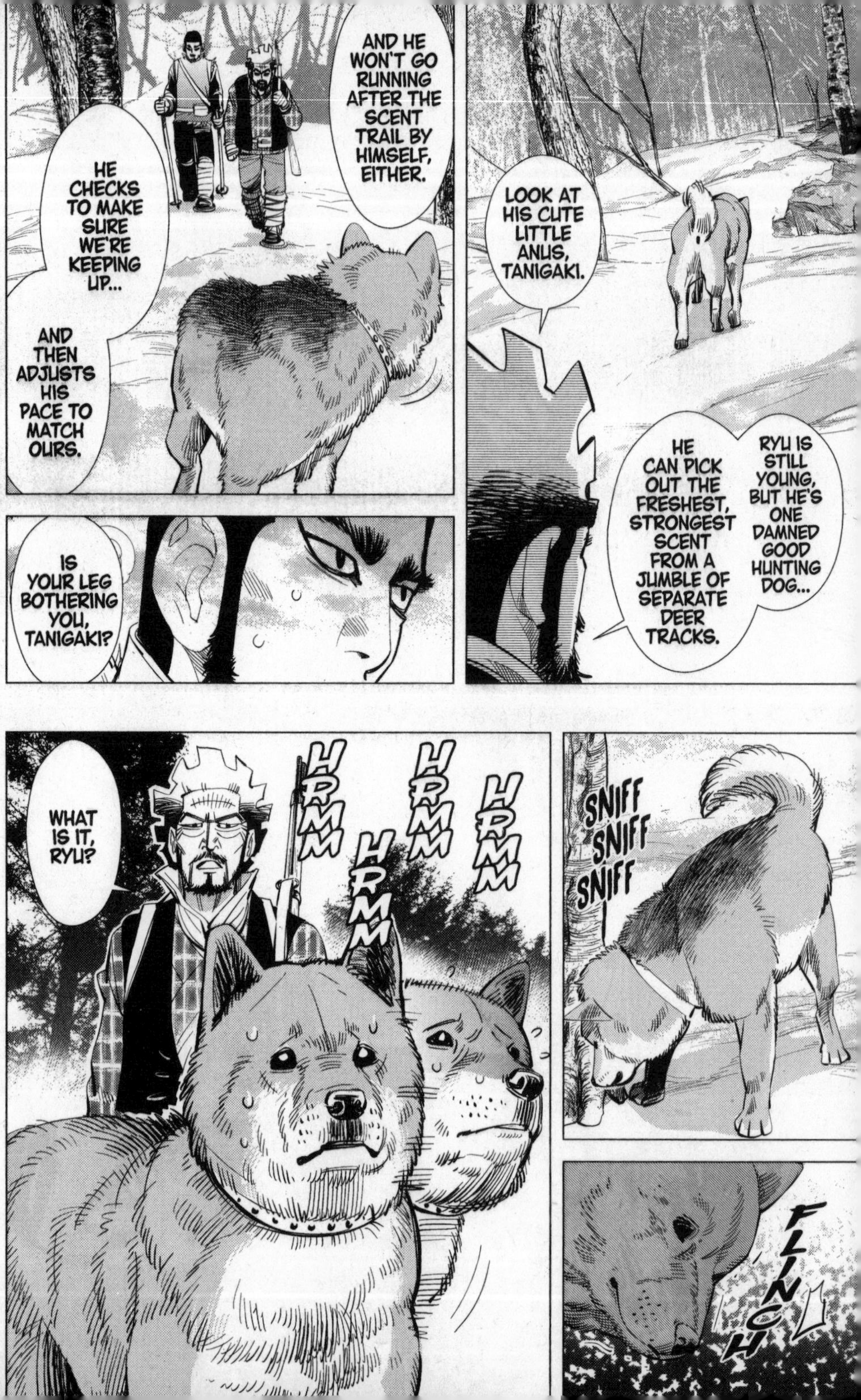

RYU IS STILL YOUNG, BUT HE'S ONE DAMNED GOOD HUNTING DOG...
HE CAN PICK OUT THE FRESHEST, STRONGEST SCENT FROM A JUMBLE OF SEPARATE DEER TRACKS.
AND HE WON'T GO RUNNING AFTER THE SCENT TRAIL BY HIMSELF, EITHER.
HE CHECKS TO MAKE SURE WE'RE KEEPING UP...
AND THEN ADJUSTS HIS PACE TO MATCH OURS.
LOOK AT HIS CUTE LITTLE ANUS, TANIGAKI.
IS YOUR LEG BOTHERING YOU, TANIGAKI?
SNIFF SNIFF SNIFF
FLINCH
HRMM
HRMM
HRMM
HRMM
WHAT IS IT, RYU?

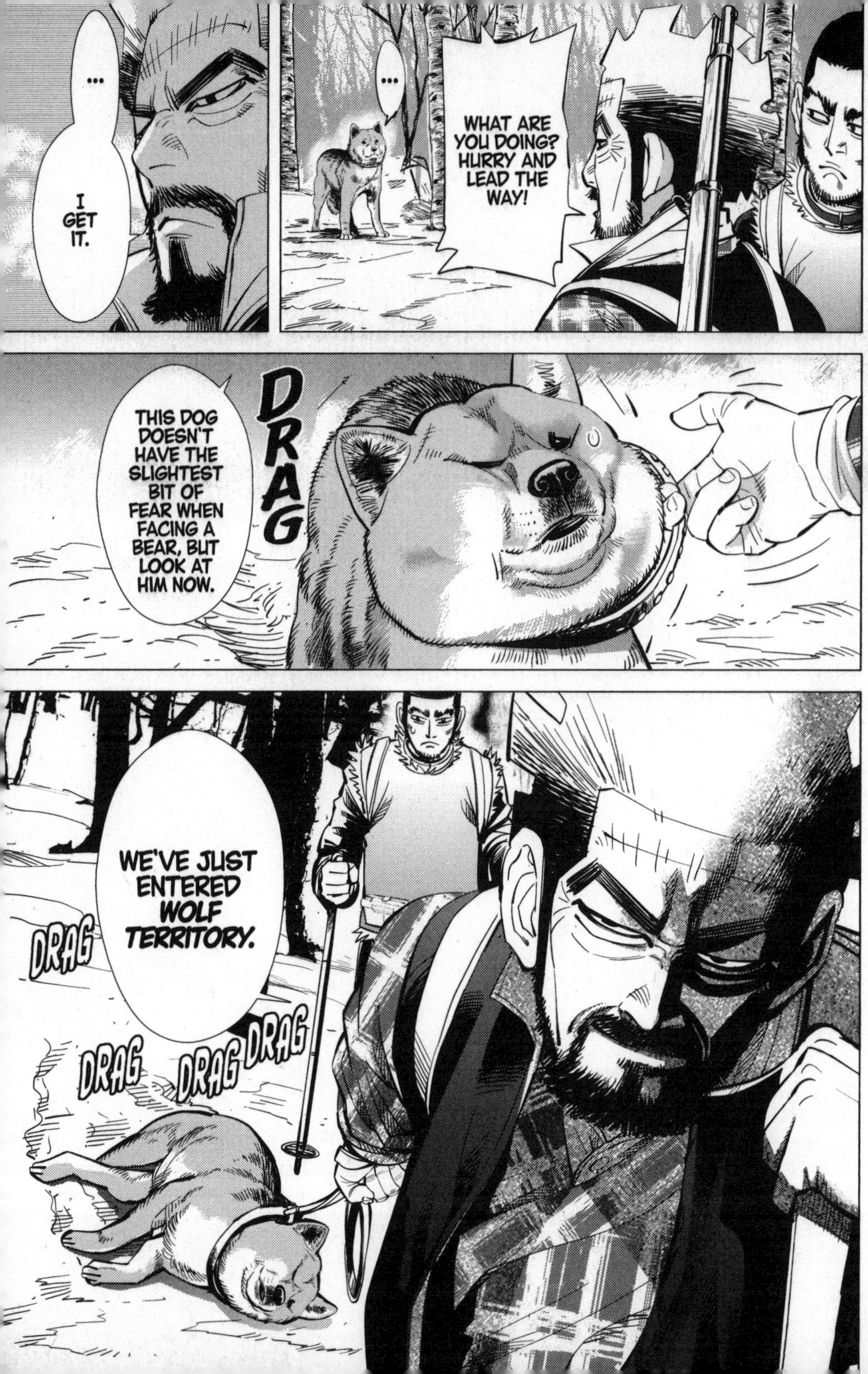
WHAT ARE YOU DOING? HURRY AND LEAD THE WAY!
...
... I GET IT.
DRAG
THIS DOG DOESN'T HAVE THE SLIGHTEST BIT OF FEAR WHEN FACING A BEAR, BUT LOOK AT HIM NOW.
WE'VE JUST ENTERED WOLF TERRITORY.
DRAG
DRAG DRAG
DRAG
DRAG

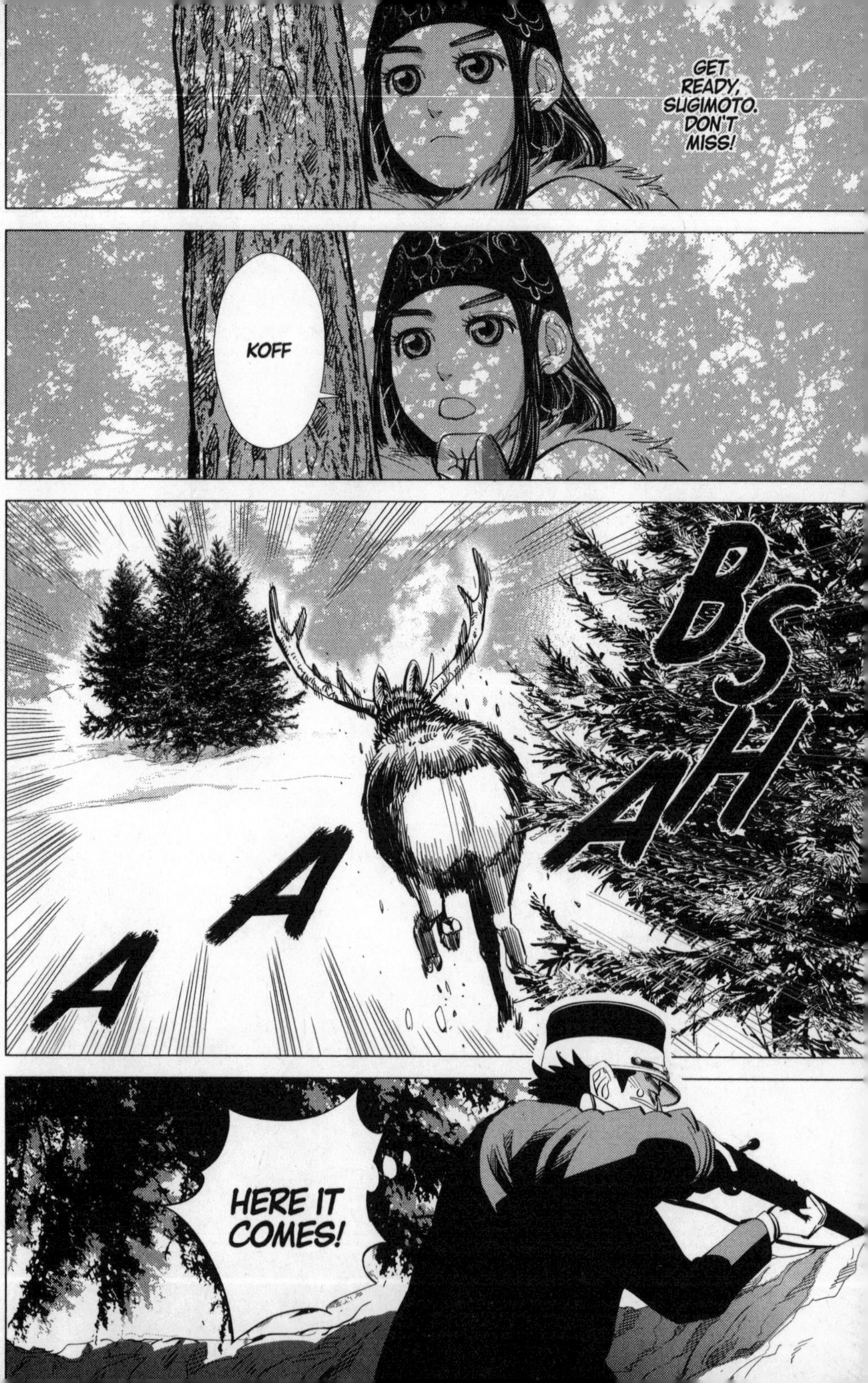
GET READY, SUGIMOTO. DON'T MISS!
KOFF
BSHAAAA
HERE IT COMES!

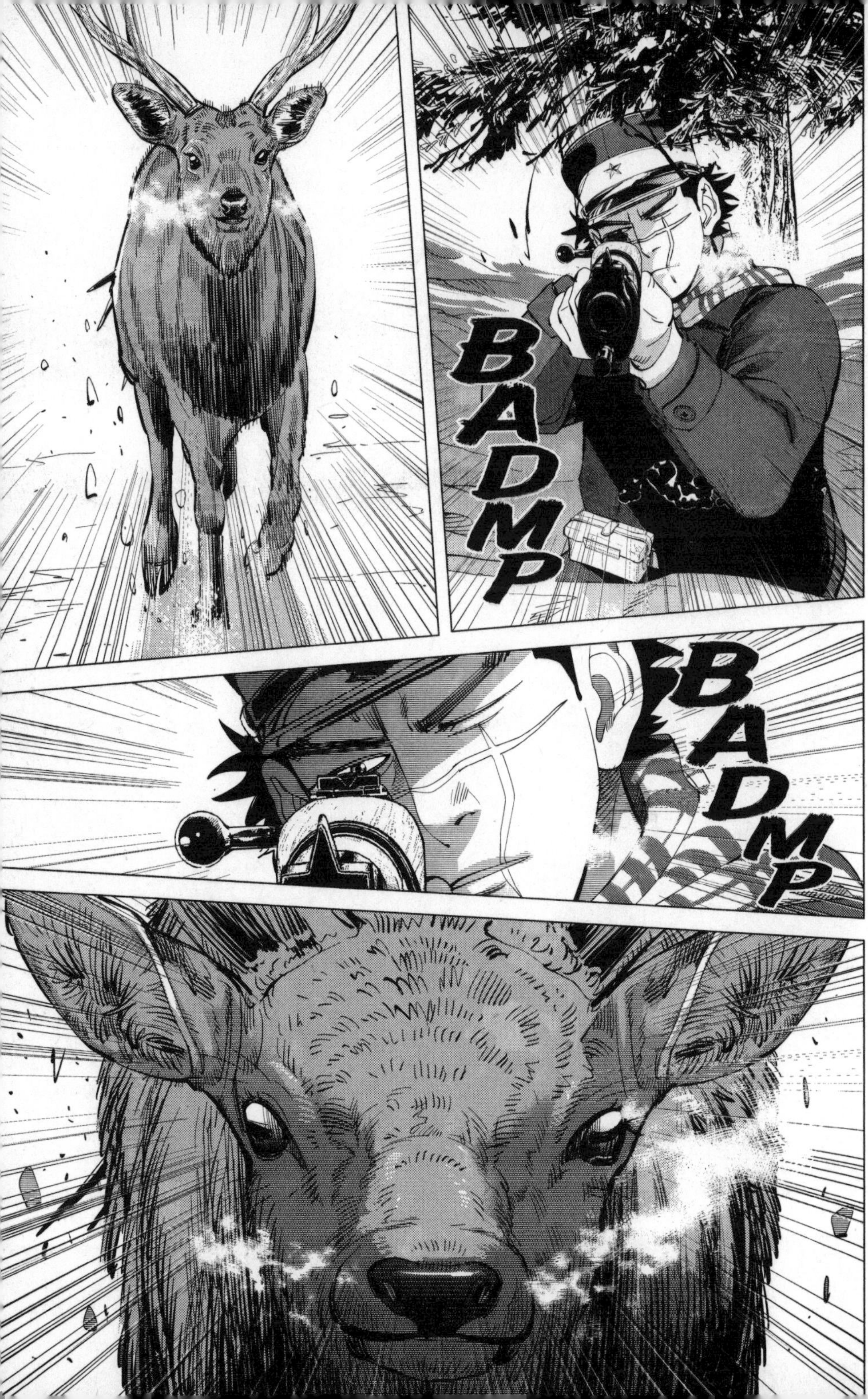
BADMP
BADMP

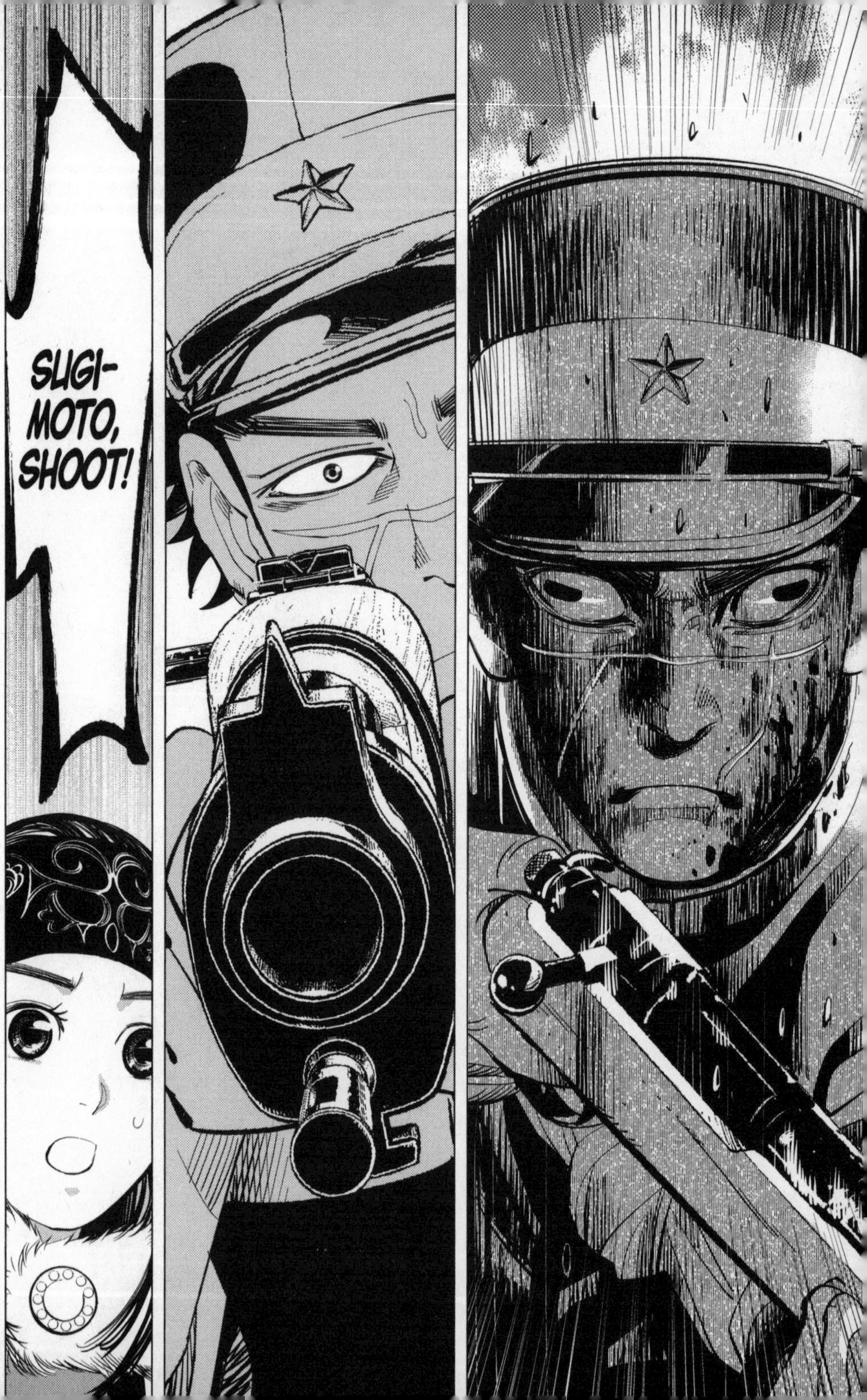
SUGI-MOTO, SHOOT!

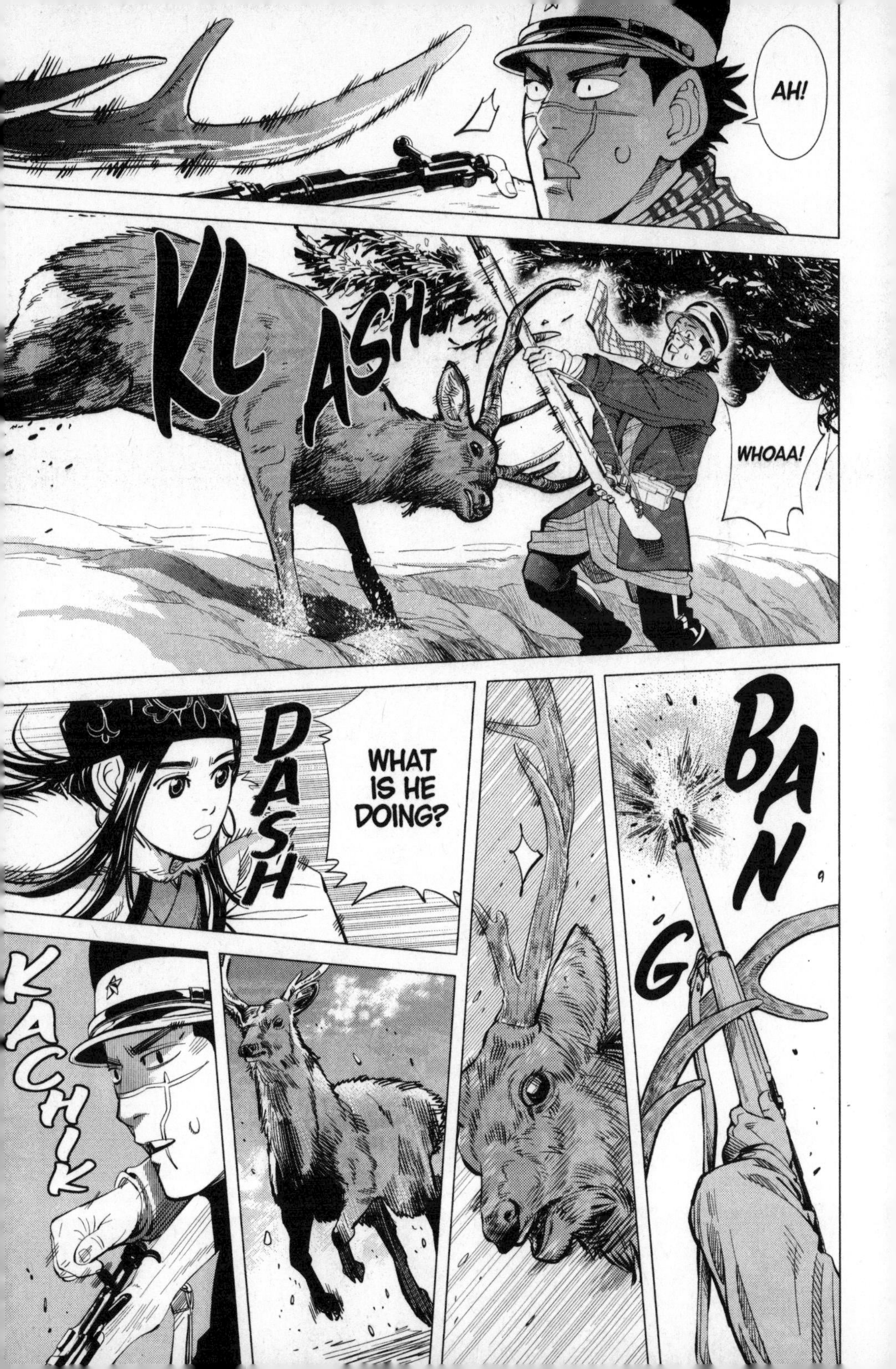
AH!
KLASH
WHOAA!
BANG
WHAT IS HE DOING?
DASH
KACHIK

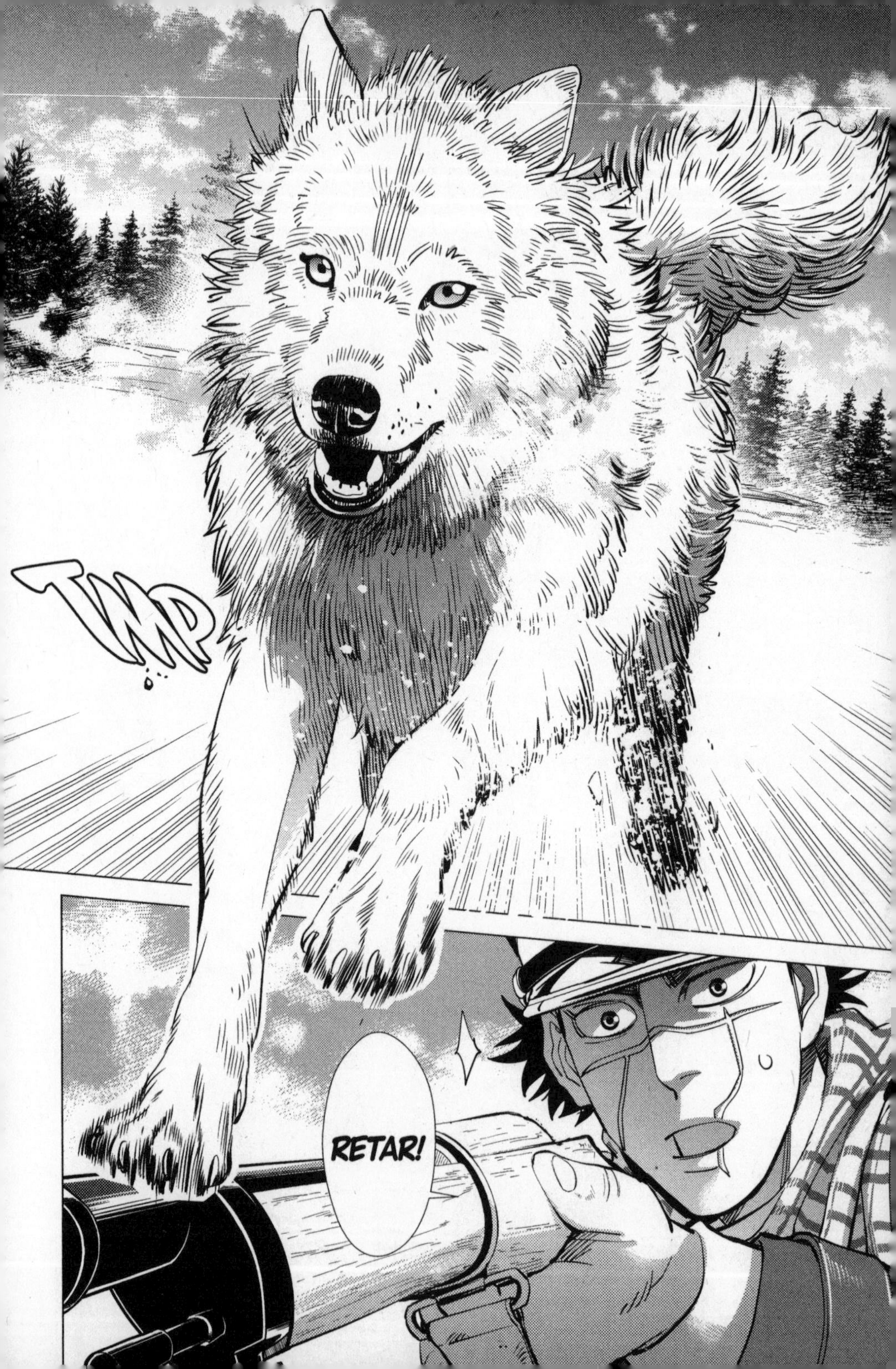
TMP
RETAR!

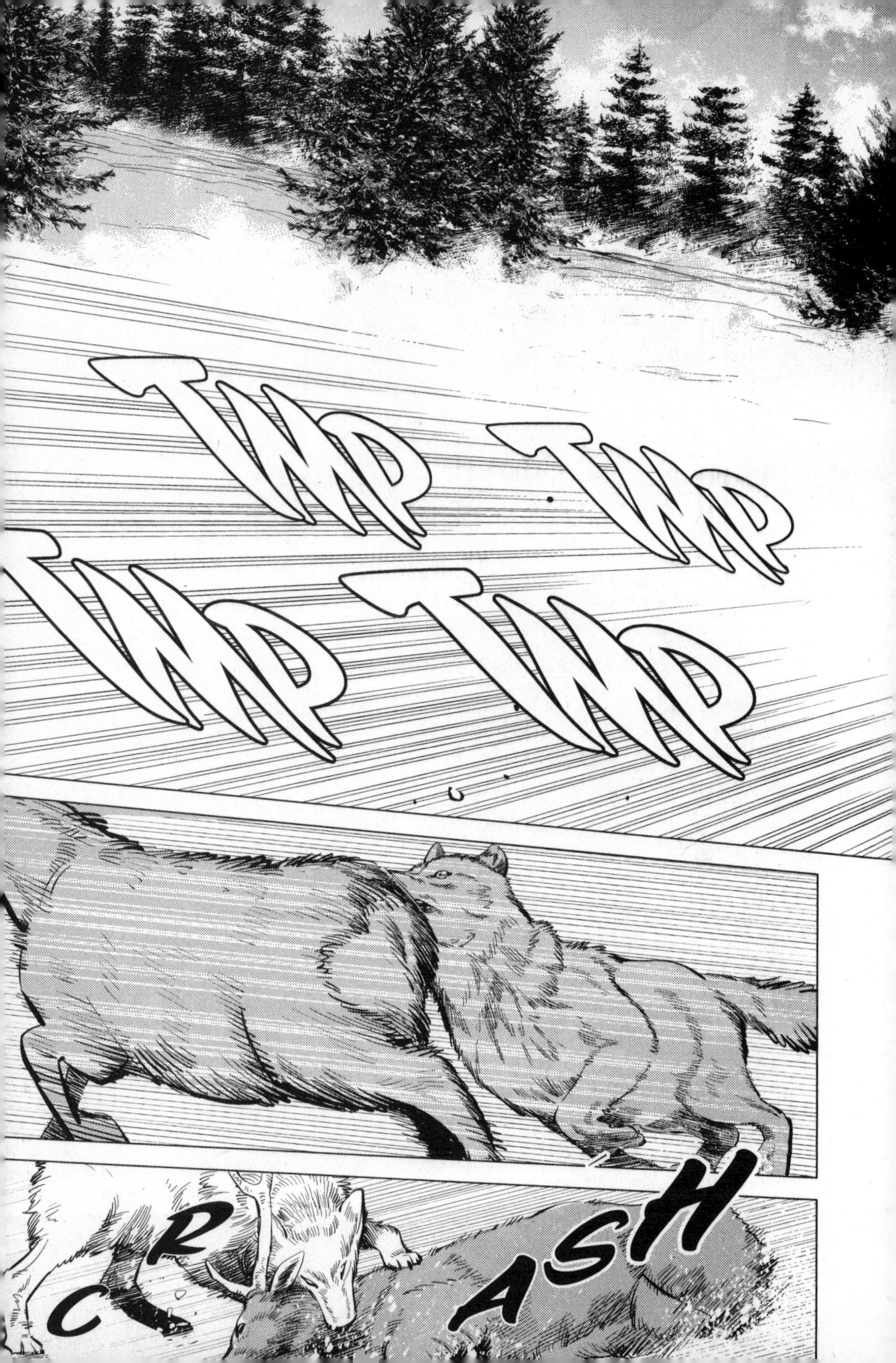
THMP
THMP
THMP
THMP
CRASH

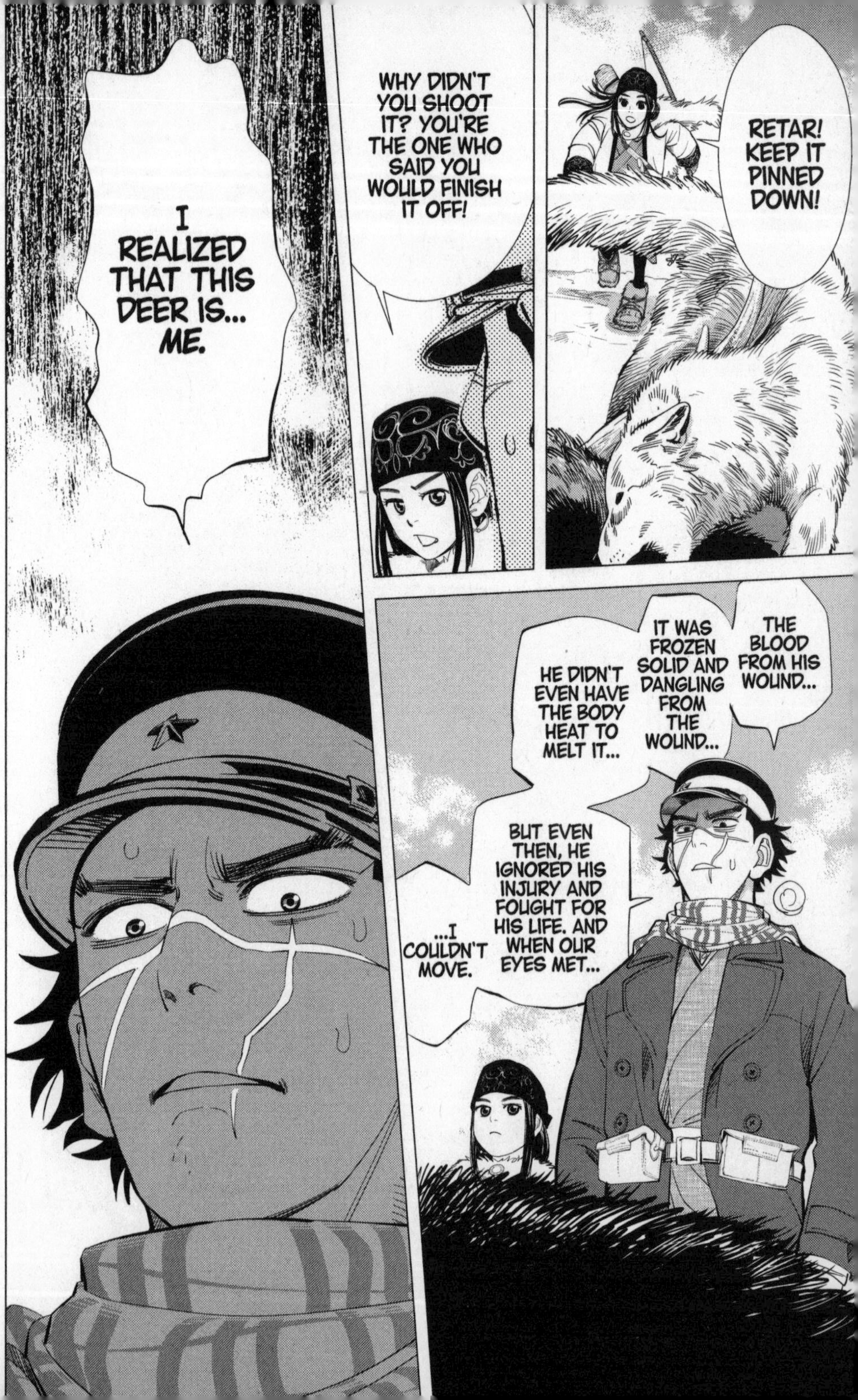
RETAR! KEEP IT PINNED DOWN!
WHY DIDN'T YOU SHOOT IT? YOU'RE THE ONE WHO SAID YOU WOULD FINISH IT OFF!
THE BLOOD FROM HIS WOUND...
IT WAS FROZEN SOLID AND DANGLING FROM THE WOUND...
HE DIDN'T EVEN HAVE THE BODY HEAT TO MELT IT...
BUT EVEN THEN, HE IGNORED HIS INJURY AND FOUGHT FOR HIS LIFE. AND WHEN OUR EYES MET...
...I COULDN'T MOVE.
I REALIZED THAT THIS DEER IS... ME.

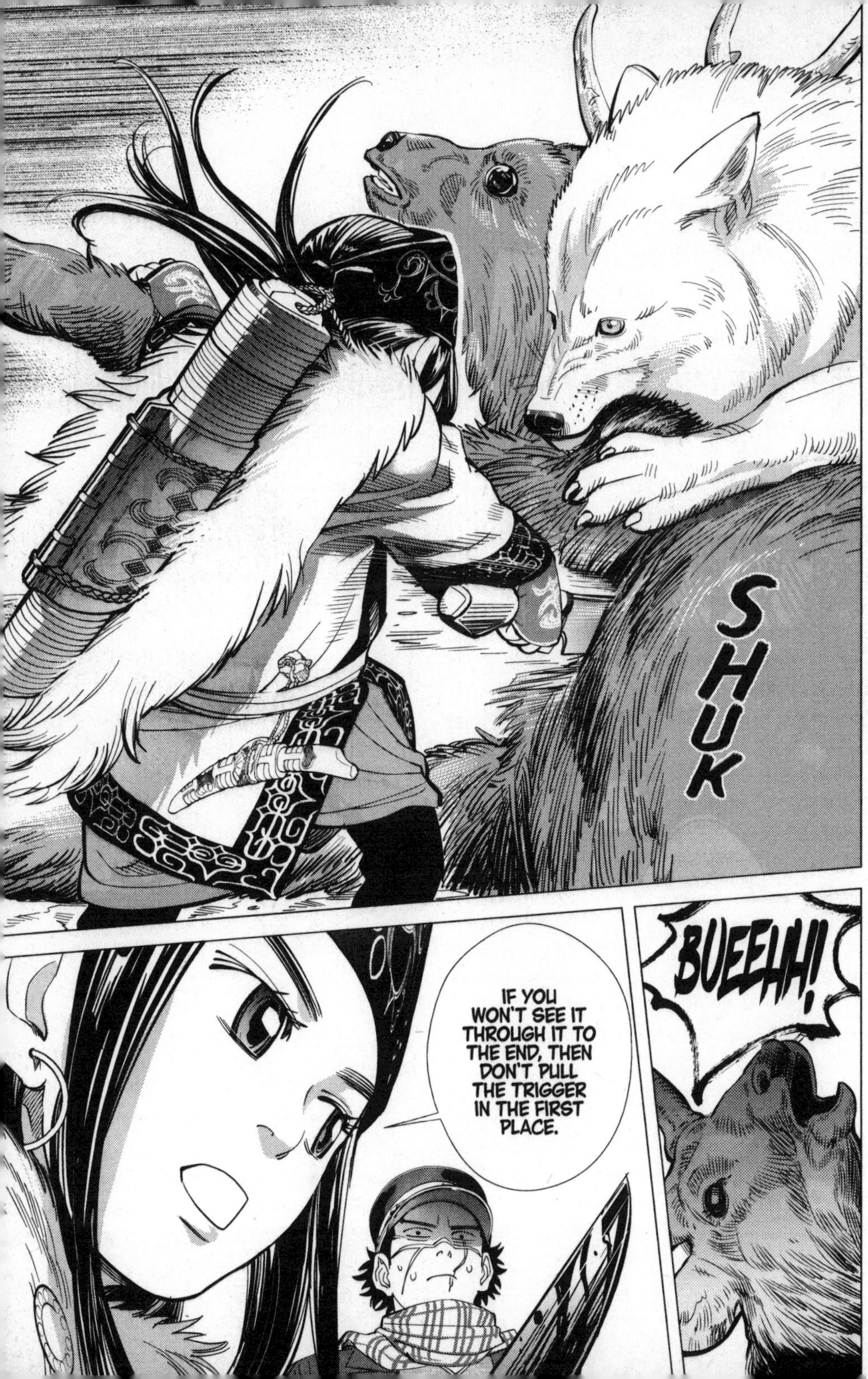
SHUK
BUEEHH!
IF YOU WON'T SEE IT THROUGH IT TO THE END, THEN DON'T PULL THE TRIGGER IN THE FIRST PLACE.

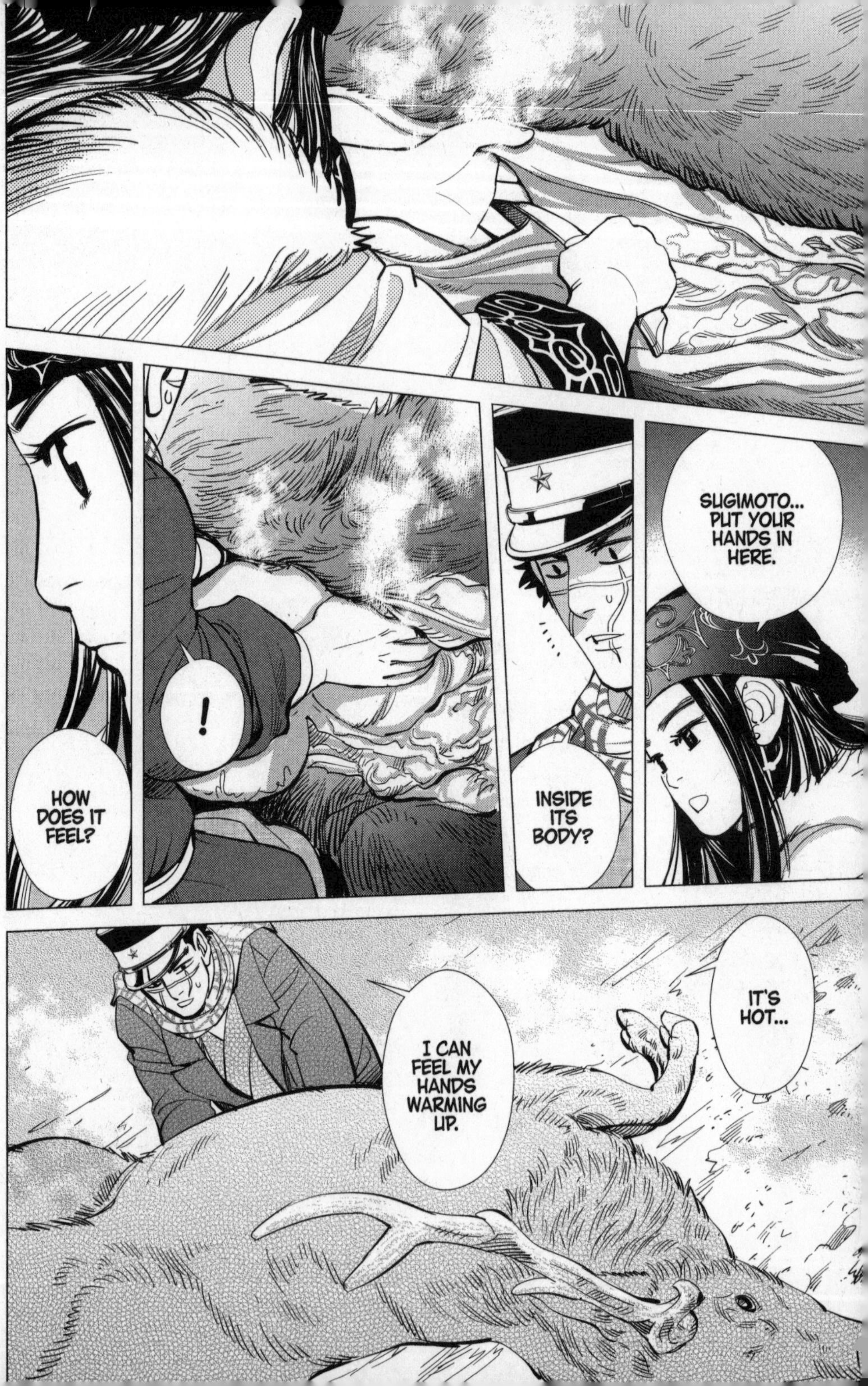
SUGIMOTO... PUT YOUR HANDS IN HERE.
...
INSIDE ITS BODY?
!
HOW DOES IT FEEL?
IT'S HOT...
I CAN FEEL MY HANDS WARMING UP.

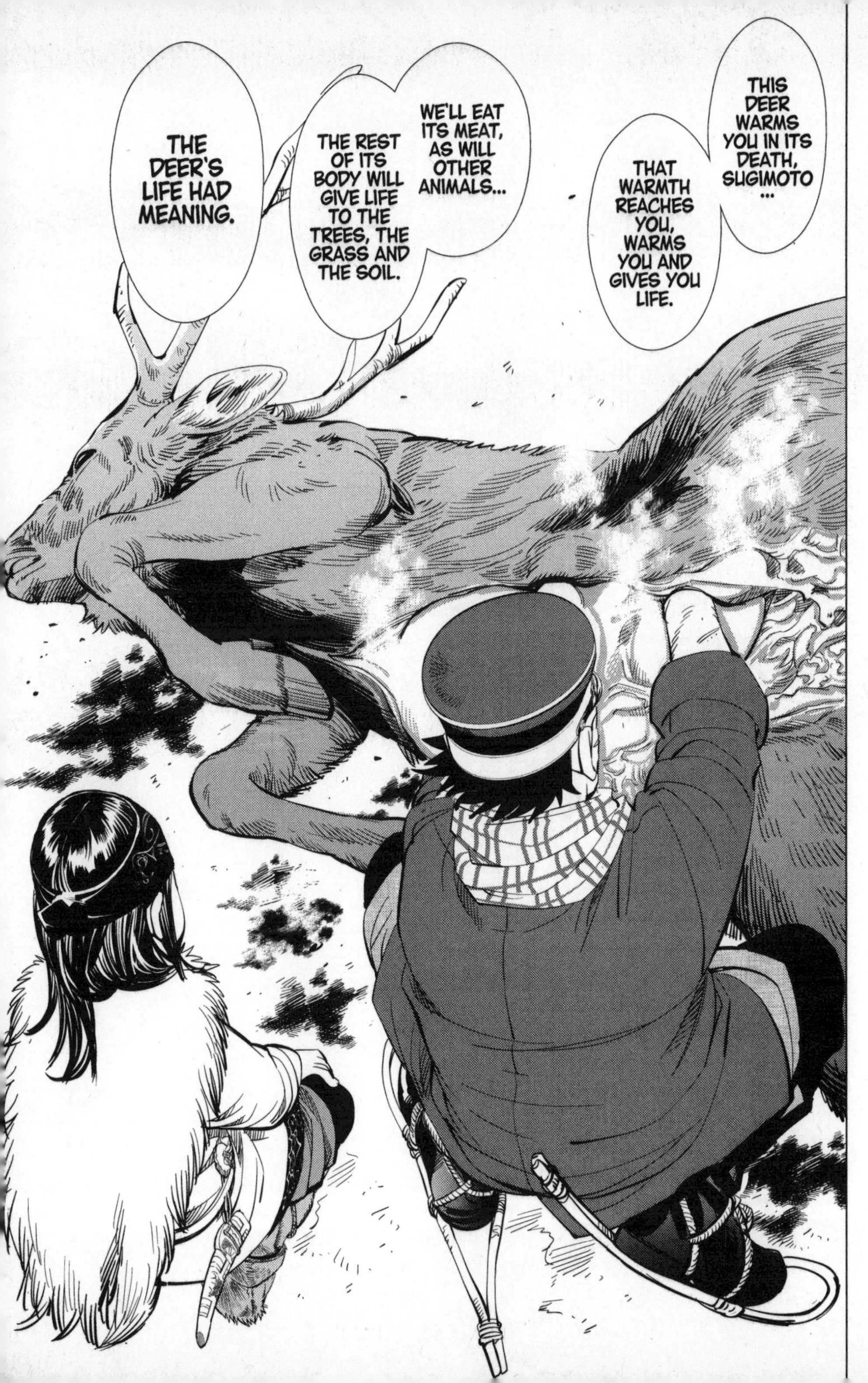
THIS DEER WARMS YOU IN ITS DEATH, SUGIMOTO...
THAT WARMTH REACHES YOU, WARMS YOU AND GIVES YOU LIFE.
WE'LL EAT ITS MEAT, AS WILL OTHER ANIMALS...
THE REST OF ITS BODY WILL GIVE LIFE TO THE TREES, THE GRASS AND THE SOIL.
THE DEER'S LIFE HAD MEANING.

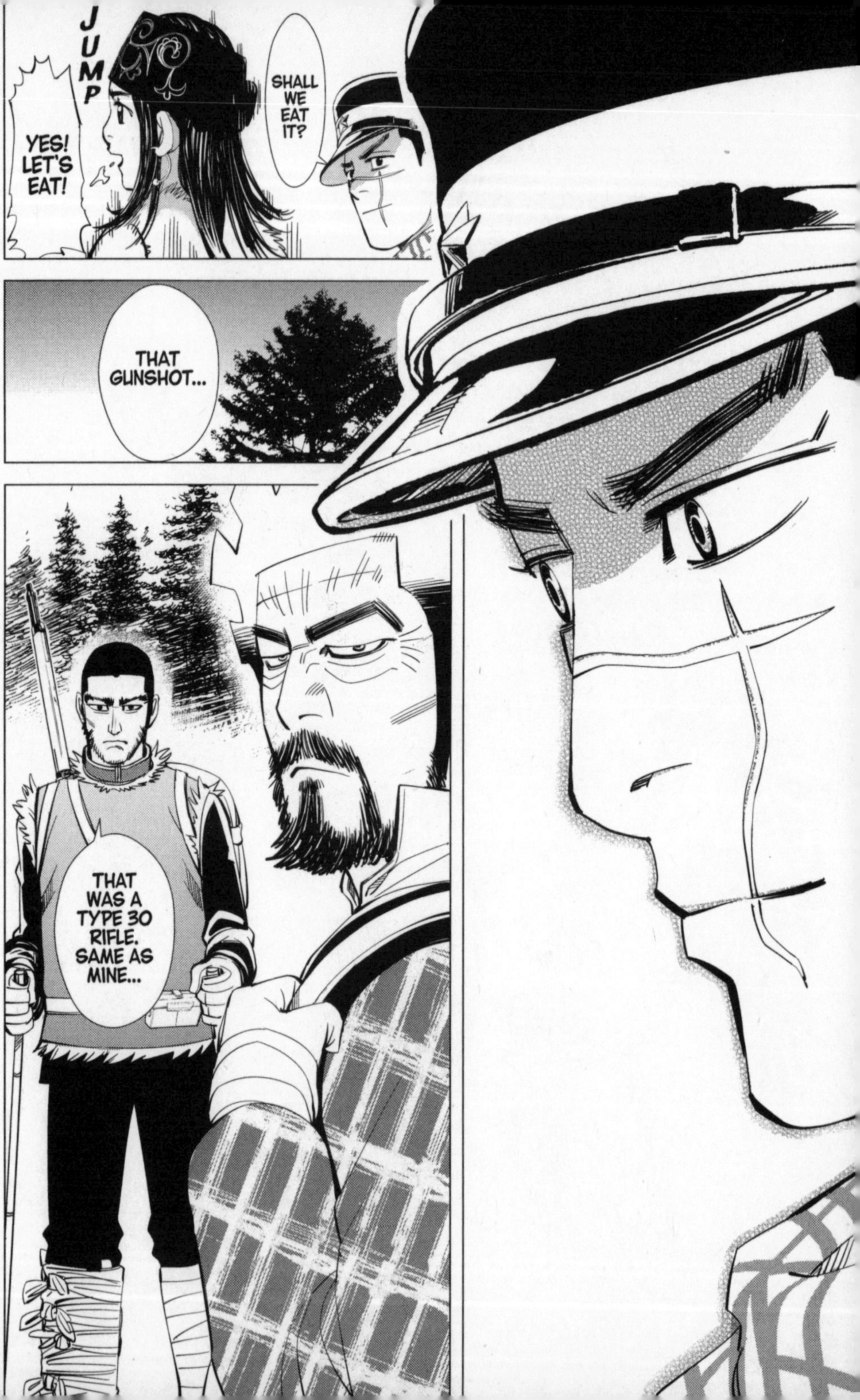
SHALL WE EAT IT?
JUMP
YES! LET'S EAT!
THAT GUNSHOT...
THAT WAS A TYPE 30 RIFLE. SAME AS MINE...

Chapter 25: Yuk

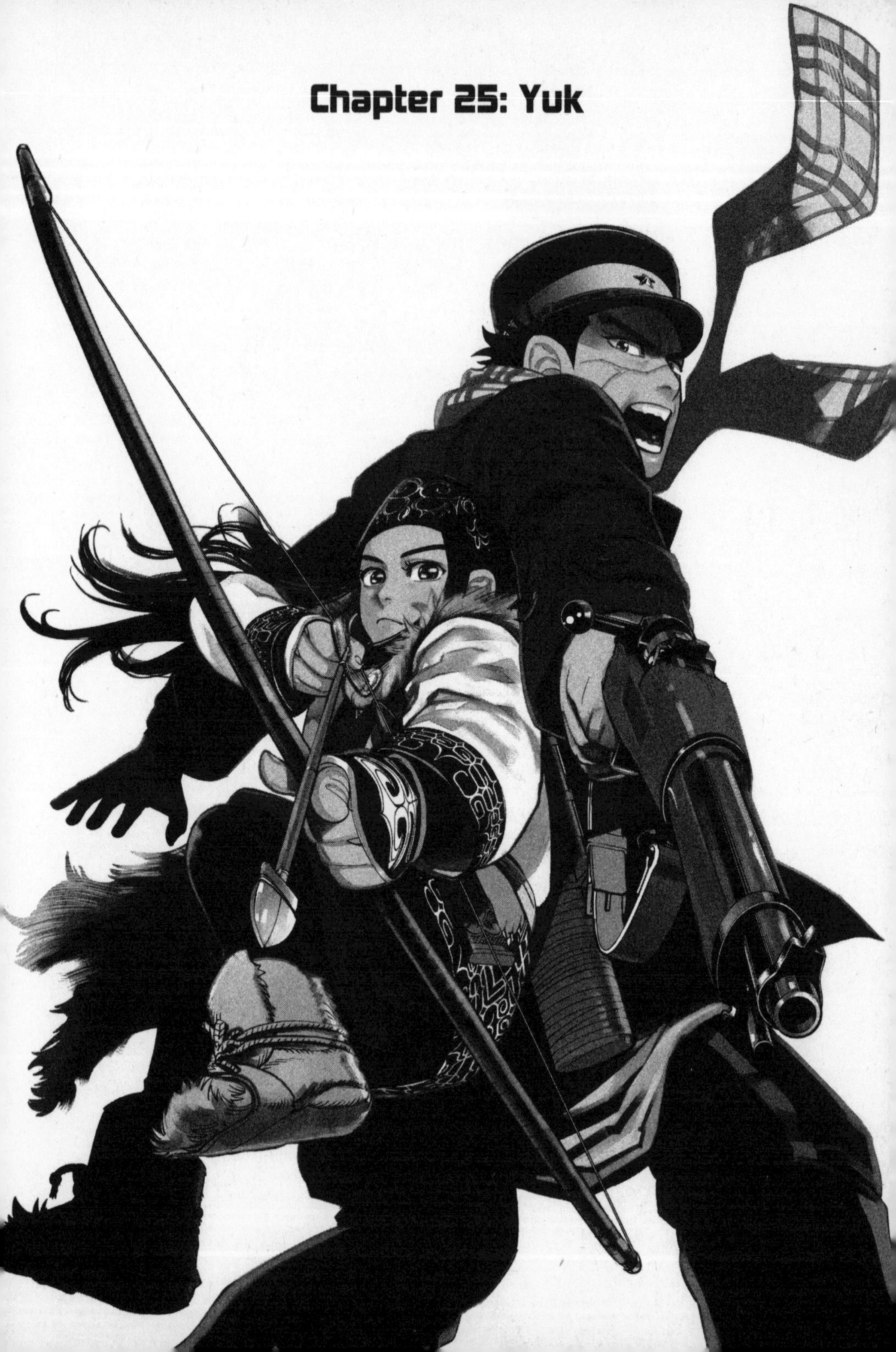

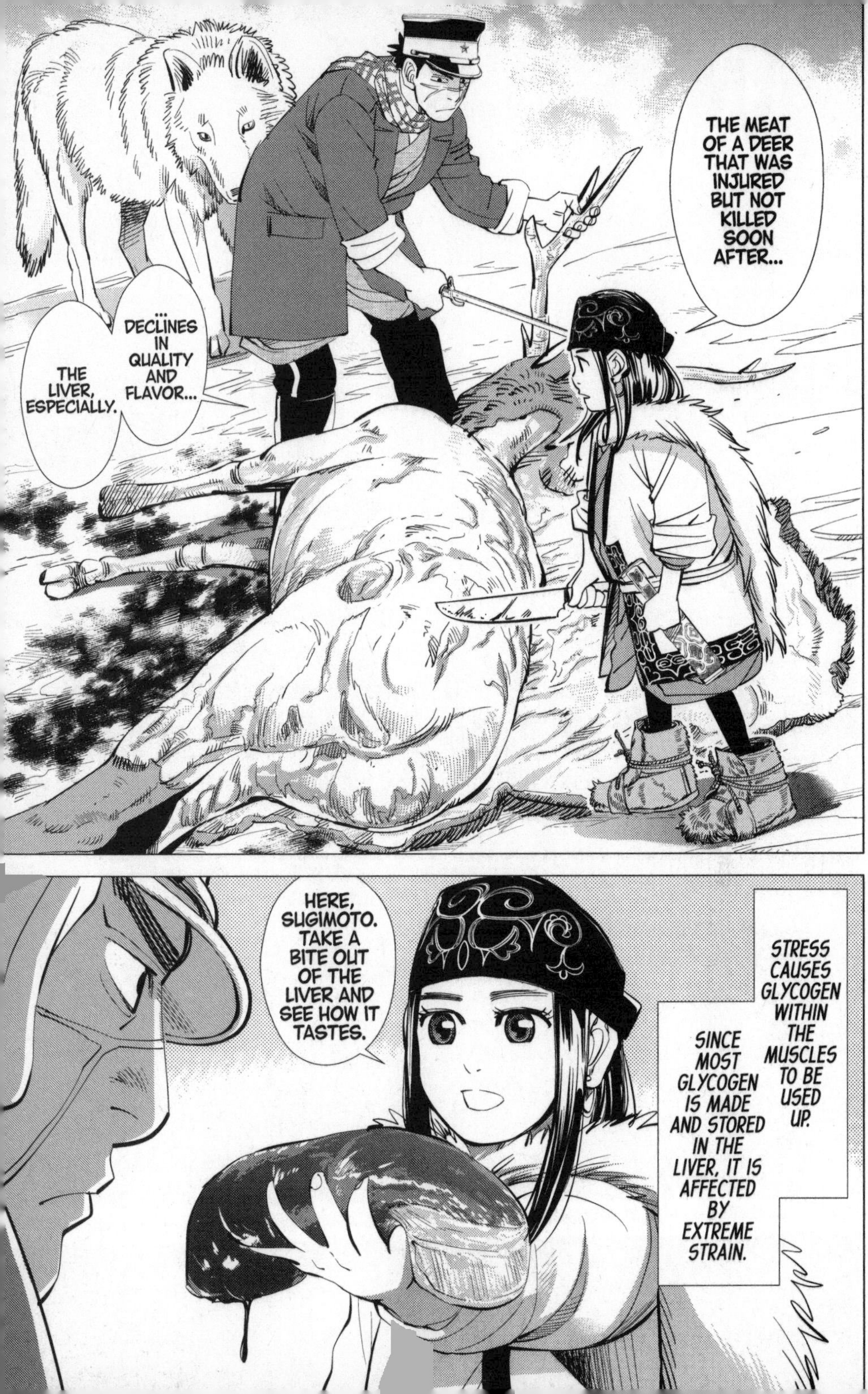
THE MEAT OF A DEER THAT WAS INJURED BUT NOT KILLED SOON AFTER...
...DECLINES IN QUALITY AND FLAVOR...
THE LIVER, ESPECIALLY.
STRESS CAUSES GLYCOGEN WITHIN THE MUSCLES TO BE USED UP.
SINCE MOST GLYCOGEN IS MADE AND STORED IN THE LIVER, IT IS AFFECTED BY EXTREME STRAIN.
HERE, SUGIMOTO. TAKE A BITE OUT OF THE LIVER AND SEE HOW IT TASTES.

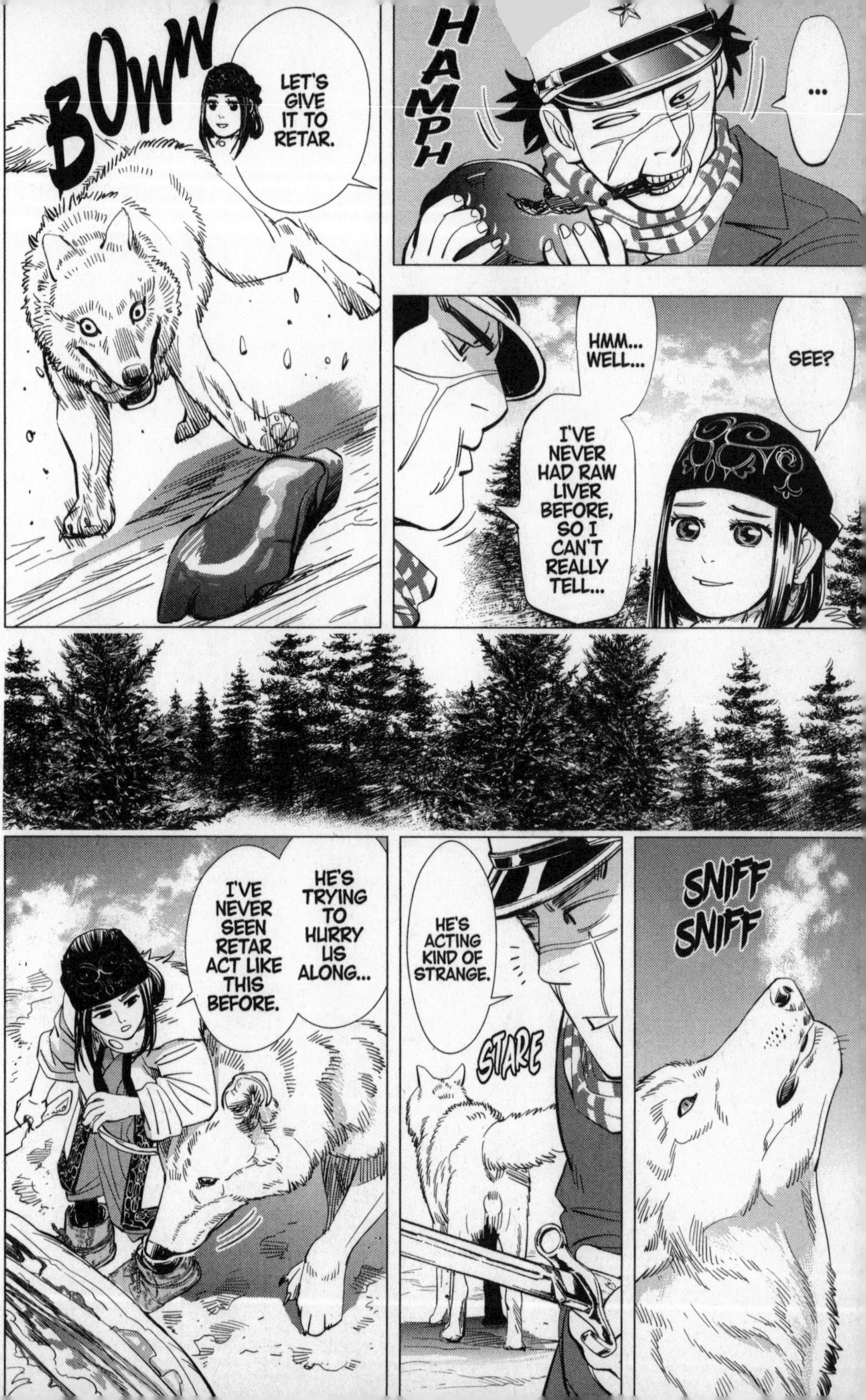
HAMPH
...
SEE?
HMM... WELL...
I'VE NEVER HAD RAW LIVER BEFORE, SO I CAN'T REALLY TELL...
BOWW
LET'S GIVE IT TO RETAR.
SNIFF SNIFF
HE'S ACTING KIND OF STRANGE.
STARE
HE'S TRYING TO HURRY US ALONG...
I'VE NEVER SEEN RETAR ACT LIKE THIS BEFORE.

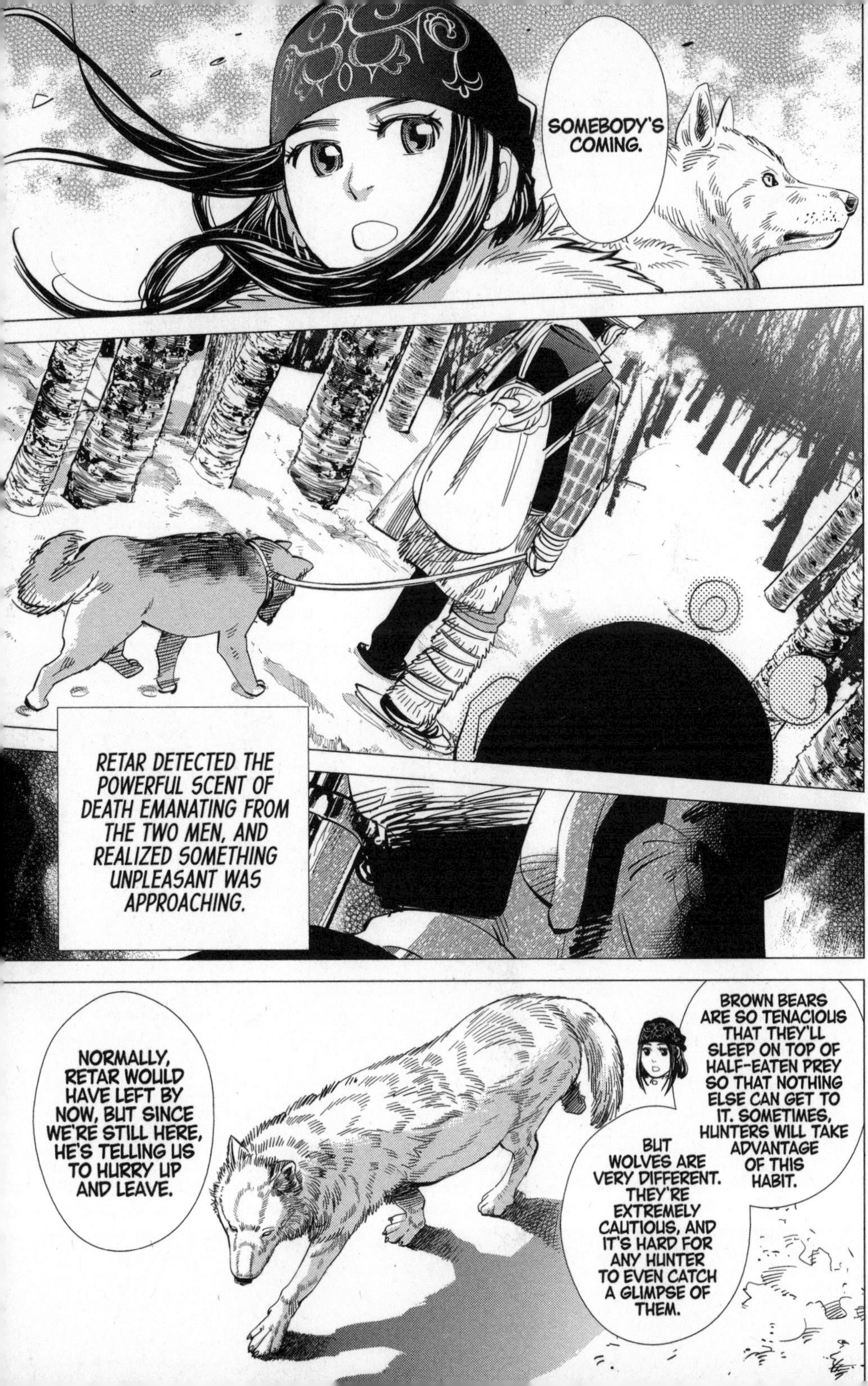
SOMEBODY'S COMING.
RETAR DETECTED THE POWERFUL SCENT OF DEATH EMANATING FROM THE TWO MEN, AND REALIZED SOMETHING UNPLEASANT WAS APPROACHING.
BROWN BEARS ARE SO TENACIOUS THAT THEY'LL SLEEP ON TOP OF HALF-EATEN PREY SO THAT NOTHING ELSE CAN GET TO IT. SOMETIMES, HUNTERS WILL TAKE ADVANTAGE OF THIS HABIT.
BUT WOLVES ARE VERY DIFFERENT. THEY'RE EXTREMELY CAUTIOUS, AND IT'S HARD FOR ANY HUNTER TO EVEN CATCH A GLIMPSE OF THEM.
NORMALLY, RETAR WOULD HAVE LEFT BY NOW, BUT SINCE WE'RE STILL HERE, HE'S TELLING US TO HURRY UP AND LEAVE.

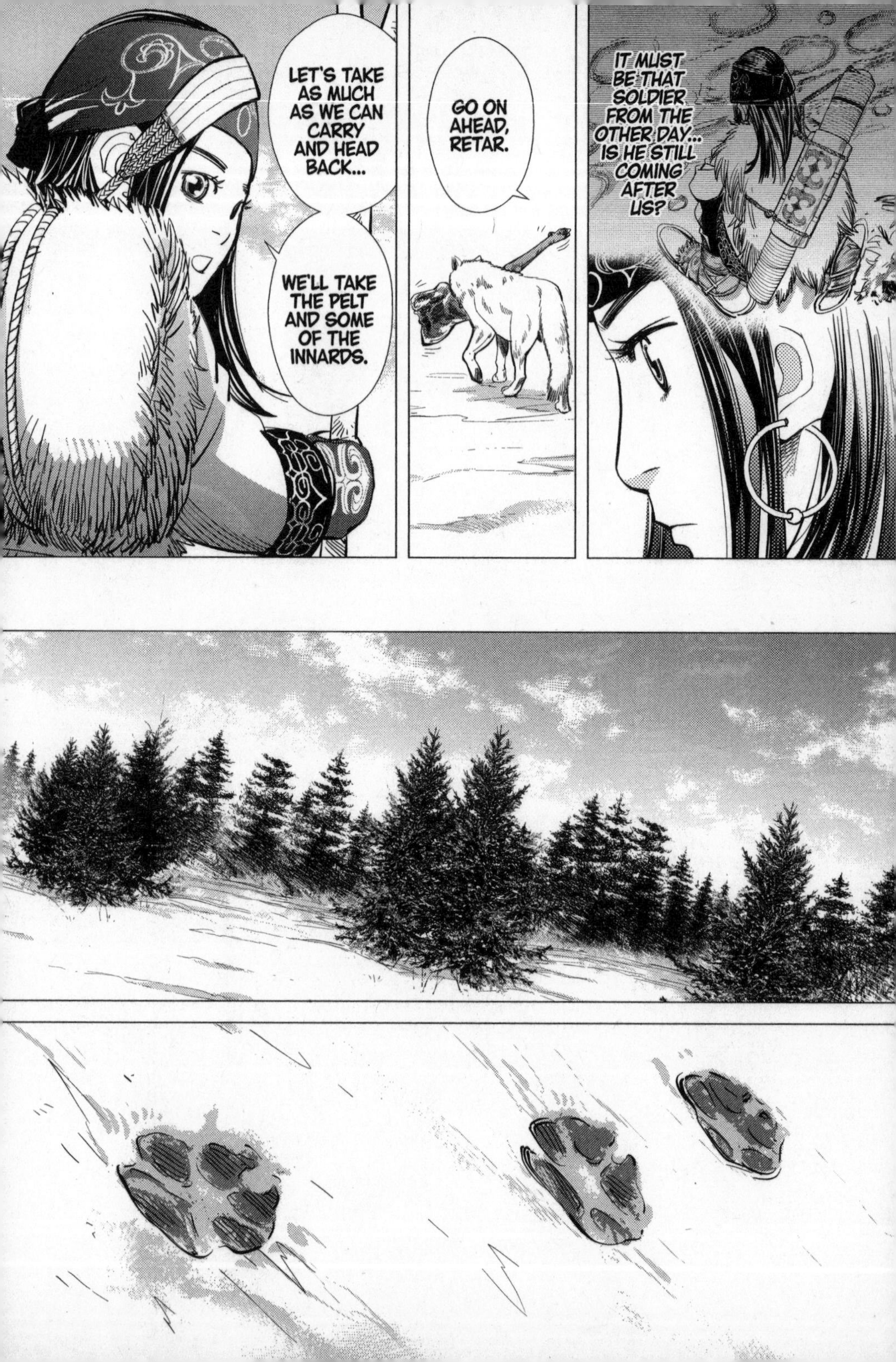
IT MUST BE THAT SOLDIER FROM THE OTHER DAY... IS HE STILL COMING AFTER US?
GO ON AHEAD, RETAR.
LET'S TAKE AS MUCH AS WE CAN CARRY AND HEAD BACK...
WE'LL TAKE THE PELT AND SOME OF THE INNARDS.

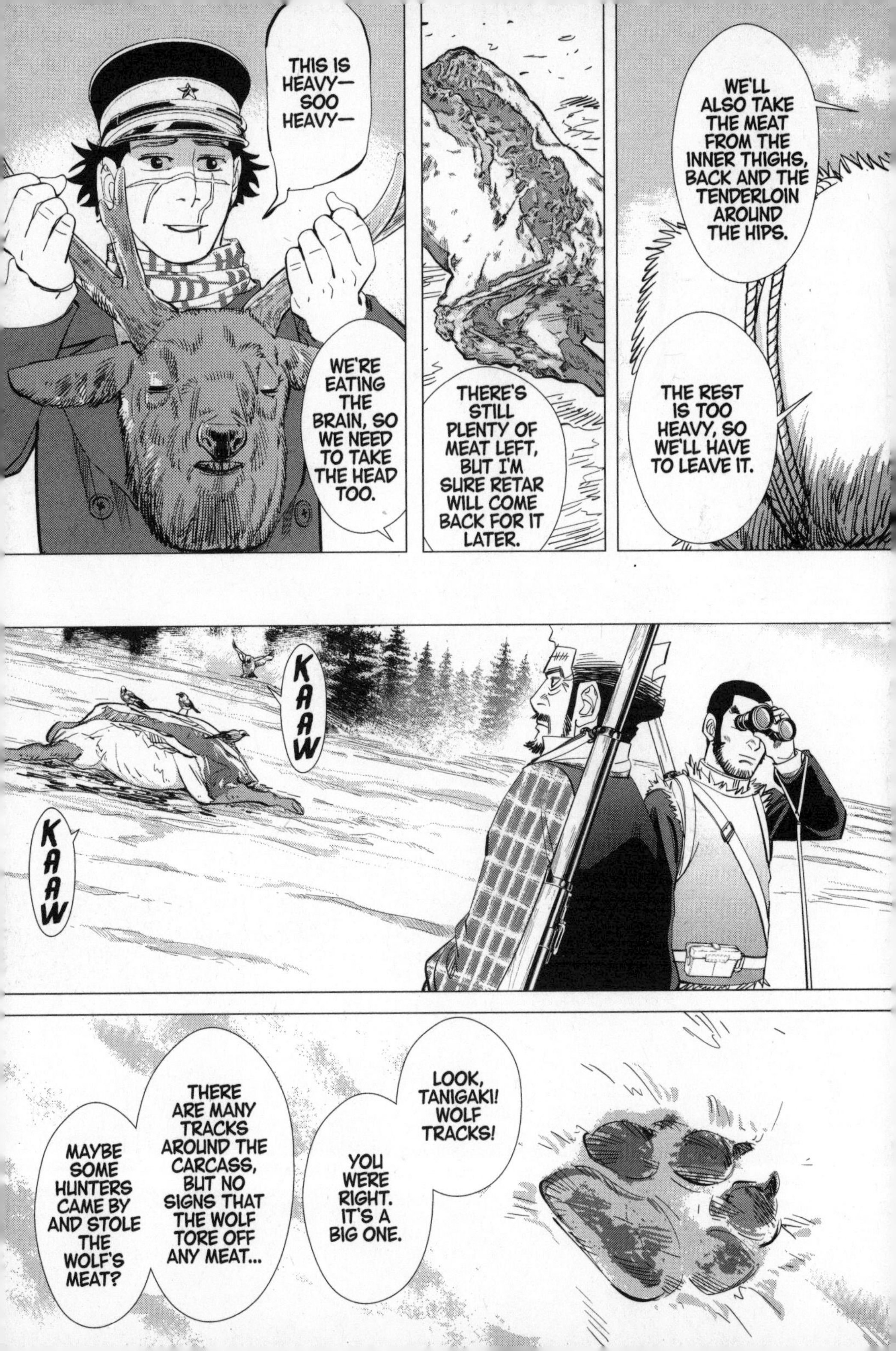
WE'LL ALSO TAKE THE MEAT FROM THE INNER THIGHS, BACK AND THE TENDERLOIN AROUND THE HIPS.
THE REST IS TOO HEAVY, SO WE'LL HAVE TO LEAVE IT.
THERE'S STILL PLENTY OF MEAT LEFT, BUT I'M SURE RETAR WILL COME BACK FOR IT LATER.
THIS IS HEAVY— SOO HEAVY—
WE'RE EATING THE BRAIN, SO WE NEED TO TAKE THE HEAD TOO.
KAAW
KAAW
LOOK, TANIGAKI! WOLF TRACKS!
YOU WERE RIGHT. IT'S A BIG ONE.
THERE ARE MANY TRACKS AROUND THE CARCASS, BUT NO SIGNS THAT THE WOLF TORE OFF ANY MEAT...
MAYBE SOME HUNTERS CAME BY AND STOLE THE WOLF'S MEAT?

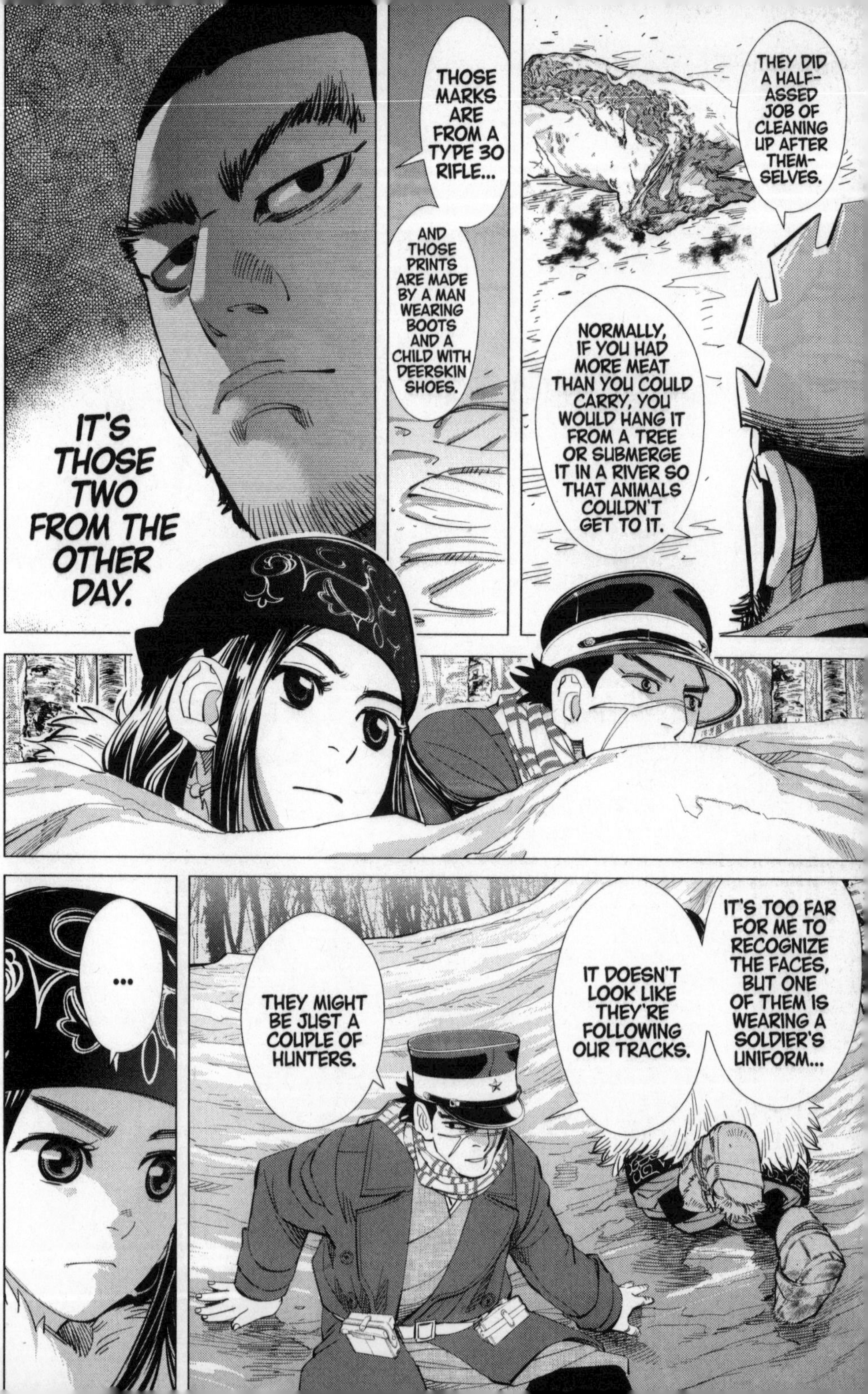
THEY DID A HALF-ASSED JOB OF CLEANING UP AFTER THEMSELVES.
NORMALLY, IF YOU HAD MORE MEAT THAN YOU COULD CARRY, YOU WOULD HANG IT FROM A TREE OR SUBMERGE IT IN A RIVER SO THAT ANIMALS COULDN'T GET TO IT.
THOSE MARKS ARE FROM A TYPE 30 RIFLE...
AND THOSE PRINTS ARE MADE BY A MAN WEARING BOOTS AND A CHILD WITH DEERSKIN SHOES.
IT'S THOSE TWO FROM THE OTHER DAY.
IT'S TOO FAR FOR ME TO RECOGNIZE THE FACES, BUT ONE OF THEM IS WEARING A SOLDIER'S UNIFORM...
IT DOESN'T LOOK LIKE THEY'RE FOLLOWING OUR TRACKS.
THEY MIGHT BE JUST A COUPLE OF HUNTERS.
...

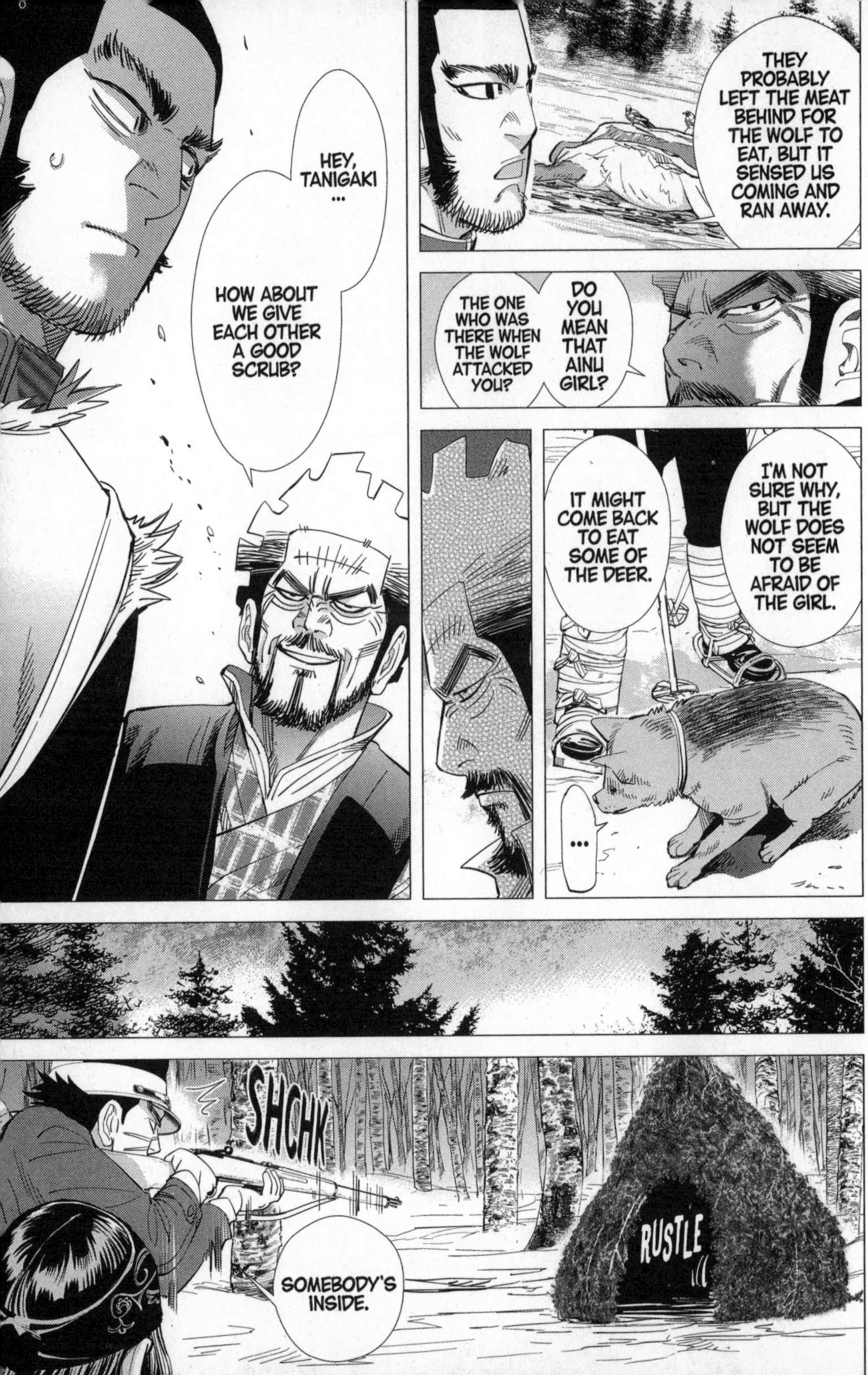
THEY PROBABLY LEFT THE MEAT BEHIND FOR THE WOLF TO EAT, BUT IT SENSED US COMING AND RAN AWAY.
DO YOU MEAN THAT AINU GIRL?
THE ONE WHO WAS THERE WHEN THE WOLF ATTACKED YOU?
I'M NOT SURE WHY, BUT THE WOLF DOES NOT SEEM TO BE AFRAID OF THE GIRL.
IT MIGHT COME BACK TO EAT SOME OF THE DEER.
...
HEY, TANIGAKI ...
HOW ABOUT WE GIVE EACH OTHER A GOOD SCRUB?
SHCHK
RUSTLE
SOMEBODY'S INSIDE.

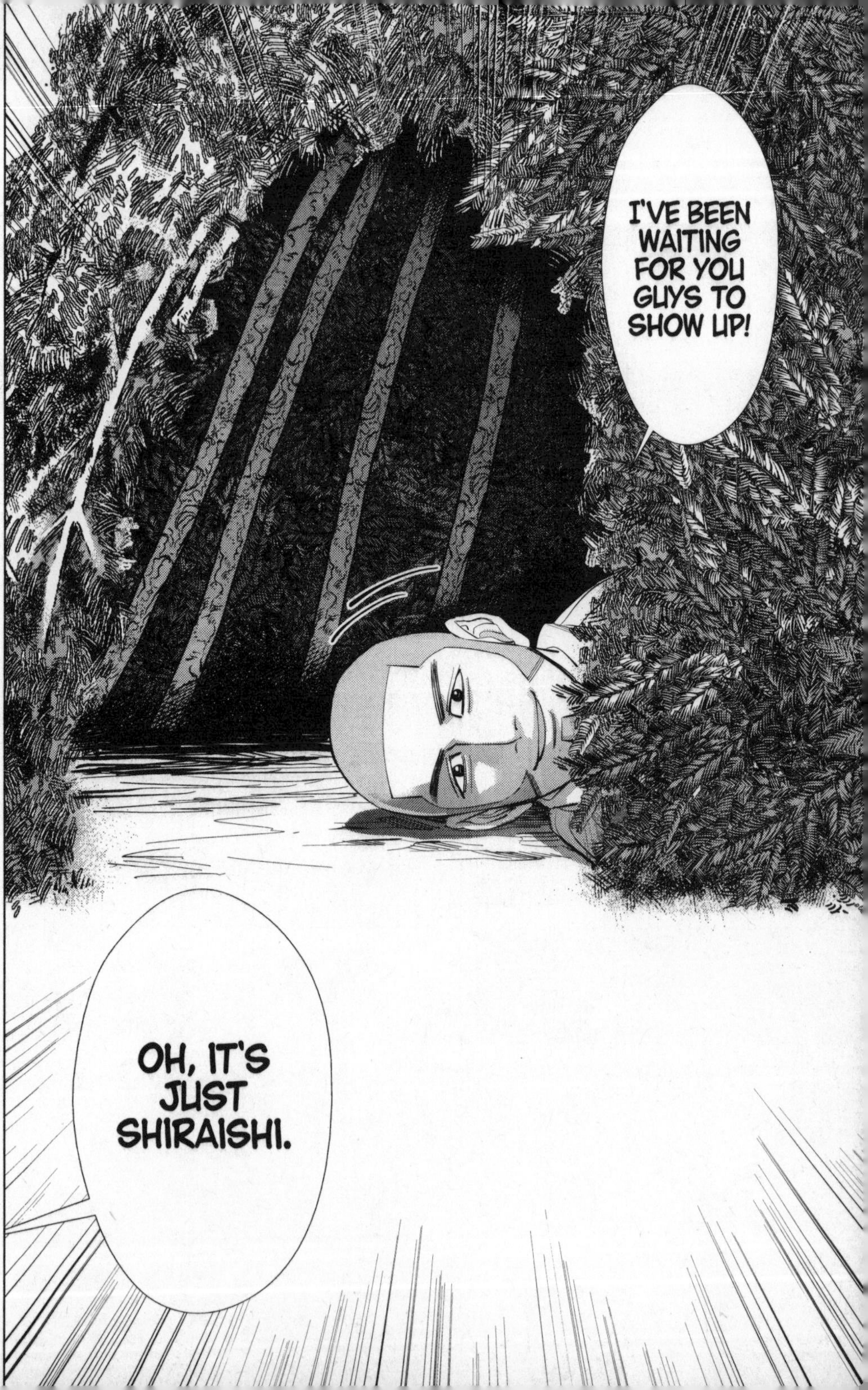
I'VE BEEN WAITING FOR YOU GUYS TO SHOW UP!
OH, IT'S JUST SHIRAISHI.

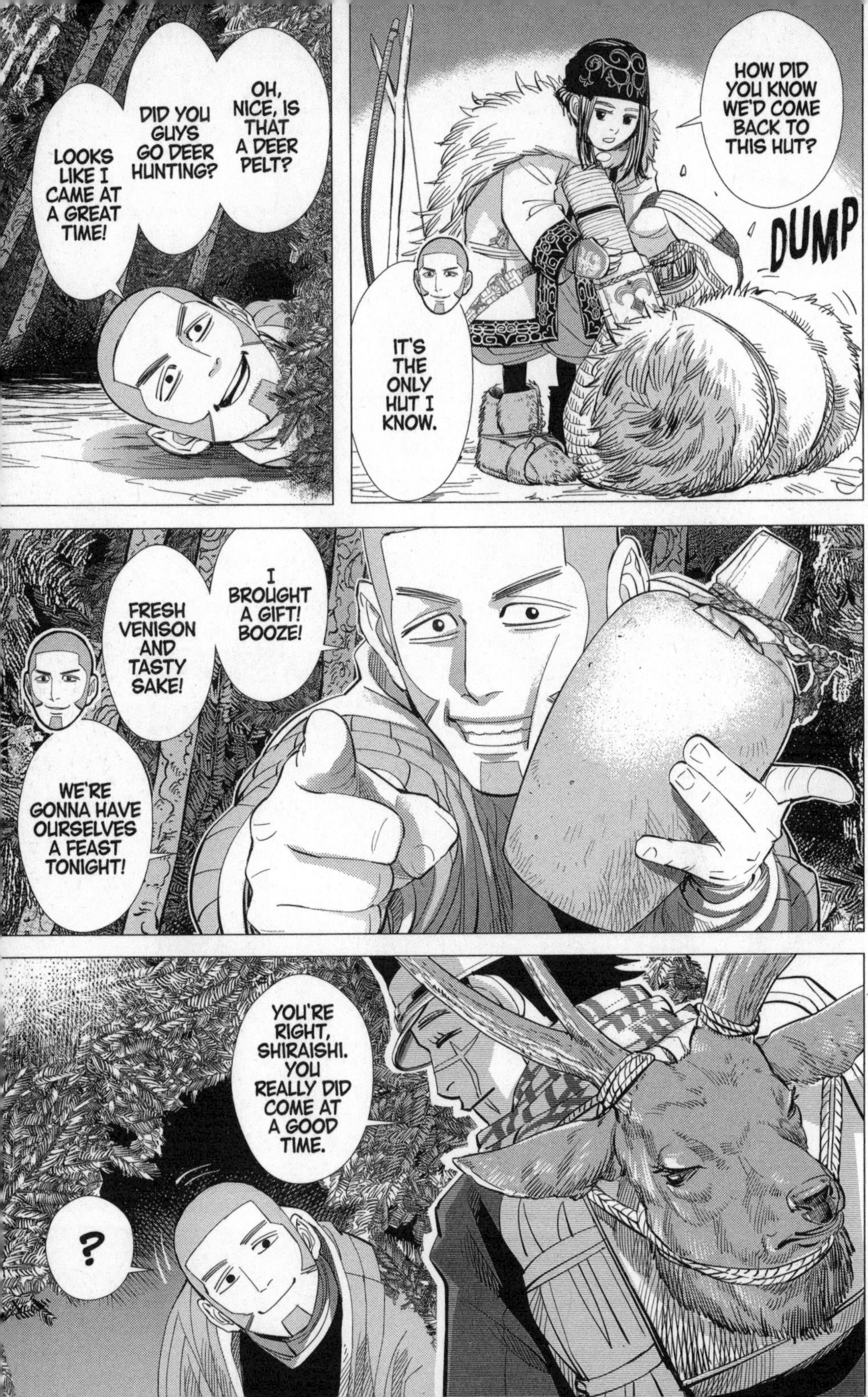
HOW DID YOU KNOW WE'D COME BACK TO THIS HUT?
DUMP
IT'S THE ONLY HUT I KNOW.
OH, NICE, IS THAT A DEER PELT?
DID YOU GUYS GO DEER HUNTING?
LOOKS LIKE I CAME AT A GREAT TIME!
I BROUGHT A GIFT! BOOZE!
FRESH VENISON AND TASTY SAKE!
WE'RE GONNA HAVE OURSELVES A FEAST TONIGHT!
YOU'RE RIGHT, SHIRAISHI. YOU REALLY DID COME AT A GOOD TIME.
?

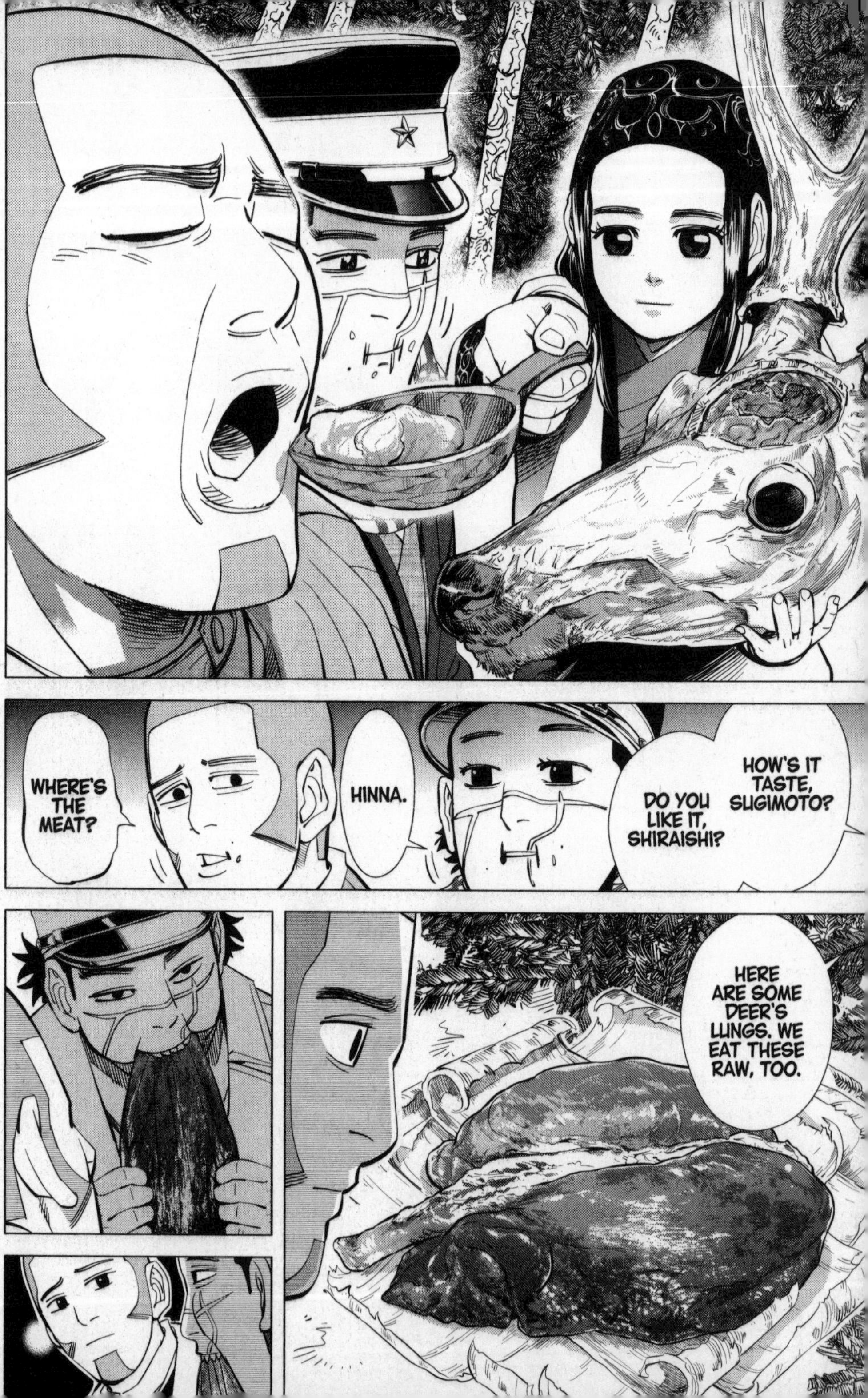
HOW'S IT TASTE, SUGIMOTO?
DO YOU LIKE IT, SHIRAISHI?
HINNA.
WHERE'S THE MEAT?
HERE ARE SOME DEER'S LUNGS. WE EAT THESE RAW, TOO.

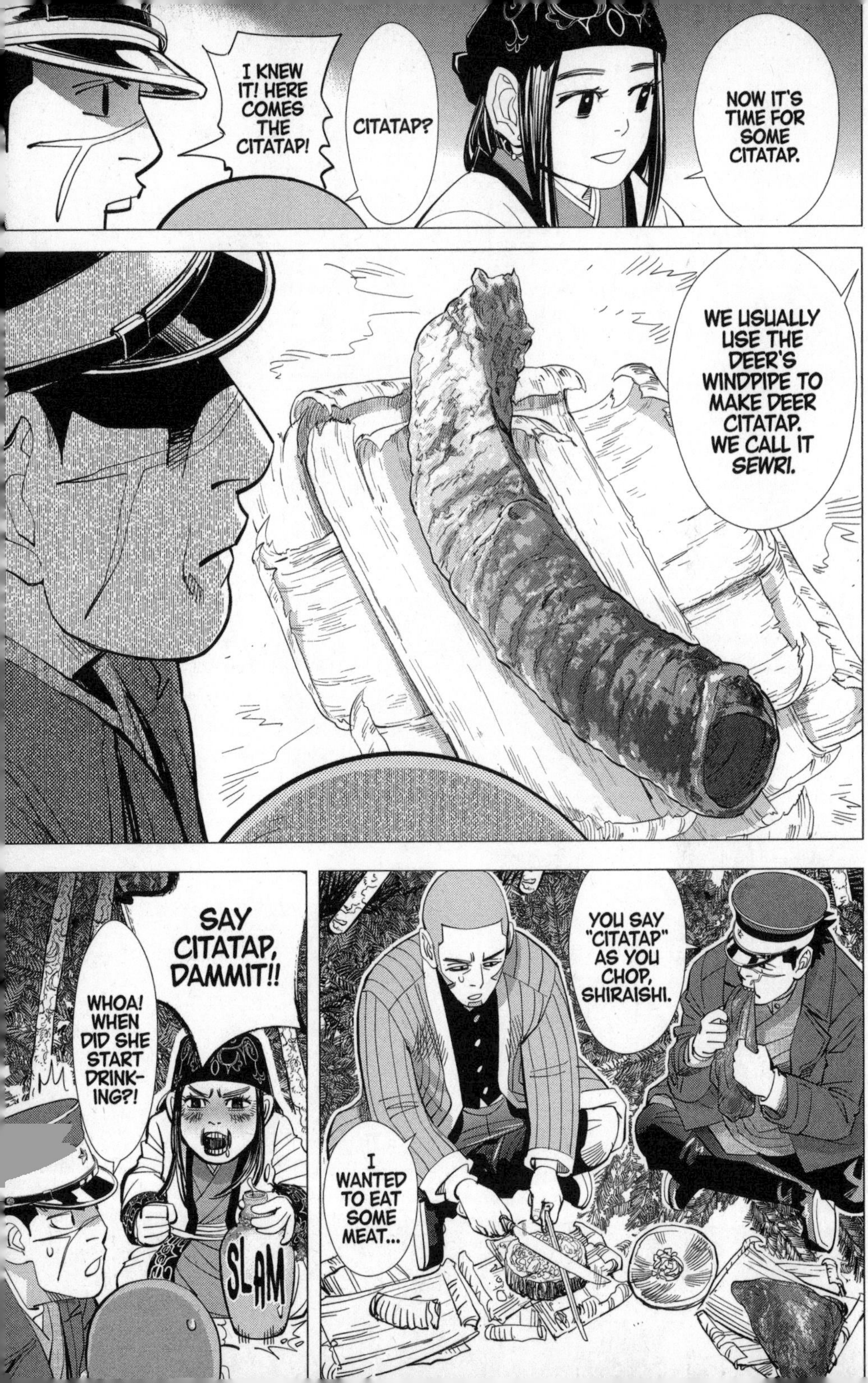
NOW IT'S TIME FOR SOME CITATAP.
CITATAP?
I KNEW IT! HERE COMES THE CITATAP!
WE USUALLY USE THE DEER'S WINDPIPE TO MAKE DEER CITATAP. WE CALL IT SEWRI.
YOU SAY "CITATAP" AS YOU CHOP, SHIRAISHI.
I WANTED TO EAT SOME MEAT...
SAY CITATAP, DAMMIT!!
WHOA! WHEN DID SHE START DRINKING?!
SLAM

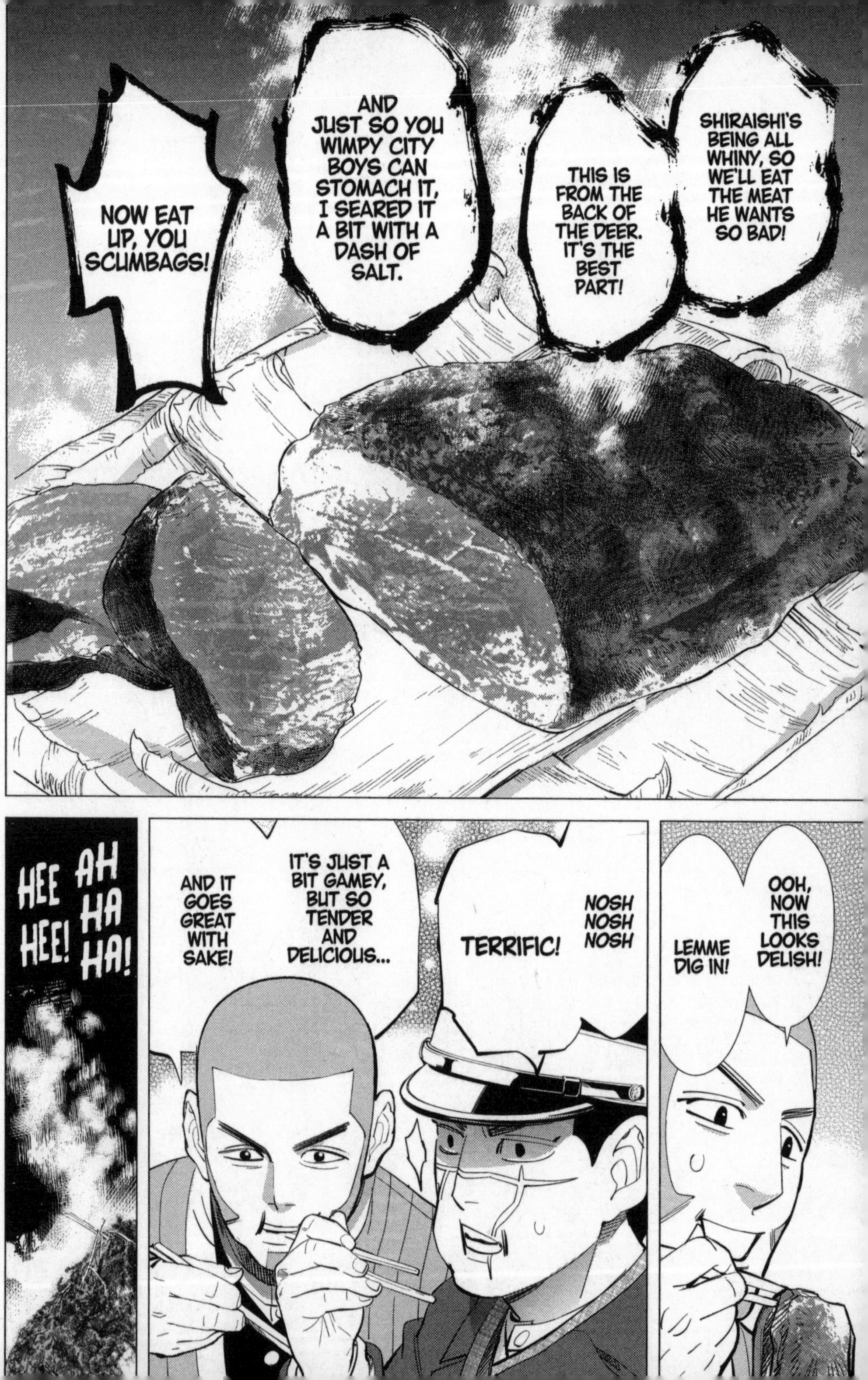
SHIRAISHI'S BEING ALL WHINY, SO WE'LL EAT THE MEAT HE WANTS SO BAD!
THIS IS FROM THE BACK OF THE DEER. IT'S THE BEST PART!
AND JUST SO YOU WIMPY CITY BOYS CAN STOMACH IT, I SEARED IT A BIT WITH A DASH OF SALT.
NOW EAT UP, YOU SCUMBAGS!
OOH, NOW THIS LOOKS DELISH!
LEMME DIG IN!
NOSH NOSH NOSH
TERRIFIC!
IT'S JUST A BIT GAMEY, BUT SO TENDER AND DELICIOUS...
AND IT GOES GREAT WITH SAKE!
AH HA HA!
HEE HEE!

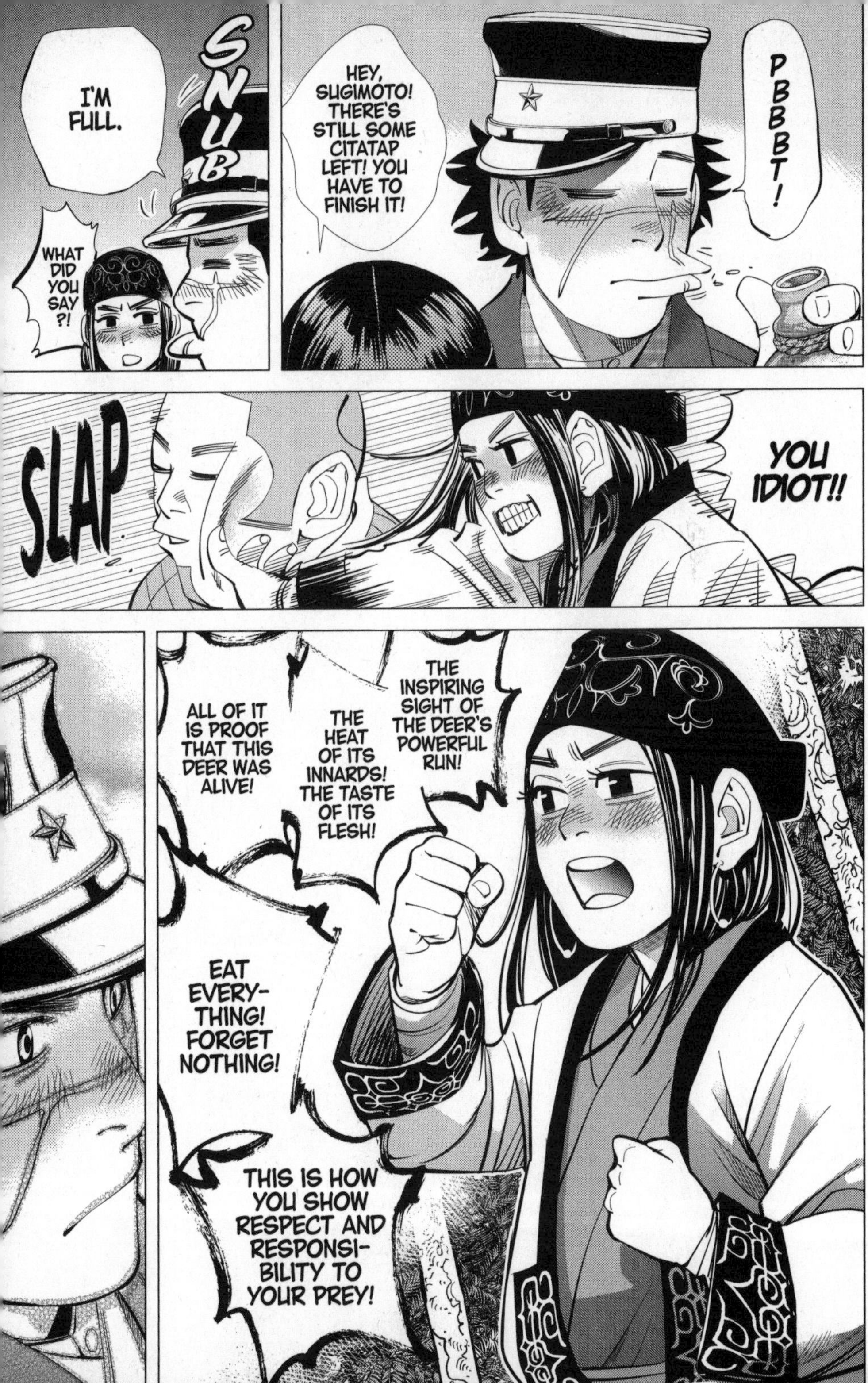
PBBBT!
HEY, SUGIMOTO! THERE'S STILL SOME CITATAP LEFT! YOU HAVE TO FINISH IT!
SNUB
I'M FULL.
WHAT DID YOU SAY?!
YOU IDIOT!!
SLAP
THE INSPIRING SIGHT OF THE DEER'S POWERFUL RUN!
THE HEAT OF ITS INNARDS! THE TASTE OF ITS FLESH!
ALL OF IT IS PROOF THAT THIS DEER WAS ALIVE!
EAT EVERY-THING! FORGET NOTHING!
THIS IS HOW YOU SHOW RESPECT AND RESPONSI-BILITY TO YOUR PREY!

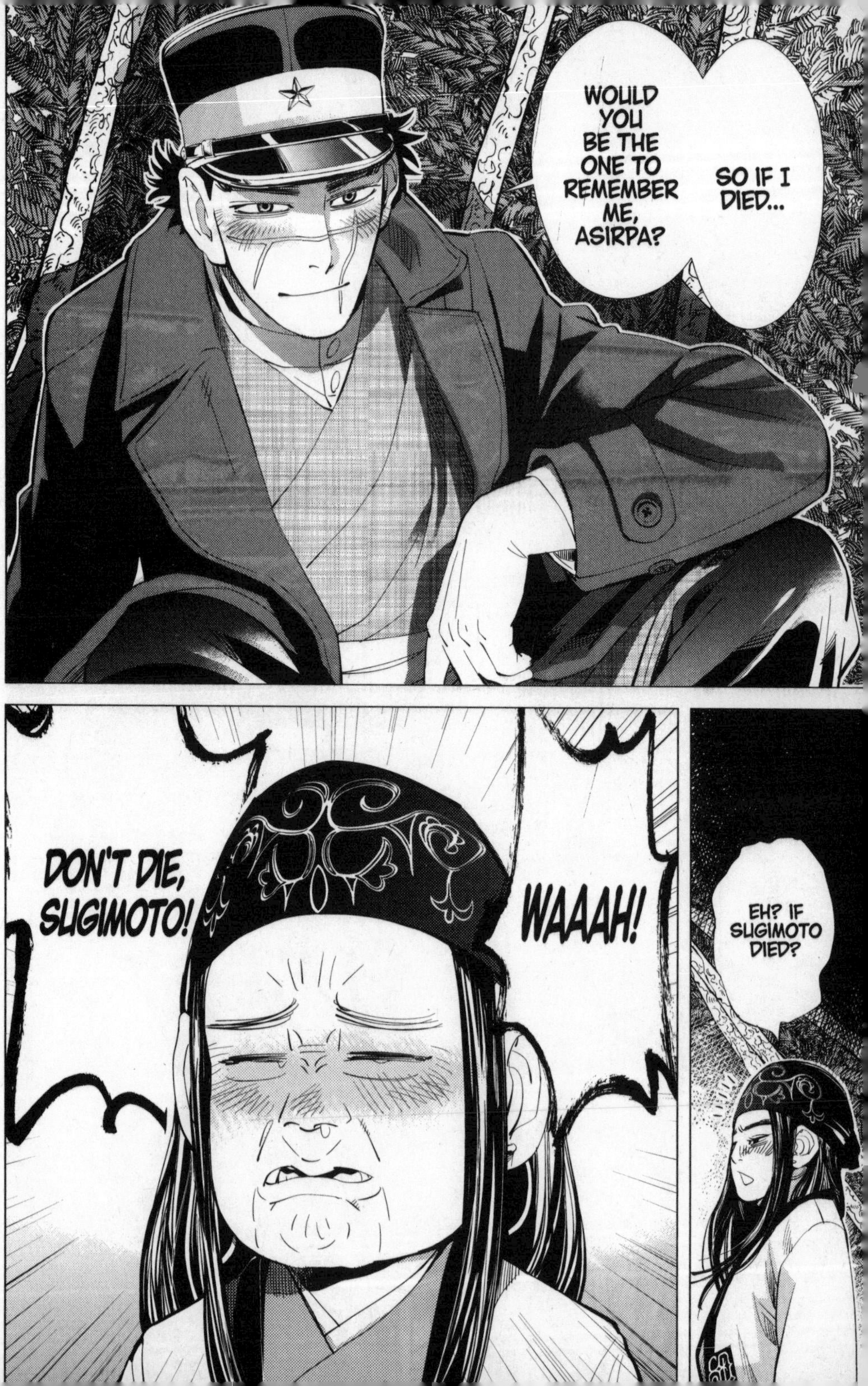
SO IF I DIED...
WOULD YOU BE THE ONE TO REMEMBER ME, ASIRPA?
EH? IF SUGIMOTO DIED?
WAAAH!
DON'T DIE, SUGIMOTO!

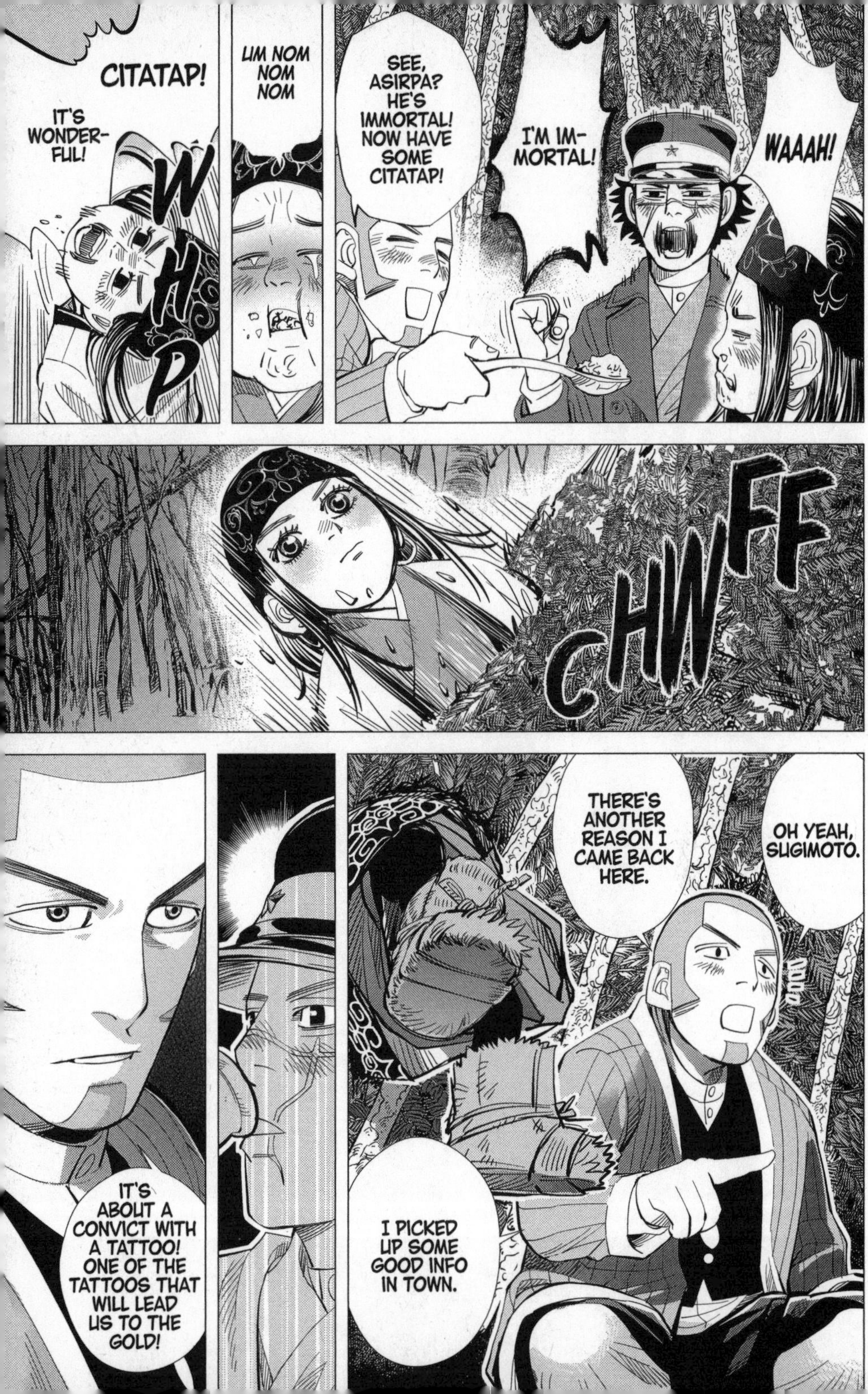
WAAAH!
I'M IM-MORTAL!
SEE, ASIRPA? HE'S IMMORTAL! NOW HAVE SOME CITATAP!
UM NOM NOM NOM
CITATAP!
IT'S WONDER-FUL!
WHP
CHWFF
OH YEAH, SUGIMOTO.
THERE'S ANOTHER REASON I CAME BACK HERE.
I PICKED UP SOME GOOD INFO IN TOWN.
IT'S ABOUT A CONVICT WITH A TATTOO! ONE OF THE TATTOOS THAT WILL LEAD US TO THE GOLD!

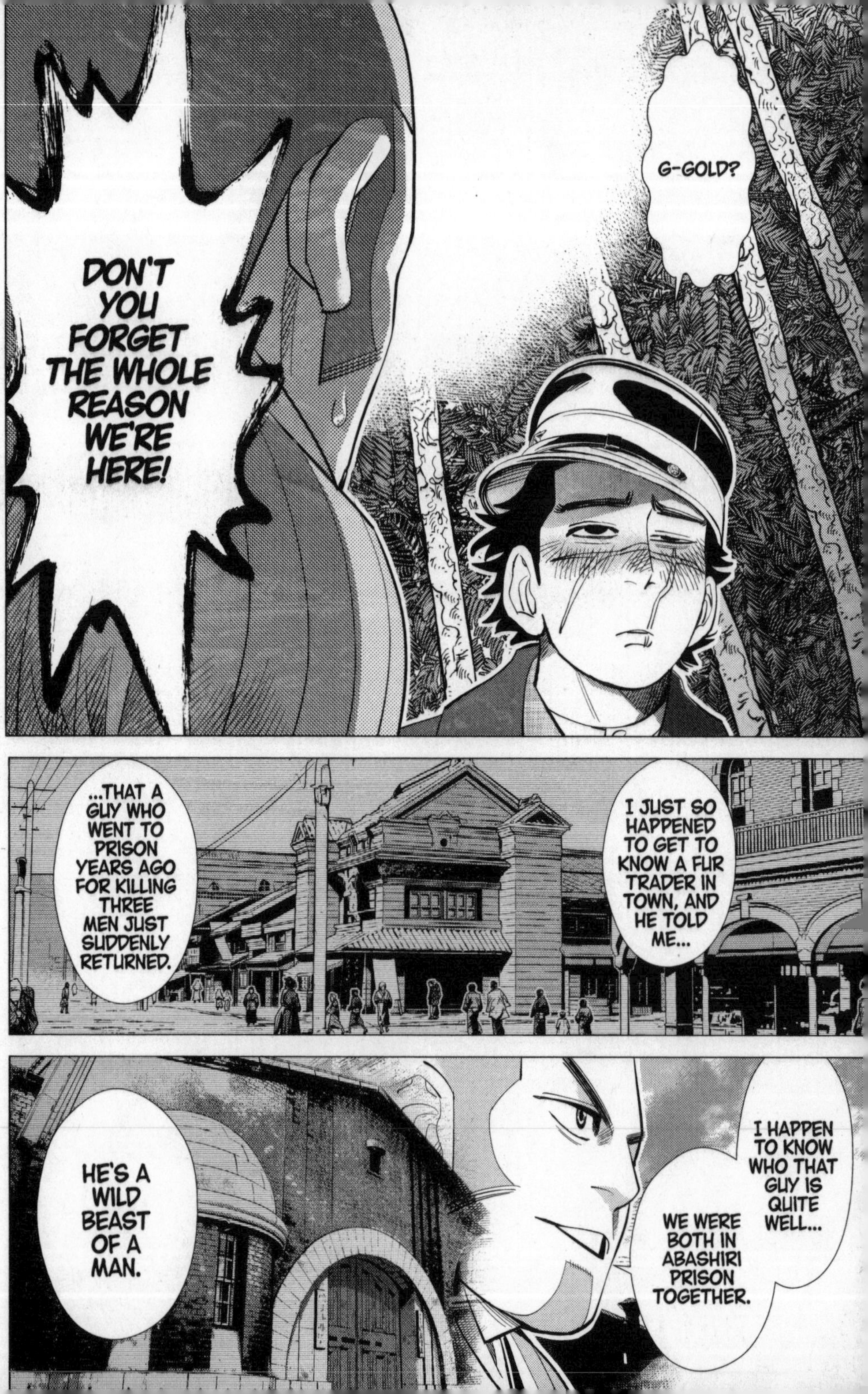
G-GOLD?
DON'T YOU FORGET THE WHOLE REASON WE'RE HERE!
I JUST SO HAPPENED TO GET TO KNOW A FUR TRADER IN TOWN, AND HE TOLD ME...
...THAT A GUY WHO WENT TO PRISON YEARS AGO FOR KILLING THREE MEN JUST SUDDENLY RETURNED.
I HAPPEN TO KNOW WHO THAT GUY IS QUITE WELL...
WE WERE BOTH IN ABASHIRI PRISON TOGETHER.
HE'S A WILD BEAST OF A MAN.

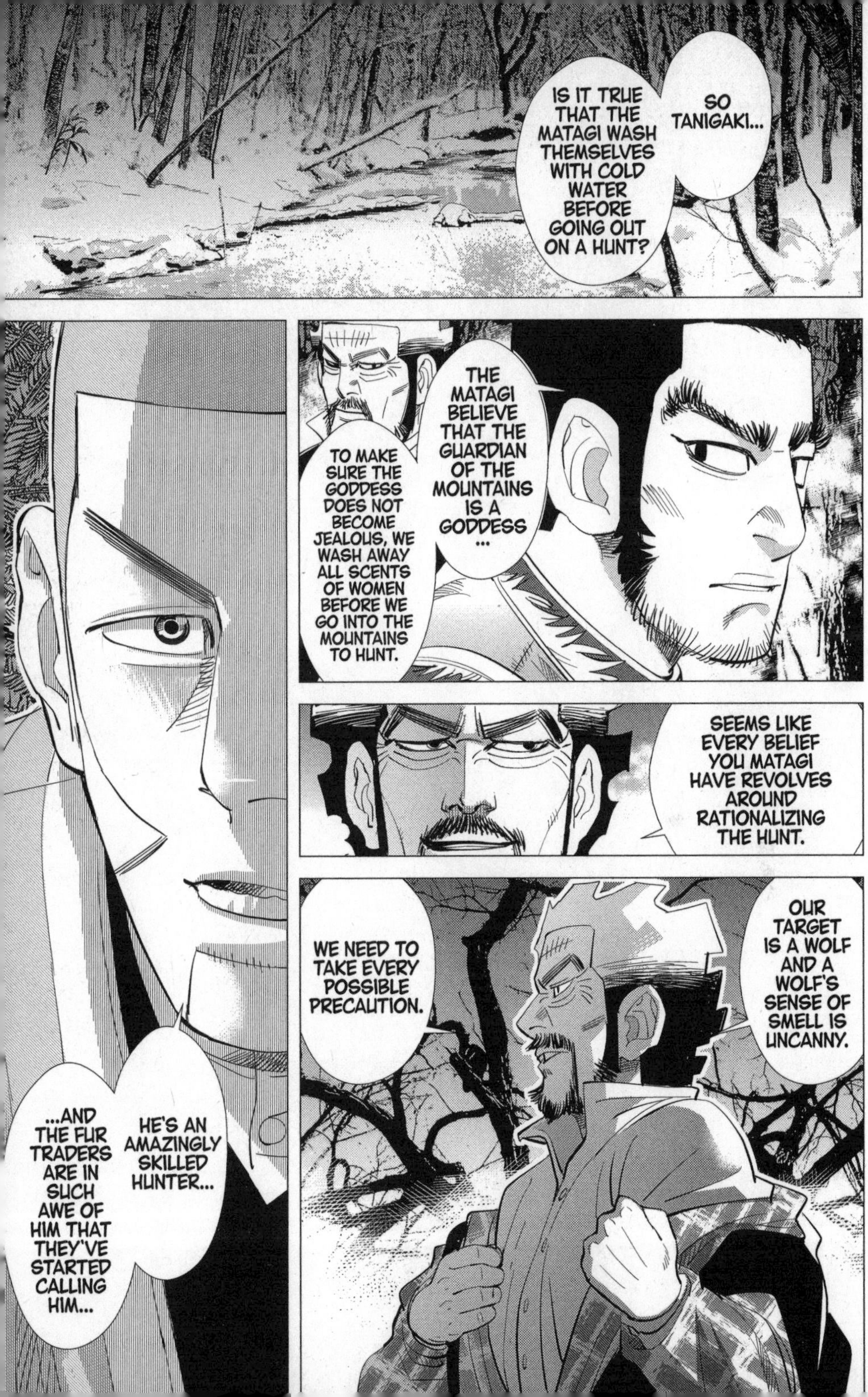
SO TANIGAKI...
IS IT TRUE THAT THE MATAGI WASH THEMSELVES WITH COLD WATER BEFORE GOING OUT ON A HUNT?
THE MATAGI BELIEVE THAT THE GUARDIAN OF THE MOUNTAINS IS A GODDESS...
TO MAKE SURE THE GODDESS DOES NOT BECOME JEALOUS, WE WASH AWAY ALL SCENTS OF WOMEN BEFORE WE GO INTO THE MOUNTAINS TO HUNT.
SEEMS LIKE EVERY BELIEF YOU MATAGI HAVE REVOLVES AROUND RATIONALIZING THE HUNT.
OUR TARGET IS A WOLF AND A WOLF'S SENSE OF SMELL IS UNCANNY.
WE NEED TO TAKE EVERY POSSIBLE PRECAUTION.
HE'S AN AMAZINGLY SKILLED HUNTER...
...AND THE FUR TRADERS ARE IN SUCH AWE OF HIM THAT THEY'VE STARTED CALLING HIM...

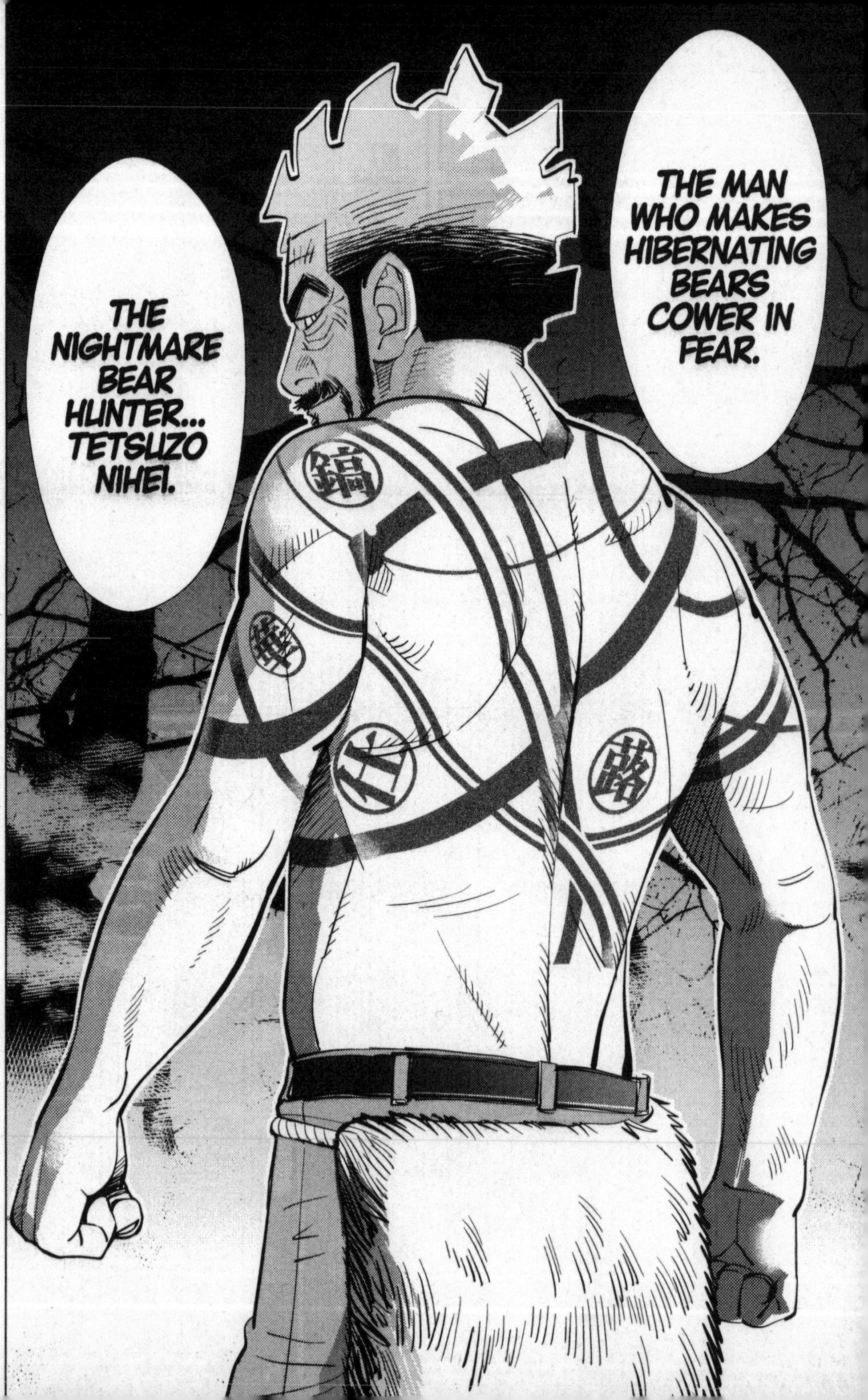
THE MAN WHO MAKES HIBERNATING BEARS COWER IN FEAR.
THE NIGHTMARE BEAR HUNTER... TETSUZO NIHEI.

Chapter 26: The Law of the Mountain

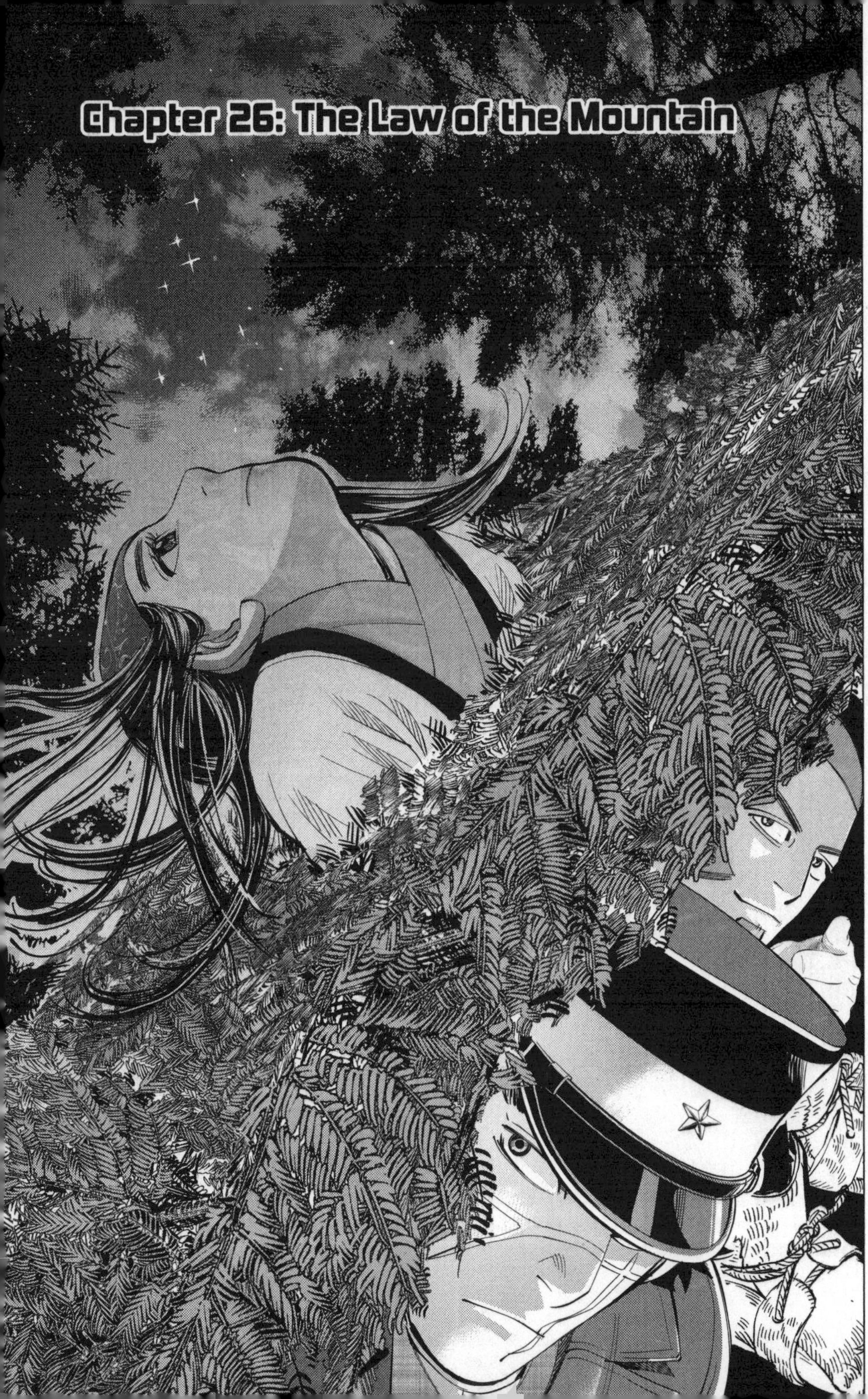

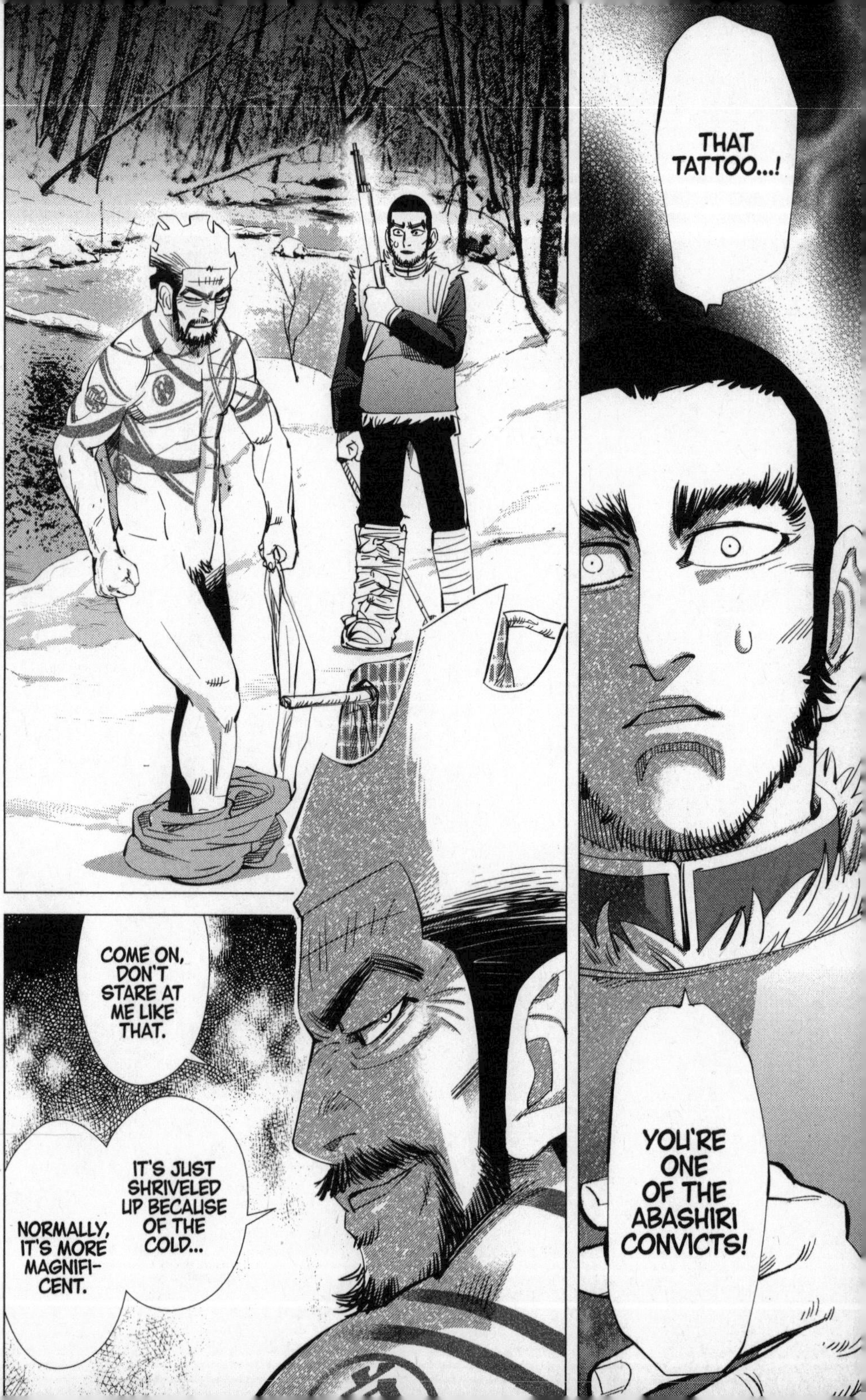
THAT TATTOO...!
YOU'RE ONE OF THE ABASHIRI CONVICTS!
COME ON, DON'T STARE AT ME LIKE THAT.
IT'S JUST SHRIVELED UP BECAUSE OF THE COLD...
NORMALLY, IT'S MORE MAGNIFI-CENT.

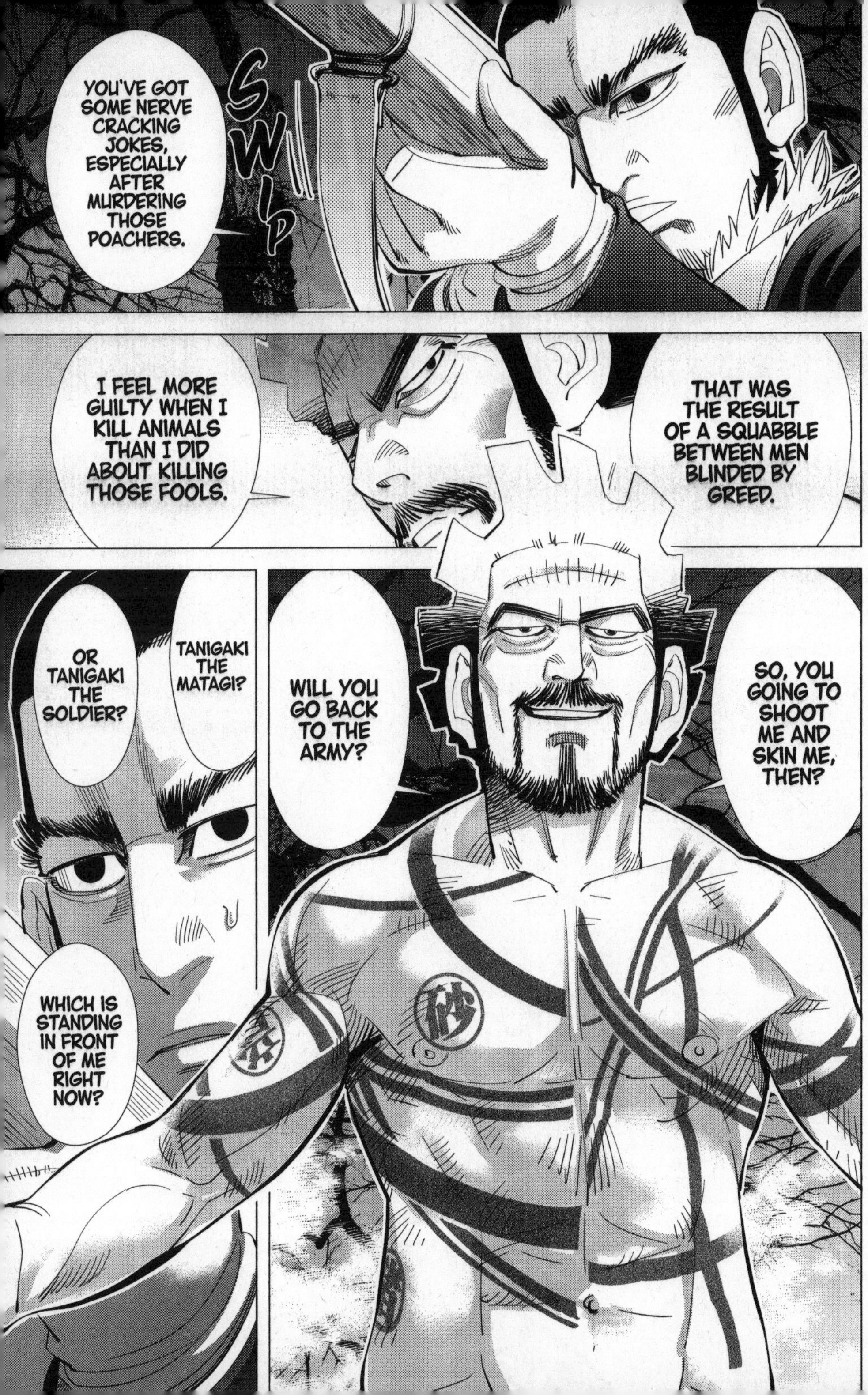
SWIP
YOU'VE GOT SOME NERVE CRACKING JOKES, ESPECIALLY AFTER MURDERING THOSE POACHERS.
THAT WAS THE RESULT OF A SQUABBLE BETWEEN MEN BLINDED BY GREED.
I FEEL MORE GUILTY WHEN I KILL ANIMALS THAN I DID ABOUT KILLING THOSE FOOLS.
SO, YOU GOING TO SHOOT ME AND SKIN ME, THEN?
WILL YOU GO BACK TO THE ARMY?
TANIGAKI THE MATAGI?
OR TANIGAKI THE SOLDIER?
WHICH IS STANDING IN FRONT OF ME RIGHT NOW?

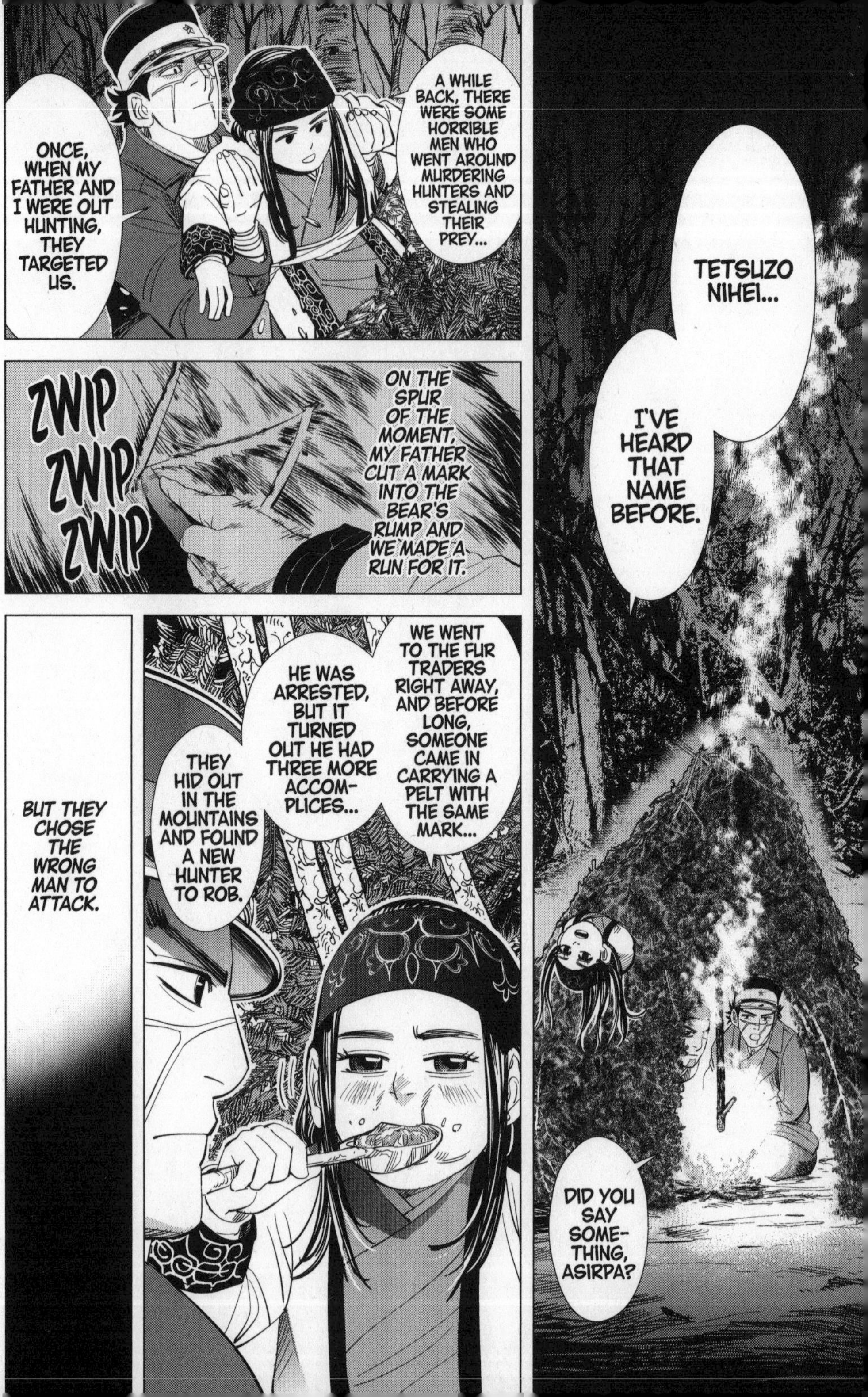
TETSUZO NIHEI...
I'VE HEARD THAT NAME BEFORE.
DID YOU SAY SOME-THING, ASIRPA?
A WHILE BACK, THERE WERE SOME HORRIBLE MEN WHO WENT AROUND MURDERING HUNTERS AND STEALING THEIR PREY...
ONCE, WHEN MY FATHER AND I WERE OUT HUNTING, THEY TARGETED US.
ON THE SPUR OF THE MOMENT, MY FATHER CUT A MARK INTO THE BEAR'S RUMP AND WE MADE A RUN FOR IT.
ZWIP ZWIP ZWIP
WE WENT TO THE FUR TRADERS RIGHT AWAY, AND BEFORE LONG, SOMEONE CAME IN CARRYING A PELT WITH THE SAME MARK...
HE WAS ARRESTED, BUT IT TURNED OUT HE HAD THREE MORE ACCOM-PLICES...
THEY HID OUT IN THE MOUNTAINS AND FOUND A NEW HUNTER TO ROB.
BUT THEY CHOSE THE WRONG MAN TO ATTACK.

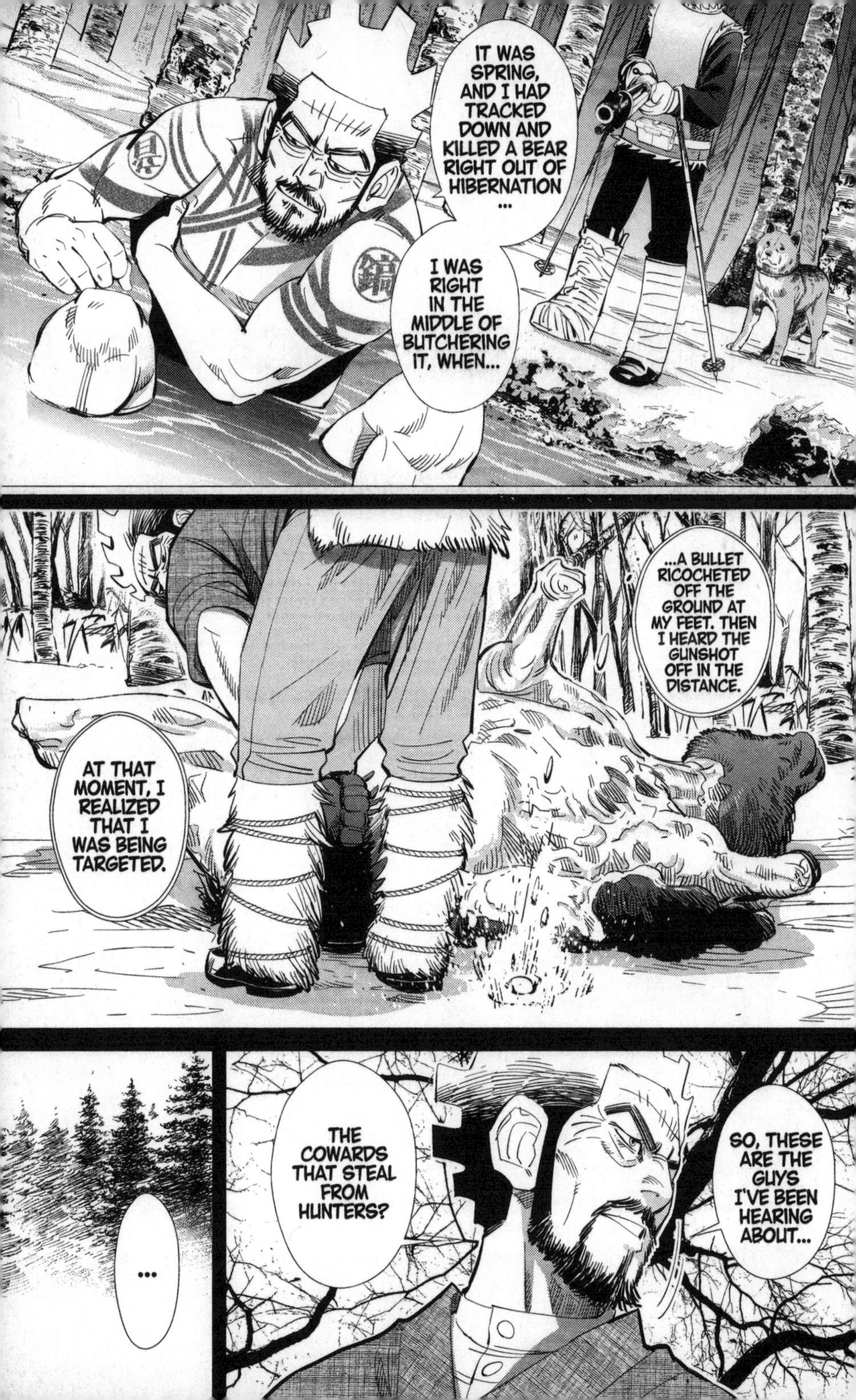
IT WAS SPRING, AND I HAD TRACKED DOWN AND KILLED A BEAR RIGHT OUT OF HIBERNATION...
I WAS RIGHT IN THE MIDDLE OF BUTCHERING IT, WHEN...
...A BULLET RICOCHETED OFF THE GROUND AT MY FEET. THEN I HEARD THE GUNSHOT OFF IN THE DISTANCE.
AT THAT MOMENT, I REALIZED THAT I WAS BEING TARGETED.
SO, THESE ARE THE GUYS I'VE BEEN HEARING ABOUT...
THE COWARDS THAT STEAL FROM HUNTERS?
...

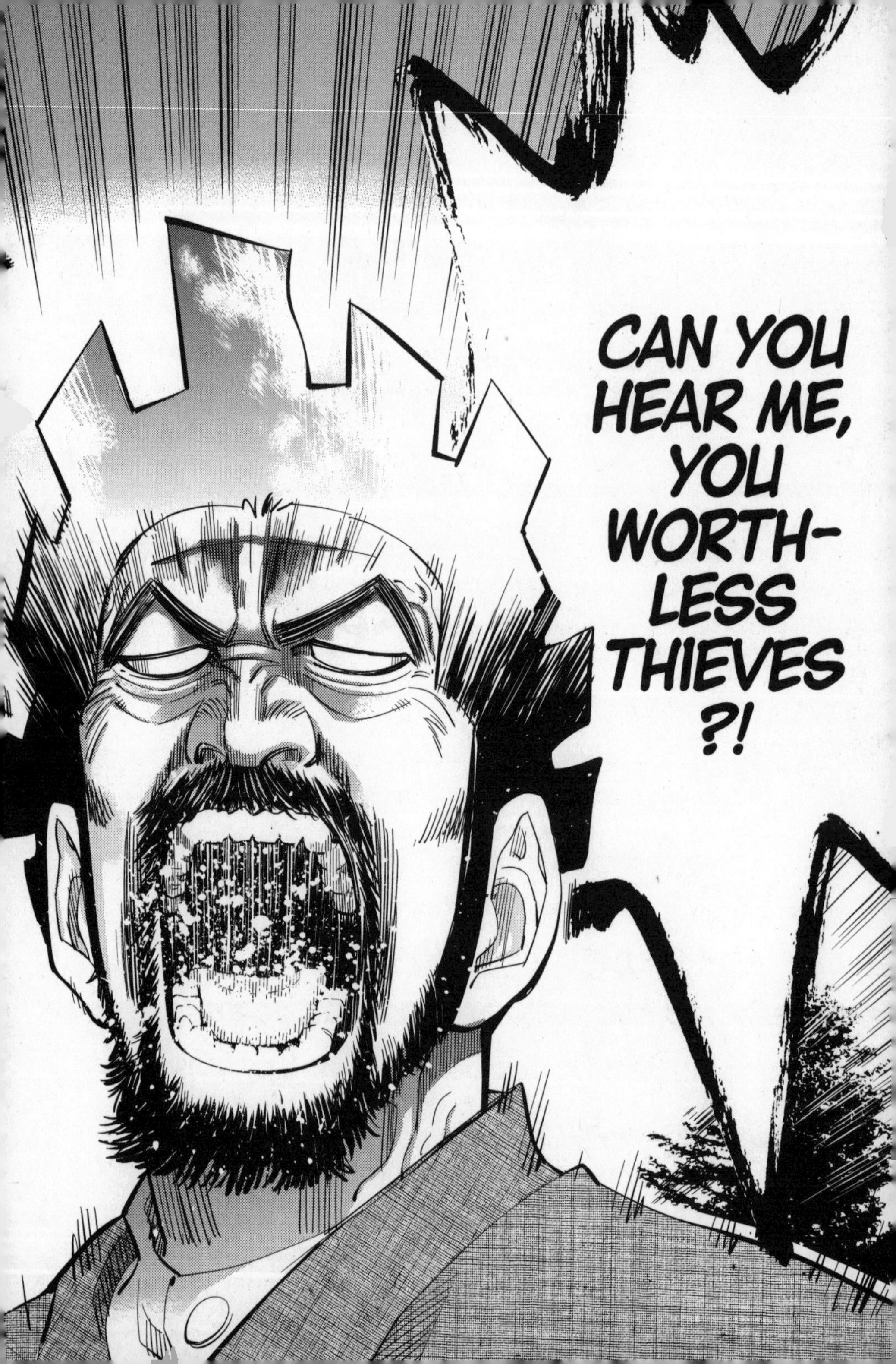
CAN YOU HEAR ME, YOU WORTH-LESS THIEVES ?!

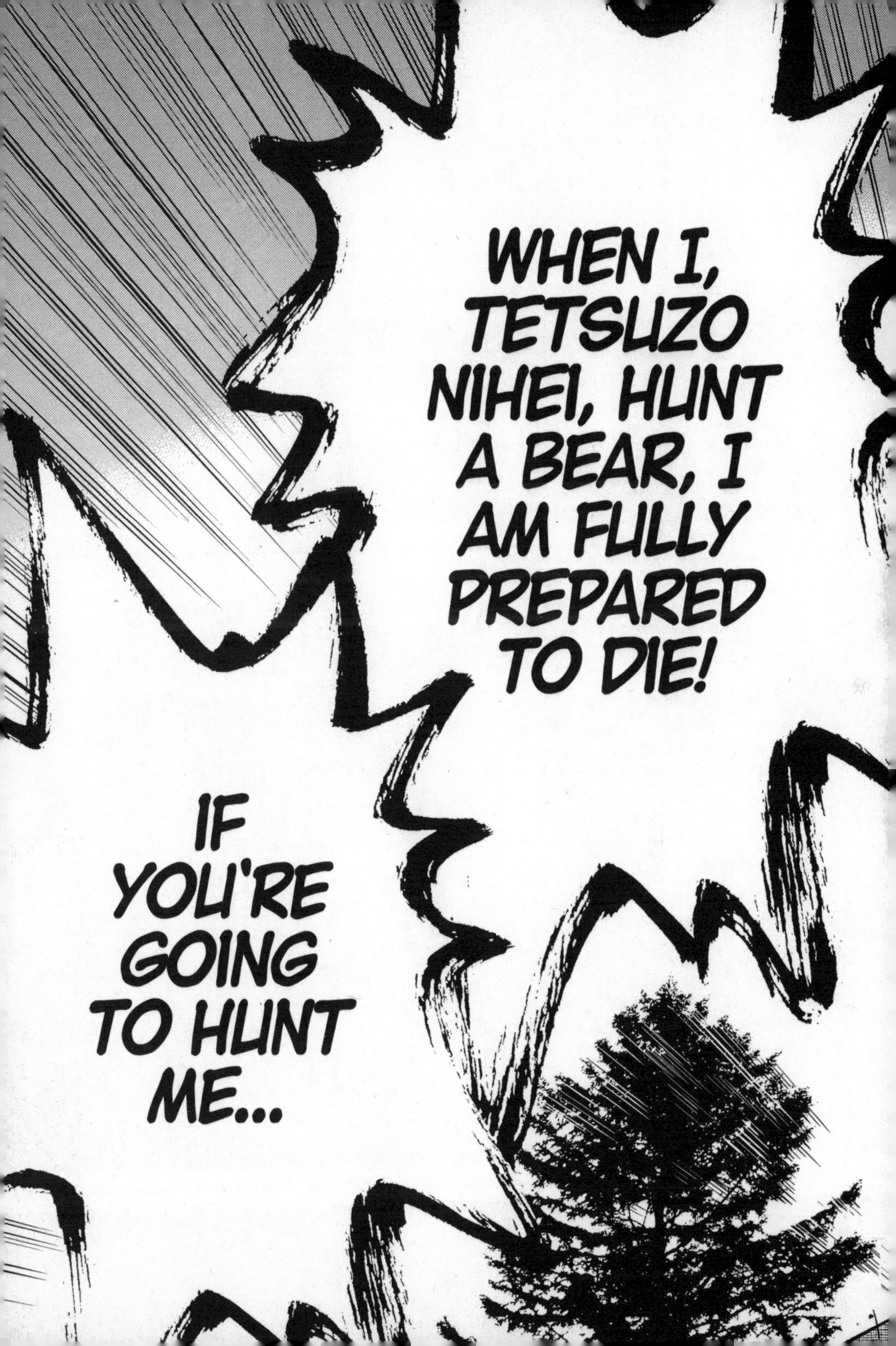
WHEN I, TETSUZO NIHEI, HUNT A BEAR, I AM FULLY PREPARED TO DIE!
IF YOU'RE GOING TO HUNT ME...

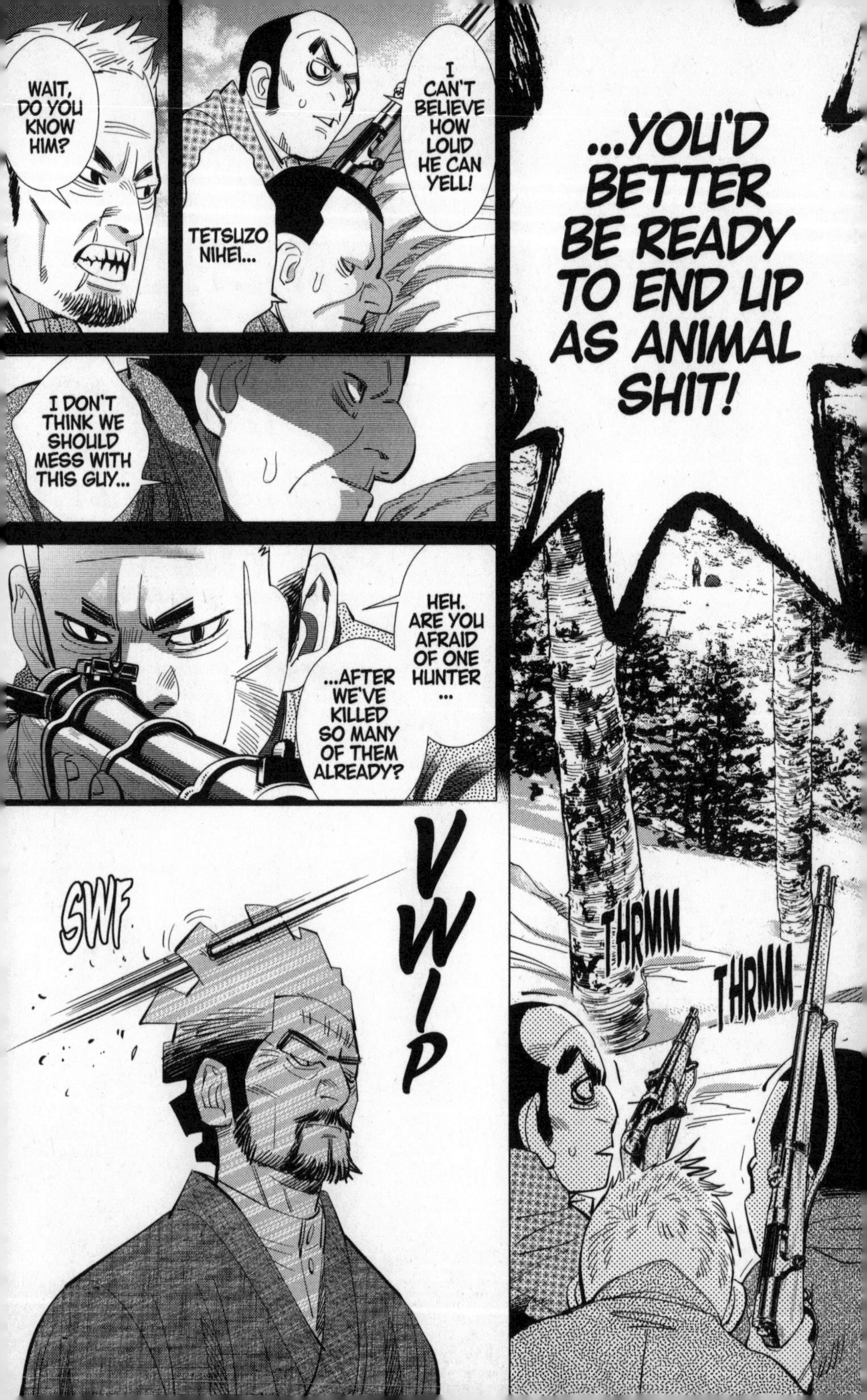
...YOU'D BETTER BE READY TO END UP AS ANIMAL SHIT!
THRMM
THRMM
I CAN'T BELIEVE HOW LOUD HE CAN YELL!
TETSUZO NIHEI...
WAIT, DO YOU KNOW HIM?
I DON'T THINK WE SHOULD MESS WITH THIS GUY...
HEH. ARE YOU AFRAID OF ONE HUNTER ...
...AFTER WE'VE KILLED SO MANY OF THEM ALREADY?
VWIP
SWF

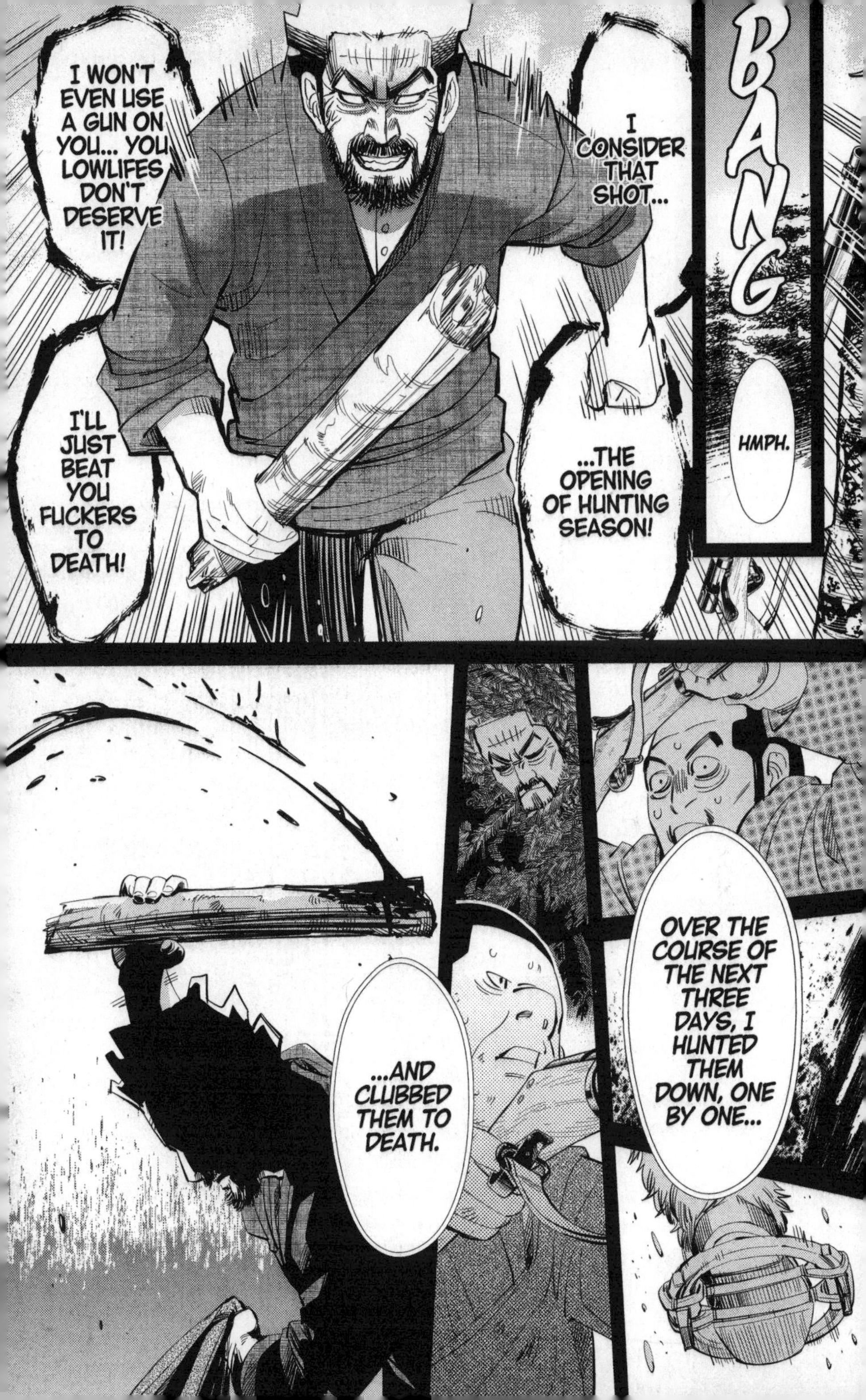
BANG
HMPH.
I CONSIDER THAT SHOT...
...THE OPENING OF HUNTING SEASON!
I WON'T EVEN USE A GUN ON YOU... YOU LOWLIFES DON'T DESERVE IT!
I'LL JUST BEAT YOU FUCKERS TO DEATH!
OVER THE COURSE OF THE NEXT THREE DAYS, I HUNTED THEM DOWN, ONE BY ONE...
...AND CLUBBED THEM TO DEATH.

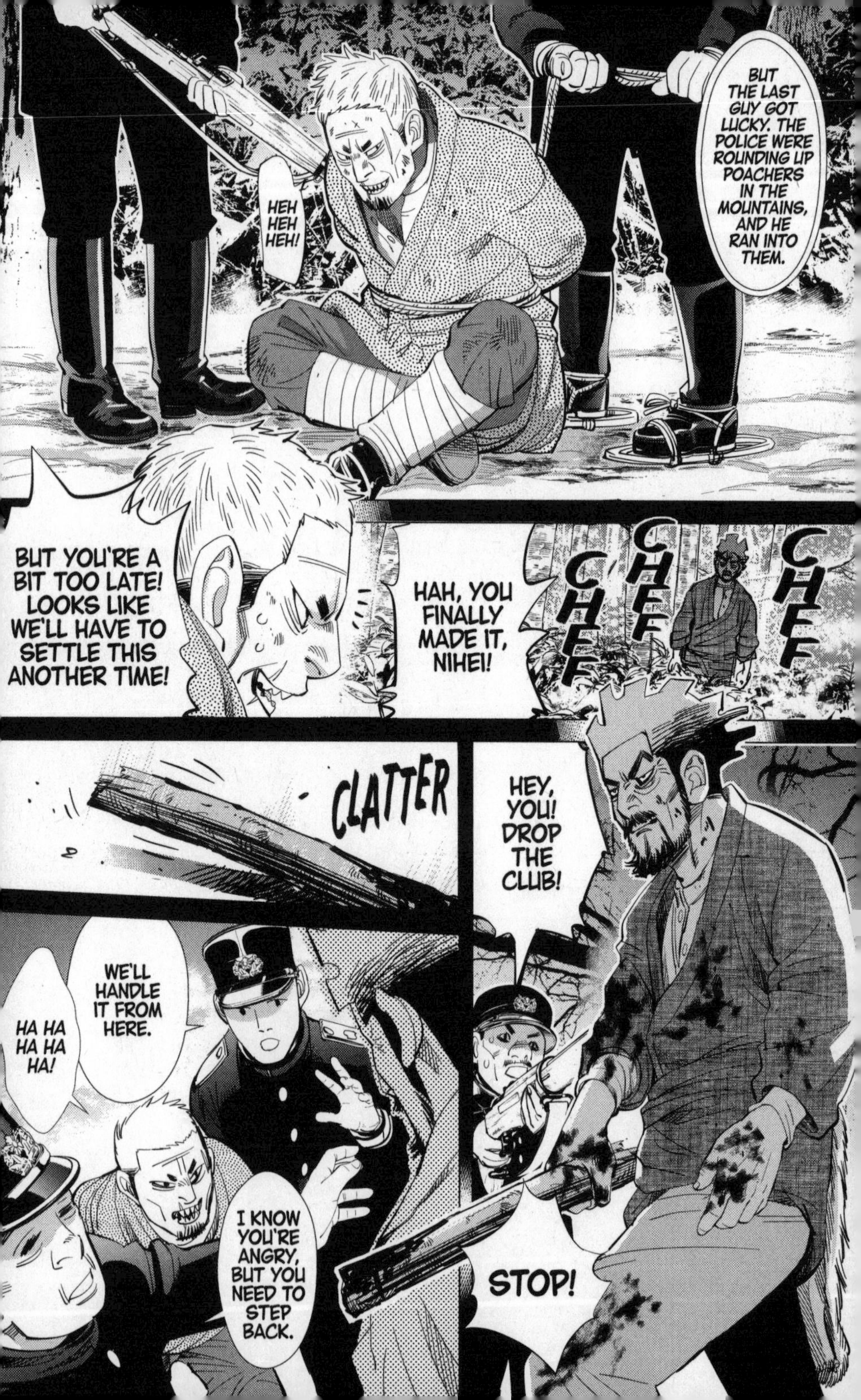
BUT THE LAST GUY GOT LUCKY. THE POLICE WERE ROUNDING UP POACHERS IN THE MOUNTAINS, AND HE RAN INTO THEM.
HEH HEH HEH!
CHEF CHEF CHEF
HAH, YOU FINALLY MADE IT, NIHEI!
BUT YOU'RE A BIT TOO LATE! LOOKS LIKE WE'LL HAVE TO SETTLE THIS ANOTHER TIME!
HEY, YOU! DROP THE CLUB!
STOP!
CLATTER
WE'LL HANDLE IT FROM HERE.
HA HA HA HA HA!
I KNOW YOU'RE ANGRY, BUT YOU NEED TO STEP BACK.

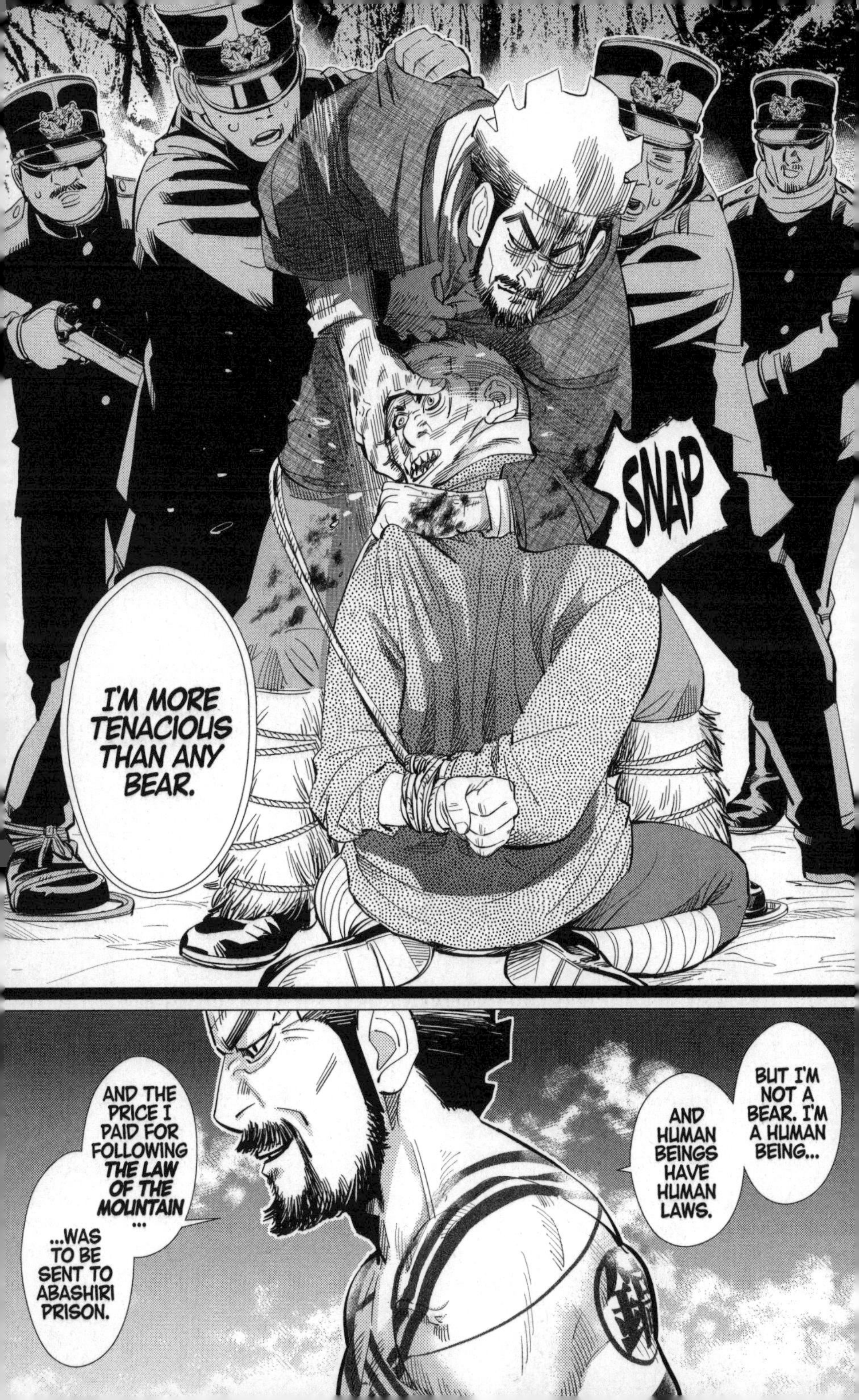
SNAP
I'M MORE TENACIOUS THAN ANY BEAR.
BUT I'M NOT A BEAR. I'M A HUMAN BEING...
AND HUMAN BEINGS HAVE HUMAN LAWS.
AND THE PRICE I PAID FOR FOLLOWING THE LAW OF THE MOUNTAIN...
...WAS TO BE SENT TO ABASHIRI PRISON.

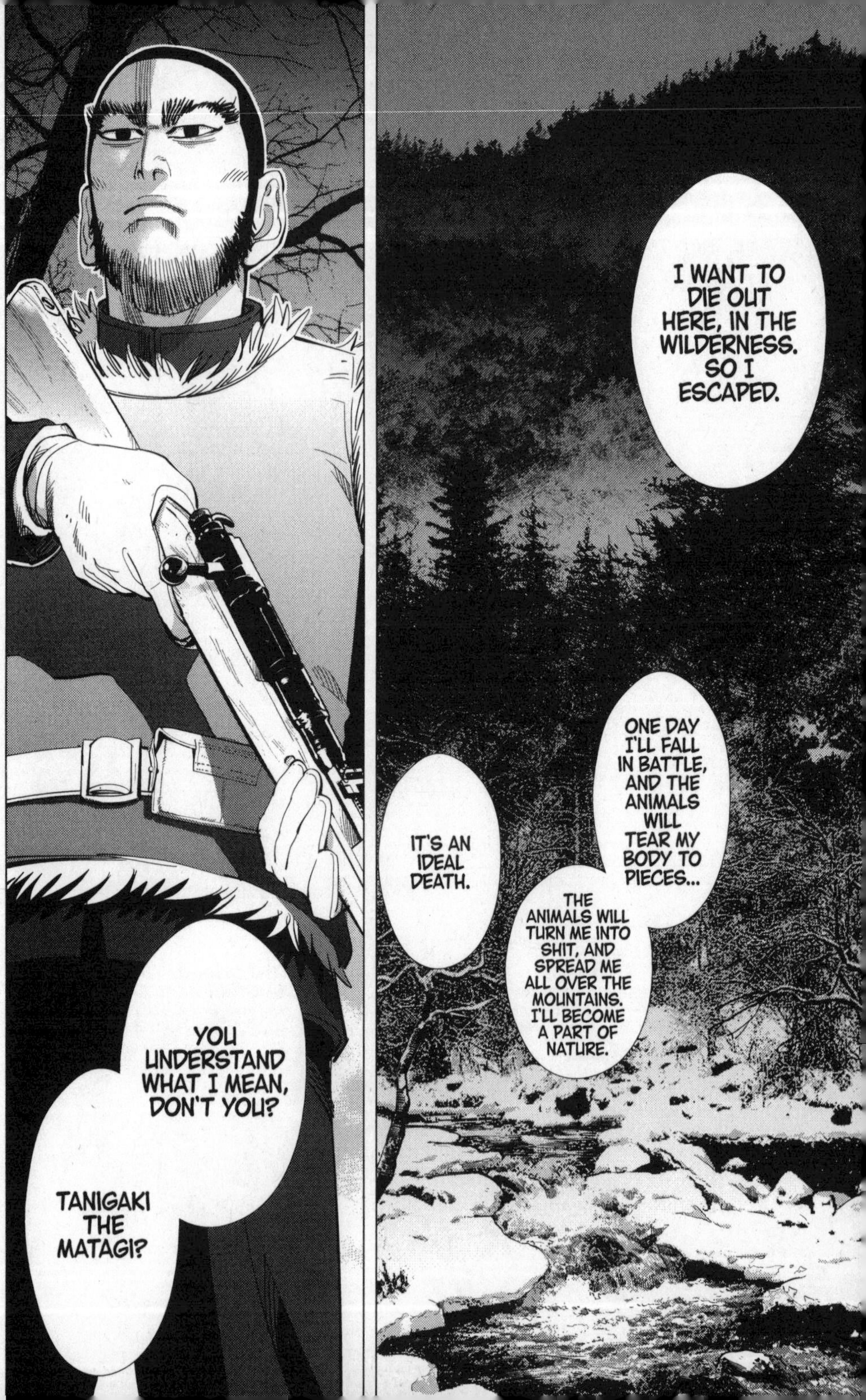
I WANT TO DIE OUT HERE, IN THE WILDERNESS. SO I ESCAPED.
ONE DAY I'LL FALL IN BATTLE, AND THE ANIMALS WILL TEAR MY BODY TO PIECES...
THE ANIMALS WILL TURN ME INTO SHIT, AND SPREAD ME ALL OVER THE MOUNTAINS. I'LL BECOME A PART OF NATURE.
IT'S AN IDEAL DEATH.
YOU UNDERSTAND WHAT I MEAN, DON'T YOU?
TANIGAKI THE MATAGI?

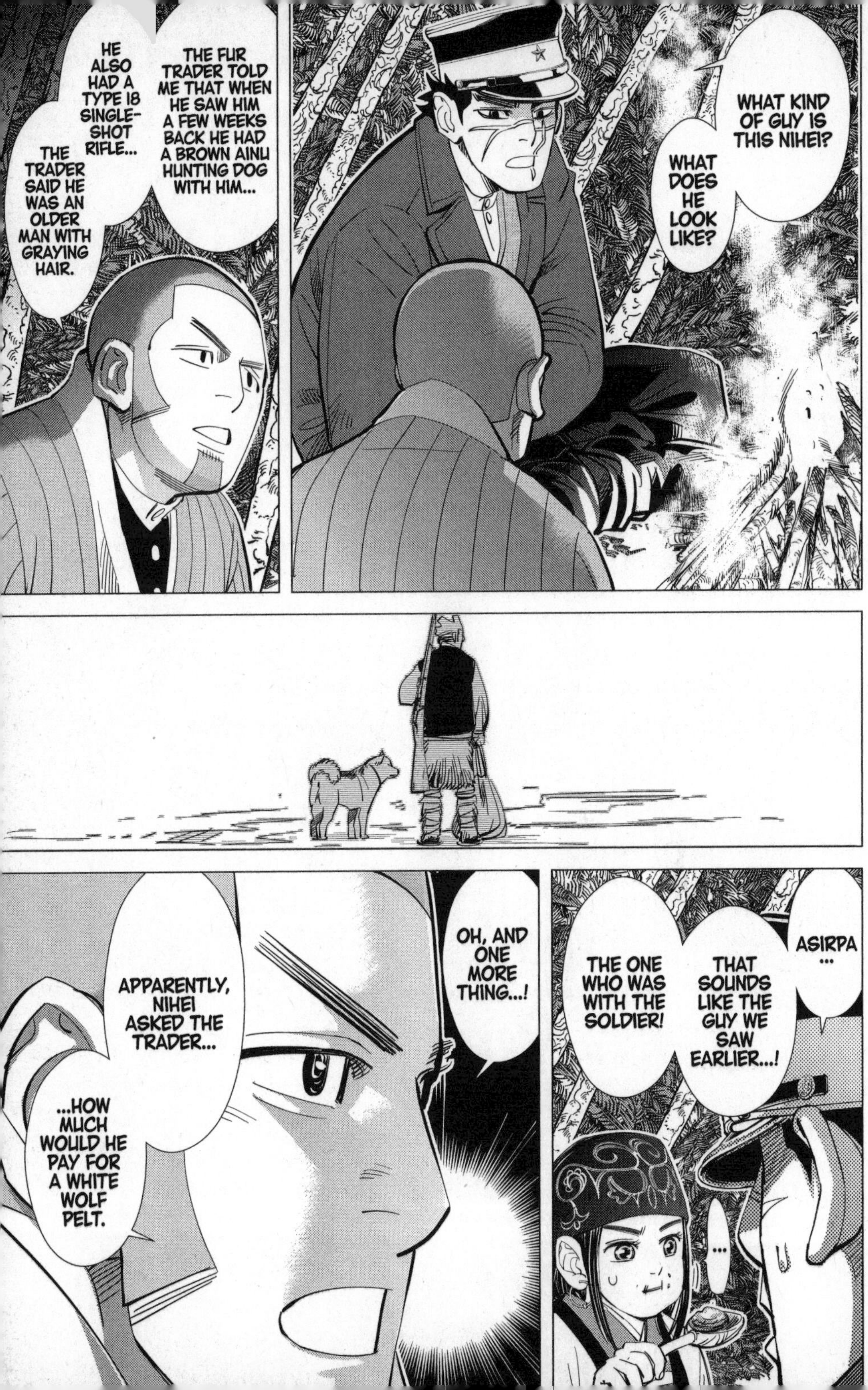
WHAT KIND OF GUY IS THIS NIHEI?
WHAT DOES HE LOOK LIKE?
THE FUR TRADER TOLD ME THAT WHEN HE SAW HIM A FEW WEEKS BACK HE HAD A BROWN AINU HUNTING DOG WITH HIM...
HE ALSO HAD A TYPE 18 SINGLE-SHOT RIFLE...
THE TRADER SAID HE WAS AN OLDER MAN WITH GRAYING HAIR.
ASIRPA ...
THAT SOUNDS LIKE THE GUY WE SAW EARLIER...!
THE ONE WHO WAS WITH THE SOLDIER!
...
OH, AND ONE MORE THING...!
APPARENTLY, NIHEI ASKED THE TRADER...
...HOW MUCH WOULD HE PAY FOR A WHITE WOLF PELT.

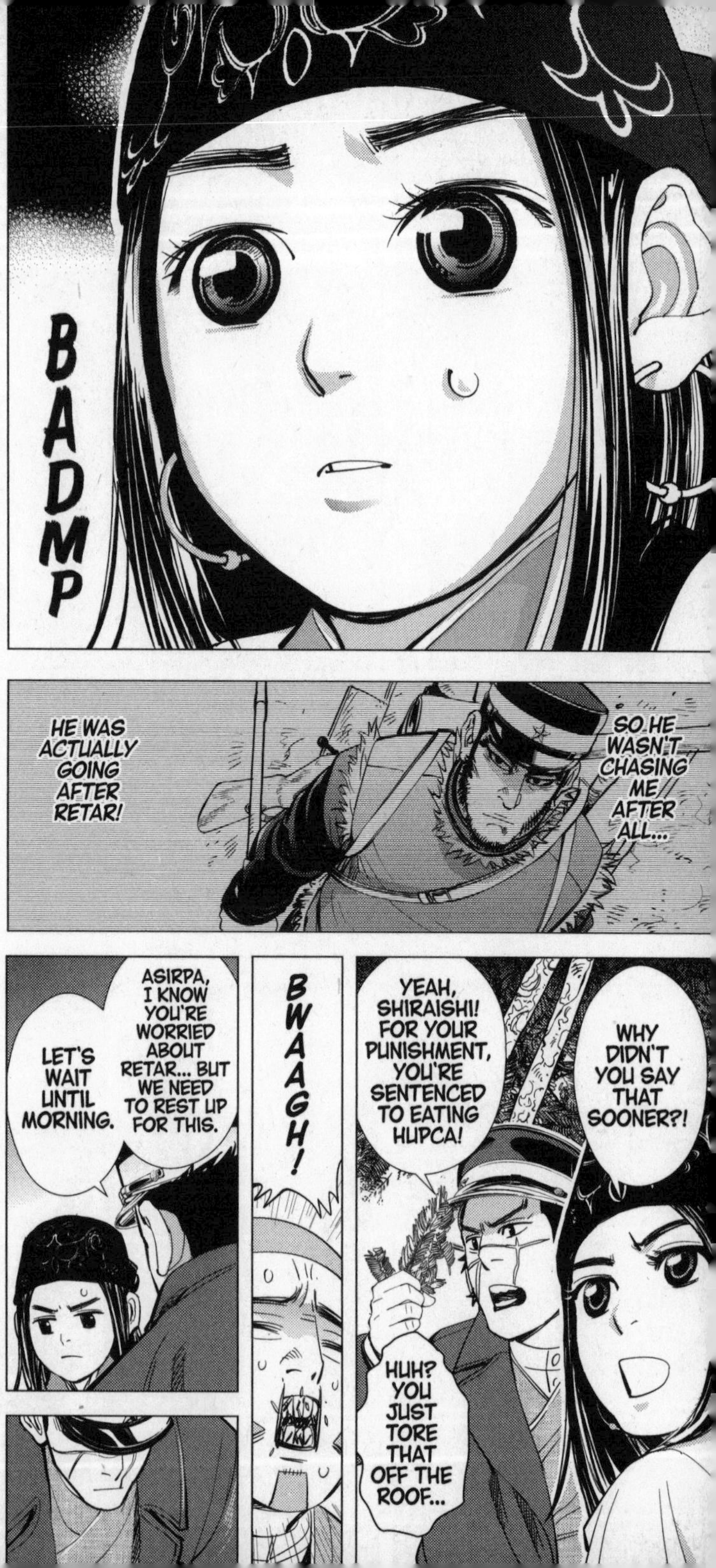
BADMP
SO HE WASN'T CHASING ME AFTER ALL...
HE WAS ACTUALLY GOING AFTER RETAR!
WHY DIDN'T YOU SAY THAT SOONER?!
YEAH, SHIRAISHI! FOR YOUR PUNISHMENT, YOU'RE SENTENCED TO EATING HUPCA!
HUH? YOU JUST TORE THAT OFF THE ROOF...
BWAAAGH!
ASIRPA, I KNOW YOU'RE WORRIED ABOUT RETAR... BUT WE NEED TO REST UP FOR THIS.
LET'S WAIT UNTIL MORNING.

THERE IT IS... ANOTHER CLUE TO THE GOLD...!

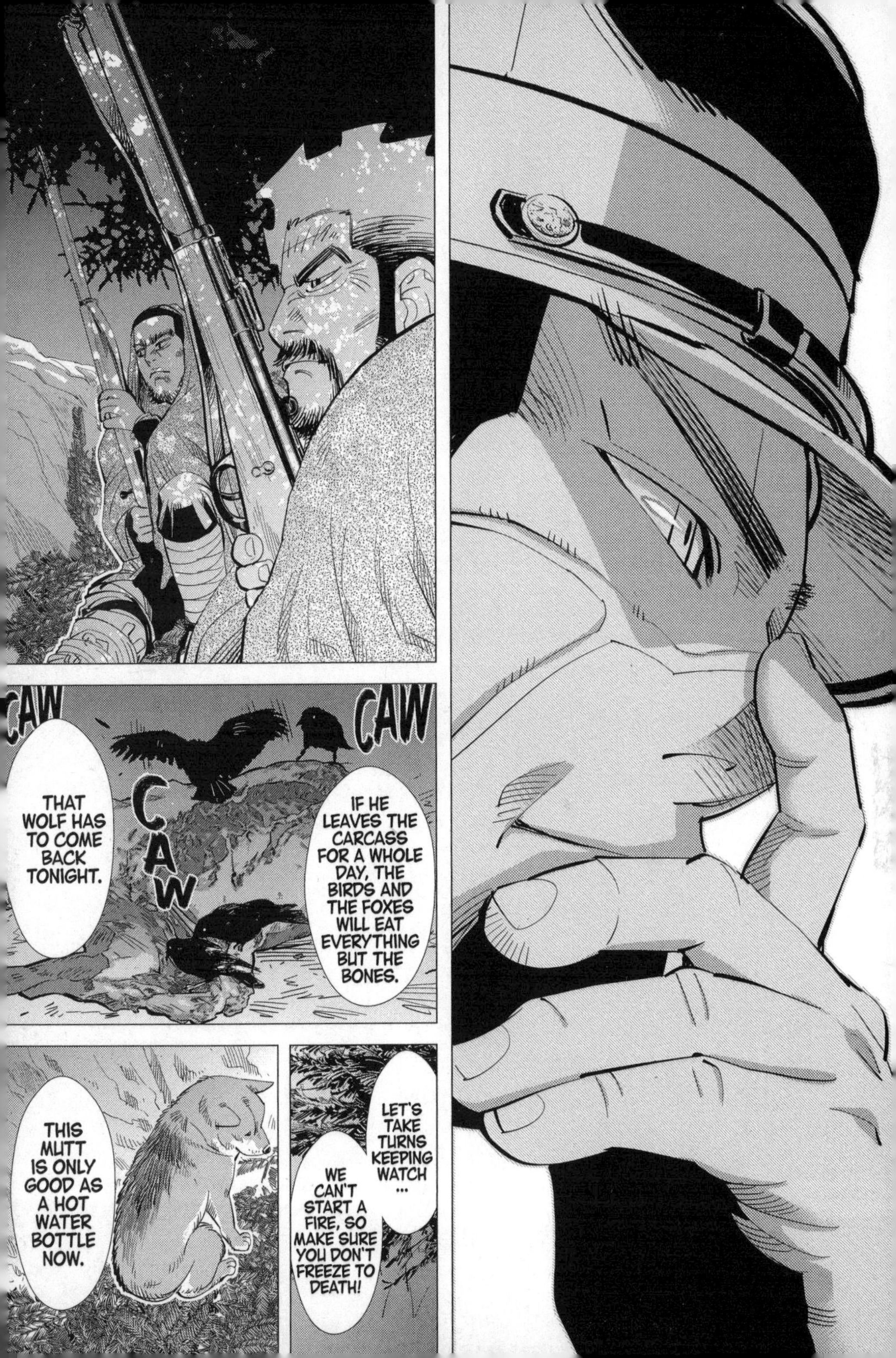
CAW
IF HE LEAVES THE CARCASS FOR A WHOLE DAY, THE BIRDS AND THE FOXES WILL EAT EVERYTHING BUT THE BONES.
CAW
CAW
THAT WOLF HAS TO COME BACK TONIGHT.
LET'S TAKE TURNS KEEPING WATCH ...
WE CAN'T START A FIRE, SO MAKE SURE YOU DON'T FREEZE TO DEATH!
THIS MUTT IS ONLY GOOD AS A HOT WATER BOTTLE NOW.

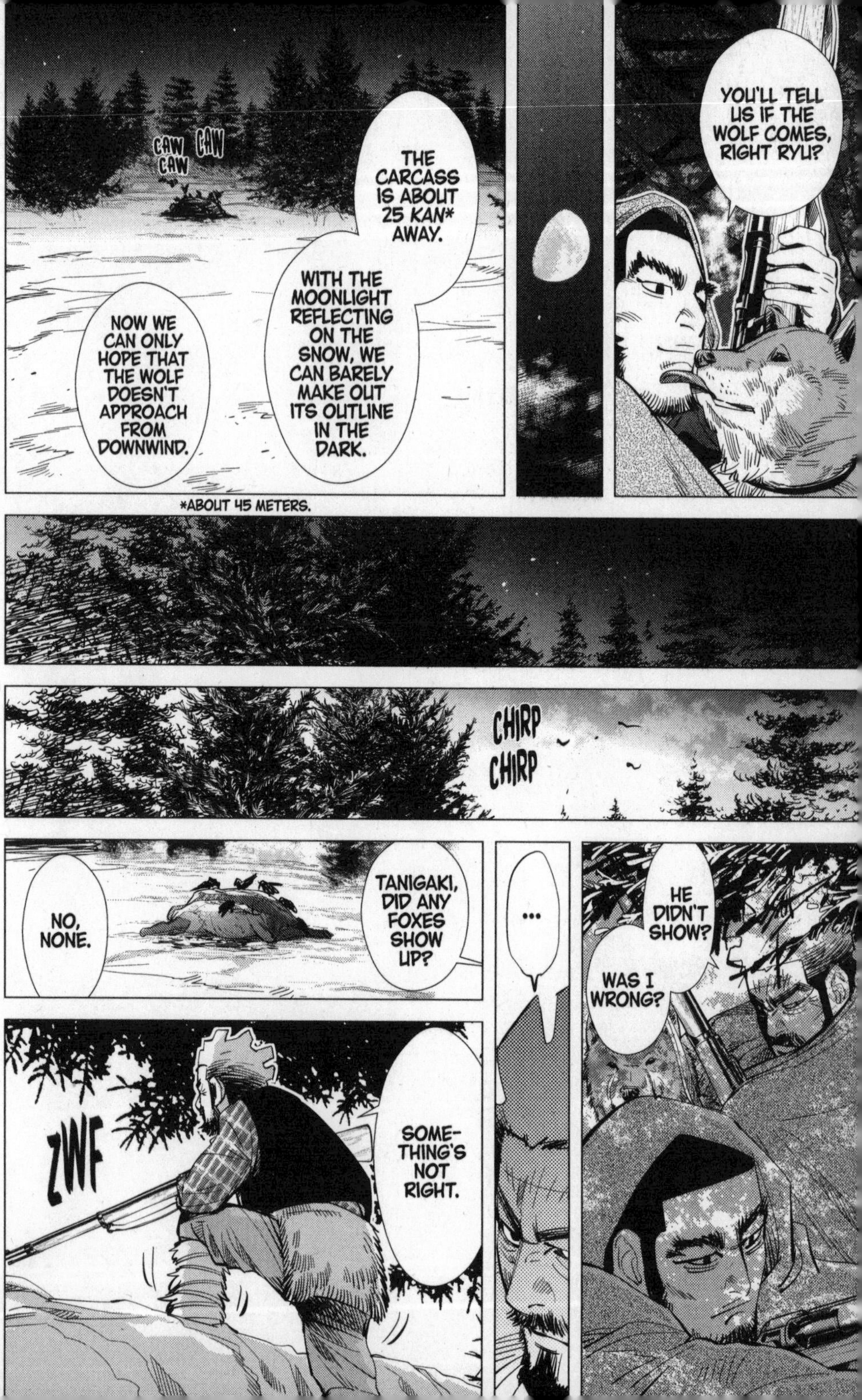
YOU'LL TELL US IF THE WOLF COMES, RIGHT RYU?
THE CARCASS IS ABOUT 25 KAN* AWAY.
WITH THE MOONLIGHT REFLECTING ON THE SNOW, WE CAN BARELY MAKE OUT ITS OUTLINE IN THE DARK.
NOW WE CAN ONLY HOPE THAT THE WOLF DOESN'T APPROACH FROM DOWNWIND.
CAW CAW
CAW
CHIRP
CHIRP
HE DIDN'T SHOW?
WAS I WRONG?
...
TANIGAKI, DID ANY FOXES SHOW UP?
NO, NONE.
SOME-THING'S NOT RIGHT.
ZWF

*ABOUT 45 METERS.

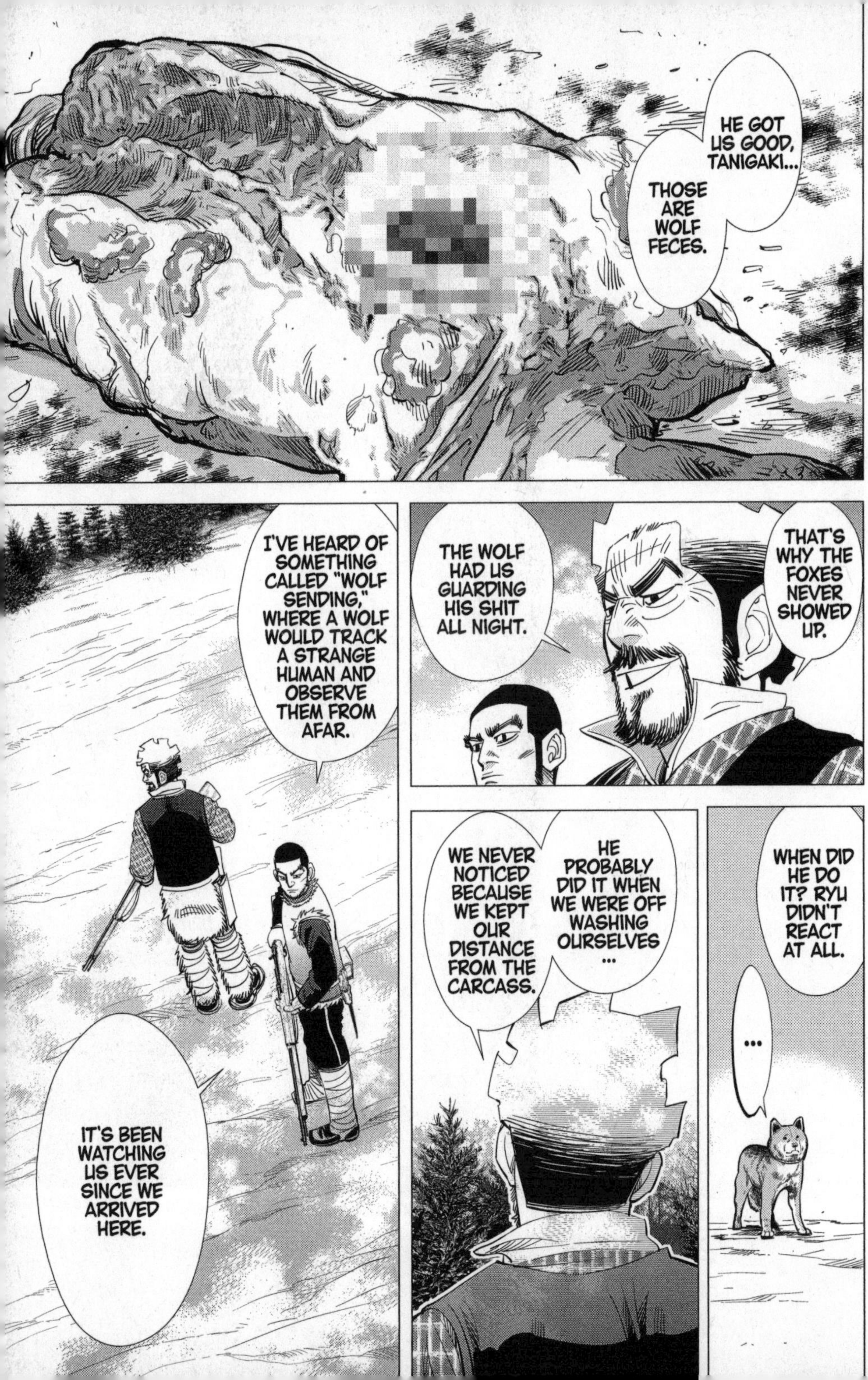
HE GOT US GOOD, TANIGAKI...
THOSE ARE WOLF FECES.
THAT'S WHY THE FOXES NEVER SHOWED UP.
THE WOLF HAD US GUARDING HIS SHIT ALL NIGHT.
WHEN DID HE DO IT? RYU DIDN'T REACT AT ALL.
...
HE PROBABLY DID IT WHEN WE WERE OFF WASHING OURSELVES...
WE NEVER NOTICED BECAUSE WE KEPT OUR DISTANCE FROM THE CARCASS.
I'VE HEARD OF SOMETHING CALLED "WOLF SENDING," WHERE A WOLF WOULD TRACK A STRANGE HUMAN AND OBSERVE THEM FROM AFAR.
IT'S BEEN WATCHING US EVER SINCE WE ARRIVED HERE.

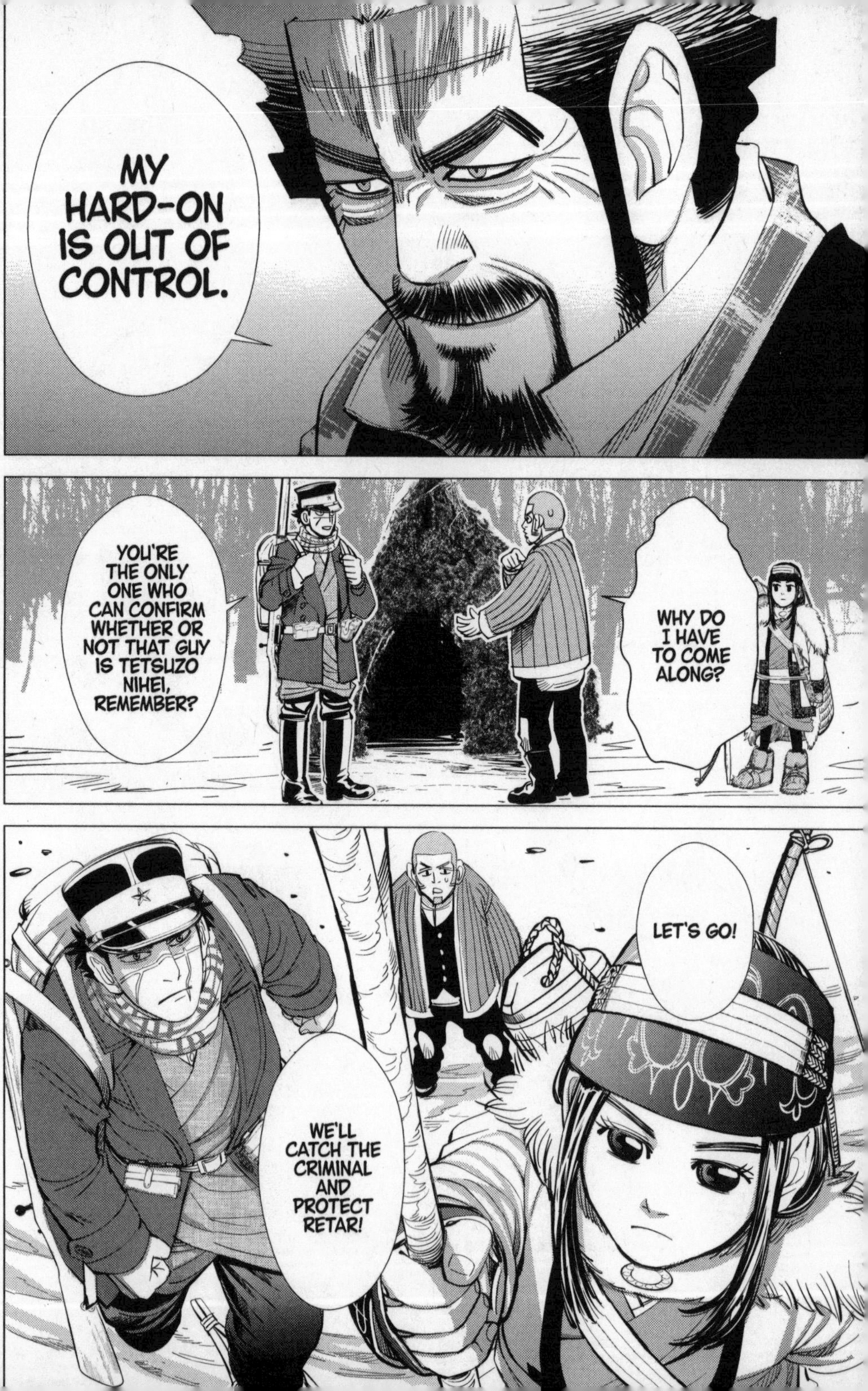
MY HARD-ON IS OUT OF CONTROL.
WHY DO I HAVE TO COME ALONG?
YOU'RE THE ONLY ONE WHO CAN CONFIRM WHETHER OR NOT THAT GUY IS TETSUZO NIHEI, REMEMBER?
LET'S GO!
WE'LL CATCH THE CRIMINAL AND PROTECT RETAR!

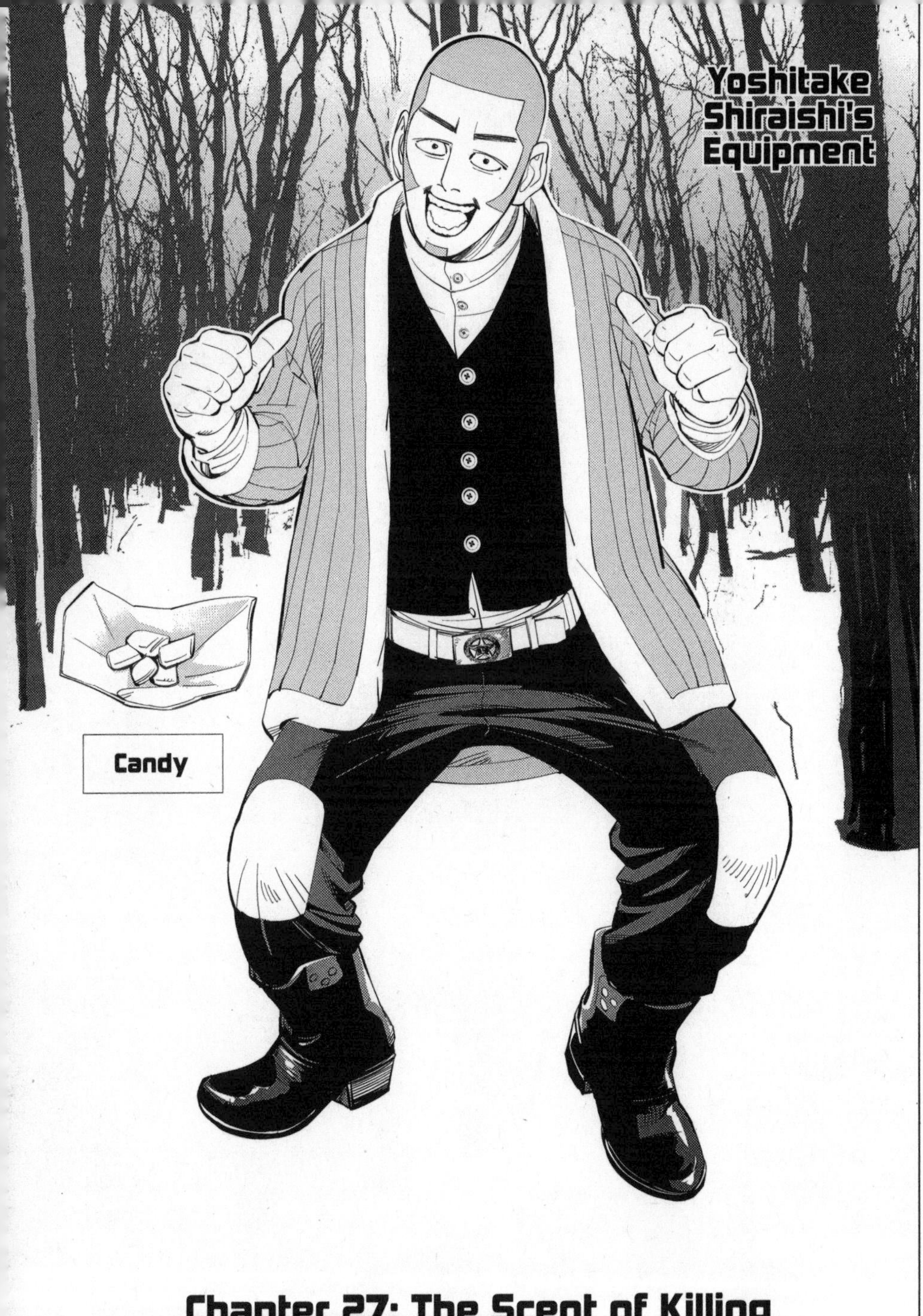
Yoshitake Shiraishi's Equipment
Candy

Chapter 27: The Scent of Killing

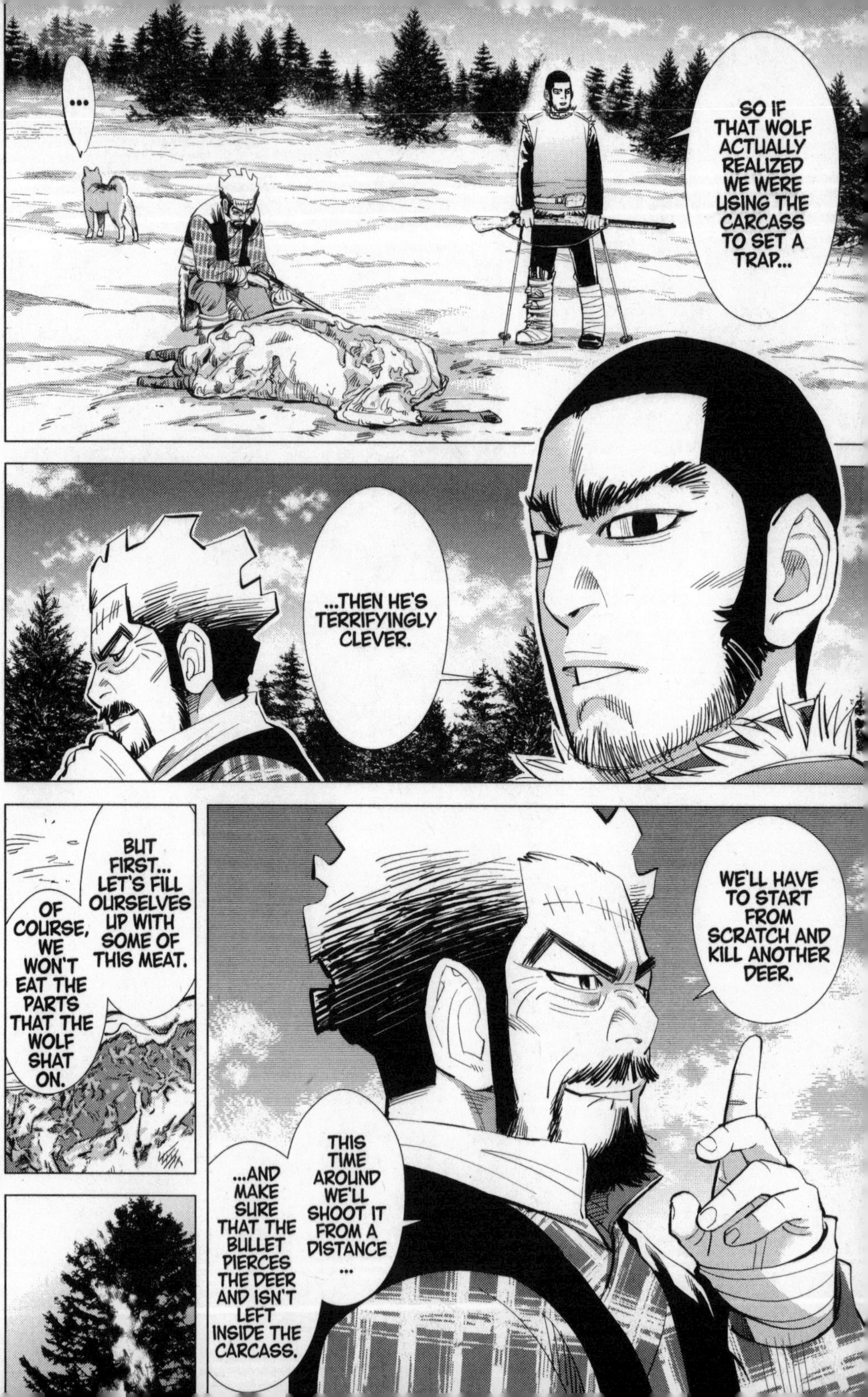

SO IF THAT WOLF ACTUALLY REALIZED WE WERE USING THE CARCASS TO SET A TRAP...
...
...THEN HE'S TERRIFYINGLY CLEVER.
WE'LL HAVE TO START FROM SCRATCH AND KILL ANOTHER DEER.
THIS TIME AROUND WE'LL SHOOT IT FROM A DISTANCE ...
...AND MAKE SURE THAT THE BULLET PIERCES THE DEER AND ISN'T LEFT INSIDE THE CARCASS.
BUT FIRST... LET'S FILL OURSELVES UP WITH SOME OF THIS MEAT.
OF COURSE, WE WON'T EAT THE PARTS THAT THE WOLF SHAT ON.

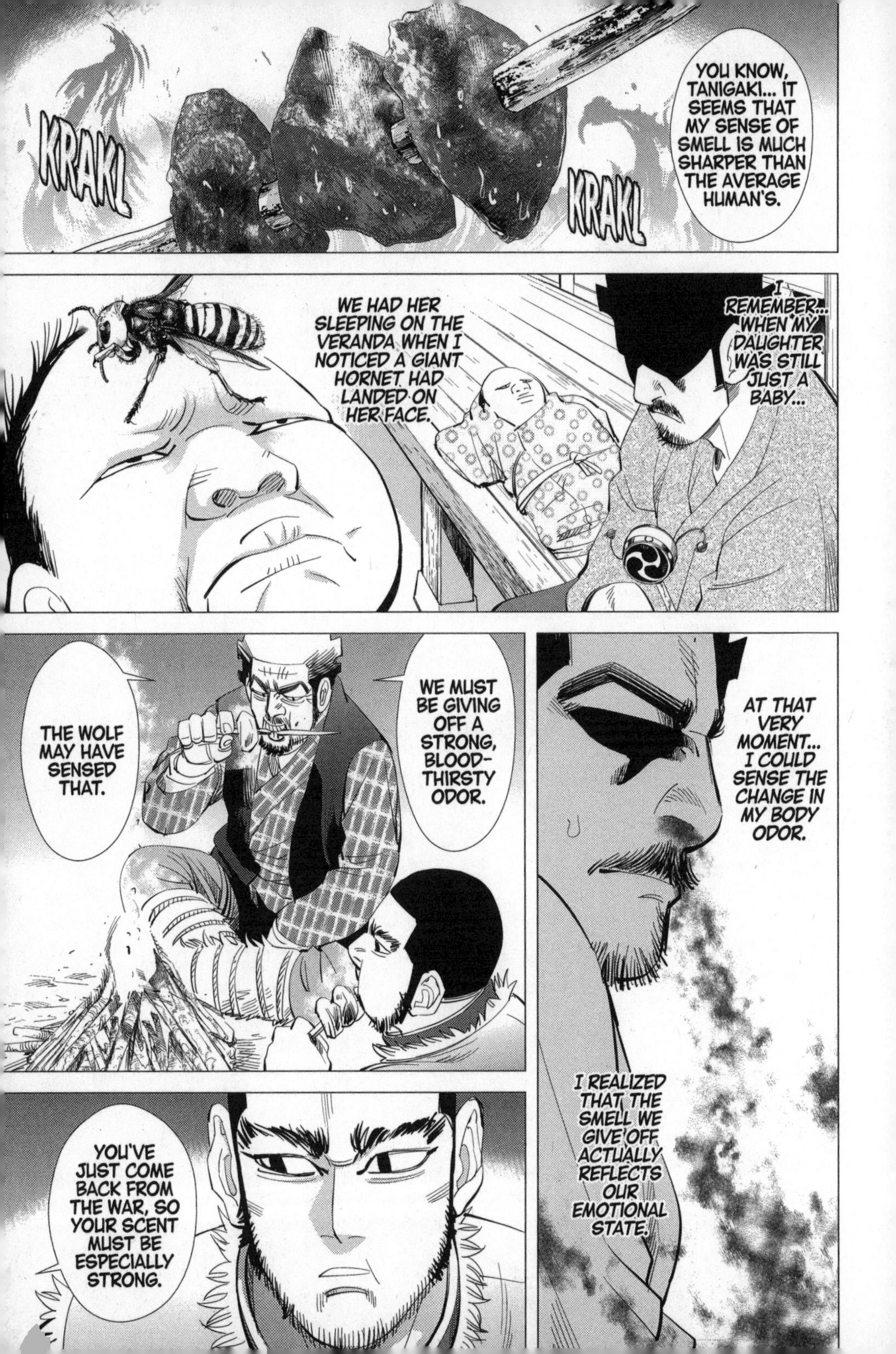
YOU KNOW, TANIGAKI... IT SEEMS THAT MY SENSE OF SMELL IS MUCH SHARPER THAN THE AVERAGE HUMAN'S.
KRAKL
KRAKL
I REMEMBER... WHEN MY DAUGHTER WAS STILL JUST A BABY...
WE HAD HER SLEEPING ON THE VERANDA WHEN I NOTICED A GIANT HORNET HAD LANDED ON HER FACE.
AT THAT VERY MOMENT... I COULD SENSE THE CHANGE IN MY BODY ODOR.
I REALIZED THAT THE SMELL WE GIVE OFF ACTUALLY REFLECTS OUR EMOTIONAL STATE.
WE MUST BE GIVING OFF A STRONG, BLOOD-THIRSTY ODOR.
THE WOLF MAY HAVE SENSED THAT.
YOU'VE JUST COME BACK FROM THE WAR, SO YOUR SCENT MUST BE ESPECIALLY STRONG.

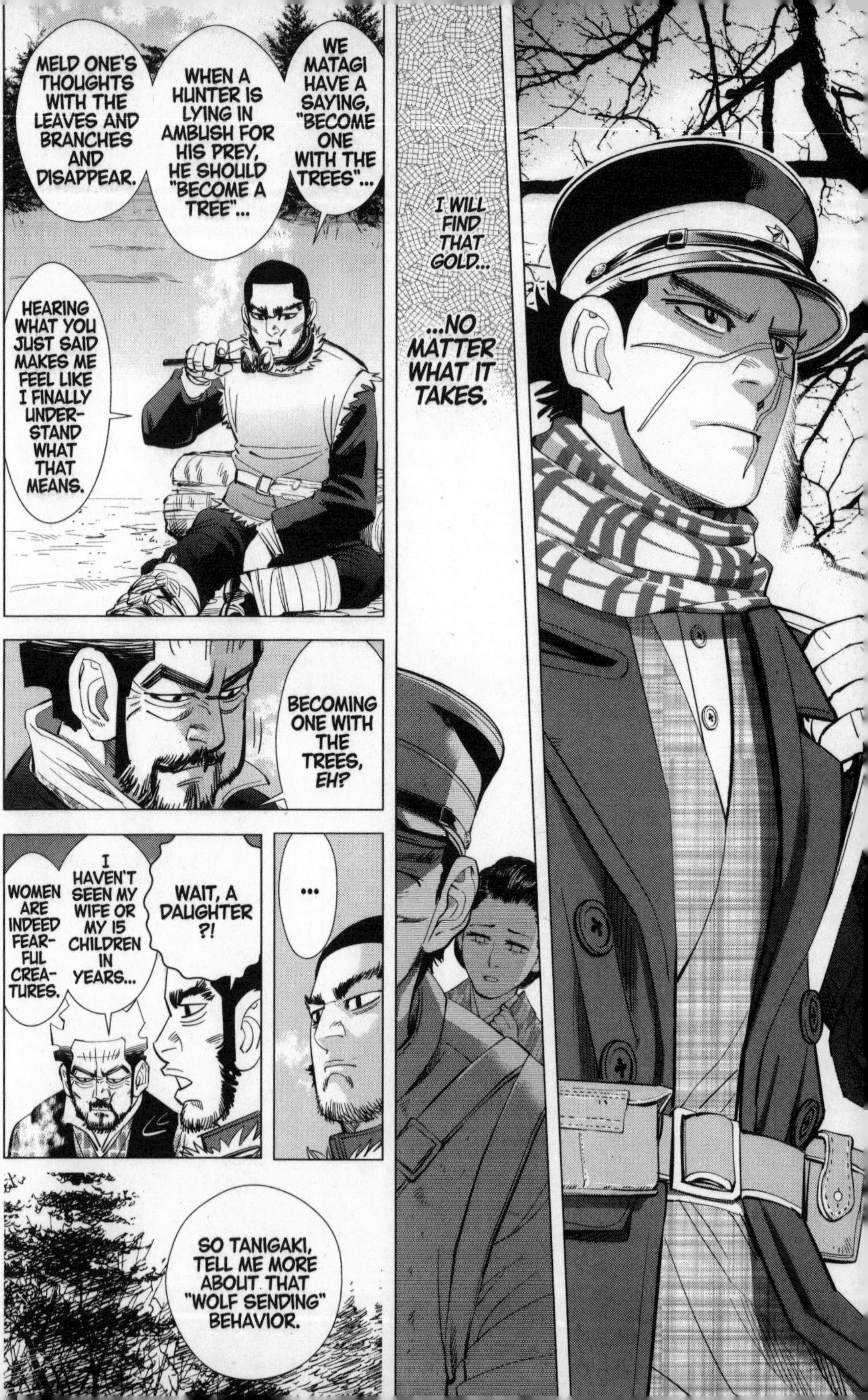
I WILL FIND THAT GOLD...
...NO MATTER WHAT IT TAKES.
WE MATAGI HAVE A SAYING, "BECOME ONE WITH THE TREES"...
WHEN A HUNTER IS LYING IN AMBUSH FOR HIS PREY, HE SHOULD "BECOME A TREE"...
MELD ONE'S THOUGHTS WITH THE LEAVES AND BRANCHES AND DISAPPEAR.
HEARING WHAT YOU JUST SAID MAKES ME FEEL LIKE I FINALLY UNDER-STAND WHAT THAT MEANS.
BECOMING ONE WITH THE TREES, EH?
...
WAIT, A DAUGHTER ?!
I HAVEN'T SEEN MY WIFE OR MY 15 CHILDREN IN YEARS...
WOMEN ARE INDEED FEAR-FUL CREA-TURES.
SO TANIGAKI, TELL ME MORE ABOUT THAT "WOLF SENDING" BEHAVIOR.

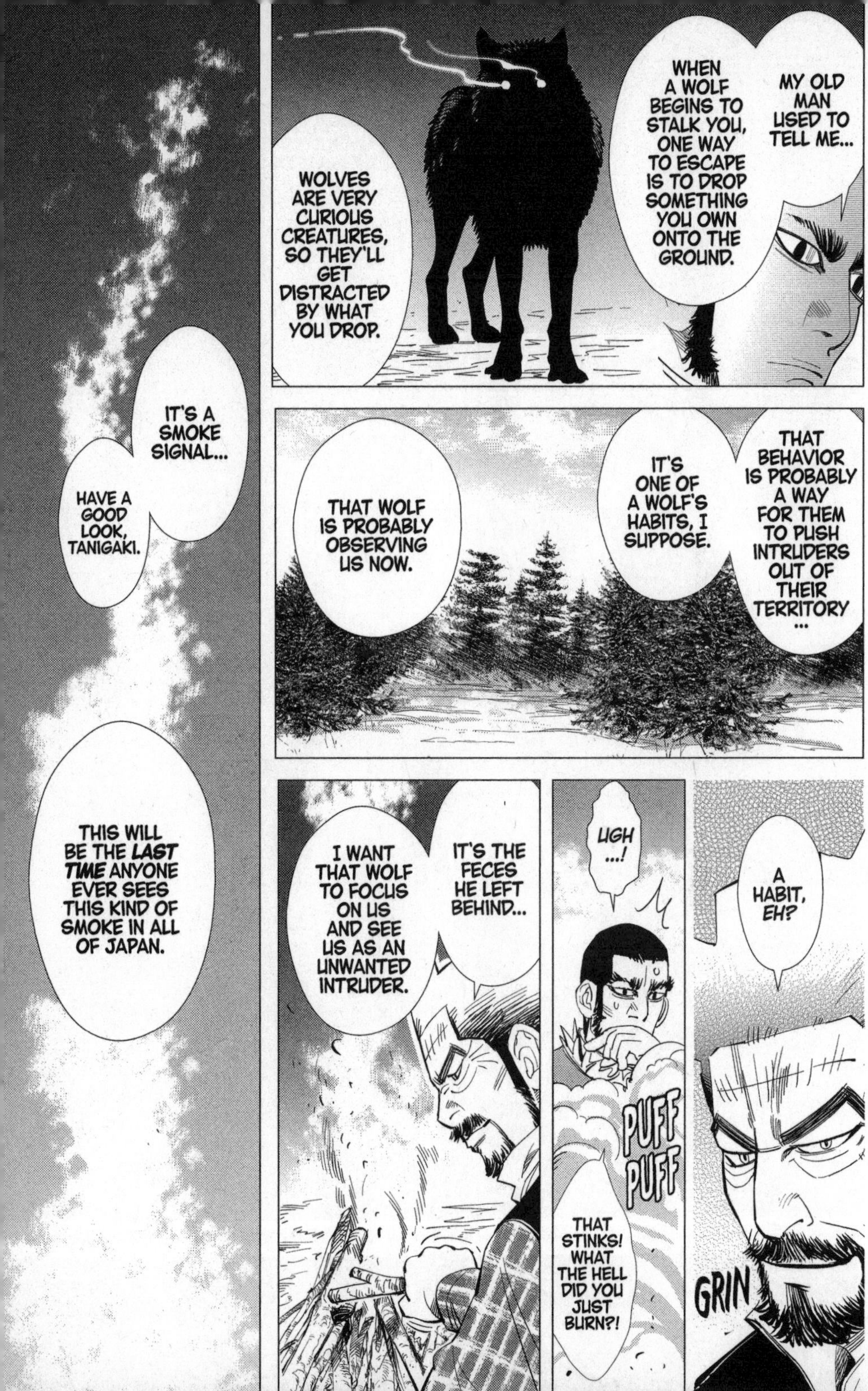
MY OLD MAN USED TO TELL ME...
WHEN A WOLF BEGINS TO STALK YOU, ONE WAY TO ESCAPE IS TO DROP SOMETHING YOU OWN ONTO THE GROUND.
WOLVES ARE VERY CURIOUS CREATURES, SO THEY'LL GET DISTRACTED BY WHAT YOU DROP.
THAT BEHAVIOR IS PROBABLY A WAY FOR THEM TO PUSH INTRUDERS OUT OF THEIR TERRITORY...
IT'S ONE OF A WOLF'S HABITS, I SUPPOSE.
THAT WOLF IS PROBABLY OBSERVING US NOW.
A HABIT, EH?
GRIN
UGH ...!
PUFF PUFF
THAT STINKS! WHAT THE HELL DID YOU JUST BURN?!
IT'S THE FECES HE LEFT BEHIND...
I WANT THAT WOLF TO FOCUS ON US AND SEE US AS AN UNWANTED INTRUDER.
IT'S A SMOKE SIGNAL...
HAVE A GOOD LOOK, TANIGAKI.
THIS WILL BE THE *LAST TIME* ANYONE EVER SEES THIS KIND OF SMOKE IN ALL OF JAPAN.

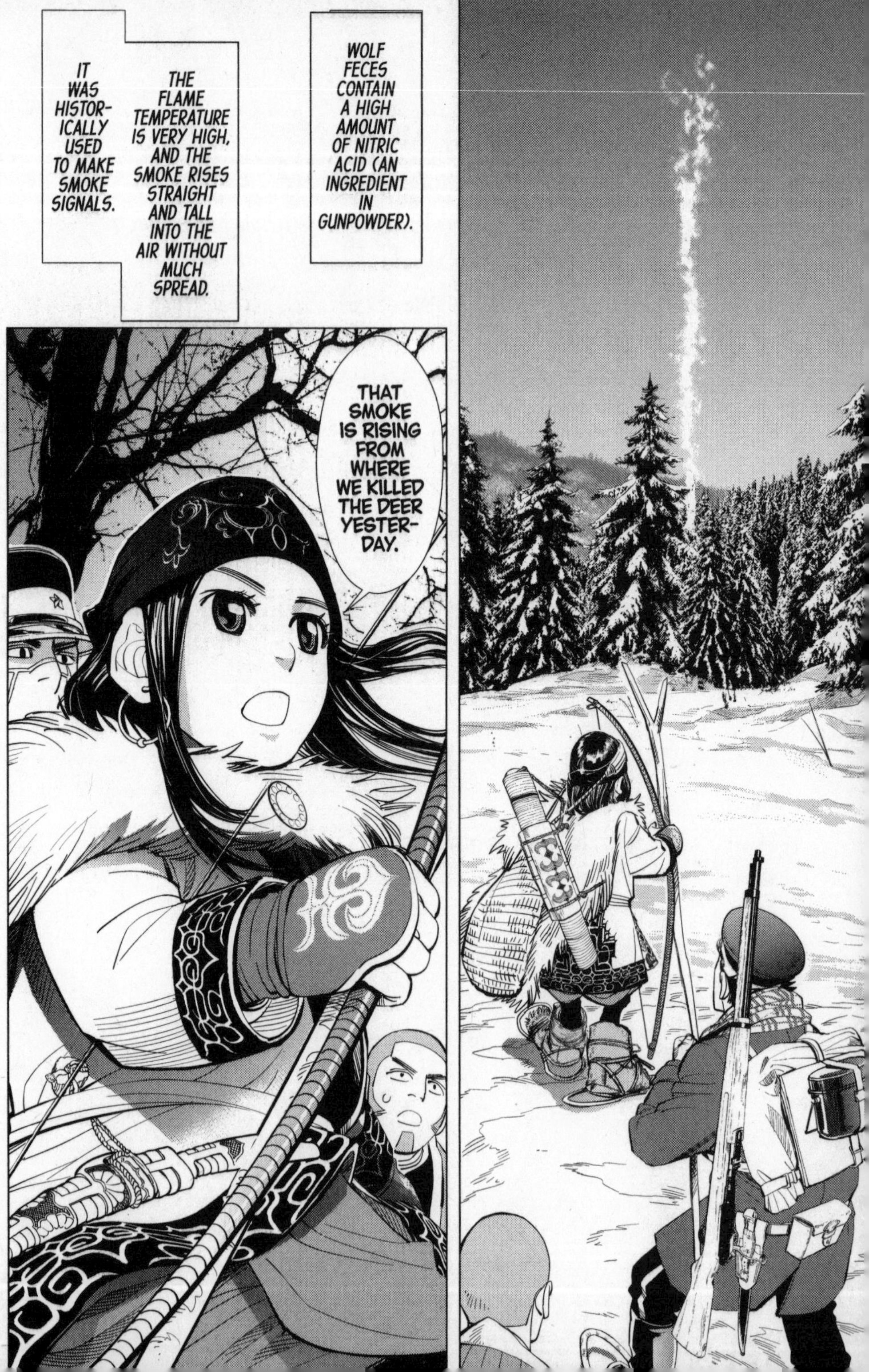
WOLF FECES CONTAIN A HIGH AMOUNT OF NITRIC ACID (AN INGREDIENT IN GUNPOWDER).
THE FLAME TEMPERATURE IS VERY HIGH, AND THE SMOKE RISES STRAIGHT AND TALL INTO THE AIR WITHOUT MUCH SPREAD.
IT WAS HISTORICALLY USED TO MAKE SMOKE SIGNALS.
THAT SMOKE IS RISING FROM WHERE WE KILLED THE DEER YESTERDAY.

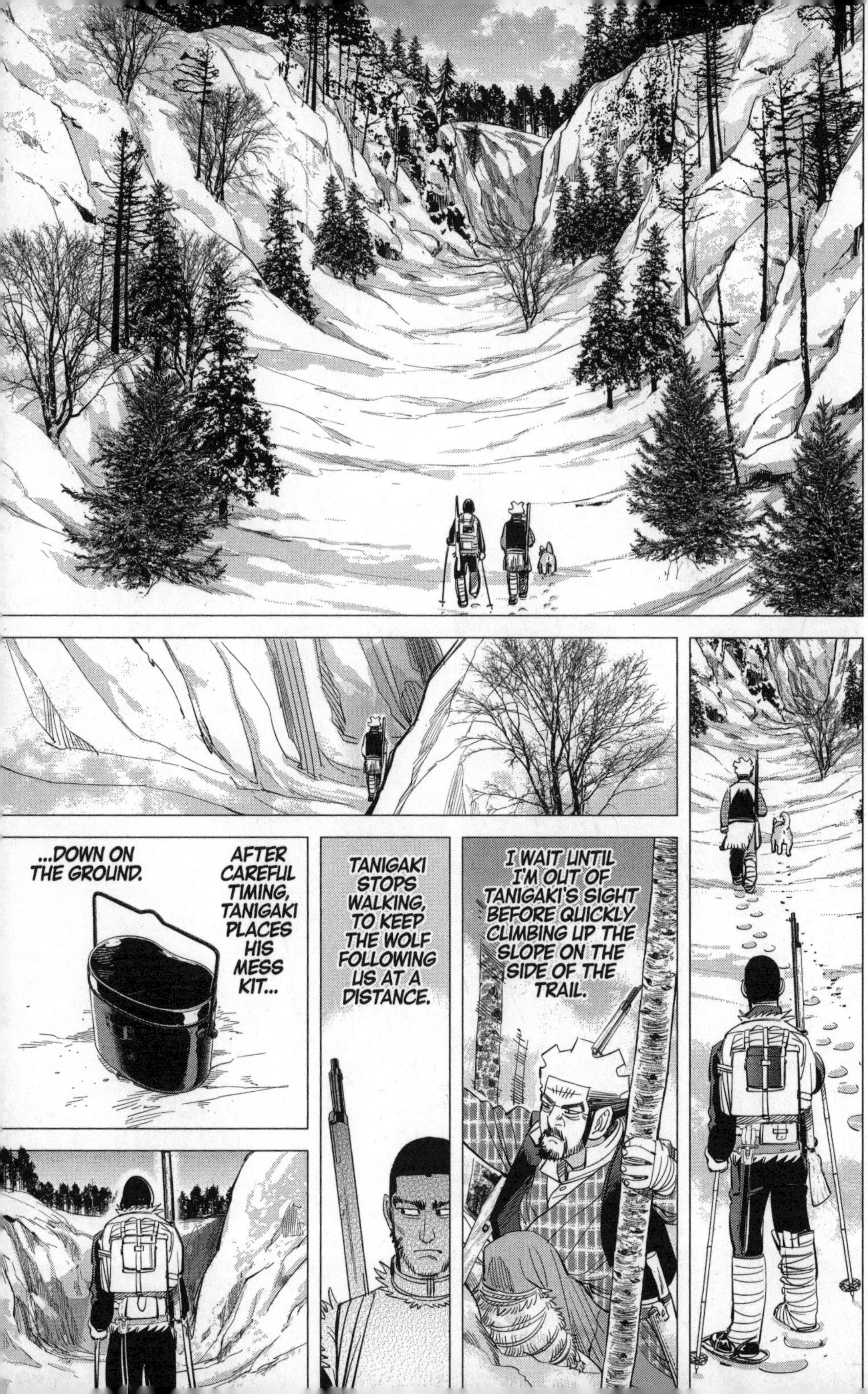
I WAIT UNTIL I'M OUT OF TANIGAKI'S SIGHT BEFORE QUICKLY CLIMBING UP THE SLOPE ON THE SIDE OF THE TRAIL.
TANIGAKI STOPS WALKING, TO KEEP THE WOLF FOLLOWING US AT A DISTANCE.
AFTER CAREFUL TIMING, TANIGAKI PLACES HIS MESS KIT...
...DOWN ON THE GROUND.

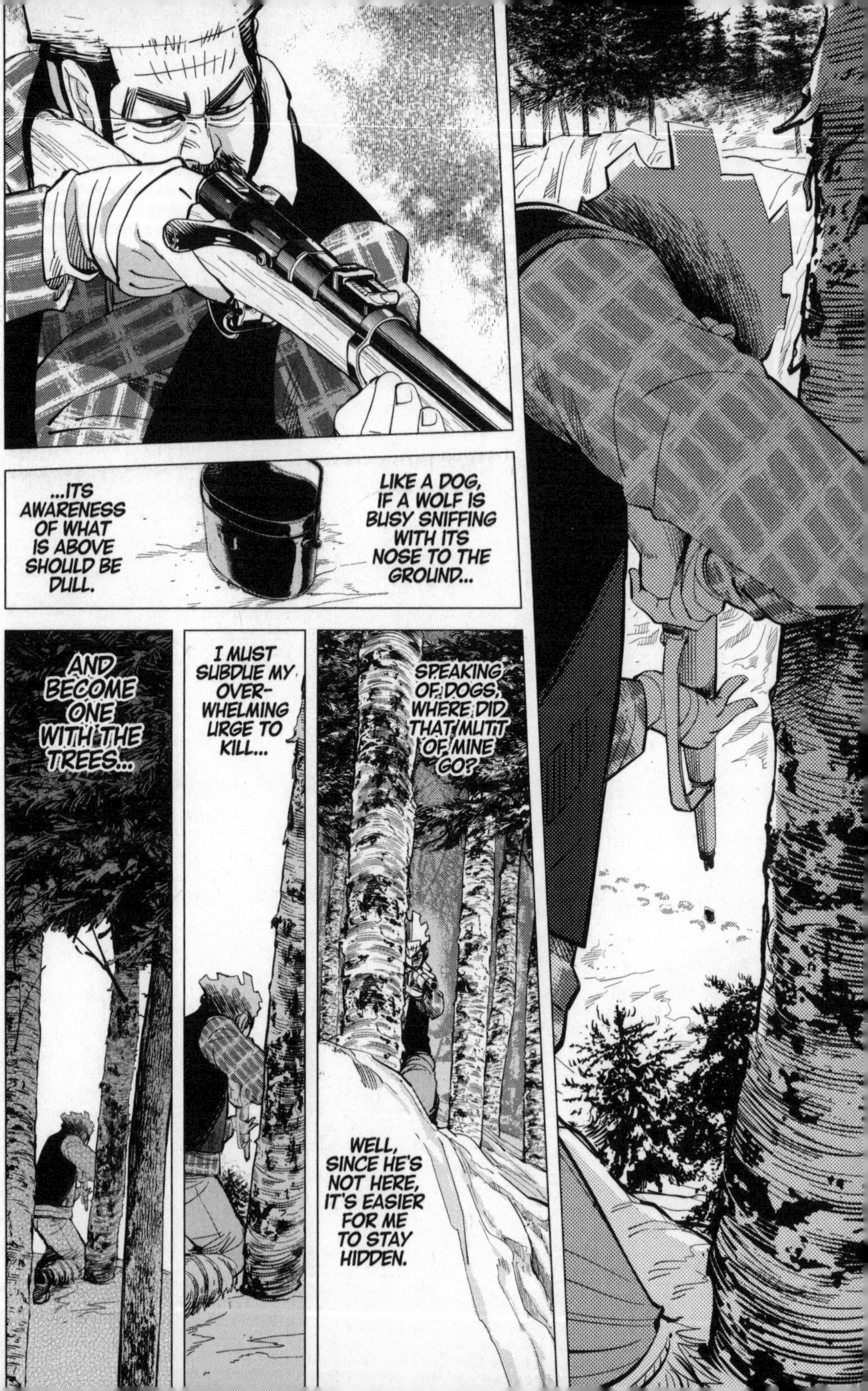
LIKE A DOG, IF A WOLF IS BUSY SNIFFING WITH ITS NOSE TO THE GROUND...
...ITS AWARENESS OF WHAT IS ABOVE SHOULD BE DULL.
SPEAKING OF DOGS, WHERE DID THAT MUTT OF MINE GO?
WELL, SINCE HE'S NOT HERE, IT'S EASIER FOR ME TO STAY HIDDEN.
I MUST SUBDUE MY OVER-WHELMING URGE TO KILL...
AND BECOME ONE WITH THE TREES...

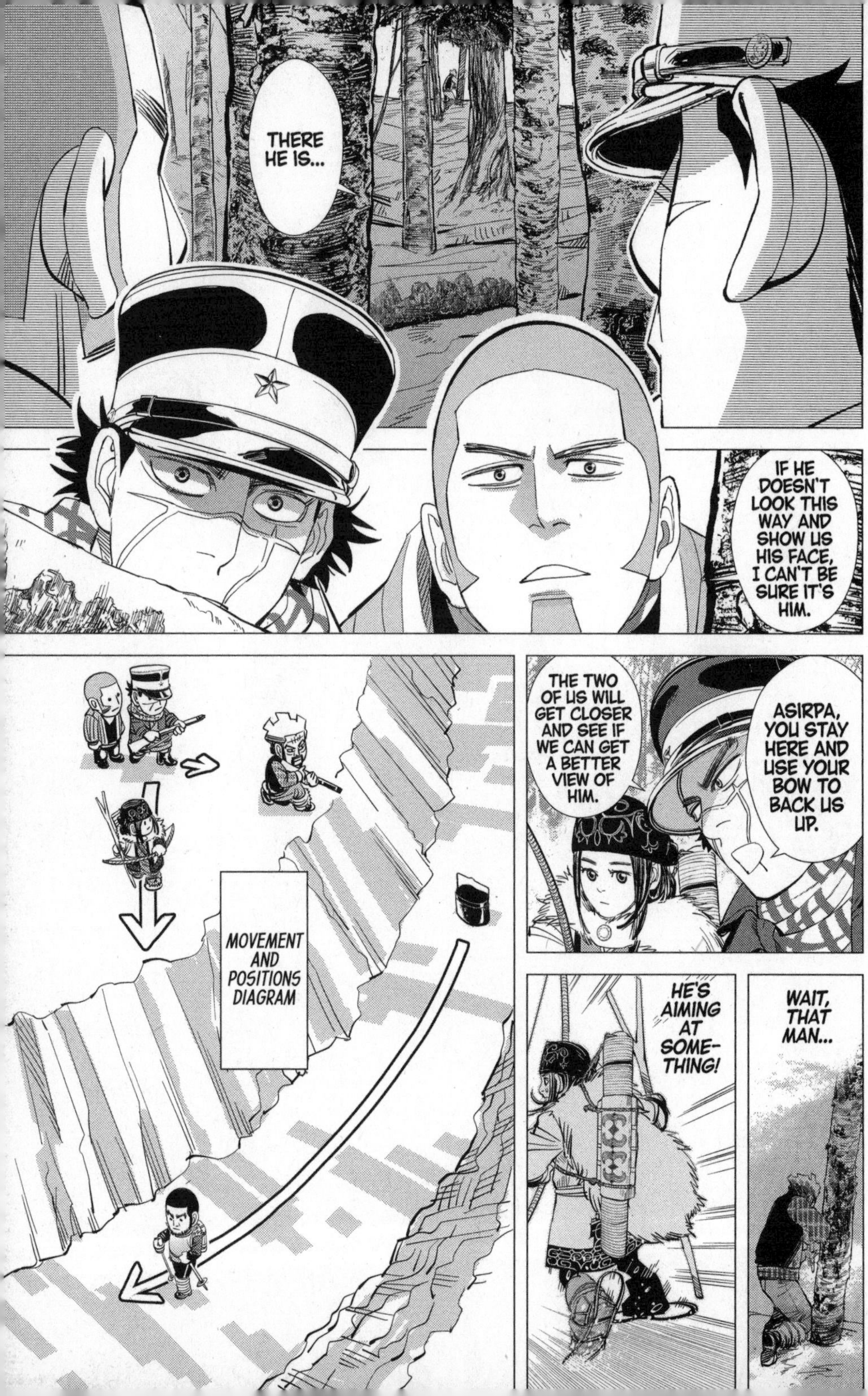
THERE HE IS...
IF HE DOESN'T LOOK THIS WAY AND SHOW US HIS FACE, I CAN'T BE SURE IT'S HIM.
ASIRPA, YOU STAY HERE AND USE YOUR BOW TO BACK US UP.
THE TWO OF US WILL GET CLOSER AND SEE IF WE CAN GET A BETTER VIEW OF HIM.
WAIT, THAT MAN...
HE'S AIMING AT SOME-THING!
MOVEMENT AND POSITIONS DIAGRAM

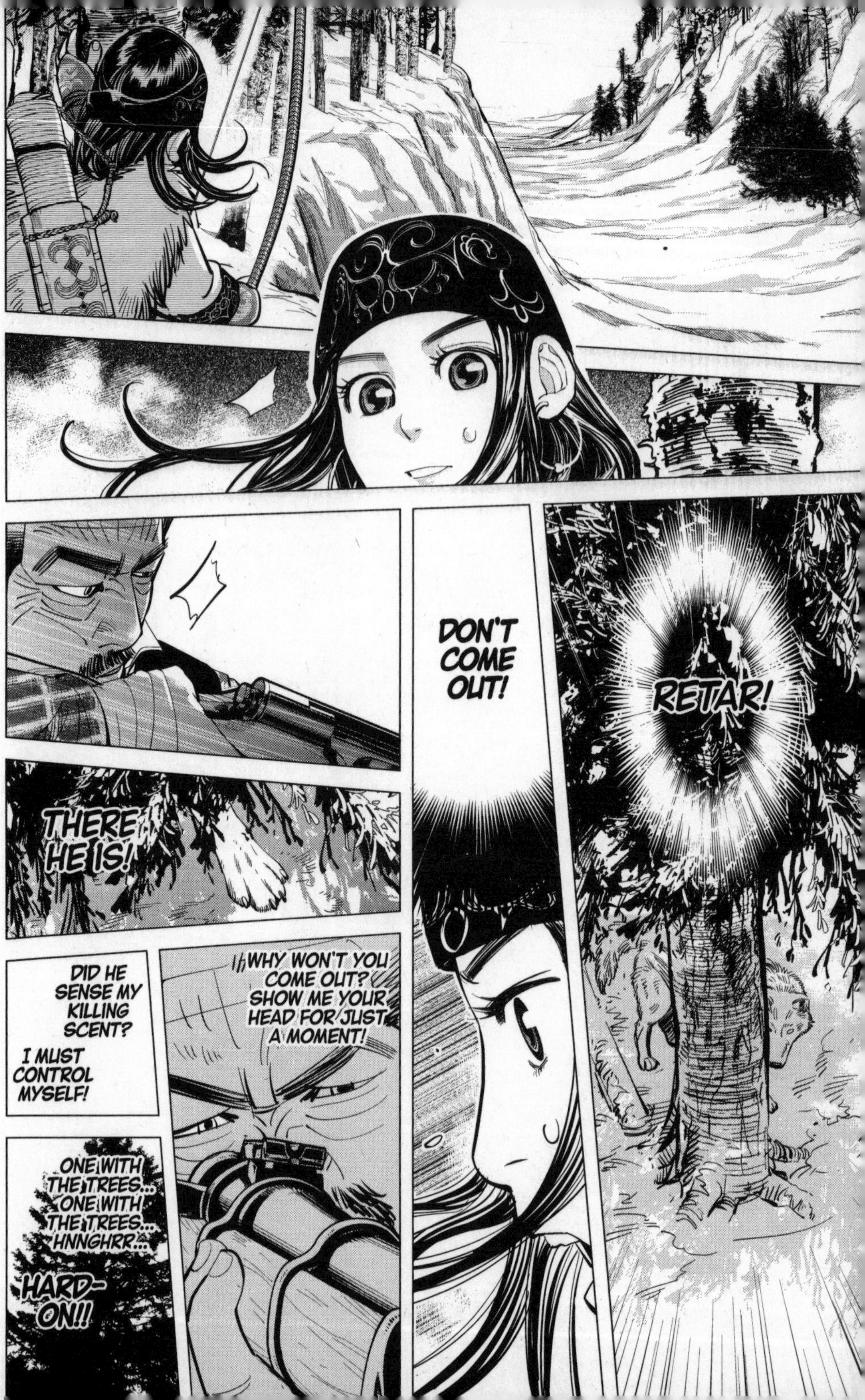
RETAR!
DON'T COME OUT!
THERE HE IS!
WHY WON'T YOU COME OUT? SHOW ME YOUR HEAD FOR JUST A MOMENT!
DID HE SENSE MY KILLING SCENT?
I MUST CONTROL MYSELF!
ONE WITH THE TREES... ONE WITH THE TREES... HNNGHRR...
HARD-ON!!

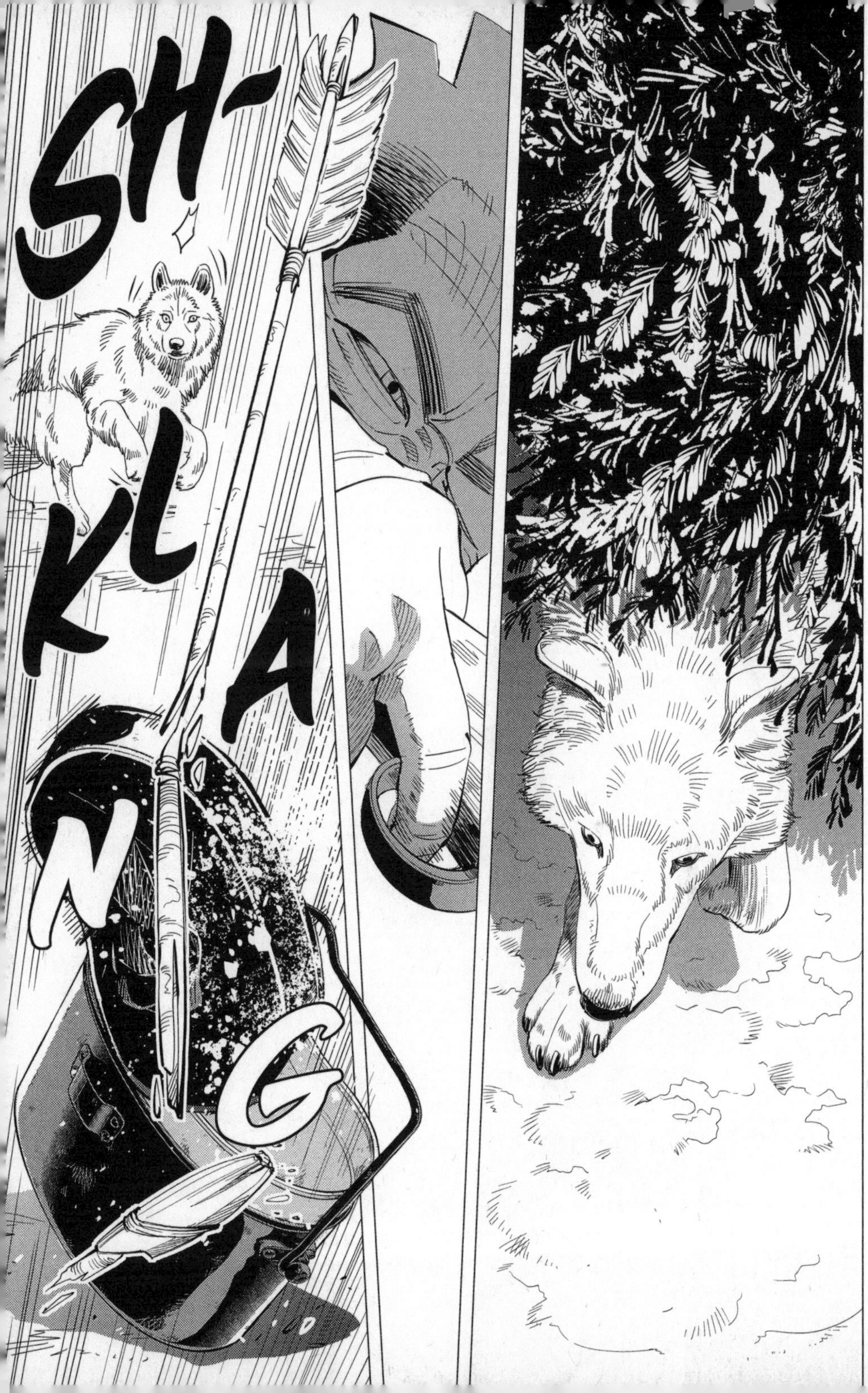
SH-KLANG

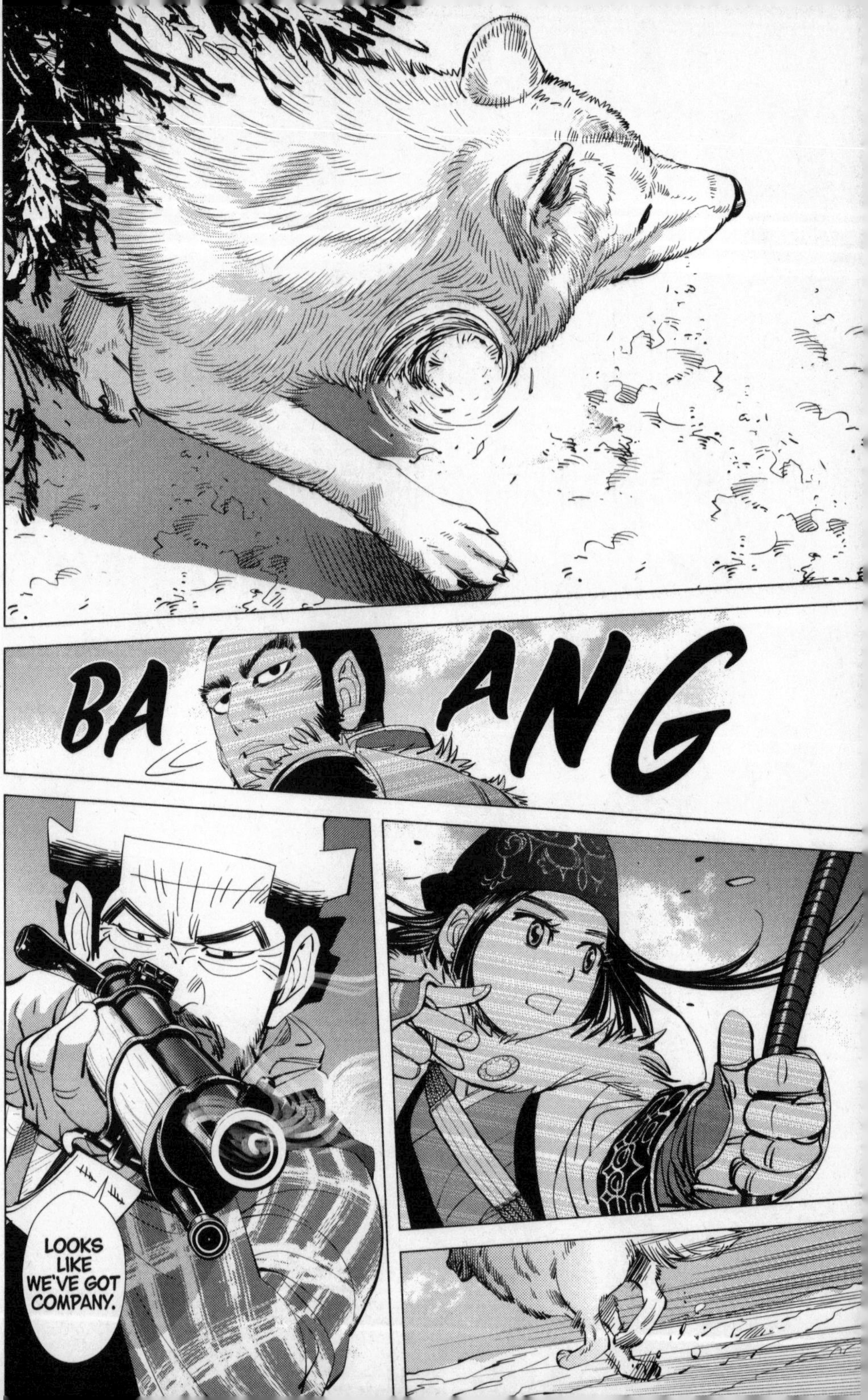
BA ANG
LOOKS LIKE WE'VE GOT COMPANY.

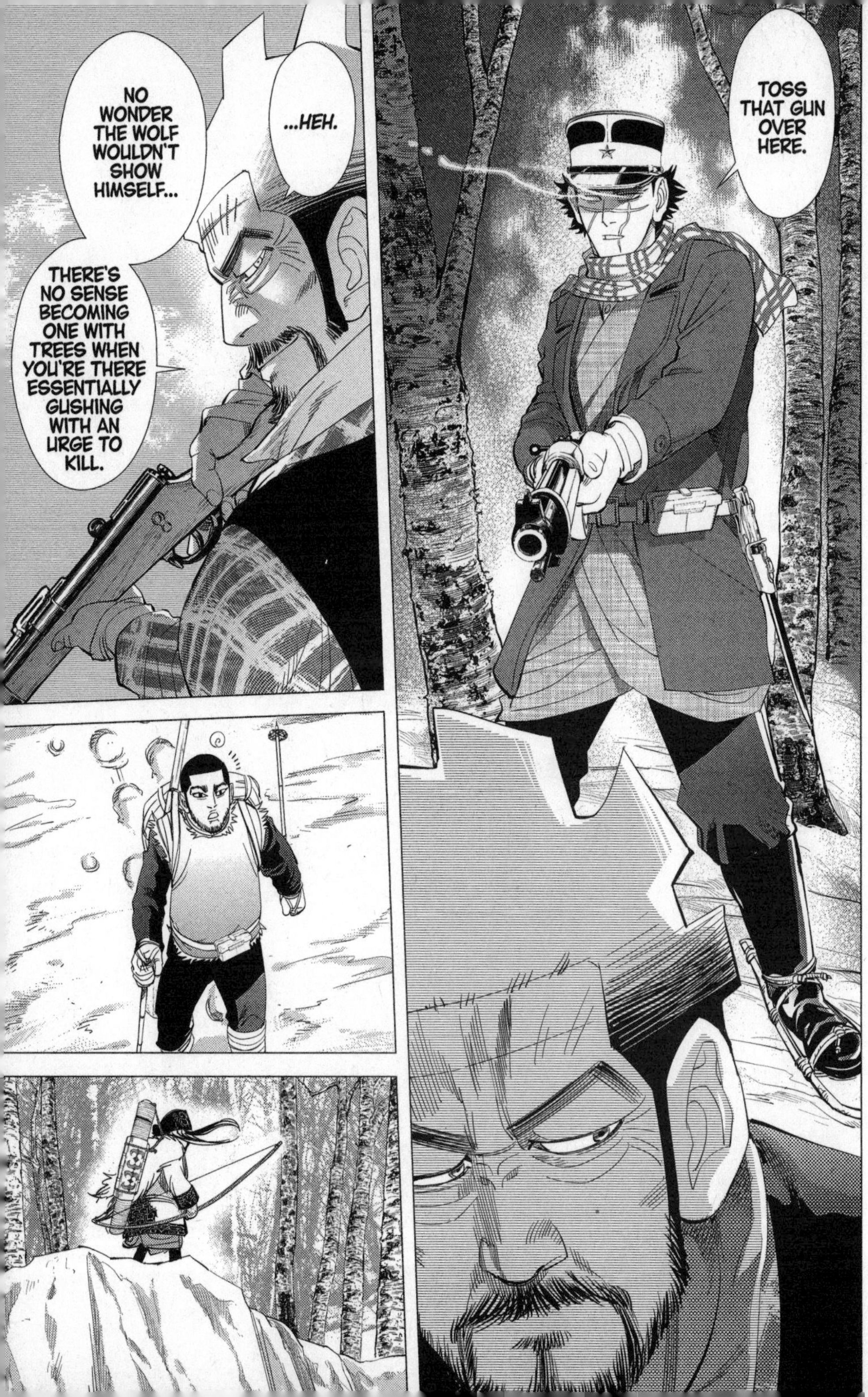
TOSS THAT GUN OVER HERE.
...HEH.
NO WONDER THE WOLF WOULDN'T SHOW HIMSELF...
THERE'S NO SENSE BECOMING ONE WITH TREES WHEN YOU'RE THERE ESSENTIALLY GUSHING WITH AN URGE TO KILL.

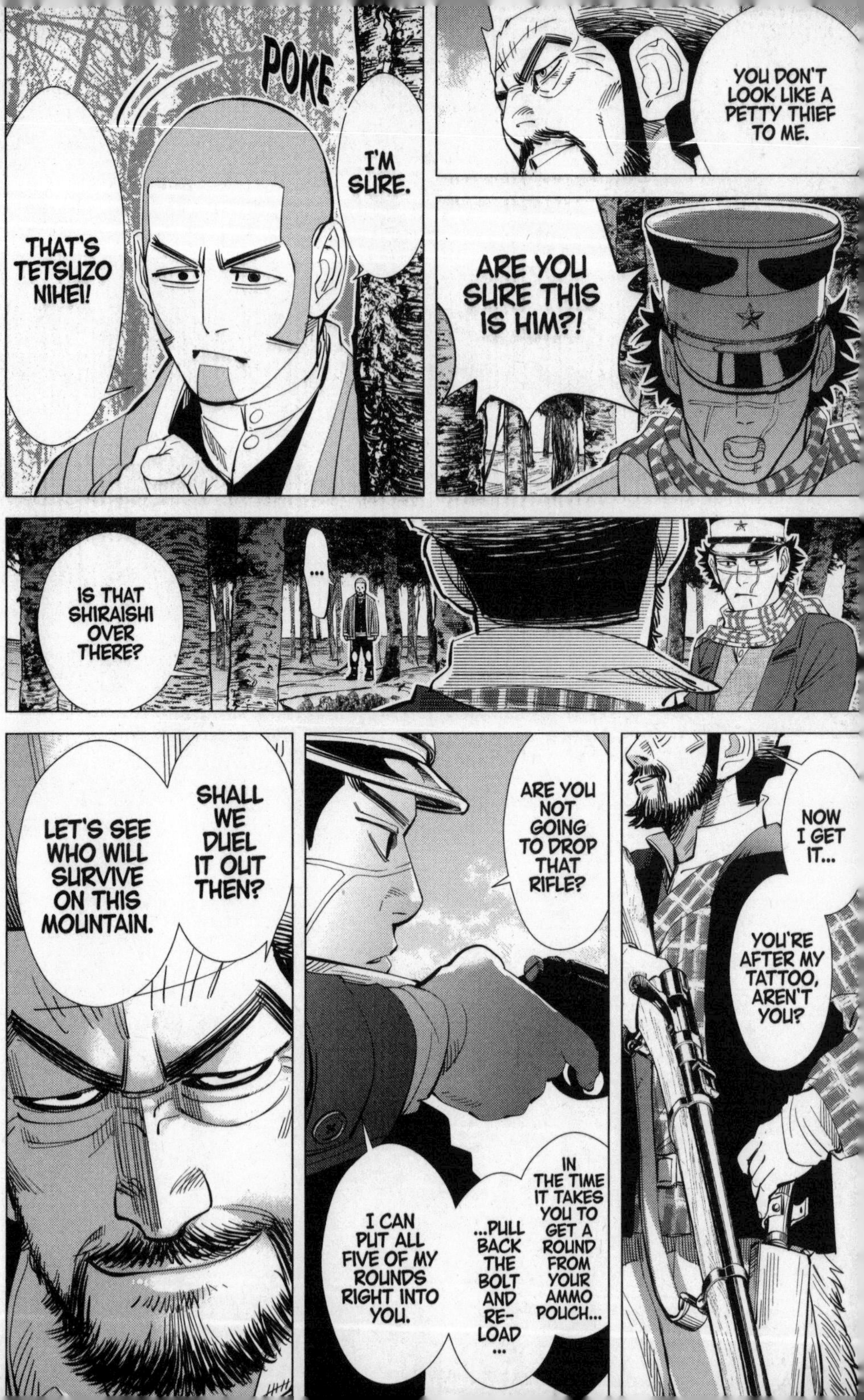
YOU DON'T LOOK LIKE A PETTY THIEF TO ME.
ARE YOU SURE THIS IS HIM?!
POKE
I'M SURE.
THAT'S TETSUZO NIHEI!
...
IS THAT SHIRAISHI OVER THERE?
NOW I GET IT...
YOU'RE AFTER MY TATTOO, AREN'T YOU?
ARE YOU NOT GOING TO DROP THAT RIFLE?
IN THE TIME IT TAKES YOU TO GET A ROUND FROM YOUR AMMO POUCH...
...PULL BACK THE BOLT AND RE-LOAD...
I CAN PUT ALL FIVE OF MY ROUNDS RIGHT INTO YOU.
SHALL WE DUEL IT OUT THEN?
LET'S SEE WHO WILL SURVIVE ON THIS MOUNTAIN.

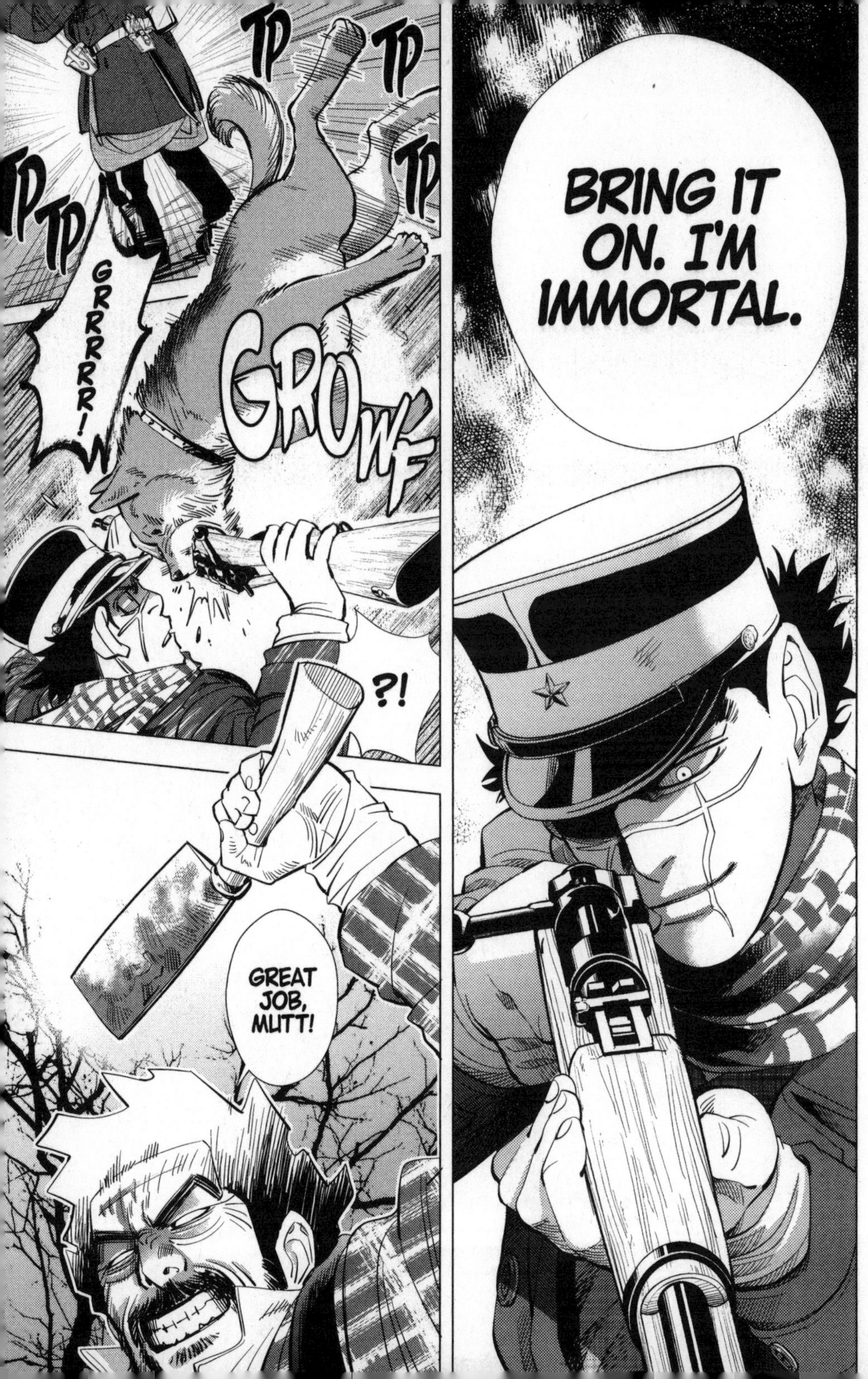
BRING IT ON. I'M IMMORTAL.
TP
TP
TP
TP
TP
GRRRRR!
GROWF
?!
GREAT JOB, MUTT!

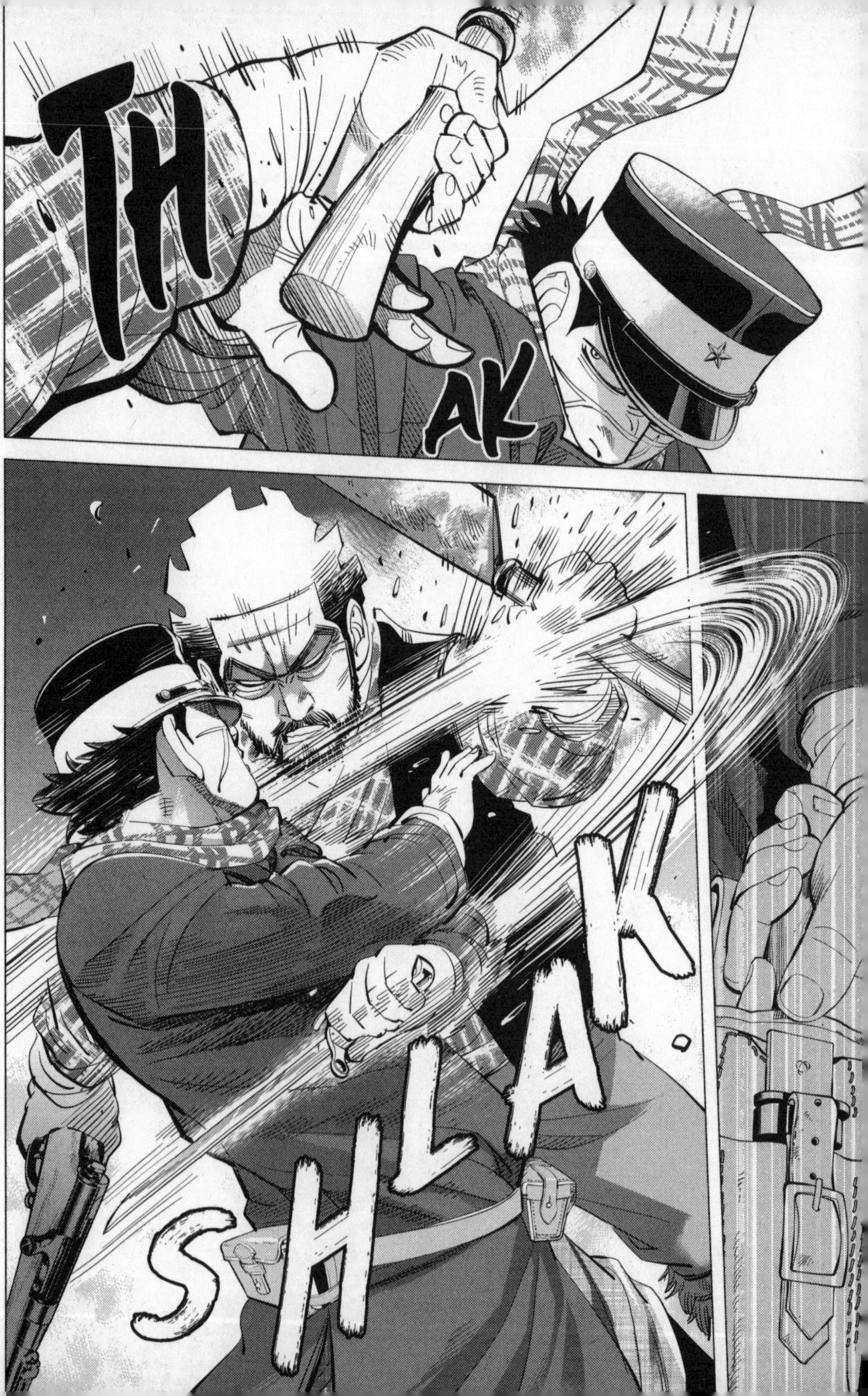
THAK
SHLAK

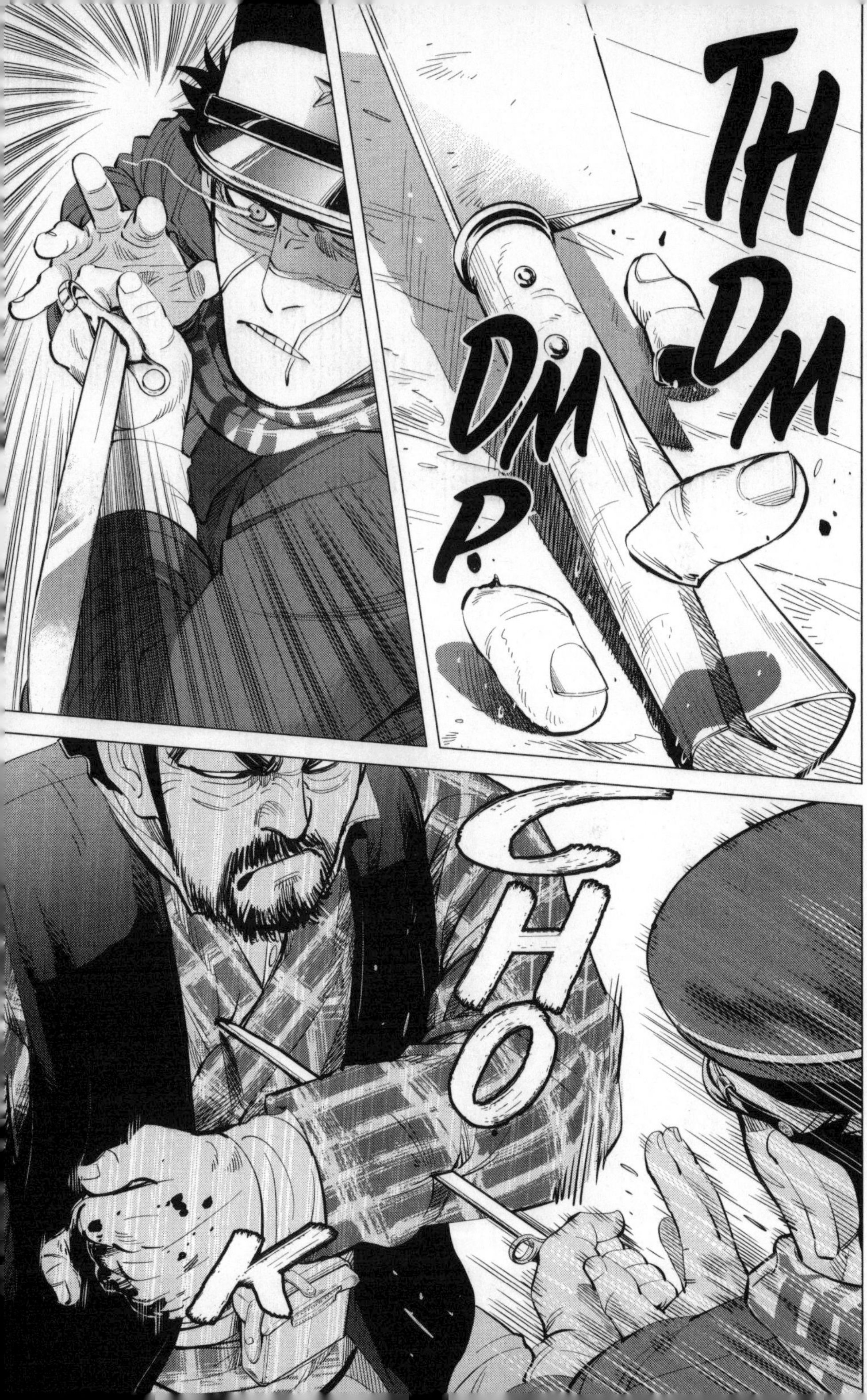
THDM
DMP
CHOK

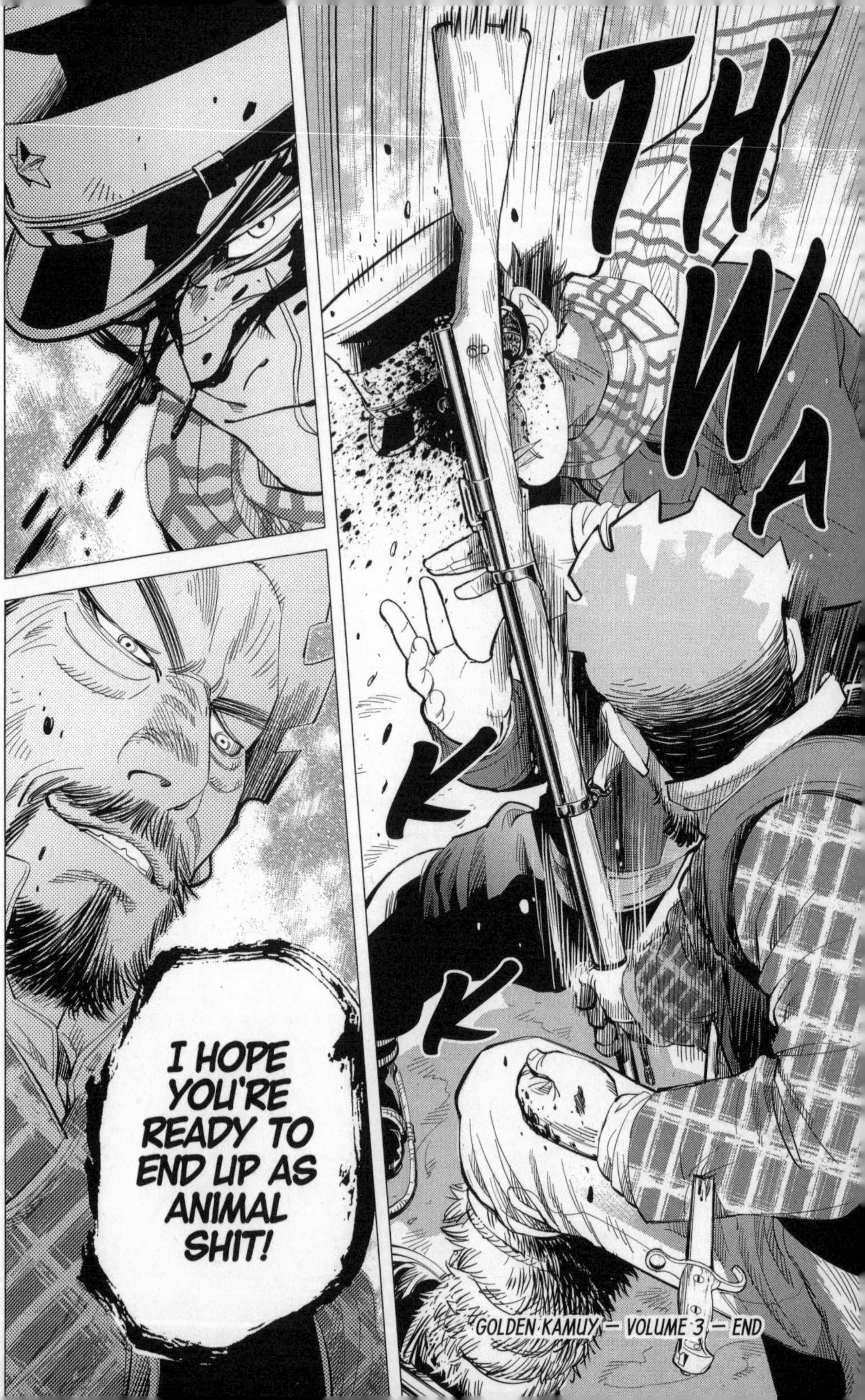
THWAAKK
GOLDEN KAMUY — VOLUME 3 — END
I HOPE YOU'RE READY TO END UP AS ANIMAL SHIT!

Ainu Language Supervision • Hiroshi Nakagawa

Cooperation from • Hokkaido Ainu Association
and the Abashiri Prison Museum

Ainu Culture References

Chiri, Takanaka and Yokoyama, Takao. *Ainugo Eiri Jiten*
(Ainu Language Illustrated Dictionary). Tokyo: Kagyusha, 1994

Kayano, Shigeru. *Ainu no Mingu* (Ainu Folkcrafts).
Kawagoe: Suzusawa Book Store, 1978

Kayano, Shigeru. *Kayano Shigeru no Ainugo Jiten* (Kayano Shigeru's Ainu
Language Dictionary). Tokyo: Sanseido, 1996

Musashino Art University - The Research Institute for Culture and Cultural History.
Ainu no Mingu Jissoku Zushu (Ainu Folkcrafts – Collection of Drawing and
Figures). Biratori: Biratori-cho Council for Promoting Ainu Culture, 2014

Satouchi, Ai. *Ainu-shiki ekoroji-seikatsu: Haruzo Ekashi ni manabu shizen no chie*
(Ainu Style Ecological Living: Haruzo Ekashi Teaches the Wisdom of Nature).
Tokyo: Kabushiki gaisha Shogakukan, 2008

Chiri, Yukie. *Ainu Shin'yoshu* (Chiri Yukie's Ainu Epic Tales).
Tokyo: Iwanami Shoten, 1978

Namikawa, Kenji. *Ainu Minzoku no Kiseki* (The Path of the Ainu People).
Tokyo: Yamakawa Publishing, 2004

Mook. *Senjuumin Ainu Minzoku* (Bessatsu Taiyo) (The
Ainu People (Extra Issue Taiyo). Tokyo: Heibonsha, 2004

Kinoshita, Seizo. *Shiraoikotan Kinoshita Seizo Isaku Shashin Shu* (Shiraoikotan:
Kinoshita Seizo's Posthumous Photography Collection). Hokkaido Shiraoi-gun
Shiraoi-cho: Shiraoi Heritage Conservation Foundation, 1988

The Ainu Museum. *Ainu no Ifuku Bunka* (The Culture of Ainu Clothing). Hokkaido
Shiraoi-gun Shiraoi-cho: Shiraoi Ainu Museum, 1991.

Keira, Tomoko and Kaji, Sayaka. *Ainu no Shiki* (Ainu's Four Seasons).
Tokyo: Akashi Shoten, 1995

Fukuoka, Itoko and Sato, Kazuko. *Ainu Shokubutsushi* (Ainu Botanical Journal).
Chiba Urayasu-Shi: Sofukan, 1995

Hayakawa, Noboru. *Ainu no Minzoku* (Ainu Folklore).
Iwasaki Bijutsusha, 1983

Sunazawa, Kura. *Ku Sukuppu Orushibe* (The Memories of My Generation).
Hokkaido, Sapporo-shi: Miyama Shobo, 1983

Haginaka, Miki et al., *Kikigaki Ainu no Shokuji* (Oral History of Ainu Diet). Tokyo:
Rural Culture Association Japan, 1992

Nakagawa, Hiroshi. *New Express Ainu Go.* Tokyo: Hakusuisha, 2013

Nakagawa, Hiroshi. *Ainugo Chitose Hogen Jiten* (The Ainu-Japanese dictionary).
Chiba Urayasu-Shi: Sofukan, 1995

Nakagawa, Hiroshi and Nakamoto, Mutsuko. *Kamuy Yukara de Ainu Go wo
Manabu* (Learning Ainu with Kamuy Yukar). Tokyo: Hakusuisha, 2007

Nakagawa, Hiroshi. *Katari au Kotoba no Chikara – Kamuy tachi to Ikiru Sekai*
(The Power of Spoken Words – Living in a World with Kamuy).
Tokyo: Iwanami Shoten, 2010

Sarashina, Genzo and Sarashina, Hikari. *Kotan Seibutsu Ki <1 Juki / Zassou hen>*
(Kotan Wildlife Vol. 1 – Trees and Weeds). Hosei University Publishing, 1992/2007

Sarashina, Genzo and Sarashina, Hikari. *Kotan Seibutsu Ki <2 Yacho / Kaijuu /
Gyozoku hen>* (Kotan Wildlife Vol. 2 – Birds, Sea Creatures, and Fish).
Hosei University Publishing, 1992/2007

Sarashina, Genzo and Sarashina, Hikari. *Kotan Seibutsu Ki <3 Yachou / Mizudori /
Konchu hen>* (Kotan Wildlife Vol. 3 – Shorebirds, Seabirds, and Insects).
Hosei University Publishing, 1992/2007

Kawakami Yuji. *Sarunkur Ainu Monogatari* (The Tale of Sarunkur Ainu).
Kawagoe: Suzusawa Book Store, 2003/2005

Kawakami, Yuji. *Ekashi to Fuchi wo Tazunete* (Visiting Ekashi and Fuchi)
Kawagoe: Suzusawa Book Store, 1991

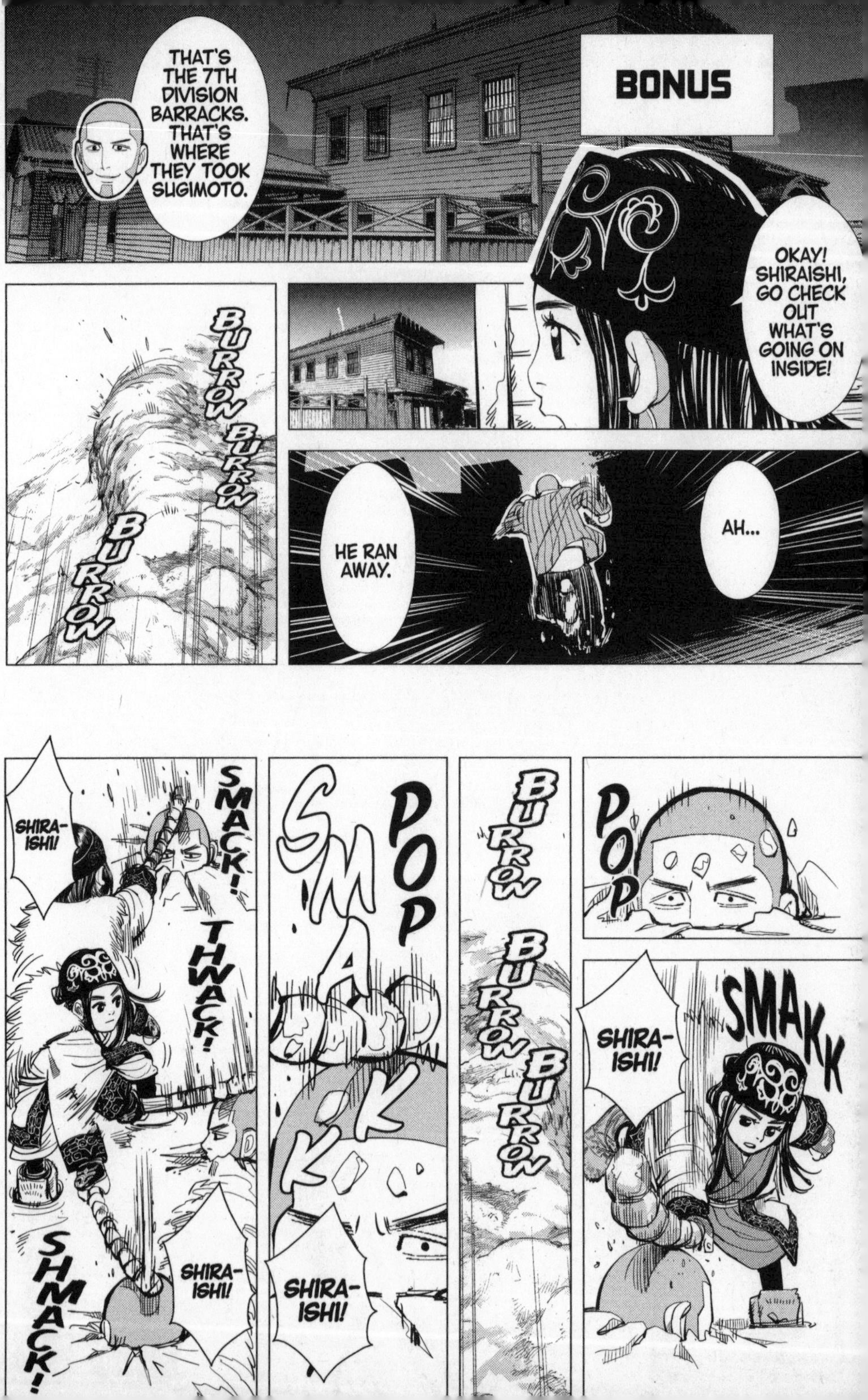
BONUS
THAT'S THE 7TH DIVISION BARRACKS. THAT'S WHERE THEY TOOK SUGIMOTO.
OKAY! SHIRAISHI, GO CHECK OUT WHAT'S GOING ON INSIDE!
AH...
HE RAN AWAY.
BURROW
BURROW
BURROW
POP
POP
SHIRA-ISHI!
SMAKK
BURROW
BURROW
BURROW
POP
POP
SMAKK
SHIRA-ISHI!
SHIRA-ISHI!
SHIRA-ISHI!
SMACK!
THWACK!
SHMACK!

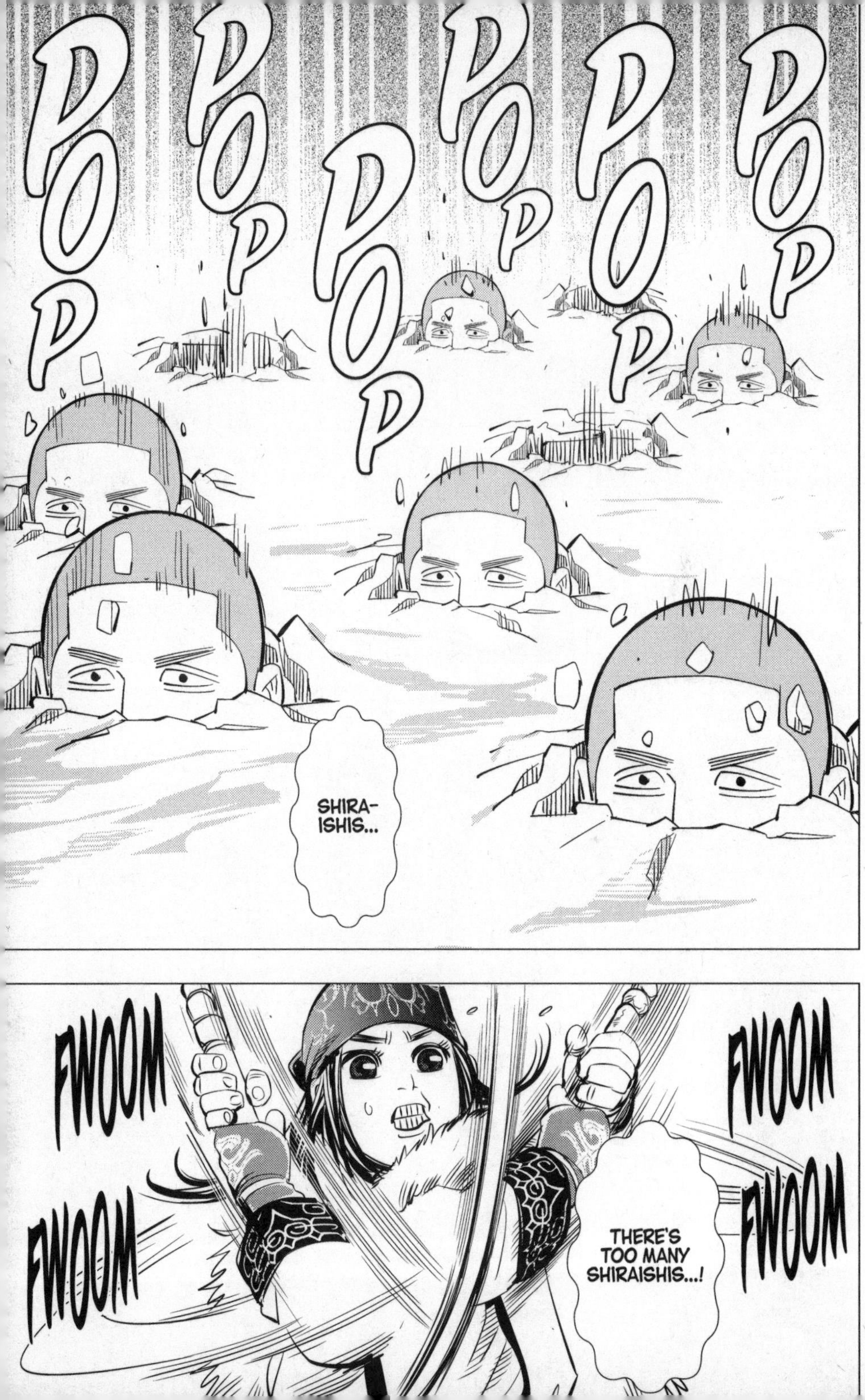
POP
POP
POP
POP
POP
POP
SHIRA-ISHIS...
FWOOM
FWOOM
THERE'S TOO MANY SHIRAISHIS...!
FWOOM
FWOOM

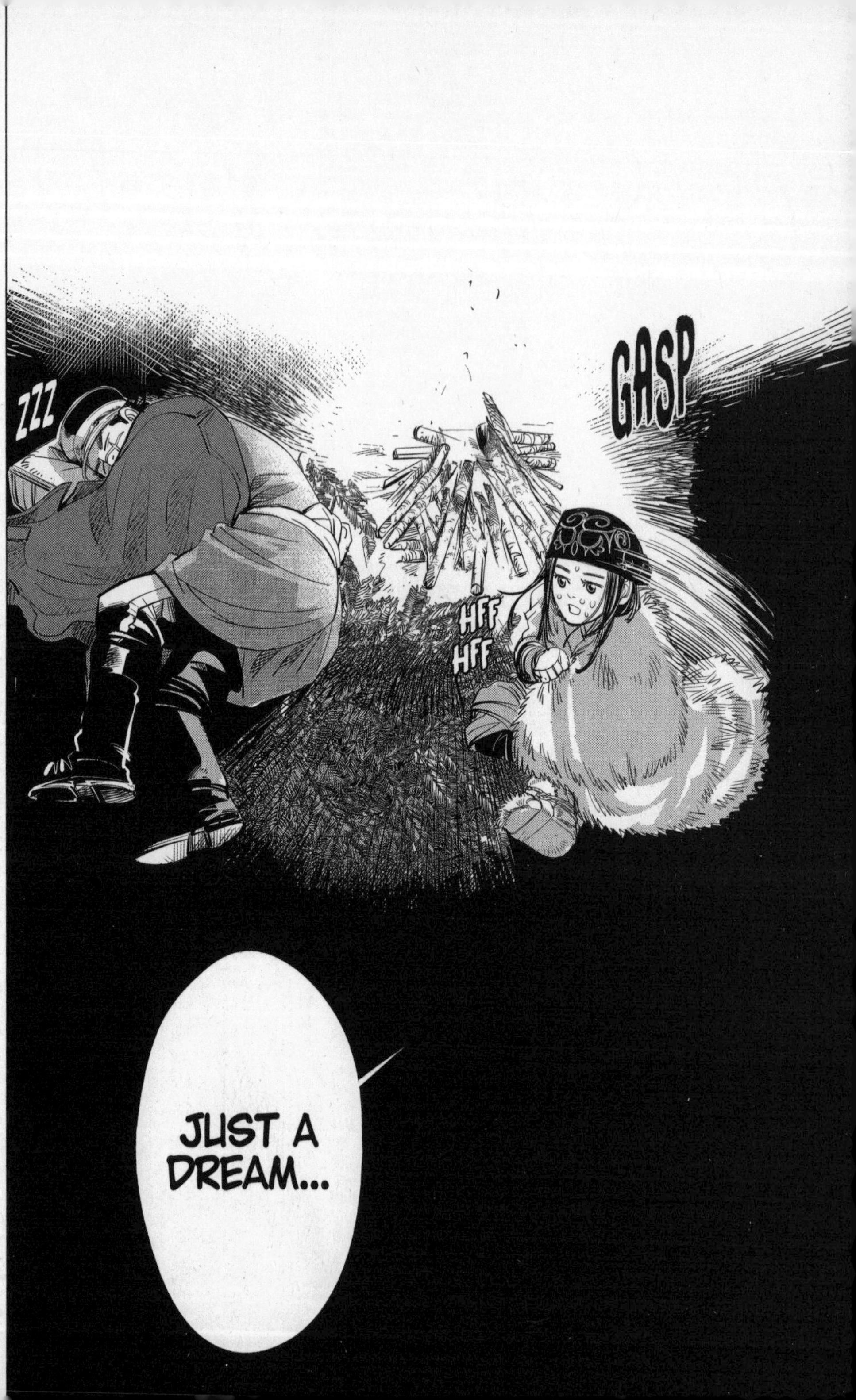
GASP
HFF HFF
ZZZ
JUST A DREAM...

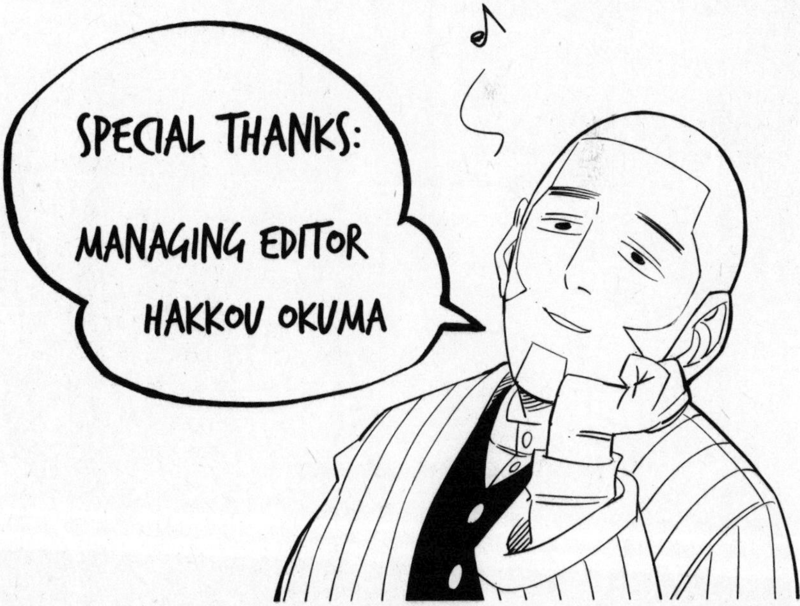
SPECIAL THANKS:
MANAGING EDITOR
HAKKOU OKUMA

GOLDEN KAMUY

Volume 3
VIZ Signature Edition

Story/Art by Satoru Noda

GOLDEN KAMUY © 2014 by Satoru Noda
All rights reserved.
First published in Japan in 2014 by SHUEISHA Inc., Tokyo.
English translation rights arranged by SHUEISHA Inc.

Translation/Eiji Yasuda
Touch-Up Art & Lettering/Steve Dutro
Design/Izumi Evers
Editor/Mike Montesa

The stories, characters and incidents mentioned in this publication are entirely fictional.

Published by VIZ Media, LLC
P.O. Box 77010
San Francisco, CA 94107

10 9 8 7 6 5 4 3 2 1
First printing, December 2017

www.viz.com

VIZ SIGNATURE